D0757686

FORENSIC SHAKESPEARE

CLARENDON LECTURES IN ENGLISH

FORENSIC SHAKESPEARE

QUENTIN SKINNER

OXFORD
UNIVERSITY PRESS

OXFORD
UNIVERSITY PRESS

Great Clarendon Street, Oxford, OX2 6DP,
United Kingdom

Oxford University Press is a department of the University of Oxford.
It furthers the University's objective of excellence in research, scholarship,
and education by publishing worldwide. Oxford is a registered trade mark of
Oxford University Press in the UK and in certain other countries

© Quentin Skinner 2014

The moral rights of the author have been asserted

First Edition published in 2014

Impression: 1

All rights reserved. No part of this publication may be reproduced, stored in
a retrieval system, or transmitted, in any form or by any means, without the
prior permission in writing of Oxford University Press, or as expressly permitted
by law, by licence or under terms agreed with the appropriate reprographics
rights organization. Enquiries concerning reproduction outside the scope of the
above should be sent to the Rights Department, Oxford University Press, at the
address above

You must not circulate this work in any other form
and you must impose this same condition on any acquirer

Published in the United States of America by Oxford University Press
198 Madison Avenue, New York, NY 10016, United States of America

British Library Cataloguing in Publication Data
Data available

Library of Congress Control Number: 2014933919

ISBN 978-0-19-955824-7

Printed in Great Britain by
Clays Ltd, St Ives plc

Links to third party websites are provided by Oxford in good faith and
for information only. Oxford disclaims any responsibility for the materials
contained in any third party website referenced in this work.

Acknowledgements

I first presented the argument of this book as the Clarendon Lectures at the University of Oxford in the Hilary Term 2011. I feel deeply honoured to have been asked to contribute to this series, and must begin by thanking those who made my visits to Oxford such an enjoyable as well as instructive experience. Richard McCabe and Seamus Perry were my official hosts, and both were warmly welcoming, as was David Norbrook, who organized a helpful seminar in connection with the lectures. Katy Routh of the Faculty of English took care of all practical arrangements with exemplary care and efficiency. I also want to express my gratitude to all those friends and colleagues who not only came to hear me, but in many cases supplied me with additional references, suggestions for improvement, much-needed encouragement, cakes and ale. My warmest thanks to Laura Ashe, Colin Burrow, Terence Cave, John Elliott, George Garnett, Claire Landis, Rhodri Lewis, Laurie Maguire, Noel Malcolm, Sarah Mortimer, Keith Thomas, Bart van Es, Jeremy Waldron, David Womersley, and Brian Young. To Andrew McNeillie I owe a special word of thanks for having proposed that I be invited to deliver the lectures, and for continuing to show so much faith in my work.

I presented a revised version of my argument as the Clark Lectures at Trinity College Cambridge in the Lent Term 2012. This too was a series to which I felt deeply honoured to contribute, and I am very grateful to Boyd Hilton and Richard Serjeantson for putting forward my name. My hosts at Trinity College were Caroline Humphrey and Martin Rees, and I was magnificently entertained. Adrian Poole was another welcoming presence in the college, and chaired a further helpful seminar at the end of the series. To Richard Serjeantson I owe additional thanks for organizing the lectures, and for presiding at the splendid dinner after my final talk. During my weekly visits to Cambridge I also benefited from many conversations with friends and colleagues who generously attended my lectures, including Gavin Alexander, Michael Allen, Annabel Brett, John Dunn, Richard

Fisher, Raymond Geuss, Heather Glen, Fred Inglis, John Kerrigan, Subha Mukherji, Jeremy Mynott, David Reynolds, John Robertson, John Thompson, and Phil Withington. For subsequent encouragement and advice about my project I am greatly indebted to Akeel Bilgrami, Stephen Greenblatt, Peter Mack, Kari Palonen, Christopher Prendergast, David Sedley, Cathy Shrank, B. J. Sokol, James Tully, and Martin Wiggins. I owe particular thanks to Brian Vickers, who provided me with indispensable help in matters of dating and bibliography. I should also like to take this opportunity to say how much I owe to Christopher Ricks, from whom I never cease to learn.

I started thinking about this book after taking part in two conferences in 2006. The first was organized at Cambridge by Sylvia Adamson, Gavin Alexander, and Katrin Ettenhuber, who were then in the process of editing *Renaissance Figures of Speech*.[1] Contributors were asked to outline what they intended to say in the book, and I received valuable advice about my own chapter in it.[2] It was Eric Griffiths who insisted that my examples should be taken from Shakespeare, thereby setting me on my course. The other conference was organized by David Armitage, Conal Condren, and Andrew Fitzmaurice at the Humanities Research Centre of the Australian National University on the subject of Shakespeare and political thought. Ian Donaldson chaired the proceedings, and to him as well as the editors of the resulting volume I am indebted for counsel and support not merely on that occasion but over many years.[3]

I began the process of writing after moving from the University of Cambridge to Queen Mary, University of London in 2008. Queen Mary has proved an ideal place in which to work. I am profoundly grateful to Philip Ogden, then Vice-Principal, for inviting me to join the college, and more recently for the helping hand of Morag Shiach as Dean of the Humanities and Social Sciences. These may be dark days for the humanities, but at Queen Mary I could not have received a brighter welcome. I am also blessed with outstanding colleagues, and I want to thank Richard Bourke, Warren Boutcher, and David Colclough for many discussions about my research.

I finished what I hoped was a final draft in the summer of 2013 and circulated it to a number of readers. I name them with deep gratitude: Colin

---

[1] See Adamson, Alexander, and Ettenhuber (eds) 2007.   [2] Skinner 2007.
[3] See Armitage, Condren, and Fitzmaurice (eds) 2009, and cf. Skinner 2009.

Burrow, David Colclough, Lorna Hutson, Susan James, John Kerrigan, Jeremy Mynott, Eric Nelson, Markku Peltonen, Neil Rudenstine, and John Thompson. They provided me with many new ideas and much generous encouragement, but they also made it clear that my manuscript needed to be extensively revised. Colin Burrow showed me that the tone as well as the direction of my argument required reconsideration in many places. Lorna Hutson enabled me radically to improve the balance of the book by pointing out the vital importance of *Lucrece*. And John Kerrigan, who talked to me extraordinarily illuminatingly about my lectures, persuaded me that there were many things I simply could not say, thereby rescuing me from a number of absurdities.

I was able to make the necessary revisions during a year of sabbatical leave from Queen Mary, which I spent as Visiting Professor attached to the Center for Human Values at Princeton University in 2013–14. I am greatly indebted to Charles Beitz and his committee for inviting me, and grateful for many conversations with members of the Center and others associated with it, among whom I particularly want to mention David Ciepley, Melissa Lane, Tori McGeer, Philip Pettit, and Alan Ryan. To Nigel Smith of the Department of English I am grateful not merely for enlightening conversations, but also for putting me in touch with two remarkable PhD students, Andrew Miller and Daniel Blank. Both read the final draft of my manuscript with meticulous attention, checking all my quotations from Shakespeare as well as all my references and correcting many embarrassing mistakes. The Center generously paid for this wonderful help, and I owe many thanks to the Assistant Director, Maureen Killeen, for making the necessary arrangements.

The working lives of those who study early modern texts have been transformed in recent times by the availability of online concordances and databases, among which *Early English Books Online* is a resource to which we all owe a large and growing debt. But the rare book rooms of the great libraries remain indispensable, and I am happy to record how much I have once again profited from the expertise of the staff at the British Library, the Cambridge University Library, the Library of the Faculty of English at the University of Cambridge, and the Firestone Library at Princeton.

I leave my most heartfelt thanks until the end. Susan James has read each successive draft of this book, discussed it with me at every stage, improved its presentation and argument beyond recognition, and shown endless patience and enthusiasm for my project. Without her support and that of our children, Olivia and Marcus, I would not be able to manage at all.

As this book goes to press I am very pleased to be able to add two further expressions of thanks. One is to Rob Tempio and Natalie Baan of Princeton University Press for indispensable help at the proof-correcting stage. The other is to the staff of the Oxford University Press. Elizabeth Stone sub-edited my typescript with marvellous precision and thoroughness, and calmly sorted out a considerable number of last-minute difficulties. Rachel Platt and Emma Slaughter supervised the process of production with unfailing helpfulness and dispatch. And Jacqueline Baker as my Editor proved a mainstay at all times. I thank her not only for her professionalism and her many kindnesses, but more particularly for supplying me—after several failed attempts on my part—with the title of my book.

Contents

Conventions

Abbreviations. The following abbreviations are used in the footnotes:

BL: British Library
CUL: Cambridge University Library
SD: Stage direction
TLN: Through line number

Bibliographies. These are simply check-lists of the primary sources I have quoted and the secondary authorities on which I have relied. They make no pretence of being systematic guides to the critical literature on my theme. Readers in need of such a guide should consult the *World Shakespeare Bibliography*, published online for the Folger Shakespeare Library. The bibliography of primary sources lists anonymous works by title. Where a work was published anonymously but its author's name is known I place the name in square brackets.

Classical names and titles. I refer to ancient writers in their most familiar single-name style. I translate Greek titles, but all others are given in their original form.

Dates. I date by the common era. When referring to the publication dates of early modern English texts I follow my sources in treating the year as beginning on 25 March.

Gender. I try to use gender-neutral language so far as possible. The rhetoricians assume, however, that the figure of the orator will always and necessarily be male. When they say 'he' they often do *not* mean 'he or she', and in these cases I have felt obliged to follow their usage rather than change their sense.

References. I use the author–date system when quoting from primary as well as secondary sources. When I use modern editions, I add the original date of publication in square brackets. The bibliography of secondary sources gives all journal references in Arabic numerals. References in the footnotes to chapters and sections of books appear in the same style, except that, when quoting from editions published in the Loeb Classical Library, I follow their mixed system. When referring to the Bible, I simply cite the relevant Book, chapter, and verse.

References to Shakespeare. When quoting from Shakespeare's plays I give the TLN and page number from Shakespeare 1986, except where I specifically note that I am using Shakespeare 1996. I then add Act–scene–line references from the relevant New Cambridge edition in each case. These editions are listed in the bibliography of primary sources. When quoting from Shakespeare's poems I give the TLN and page number from Shakespeare 1986, followed simply by the page number from the appropriate New Cambridge edition (Blakemore Evans 2006 or Roe 2006).

Transcriptions. My general rule is to preserve original spelling (including names, although not titles) as well as capitalization, italicization, and punctuation. Even at the end of block excerpts I never alter the punctuation given in Shakespeare 1986. But I expand contractions, remove ligatures, occasionally correct obvious typographical errors, and change 'u' to 'v' and 'i' to 'j' in accordance with modern orthography. When quoting in Latin I use 'v' as well as 'u', change 'j' to 'i', expand contractions and omit diacritical marks. Sometimes I change a lower case initial letter to an upper, or vice versa, when fitting quotations around my own prose. Shakespeare's texts are often modernized, but it would obviously be self-defeating to follow this convention in the present study, given that I am trying to situate his works within the intellectual context in which they were written. This makes me all the more grateful for Stanley Wells and Gary Taylor's original-spelling edition (1986), and for Charlton Hinman's edition of the First Folio (1996), on which I have wholly relied.

Translations. When quoting from classical sources, and from early modern sources in languages other than English, all translations are my own except where specifically noted. I make extensive use of the editions published in the Loeb Classical Library, which contain facing-page versions in English, but here too I have preferred to translate for myself. One reason is that some Loeb translations are very free, and tend to obscure the technical rhetorical vocabulary that I need to highlight. A further reason is that, even when the Loeb versions are exact, I have still needed to make my own translations in order to fit them around my prose. I must emphasize, however, that I am extremely grateful for the availability of the Loeb editions, and have generally been guided by them, often to the extent of adopting turns of phrase. I am no less grateful for the *Oxford Latin Dictionary*, to which I have invariably deferred in giving definitions of terms.

Introduction

With this book I am publishing the third instalment in my continuing efforts to understand the place of the *ars rhetorica* in the history of Renaissance culture. I began by tracing the re-emergence of Roman rhetorical ideas in the city-republics of Renaissance Italy and the influence they exerted on the theory and conduct of public life.[1] I then shifted to the period in which the teaching of rhetoric began to be questioned and discredited in the course of the seventeenth century.[2] The present study returns to the heyday of rhetorical instruction in the grammar schools of Elizabethan and Jacobean England, and attempts to trace some of the complex links between that system of education and the unmatched efflorescence of the drama during the same period.

My central claim is that among Shakespeare's plays there are several in which the dramaturgy is extensively drawn from classical and Renaissance treatises on judicial rhetoric. Shakespeare first made use of these sources in five of the works he composed between 1594 and c.1600: in his narrative poem *Lucrece*, and then in *Romeo and Juliet*, *The Merchant of Venice*, *Julius Caesar*, and *Hamlet*. He subsequently returned to the same sources in three further plays that he seems to have completed between the summer of 1603 and the beginning of 1605: *Othello*, *Measure for Measure*, and *All's Well That Ends Well*.[3] Neither before nor after this period did he display any comparable interest in the technicalities of forensic eloquence. But in the works I am singling out—and especially in *Hamlet* and his early Jacobean dramas—his engagement with the *genus iudiciale* is so intense that one might even think of these as his forensic plays. My aim in grouping them together will

1. Skinner 1978; Skinner 1995.   2. Skinner 1996; Skinner 2002b; Skinner 2002c.
3. This dating is contentious only in the case of *All's Well That Ends Well*. For evidence that *All's Well* was written in late 1604 or early 1605 see the Appendix.

be to show that a number of major speeches, as well as several sequences of
scenes, are assembled according to a set of rhetorical precepts about how to
develop a persuasive case in accusation or defence. My overall aspiration
will be to say something about the dynamics of Shakespeare's creative
processes by way of excavating the intellectual materials out of which
these passages are constructed. To express the same thought differently,
I am trying to identify some of the sources that Shakespeare used in order to
get his imagination on the move.

What can we learn about these works by scrutinizing them from this
perspective? Here I need to make a rough distinction between explaining
and interpreting texts.[4] I am not primarily concerned with interpretation, if
by that term we understand the process of analysing or deconstructing texts
and passing judgement on their worth. Like many in our historically
minded days I am more concerned with explanation, with the attempt to
determine why the works I am considering possess their distinctive characteristics. By focusing on the theory of judicial rhetoric we can hope in the
first place to help explain why certain of Shakespeare's scenes have a
particular shape, and why a number of individual speeches conform to a
recurrent pattern and arrangement. We can even hope to identify what
might be described as Shakespeare's rhetorical silences. Generally he follows
the rules of judicial rhetoric sufficiently closely to set up clear expectations
about how his forensic scenes will unfold, but sometimes he defeats our
expectations by failing to say something that anyone acquainted with the art
of rhetoric would expect to be said. An understanding of the rhetorical
conventions enables us to hear these silences.[5] Perhaps most important, we
can also hope to account for some distinctive features of Shakespeare's
vocabulary. I am especially interested in his use of the terms 'foul' and
'honest' in the evaluation of actions and character. These were pivotal terms
of moral appraisal in forensic rhetoric, but they also recur with striking
frequency in the works I discuss,[6] and I attempt to trace the extent to which
these continuities reflect Shakespeare's engagement with specific rhetorical
texts. The claims I am making here can also be expressed more boldly in
negative terms. Through lack of a sufficiently detailed understanding of

---

4. For a fuller explication and defence of this approach to textual analysis see Skinner 2002a.
5. My concern is not with the 'open' silences discussed in McGuire 1985, but with moments
   when a character fails to say something expected.
6. According to the Concordances, 'foul' occurs 59 times in the nine works I discuss and 'honest'
   or 'honesty' 136 times.

Shakespeare's use of judicial rhetoric, I shall argue, all these dimensions of meaning have tended to be missed or misunderstood.

By revealing the extent of Shakespeare's knowledge of classical rhetoric I hope to fulfil another and related purpose, that of expanding our awareness of his reading in ancient literature.[7] It is not of course essential to my argument to show that he was drawing on any specific classical authorities in the plays I have singled out. He was influenced by a whole tradition of thought encompassing a large number of vernacular as well as classical texts. As we shall see, however, he sometimes quotes directly from Cicero's *De inventione* and the anonymous *Rhetorica ad Herennium*, and it is clear that he also studied some contemporary neo-Ciceronian treatises, among which Thomas Wilson's *Arte of Rhetorique* stands out as a work to which he makes explicit reference, and which he may even have bought.[8] There have been many recent inventories of Shakespeare's books and reading,[9] but in none of them do we find it suggested that he may have owned any rhetorical texts.[10] As I hope to show, however, there can be little doubt that, in composing the works I shall be discussing, he must frequently have had one or other of the classical or Elizabethan manuals at the front of his mind—possibly even in front of him—as he wrote.[11] My broader purpose, in sum, is to illustrate the extent to which Shakespeare's dramaturgy in the plays I am considering is classical and humanist in its intellectual allegiances.

While my aim is to extend our knowledge of Shakespeare's rhetoric, I am anxious at the same time to acknowledge the large body of valuable research that has already been published on his use of classical rhetorical techniques. If I have a criticism of this literature, it is only that it sometimes seems to me

---

7. This general theme has now been thoroughly explored in Burrow 2013. Burrow does not examine classical rhetoric, so my discussion might perhaps be read as a supplement to his, but he closely examines Shakespeare's use of Roman moral philosophy as well as poetry and comedy.

8. As noted in Forker 2004, p. 112, who observes that a copy of the 1580 edition would have cost him one shilling.

9. For recent discussions see Ackroyd 2005, pp. 403–6; Nicholl 2007, pp. 80–6; Bate 2008, pp. 141–61, Potter 2012, pp. 26–9. None of these surveys mentions any rhetorical texts. Miola 2000, p. 16 prints a table of 'Principal source texts' of Shakespeare's plays, but no work of classical or Renaissance rhetoric is mentioned. Martindale and Martindale 1990, an account of Shakespeare's 'uses of antiquity' makes no mention of the *Ad Herennium* or Quintilian; nor does Gillespie 2001, a dictionary of Shakespeare's books.

10. This is not to say that Shakespeare's knowledge of classical rhetoric has remained unexplored. See Kennedy 1942; Baldwin 1944; Jones 1977; Platt 1999; Plett 2004; Burrow 2004 and 2013.

11. Struever 1988 raises doubts about Shakespeare's knowledge of rhetorical theory, but they are not tenable, as I hope to show.

too narrowly focused.[12] The Ciceronian conception of the *ars rhetorica* encompassed five elements: *inventio, dispositio, elocutio, pronuntiatio,* and *memoria*.[13] But in the literature on Shakespeare's rhetoric there has been a tendency to concentrate almost exclusively on *elocutio*, the study of rhetorical 'exornation', especially in the form of the figures and tropes of speech.[14] I have of course no complaint about this emphasis in itself, but a number of critics have in turn equated *elocutio* with the whole art of eloquence, speaking of 'Shakespeare's rhetoric' when they are merely referring to his wordplay and other verbal effects.[15] This sense of priorities is strikingly at variance with that of the classical rhetoricians themselves.[16] They always treat the art of rhetoric essentially as a theory of argument, especially legal argument, and they like to stress its practical usefulness.[17] They accordingly place their main emphasis on *inventio* and *dispositio*, and tend in addition to treat the topic of *dispositio* largely as an ancillary element in the successful 'invention' of arguments.[18] This is likewise Shakespeare's sense of priorities. He never speaks about 'elocution' or 'exornation'; whenever he mentions the art of rhetoric it is always the concept of invention that he seems to have at the forefront of his mind. When he

12. For a similar criticism see Enders 1992, pp. 5–6.
13. See Cicero 1949a, I. VII. 9, pp. 18–20. Cf. *Rhetorica ad Herennium* 1954, I. II. 3, p. 6; Quintilian 2001, 3. 3. 1, vol. 2, p. 22.
14. Crider 2009, which focuses on Aristotle, is an exception. For discussions of 'exornation' in the English vernacular rhetorics of the later sixteenth century see Sherry 1550, Sig. C, 4ʳ; Wilson 1553, Sig. Z, 2ʳ; [Puttenham] 1589, p. 114; Peacham 1593, p. 1.
15. For example, Levenson 2004, writing about *Romeo and Juliet*, claims (p. 134) to provide an analysis of 'the play's use of rhetoric' but concentrates wholly on figures of speech. McNeely 2004, p. 132 speaks of disclosing Shakespeare's 'mastery of technical rhetoric', but illustrates the claim almost exclusively by reference to elocutionary effects. Clark 2007, p. 117 promises 'a formal rhetorical approach' to *Measure for Measure* and *All's Well That Ends Well*, but this turns out to mean a study of certain organizing figures. Nicholson 2010, p. 61 declares that *Othello* 'is a play about rhetoric', but speaks only about figures and commonplaces. Wills 2011 examines the 'rhetoric' of *Julius Caesar*, but focuses almost entirely on figures and tropes. Lyne 2011, p. 172 sees in rhetoric 'a representation of the process of thinking' but limits himself to illustrating it from Shakespeare's use of tropes. For the equation between the 'rhetoric' of Shakespeare's plays and their deployment of figures and tropes see also Evans 1966; Brook 1976, pp. 166–76; Horvei 1984; Wells and Taylor 1987, p. 97; Thorne 2000, p. xii; McDonald 2001, pp. 23, 43–4; Menon, 2004; Roe 2006, p. 4; Keller 2009. Joseph 1947 is more broadly based, and includes a discussion (pp. 308–53) of the 'places' in which we can hope to find out (*invenire*) arguments. But when she turns to Shakespeare's texts (pp. 90–173) she likewise focuses almost exclusively on figures and tropes.
16. As noted in Kennedy 1978, pp. 1–19; Donker 1992, pp. 46–9.
17. See Meerhoff 1994, pp. 46–8; Wels 2008.
18. As noted in Joseph 1947, pp. 22–31; Hutson 2007, pp. 1–3, 78–80, 251–3. For the residual treatment of *dispositio* see *Rhetorica ad Herennium* 1954, III. IX. 16–17, pp. 184–6. Cicero 1949a includes no separate discussion of *dispositio* at all.

invokes his muse at the beginning of *The Life of Henry the Fift*, the ambition he voices is that of scaling 'the brightest Heaven of Invention'.[19] When he repeatedly bemoans the poverty of his talent in the Sonnets, it is his 'blunt invention' to which he addresses his complaint.[20] On the one occasion when he comments on his own poetry it is the element of *inventio* that he again chooses to emphasize, speaking of his *Venus and Adonis* as 'the first heire of my invention'.[21]

I do not mean to imply that my own emphasis on 'invention' and 'disposition' represents a new departure in the study of Shakespeare's deployment of rhetorical techniques. I am deeply indebted to a number of important works that have already underlined the primary role played by these elements in the Renaissance art of eloquence. Brian Vickers's classic survey of the Ciceronian ideal of rhetoric as a fivefold art originally quickened my interest in the theory of rhetorical invention.[22] Wilbur Howell's pioneering analysis of the connections between logic and rhetoric was another of my early guides,[23] and I have also benefited greatly from Peter Mack's exposition of the shifting relationship between rhetorical and dialectical invention in the sixteenth century.[24] Coming yet closer to the theme of my present book, I also want to pay tribute to several studies of the place of rhetorical invention in Shakespeare's works. Heinrich Plett and Joel Altman have both called attention to the rhetorical plotting of *Othello*, and although I follow a contrasting approach I have profited from some of their arguments.[25] Lorna Hutson has uncovered the influence of judicial rhetoric in the construction of many late sixteenth-century plays, and to her pathfinding research I owe a large and obvious debt. The dramatists, as she shows, increasingly availed themselves of the idea that the best way to proceed in the 'conjectural' form of a judicial cause—where some mystery needs to be resolved—is to 'invent' arguments that enable some initial

---

19. *The Life of Henry the Fift*, TLN 1–2, p. 639 (Prologue, lines 1–2). Gurr 2005, pp. 7–8 discusses the suggestion that the Chorus's lines may have been inserted later.
20. Shakespeare 1986, Sonnet 103, line 7, p. 866; cf. Sonnet 38, lines 1–2, p. 855; Sonnet 59, lines 1–4, p. 858; Sonnet 76, line 6, p. 861 (pp. 45, 56, 64, 78). For this theme in the Sonnets see Orgel 2006, pp. 20–2.
21. Shakespeare 1986, *Venus and Adonis*, Epistle Dedicatory, p. 254 (p. 86).
22. See Vickers 1988, pp. 52–82, on which I gratefully draw in chapter 1.
23. See Howell 1956, esp. pp. 68–102 on Renaissance theories of rhetorical *inventio* and their antecedents.
24. See Mack 1993 and cf. Mack 2011, esp. pp. 56–75. On the *quattrocento* background to this shift, especially in the work of Lorenzo Valla, see Jardine 1977.
25. See Plett 2004, esp. pp. 464–70; Altman 2010, esp. pp. 33–85.

suspicion to be confirmed or disconfirmed.[26] As I hope to demonstrate, several of Shakespeare's plots conform to this view of what it means to build up a rhetorical confirmation in the prosecution of a judicial cause.[27]

Drawing on these lines of research, I have tried to sketch a more detailed picture of Shakespeare's use of the precepts of judicial rhetoric, especially in the two phases of his literary career in which he became deeply absorbed by the dramatic possibilities of forensic eloquence. As a result, I have something to say about each of the five elements in the classical understanding of the *ars rhetorica*. I speak only briefly about *pronuntiatio* and *memoria*, although I stress the relevance for Shakespeare of Ramist discussions about the control of voice and bodily movement, the two main aspects of *pronuntiatio*. I have more to say about *elocutio*, and especially about Shakespeare's use of the range of figures and tropes that are said to be capable of eliciting feelings of *miseratio* and *ira*, pity and rage. But my principal aspiration is to revise the usual priorities in the study of Shakespeare's rhetoric, in consequence of which my emphasis falls squarely on the place of *inventio* and *dispositio* in the construction of judicial arguments.

Having proposed a tentative grouping of the works I shall be considering, I need to note that several of them have often been linked together in a different way. Traditionally they have been classified as 'problem plays', and one remarkable feature of recent Shakespearean scholarship has been the attempt to revive this concept as a useful critical category.[28] The term was originally introduced by F. S. Boas, who used it to bring together four works: *Hamlet, Troilus and Cressida, Measure for Measure*, and *All's Well That Ends Well*.[29] Boas's list has been extended and modified by more recent commentators, but his original formulation of what helps to identify an alleged problem play has continued to be invoked. He spoke of how 'the issues raised preclude a completely satisfactory outcome', so that there is no 'settlement of difficulties'.[30] Recent critics have likewise remarked that we

---

26. See Hutson 2007, esp. pp. 67, 141, 164–5 on detective plots and the attempted confirmation of conjectures.

27. By contrast with Hutson 2007, I am not concerned to establish the novelty of these dramaturgical developments. The discussion in Enders 1992, esp. pp. 56–68 on mimesis in medieval forensic oratory, suggests that they may not have been without precedent. But Hutson is surely right to emphasize that the handling of conjectural issues is newly central in sixteenth-century drama.

28. See Wheeler 1981; Thomas 1987; Hillman 1993; Maquerlot 1995; McCandless 1997; Marsh 2003; Harmon 2004; Clark 2007; Margolies 2012.

29. Boas 1896, pp. 344–5. Traversi 1969, vol. 2, p. 25 repeats the list.

30. Boas 1896, p. 345, approvingly quoted in Wheeler 1981, p. 3.

are presented with 'a set of contentions and intractable issues that seem irresolvable'; that 'we are left pondering the questions raised'; and that the issues are examined 'in such a way that they cannot be resolved'.[31] A number of reasons for these similarities have been suggested, and one of my aims will be to explore a further explanation that has not hitherto been much discussed. If we return to the four plays that Boas analysed, we find that three of them, together with *Othello*, are at the same time Shakespeare's most intensely forensic works. They are all plays in which accusations are put forward, in which they are met with counter-arguments and debated *in utramque partem*, and in which there is often no final agreement as to how the questions at issue should be assessed.[32] These are all plays, in other words, of which it seems natural to say that there is no unequivocal 'settlement of difficulties'. If we focus on the forensic properties of these four works, I shall argue, we may be able to shed further light on how they come to possess the commonalities of tone and argument that many critics have continued to observe.

A wealth of valuable research has lately been published on the subject of Shakespeare and the law.[33] It is arguable, however, that some of this scholarship has shown a tendency to exaggerate the extent of Shakespeare's legal competence. Sometimes he is taken to be making use of legal sources when he can instead be shown to be drawing on rhetorical texts. One play in which this confusion has arguably led to misinterpretation is *The Merchant of Venice*. Repeated attempts have been made to read the trial scene in Act 4 as a confrontation between the claims of equity and the strict letter of the law.[34] As I seek to show, however, Shakespeare's argument has no connection with the principles of equitable jurisdiction; it is wholly structured around the rhetorical rules governing the presentation of a *constitutio iuridicalis* of a purportedly 'absolute' kind. A related doubt needs to be registered about recent discussions of the means by which narratives and other forms of testimony gained authority in the drama and more broadly in the culture of Shakespeare's England. To explain these developments we are urged to

31. Thomas 1987, p. 14; Clark 2007, p. 117; Margolies 2012, p. 2.
32. See also Rhodes 2004, pp. 89–98, 105–9, in which he analyses—with special reference to *Measure for Measure*—Shakespeare's use of judicial *controversiae* as a basis for several of his plots.
33. See, for example, Ward 1999; Wilson 2000; Shapiro 2001; Mukherji 2006; Cormack 2007; Hutson 2007; Jordan and Cunningham 2007; Raffield and Watt 2008; Zurcher 2010; Syme 2012; Cormack, Nussbaum, and Strier 2013.
34. For a list see Bilello 2007, pp. 109–10, to which should be added Platt 2009, pp. 112–15.

think about the practice of the law, and especially about changing procedures of criminal prosecution in the course of the sixteenth century.[35] These
changes were undoubtedly important, but in many instances they were
inspired by works of forensic rhetoric, and it was from these sources that
the legal writers derived most of their organizing categories, as Barbara
Shapiro and Lorna Hutson have fully documented.[36] It is likewise one of
my principal arguments in this book that, if we wish to explain the
distinctive vocabulary and arrangement of Shakespeare's forensic scenes, it
is to the rhetorical sources that we need basically to turn.

I ought perhaps to say a word about the bearing of my argument on
the continuing dispute in Shakespearean studies about the relative significance of text and performance. Until recently the fashion was to regard
Shakespeare as a jobbing playwright collaboratively engaged in getting his
works ready to be acted.[37] Of late, however, the trend has been to question
this privileging of stage over page, and to revert to viewing Shakespeare
primarily as an author shaping a literary career.[38] My present study is
obviously aligned with the latter approach. I treat the play scripts chiefly
as literary artefacts, and I focus on their explanatory relationship with other
bodies of texts. But this is not to say that I endorse any strong separation
between Shakespeare as literary dramatist and as man of the theatre. On the
contrary, the claims I make about his use of judicial rhetoric carry a number
of implications for performance, as will become clear in the course of my
argument. Once we understand the nature of the rhetorical confrontations
that are being dramatized, we may even decide that the staging of some
famous passages will have to be reconsidered.

Shakespeare has often been praised for 'presenting life directly' and being
'true to life'.[39] But it is worth noting that, if we view his plays from the
perspective I am describing, it becomes hard to endorse this kind of

---

35. See, for example, Syme 2012, pp. 18–20. Hutson 2007, pp. 3–5 begins by laying out her
    argument in similar terms, but subsequently examines in detail the rhetorical background to
    many of these texts. See Hutson 2007, esp. pp. 78–80, 92, 213–14, 251–3, a series of
    discussions to which I am greatly indebted.
36. See Shapiro 2001; Hutson 2007, esp. pp. 251–2.
37. For a strong affirmation of this perspective see Bulman 1996. For a survey centred on
    theatrical effects see Peters 2000. For a historiography and partial reaffirmation see
    Weimann and Bruster 2008.
38. Cheney 2008, p. xi. See also Burrow 1998; Erne 2003; Cheney 2004. The two perspectives are
    brought together in van Es 2013.
39. See, for example, Traversi 1969, vol. 2, p. 83; Felperin 1977, pp. 60, 85–6; Nuttall 1983,
    p. viii.

assessment.[40] To illustrate the extent to which the dramaturgy of the plays I am considering is derived from a set of rhetorical principles is to draw attention to the artificial character of Shakespeare's art. It is even arguable that, in constructing so many speeches according to the rules of *inventio* and *dispositio*, this element of artifice is something to which Shakespeare draws attention himself. To take an obvious example, we are introduced in the final scene of *Romeo and Juliet* to the figure of the Chief Watchman, who is investigating the circumstances of an apparent crime. As he scrutinizes the signs that appear to point to Friar Lawrence's guilt, he begins to quote accurately (and in verse) from an untranslated Latin rhetorical handbook on how such examinations should be conducted. The scene lacks any mimetic verisimilitude, and no effort is made to disguise its fictionality. If we find ourselves engaged by it, it is not because Shakespeare has produced a successful representation of real life; it is rather because he has constructed a satisfying rhetorical and dramatic effect. The same applies, I shall argue, to all the scenes and speeches examined in this book.

The sceptic will want to know how I can be certain that the classical manuals I have listed played such a prominent role in Shakespeare's literary development. Surely many of their precepts amount to little more than common sense? Could he not have thought of them for himself? I assume of course that Shakespeare consulted his dramatic instincts at all times. I am merely contending that these instincts frequently led him in the direction of the rhetorical handbooks. While this claim is not uncontentious, it is I think hard to dispute it in the light of my argument as a whole. I am repeatedly able to point to passages in which he follows complex rhetorical arguments to the letter, and can sometimes be shown to be quoting from specific classical manuals in the course of doing so.[41] But the sceptic will have a

---

40. On the nature of Shakespeare's realism I am indebted to Kiernan 1996, pp. 1–3, 91–126; Fowler 2003, pp. 100–20; Hutson 2006, pp. 81–5; and Margolies 2012.

41. For example, the author of the *Ad Herennium* speaks of the need to ensure that our adversaries cannot refuse to accept our narratives, using the verb *refellere*. See *Rhetorica ad Herennium* 1954, I. IX. 16, p. 28. When Isabella in Act 5 of *Measure for Measure* refers to her narrative in Act 2, she complains that Angelo refused to accept it, saying that she was 'refeld'—a word that Shakespeare never uses again. See *Measure for Measure*, TLN 2259, p. 918 (5. 1. 94). There are also occasions when Shakespeare translates directly from Quintilian. For example, when Quintilian speaks of the *causa turpis* or 'foul cause' he characterizes it as one in which the *frons* is not *honesta*. See Quintilian 2001, 4. 1. 42, vol. 2, p. 200. The word *frons* was translated in Elizabethan Latin-English dictionaries as 'the foreheade: the front'. See Cooper 1565, Sig. 3G, 1ʳ and cf. Thomas 1592, Sig. X, 2ʳ. Claudius in *Hamlet* speaks of the 'forhead of our faults', while Othello refers to the 'head and front of my offending.' See *Hamlet*, TLN 2179, p. 759 (3. 3. 63); *Othello*, TLN 366, p. 933 (1. 3. 80).

further objection to raise. Even if Shakespeare consulted such bookish sources, could he not have derived some of his rhetorical knowledge from other and intermediate authorities rather than from the classical handbooks themselves? He not only could have done, but he undoubtedly did, and I make an attempt in each of the scenes I examine to tease apart the different narrative and theoretical sources on which he seems to have drawn. I am only claiming that among these sources were the rhetorical texts I have identified. I certainly believe that he made extensive use of them, but this contention is subordinate to my larger aim of illustrating the extent of his engagement with an entire tradition of classical and humanist thought.

Something needs to be said in conclusion about Shakespeare's education, if only to forestall egregious questions about how the classical learning I attribute to him could possibly have been attained by a mere grammar-school boy. One contention of the present study is that there is nothing in the erudition displayed in any of the plays I discuss that could not readily have been acquired from an education of precisely the kind that Shakespeare would have received at the King's New School in Stratford-upon-Avon in the course of the 1570s.[42] There is, in short, no mystery to be solved. John Aubrey was undoubtedly correct (as he usually is) when he said of Shakespeare in his *Brief Lives* that he not only 'understood Latine pretty well',[43] but that he kept up his study of the language in adult life.[44]

It goes without saying that in the following pages I am merely scratching the surface of my theme. The classical rhetoricians invariably distinguish between the *genus iudiciale*, the *genus deliberativum*, and the *genus demonstrativum*.[45] I limit myself exclusively to the *genus iudiciale,* saying nothing about Shakespeare's exploration of the two other forms of rhetorical utterance.[46] As my title indicates, my sole topic is forensic eloquence. Moreover, when I consider the *genus iudiciale* I speak only about Shakespeare's use of it, saying little about the other dramatists of the period who were no less well-acquainted with the classical *ars rhetorica*. What follows is merely an attempt to map one sector of a large territory that remains to be further explored.

---

42. On the probable curriculum at the King's New School see Whitaker 1953, pp. 14–44.
43. Aubrey 1898, vol. 2, p. 227.
44. Aubrey 1898, vol. 2, p. 227 maintains that Shakespeare was 'in his younger yeares a school-master' and hence a teacher of Latin. He gives as his authority the actor William Beeston, noting (vol. 1, p. 96) that he 'knew all the old English poets'.
45. See, for example, Cicero 1949a, I. V. 7, p. 16; *Rhetorica ad Herennium* 1954, I. II. 2, p. 4; Quintilian 2001, 3. 4. 14–15, vol. 2, pp. 34–6.
46. The largest number of orations in Shakespeare are in the demonstrative mode. Kennedy 1942, pp. 68–9 lists forty-five.

I

Classical Rhetoric in Shakespeare's England

The Roman rhetorical tradition

The earliest surviving works of Roman rhetorical theory are Cicero's youthful *De inventione*, written around 90 BCE,[1] and the anonymous *Rhetorica ad Herennium*, probably completed nearly a decade later.[2] The two writers appear to have worked in ignorance of one another,[3] and they disagree at a number of important points.[4] But their texts are so similar that they must almost certainly have been derived from a common teacher,[5] and their technical vocabularies are so closely matching that the teacher in question must have been giving instruction in Latin rather than Greek.[6] Cicero seems to have planned a systematic treatise, but in the event he limited himself, as his title indicates, exclusively to the theory of rhetorical invention. By contrast, the author of the *Ad Herennium* surveys the whole art of rhetoric, striking out on his own with remarkable and unfaltering confidence. While Cicero continues to pay tribute to the Greek rhetoricians,[7]

1. Kennedy 1972, p. 107; Corbeill 2002, pp. 28, 32–3.
2. Caplan 1954, p. xxvi; Corbeill 2002, p. 32. Heath 2009, p. 65n. proposes a yet later date. Kennedy 1972, pp. 111–12 revives the suggestion that Cornificius may have been the author, but the objections in Caplan 1954, pp. ix–xiv seem decisive.
3. For the clearest evidence see *Rhetorica ad Herennium* 1954, I. IX. 16, p. 28, where the author claims originality for an argument already put forward in Cicero 1949a, I. XV. 20, p. 40 and I. XVII. 23, p. 46.
4. They disagree over such central issues as the types of *constitutiones* and the number of *causae*, thereby excluding the possibility that one text is simply dependent on the other.
5. Corbeill 2002, p. 34.
6. See Caplan 1954, pp. xxvii–xxviii. See also Corbeill 2002, p. 32, noting forty places in which complete sentences are identical in the two works.
7. Cicero 1949a, II. II. 4–5, pp. 168–70.

the *Ad Herennium* speaks with contempt of their puerilities,[8] makes no reference to any earlier rhetorical texts, and evidently aspires to produce a system much more closely adapted to Roman legal and political life.[9]

Despite these differences, the young Cicero and the author of the *Ad Herennium* are in basic accord about the scope and character of the *ars rhetorica*. As we have seen, Cicero lays it down that there are five elements in the art, and that these can be listed as *inventio, dispositio, elocutio, memoria,* and *pronuntiatio*.[10] By the time he was writing, this claim had evidently become well established, and he acknowledges that 'many people have already stated it'.[11] The author of the *Ad Herennium* speaks in identical terms,[12] although he maintains that the list refers not to the *partes* of the art but rather to the *res*—the skills or abilities—that aspiring orators need to cultivate.[13] Among later Roman rhetoricians, the same taxonomy was almost invariably repeated. The mature Cicero restates it in his *De oratore*, his most considered treatise on the art of public speaking,[14] and Quintilian subsequently endorses it in his *Institutio oratoria*, in which he synthesizes the entire Roman tradition of rhetorical thought.[15] He not only agrees that 'the theory of oratory embodies five separate elements',[16] but he particularly emphasizes that these should be regarded not as skills of the orator but as *partes* of the art itself.[17]

While this conclusion was generally accepted, no one supposed that the different *partes* were of equal significance. Although few doubted the value of *memoria* (a retentive memory), and everyone agreed that *pronuntiatio* (voice and gesture) can have distinctive persuasive effects, both these elements are usually handled very briefly.[18] Even in the *De oratore*, Cicero's most comprehensive survey, he relegates the discussion of memory to a short

8. *Rhetorica ad Herennium* 1954, IV. III. 4, p. 234.   9. Corbeill 2002, pp. 34–5.
10. Cicero 1949a, I. VII. 9, pp. 18–20.
11. Cicero 1949a, I. VII. 9, p. 18: 'plerique dixerunt'.
12. *Rhetorica ad Herennium* 1954, I. II. 3, p. 6.   13. *Rhetorica ad Herennium* 1954, I. II. 2, p. 4.
14. Cicero 1942a, I. XXXI. 142, vol. 1, p. 98. Later he suggests that the taxonomy may refer to the skills of the orator. See Cicero 1942b, II. 5, p. 312. But in his last rhetorical work he reverts to speaking of the different parts of the art. See Cicero 1962b, XIV. 43, p. 338.
15. On Quintilian as teacher see Kennedy 1972, pp. 487–96.
16. Quintilian 2001, 3. 3. 1, vol. 2, p. 22: 'orandi ratio . . . quinque partibus constat'.
17. Quintilian 2001, 3. 3. 11–14, vol. 2, pp. 26–8.
18. As we shall see, however, they became important in Medieval and Renaissance rhetoric. On *pronuntiatio* see Enders 1992, esp. pp. 19–68 and Enterline 2012; on *memoria* see Yates 1966. On *pronuntiatio* in Shakespeare see Bevington 1984; Neill 2000, pp. 174–85; Weimann and Bruster 2008, pp. 3–4; on *memoria* in Shakespeare see Tribble 2005; Wilder 2010, pp. 1–3, 24–32; Lewis 2012b; Lees-Jeffries 2013.

section at the end of Book 2,[19] while his analysis of voice and gesture is confined to a scarcely less summary passage in the closing pages of the work.[20] Quintilian has more to say about *pronuntiatio*, but his treatment of the alleged 'art' of memory is similarly brief (as well as notably sceptical) and he relegates both discussions to the end of his penultimate Book.[21]

The *partes* on which the Roman rhetoricians invariably concentrate are *inventio*, *dispositio*, and *elocutio*. Among modern historians of rhetoric there has in turn been a strong inclination to focus on *elocutio*, which for the classical writers meant the study of rhetorical style, including the ornamentation of our utterances by the figures and tropes of speech.[22] The Roman rhetoricians undoubtedly considered this topic to be of great importance. The *Ad Herennium* allots more space to the figures and tropes than to any other oratorical skill, while Cicero's *Orator* is largely given over to a defence of his own flamboyant style against the objections of those who wanted less display and more lucidity.[23] This interest in *elocutio* eventually found expression in a number of works principally devoted to explicating the figures and tropes, including Rutilius Lupus's *De figuris*, Cornifius's lost work on the same subject,[24] and Longinus's treatise on the sublime, in which the power of certain figures to convey sublimity is analysed at length.[25]

If, however, we place so much emphasis on *elocutio*, we are liable to misunderstand the scope of Roman rhetoric and its impact on Renaissance culture. The view of the rhetoricians themselves was that the most important topic was *inventio*, the process of trying to find out (*invenire*) what needs to be said.[26] Cicero insists that 'among all the parts of rhetoric, invention is the principal one',[27] and the author of the *Ad Herennium* strongly agrees. 'Of the five tasks of the orator', he writes, 'invention is the primary and by far the most difficult',[28] and 'it is in the inventing of arguments that the skill

---

19. Cicero 1942a, II. LXXXV. 350 to II. LXXXVIII. 361, vol. 1, pp. 462–72.
20. Cicero 1942a, III. LVI. 213 to III. LXI. 227, vol. 2, pp. 168–82.
21. Quintilian 2001, 11. 2–3, vol. 5, pp. 58–156.
22. This is likewise true of recent works on Shakespeare's use of the rhetorical arts. For a list see Introduction, note 15.
23. See Cicero 1962b, especially his defence of the 'grand' style at XXVIII. 97–101, pp. 374–8.
24. Quintilian 2001, 9. 3. 91, vol. 4, p. 156 mentions this work.
25. Longinus 1995, secs. 16–29, pp. 225–57. On Longinus see Kennedy 1972, pp. 369–77.
26. On the Renaissance concept of invention see Langer 1999. For a survey see Watson 2001.
27. Cicero 1949a, I. VII. 9, p. 20: 'inventio . . . princeps est omnium partium [rhetoricae]'. See also Cicero 1942b, II. 5, p. 312: 'invenire primum est oratoris'.
28. *Rhetorica ad Herennium* 1954, II. I. 1, p. 58: 'De oratoris officiis quinque inventio et prima et difficillima est.'

of the orator must be expended to the highest degree'.[29] Quintilian underlines the point when he observes that there is a sense in which effective
elocutio depends on *inventio*. If we search for words without first thinking
about the subject matter, 'we shall merely do violence to what we have
found out' rather than engaging in genuine debate.[30]

When the Roman writers refer to *inventio*, what they have in mind is the
need to discover and apply whatever lines of reasoning seem most appropriate to the case in hand. As the figure of Crassus in Cicero's *De oratore* is
made to say, everyone knows that 'the fundamental task of the orator is to
speak in whatever manner is best suited to persuade'.[31] But if that is so, the
skill of 'inventing' must be that of finding out which arguments are most
likely to strike a particular audience as especially plausible. Cicero makes it
clear that he fully accepts this implication when he introduces his formal
definition of *inventio* at the outset of his *De inventione*. He lays it down that
'invention is the process of working out which specific claims—whether
true or at least possessed of verisimilitude—serve to render your cause
probable'.[32] Later he reiterates this view in his *De partitione oratoria*, in
which he defines an argument as 'something plausible which is *inventum*,
found out, with the aim of inducing belief'.[33] Quintilian subsequently
strengthens the point by way of observing that we do not even speak of
someone's having invented an argument if it turns out to be inconsistent or
absurd.[34]

The author of the *Ad Herennium* offers the same definition of invention as
Cicero,[35] but he is much more candid about pursuing the implications of
their shared belief in the supreme importance of sounding plausible. He
recurs to the issue in the course of giving advice about how to construct a
narrative 'in such a way as to lend it verisimilitude'.[36] One reason why it
is essential to follow the rhetorical rules is that, 'even if the claim you

29. *Rhetorica ad Herennium* 1954, I. X. 16, p. 28: 'de rerum inventione...in quo singulare
    consumitur oratoris artificium'. See also Quintilian 2001, 3. 1. 2, vol. 2, p. 8.
30. Quintilian 2001, Book 8, Prohoemium 22, vol. 3, p. 318: 'inventis vim adferimus'.
31. Cicero 1942a, 1. 31. 138, vol. 1, p. 96: 'Primum orationis officium esse, dicere ad persua-
    dendum accommodate'.
32. Cicero 1949a, I. VII. 9, p. 18: 'Inventio est excogitatio rerum verarum aut veri similium quae
    causam probabilem reddant'.
33. Cicero 1942b, II. 5, p. 314: 'C. F. Quid est argumentum? C. P. Probabile inventum ad
    faciendam fidem'.
34. Quintilian 2001, 3. 3. 5, vol. 2, p. 24.   35. *Rhetorica ad Herennium* 1954, I. II. 3, p. 6.
36. *Rhetorica ad Herennium* 1954, I. IX. 16, p. 28 explains how to ensure that 'veri similis narratio
    erit'.

are making is true, the unvarnished truth is often incapable of winning credibility'.[37] Sometimes what you are saying may sound so unlikely that it will be impossible, in the absence of rhetorical skill, to persuade your audience to believe it. The other reason why it is crucial to know how to sound plausible is that what you are saying may not be true, but may instead be a fiction, a fabrication, even an outright lie. Cicero prefers to avert his gaze from this possibility, and his overriding concern with *decorum* enables him to insist that a good rhetorician will never neglect the claims of morality.[38] But the author of the *Ad Herennium* acknowledges the place of such deceptions with characteristic openness, coolly concluding that 'if the things you are saying are fabricated, then it becomes all the more important to follow the rules'.[39]

Quintilian subsequently speaks with even greater frankness and practicality. Writing about the construction of narratives, in which the requirement of plausibility is of paramount importance, he agrees that 'there are many true things that are far from credible, just as there are false things that frequently look like the truth'.[40] He draws the moral that 'we should therefore take no less care to make the judge believe the true things we say and the things that we fabricate',[41] and he even inserts a section on what he calls 'false expositions' that can be made to sound like the truth.[42] Does this mean that we should be ready to lie and cheat if we think that such a strategy will help our case? Quintilian faces the question squarely in his final book, in which he asks whether it is possible at once to be a good orator and a bad man. Although he vigorously denies the possibility, he allows that sometimes it may be necessary to act badly if we believe that good may come of it: 'It is possible to adduce reasons for saying that a good man in defence of his cause will sometimes wish to lead the judge away from the truth.'[43] Even a thoroughly moral person, if his cause warrants it, 'will

---

37. *Rhetorica ad Herennium* 1954, I. IX. 16, p. 28: 'Si vera res erit...saepe veritas...fidem non potest facere'.
38. On this aspect of Cicero's rhetorical thought see Kapust 2011.
39. *Rhetorica ad Herennium* 1954, I. IX. 16, p. 28: 'sin [res] erunt ficta, eo magis erunt conservanda'.
40. Quintilian 2001, 4. 2. 34–5, vol. 2, p. 236: 'Sunt enim plurima vera quidem, sed parum credibilia, sicut falsa quoque frequenter veri similia.'
41. Quintilian 2001, 4. 2. 34–5, vol. 2, p. 236: 'Quare non minus laborandum est ut iudex quae vere dicimus quam quae fingimus credit.'
42. See Quintilian 2001, 4. 2. 88, vol. 2, p. 262 on 'falsae expositiones'.
43. Quintilian 2001, 12. 1, 36, vol. 5, p. 214: 'potest adferre ratio, ut vir bonus in defensione causae velit auferre aliquando iudici veritatem'.

defend someone with falsehoods no less than someone who is supporting a bad cause'.[44]

Some commentators have seen in this cast of mind a willingness to conflate the concepts of probability and truth.[45] But none of the rhetoricians I have cited denies the independence of the idea of truth. They merely argue that one of the skills of the rhetorician is that of creating an air of verisimilitude. What the ghost tells Hamlet about how he met his death eventually proves to be true, but when Hamlet first hears it the claim sounds incredible. One of the vital and benign functions of rhetoric is to rescue such improbable truths by showing us how to make them sound like the truth. As the rhetoricians concede, however, the same techniques can equally well be used in less benign ways. A sufficiently talented rhetorician may be able to make claims that are wholly false sound like the truth. This is what Othello discovers when duped by Iago into believing that Desdemona has been unfaithful to him. But in neither case is there any conflation of probability with truth. There is merely a suggestion that truth can be promoted, but also subverted, by means of the rhetorical arts.

The theory of invention, the rhetoricians next argue, not only requires us to 'invent' or find out suitable arguments but to deploy them in the most suitable order throughout a speech. As Cicero puts it, the further skill we need is that of ensuring 'a distribution in the correct sequence of whatever we have found out'.[46] With this commitment, the rhetoricians in effect reduce the topic of *dispositio*, the arrangement of arguments, to an aspect or element of *inventio*.[47] Cicero later reconsiders this position in his *De oratore*, but elsewhere he concurs with the *Ad Herennium* that, 'when we speak about the different parts of an oration, these must be accommodated to what the theory of invention requires in each case'.[48] Cicero agrees, in other words, that one aspect of inventing an argument will always be to 'dispose' it in the most persuasive style, as a result of which his analysis in *De inventione*

44. Quintilian 2001, 12. 1. 40, vol. 5, pp. 216–18: 'non tamen falsis defendet quam qui . . . malam causam tuetur'.
45. See, for example Altman 2010, pp. 21–22 on how, with the revival of classical rhetoric, the probable 'becomes conflated with the true'. This claim provides Altman with one of the leading themes of his book.
46. Cicero 1949a, I. VII. 9, p. 18: 'rerum inventarum in ordinem distributio'.
47. As noted in Mack 2011, p. 17.
48. *Rhetorica ad Herennium* 1954, I. III. 4, p. 10: 'de orationis partibus loqueremur . . . eas ad inventionis rationem adcommodaremus'.

of the five elements in the *ars rhetorica* includes no separate discussion of *dispositio* at all.

This emphasis on finding out which arguments are best suited to the different sections of a speech naturally prompts the rhetoricians to ask how many sections go to make a complete rhetorical performance. Aristotle had laid it down that no oration should have more than four divisions, dismissively adding that any proposal to increase this number is empty and absurd.[49] Nothing daunted, the author of the *Ad Herennium* takes a very different view.[50] 'There are six different parts of a speech,' he asserts, 'in relation to which the process of invention needs to be undertaken.'[51] The name and nature of each is then itemized:

> The *Exordium* is the beginning of our speech, by means of which our audience's mind is made ready to hear our case. The *Narratio* is the factual account of what happened or might have happened. The *Divisio* is where we indicate what is agreed and what is in dispute, and where we explain what points we plan to take up. The *Confirmatio* is the stage at which we offer an exposition of our own arguments with full seriousness. The *Confutatio* is when we demolish the arguments of our opponents. And the *Conclusio* is when we bring our speech to a resounding close.[52]

Cicero in his *De inventione* prefers to speak of the *partitio* rather than the *divisio*,[53] and the *reprehensio* rather than the *confutatio*,[54] but otherwise he is in full agreement with this anti-Aristotelian stance.

Faced with these numerous subdivisions, a number of authorities continued to recommend some version of the simpler Aristotelian scheme. By the time Cicero wrote his *De partitione oratoria*—an elementary textbook intended for his son—he had come round to the view that the only indispensable parts of an oration are the *narratio* and *confirmatio*, to which we can if we wish add a *principium* and a *peroratio*, a rhetorically persuasive

49. Aristotle 1926, III. 13. 4–5, p. 426.
50. But he may have been writing in ignorance of Aristotle's account. See Kennedy 1972, pp. 114–15 and cf. Vickers 1988, pp. 73–4.
51. *Rhetorica ad Herennium* 1954, I. III. 4, p. 8: 'Inventio in sex partes orationis consumitur'.
52. *Rhetorica ad Herennium* 1954, I. III. 4, pp. 8–10: 'Exordium est principium orationis, per quod animus auditoris constituitur ad audiendum. Narratio est rerum gestarum aut proinde ut gestarum expositio. Divisio est per quam aperimus quid conveniat, quid in controversia sit, et per quam exponimus quibus de rebus simus acturi. Confirmatio est nostrorum argumentorum expositio cum adseveratione. Confutatio est contrariorum locorum dissolutio. Conclusio est artificiosus orationis terminus.'
53. Cicero 1949a, I. XXII. 31, p. 62. 54. Cicero 1949a, I. XLII. 78, p. 122.

beginning and end.[55] Quintilian essentially agrees, although he thinks that Aristotle was mistaken in running together confirmation and refutation, and accordingly ends up with a preference for saying that any oration should be divided into five distinct parts.[56] There was little agreement as to how these should be labelled, but Quintilian always speaks of the opening section as the *prohoemium*, and most authorities describe the later parts as the *narratio*, the *confirmatio* (although Quintilian prefers *probatio*), the *refutatio*, and the *conclusio* or *peroratio*.[57]

Each of these parts has its own *telos*, which is why a mastery of *inventio* needs to include an understanding of which arguments are best suited to the different sections of a speech. The *prohoemium* must aim to establish our *ethos* or character, and in such a way as to render the judge attentive (*attentus*), responsive (*docilis*), and above all well-disposed (*benevolus*) to our side of the case.[58] The *narratio* should then furnish the judge with the salient facts, while persuading him at the same time to accept our version of events.[59] The *confirmatio* and *confutatio* should call on 'non-artificial' proofs such as written documents and the testimony of witnesses in addition to the most appropriate 'artificial' or rhetorical forms of argument.[60] Finally, the *peroratio* should not only summarize our case but make use of 'amplifications', especially in the form of *loci communes*, to excite the emotions of the judge. Sometimes the rhetoricians suggest that suitably resonant commonplaces can be inserted at any stage where they seem likely to have a powerful emotional impact,[61] but they always add that the *peroratio* is the moment at which they must chiefly and indispensably be used.[62]

The figure of the perfect orator whom these writers take themselves to be fashioning is accordingly said to be endowed with two closely related abilities: knowing how to invent or find out suitable arguments, and knowing how to

55. Cicero 1942b, I. 4, p. 312.   56. Quintilian 2001, 3. 9. 6, vol. 2, p. 152.
57. Quintilian 2001, 3. 9. 1, vol. 2, p. 148; 4. 1. 1, vol. 2, p. 180. Cf. *Rhetorica ad Herennium* 1954, I. III. 4, p. 8; Cicero 1949a, I. XIV. 19, p. 40.
58. Cicero 1949a, I. XV. 20, p. 40; *Rhetorica ad Herennium* 1954, I. IV. 6, p. 12; Cicero 1942a, II. XIX. 80, vol. 1, pp. 256–8; Quintilian 2001, 4. 1. 5, vol. 2, p. 182.
59. Cicero 1949a, I. XXI. 30, p. 62; *Rhetorica ad Herennium* 1954, I. VIII. 12, p. 22; Quintilian 2001, 4. 2. 21, vol. 2, p. 228.
60. Aristotle 1926, I. 2. 2, p. 14; I. 15. 1, p. 150 and I. 15. 17, p. 158; Cicero 1942a, II. XXVII. 116, vol. 1, pp. 280–2; Quintilian 2001, 5. 1. 1–2, vol. 2, p. 324.
61. Cicero 1949a, II. XV. 48–9, pp. 208–10. For the use of *loci communes* in the *narratio* see Quintilian 2001, 4. 2. 116–18, vol. 2, p. 276; for their use in the *confirmatio* see Cicero 1949a, I. LIII. 100, pp. 150–2.
62. *Rhetorica ad Herennium* 1954, III. VIII. 15, p. 182; cf. Cicero 1949a, I. LIII. 100 and I. LV. 106, pp. 150, 156; Quintilian 2001, 6. 1. 51, vol. 3, p. 42.

amplify and ornament them with maximum emotional force.[63] As Cicero summarizes at the start of *De inventione*—in a phrase that proved to have exceptional resonance—the ideal orator will therefore be a man (that he will be a man is, of course, taken for granted) who combines in the highest degree the power of *ratio* or reasoning with that of *oratio* or eloquent speech.[64] Reason is assumed to be an invariant quality, but Quintilian adds that eloquence can be expressed in one of three distinct *genera dicendi* or styles of rhetorical utterance, which he labels the plain, the intermediate, and the grand. The plain style is best adapted for conveying information, and ought chiefly to be used in narratives and proofs. But when it comes to arousing the emotions of our hearers we must know how to call upon the *genus grande* or grand style, enforcing our arguments with figures, amplifications, and other elocutionary effects.[65]

As Cicero notes, the earliest teachers of rhetoric, armed as they claimed to be with *ratio* as well as *oratio*, tended to have an overweening sense of the importance of their discipline. They liked to suppose that a fully trained orator will be capable of speaking effectively on any topic that may come up for debate.[66] But when Crassus attempts to revive this contention at the start of the *De oratore*, the figure of Scaevola reproves him for making an obvious overstatement.[67] There are some forms of reasoning, he retorts, in which the skills of the orator have no relevance. For example, 'we can set the mathematicians entirely to one side, with whose arts the capacity for powerful speech has no relation at all.'[68] The force of rhetoric is important only in relation to those types of argument in which we cannot hope to furnish demonstrations, but need to rest content with marshalling sufficient evidence to uphold a more or less probable case. As Quintilian observes, what this means is that oratorical skill is needed only in those disputes in which we can hope to debate with some plausibility *in utramque partem*, on

63. Cicero 1942b, I. XXVI. 118, p. 82; Quintilian 2001, Prohoemium 9, vol. 1, p. 56.
64. Cicero 1949a, I. II. 2, p. 6; for discussions see Wisse 2002 and (on *Coriolanus*) Kerrigan 2012, pp. 340–1.
65. Quintilian 2001, 12. 10, 58–62, vol. 5, pp. 312–14. On the grand style in the Renaissance see Shuger 1988, pp. 55–117.
66. Cicero 1949a, I. V. 7, p. 14. On the changing place of this contention in Cicero's rhetorical writings see Vickers 1988, pp. 29–32.
67. Pincombe 2001, pp. 22–9.
68. Cicero 1942a, I. X. 44, vol. 1, p. 32: 'Missos facio mathematicos . . . quorum artibus vestra ista dicendi vis ne minima quidem societate contingitur.'

either side of the case.[69] The perfect orator, as the practically minded Antonius is made to say in the *De oratore*, will therefore be someone whose speech is so persuasive and 'winning' that 'it has the effect of swinging his audience round, as if by some sort of machinery' in such a way that they cannot fail to end up on his side.[70]

It was Aristotle who put forward what became the standard classification of the types of argument in which these rhetorical skills are held to be indispensable. He identified three forms of oratorical utterance, and his taxonomy was subsequently adopted virtually without qualification by all the leading Roman authorities.[71] First there is epideictic or demonstrative oratory, the *genus demonstrativum*, in which the qualities of some particular person are assessed. Here it will always be possible to pronounce a *laudatio* or a *vituperatio*, speaking either in praise or in blame and hence on either side of the case. Next there is deliberative oratory, the *genus deliberativum*, the kind of speech we encounter in consultations and public assemblies. Here the aim will be to persuade someone to act or refrain from acting in some particular way, so that again there will be arguments on both sides. Finally there is judicial oratory, the *genus iudiciale*, the kind of speech most appropriate to courts of law.[72] Sometimes a judicial oration will take the form of a petition that may be met with a counter-plea or a refusal, but usually two opposed parties will present rival cases in prosecution and defence, so that once again there will be arguments on both sides.[73] These are the categories of argument, as Scaevola summarizes in Cicero's *De oratore,* in which the basic rhetorical skills of invention and disposition come into their own. You cannot do without them 'if you want the case you are pleading in the courts to seem the better and more probable one, or if you want the speeches you deliver in the assemblies to have the greatest persuasive force'.[74]

---

69. See, for example, Quintilian 2001, 3. 5. 5, vol. 2, p. 40. However, Quintilian occasionally suggests that the subject matter of rhetoric includes anything on which an orator may be asked to speak. See Quintilian 2001, 2. 21. 4, vol. 1, p. 408; 3. 3. 14, vol. 2, p. 28. This view was sometimes reiterated in the Renaissance. See, for example, Elyot 1531, Sig. F, 7ᵛ.
70. Cicero 1942a, II. XVII. 72, vol. 1, p. 252: 'machinatione aliqua ... est torquendus'.
71. For the details that follow see Cicero 1949a, I. V. 7, p. 16 and *Rhetorica ad Herennium* 1954, I. II. 2, p. 4.
72. On Aristotle's theory of forensic oratory see Hesk 2009, pp. 150–6.
73. Corbeill 2002, pp. 35–6 notes that, although advocacy was well established in the Roman courts, the rhetoricians still cleave to older Greek notions of speaking in one's own defence. As we shall see, this simplification suits Shakespeare's purposes well.
74. Cicero 1942a, I. X. 44, vol. 1, p. 32: 'ut in iudiciis ea causa, quamcumque tu dicis, melior et probabilior esse videatur; ut in concionibus et sententiis dicendis ad persuadendum'.

Of the three *genera* of rhetorical speech, everyone agreed that the *genus iudiciale* is by far the most important.[75] Aristotle refers somewhat cynically to this commitment, commenting that deliberative rhetoric is nobler, but that judicial speech is not only of more general interest but is better adapted to trickery and deceit.[76] By contrast, the Roman rhetoricians willingly endorse the special significance of forensic eloquence, and hence the need for the theory of rhetoric to focus on the *genus iudiciale*. Both Cicero and the author of the *Ad Herennium* concentrate overwhelmingly on judicial speech, while Quintilian goes so far as to affirm that the most basic question that any orator needs to put to himself is whether or not he is arguing in a court of law.[77] This sense of priorities has usually been explained in terms of the fact that the Roman rhetoricians were much employed in the training of young men for legal careers, but they may also have been seeking to vindicate a loftier claim about their discipline: that society is constantly subject to wounding divisions, and that these can most readily be healed by the mediating power of eloquent speech.[78]

Whatever their reasons, there is no doubt that the rhetoricians generally focus on the *genus iudiciale* when they turn to consider the orator's *officium* or distinctive role.[79] They begin by affirming that an orator will best fulfil his function if he undertakes to examine some *res* or issue of public importance.[80] The term *res* was sometimes used to refer to the entire content of the rhetorician's art,[81] but was usually applied to describe the 'matter' (as the vernacular rhetoricians liked to say)[82] that was taken to stand in need of investigation in a judicial case.[83] Cicero lays it down at the start of his *De inventione* that there will always be some single *res* under examination in such cases.[84] Quintilian, more expansive as always, prefers to say that 'in any instance in which there is a plaintiff on one side and a defendant on the other' there will

75. As Vickers 1988, pp. 53–62 points out, however, this commitment was already at odds with the realities of Roman public life, and he traces the rise of demonstrative and decline of judicial rhetoric in later antiquity.
76. Aristotle 1926, I. 1. 10, pp. 6–8.   77. Quintilian 2001, 3. 4. 7, vol. 2, p. 32.
78. Connolly 2007, pp. 27, 65–76.
79. On the *officium oratoris* see *Rhetorica ad Herennium* 1954, I. II. 2, p. 4. The focus on judicial oratory is particularly marked in Cicero 1949a, I. VIII. 10 *et seq.*
80. *Rhetorica ad Herennium* 1954, I. II. 2, p. 4; cf. Quintilian 2001, 3. 6. 21, vol. 2, p. 58.
81. See, for example, Cicero 1949a, I. V. 7, p. 16; Quintilian 2001, 3. 1. 1, vol. 2, p. 8.
82. The translation of *res* as 'matter' is also standard in the Latin–English dictionaries of Shakespeare's time. See, for example, Cooper 1565, Sig. 5P, 6ʳ: 'Res...A thyng...the mattier'.
83. See, for example, Cicero 1949a, I. VIII. 10, p. 20; *Rhetorica ad Herennium* 1954, I. II. 2, p. 4.
84. Cicero 1949a, I. VIII. 10, p. 20.

be a dispute centring 'either on a single *res* or matter, or else on a number of them'.[85]

The distinguishing feature of the matters handled in judicial causes is that they centre on *controversiae*, disputes between two opposing sides. 'An enquiry is judicial', the *Ad Herennium* explains, 'when something is put forward in controversy, and when there is either a process of accusation or a petition and defence.'[86] Quintilian agrees that, whenever we encounter a plaintiff and a defendant, there must obviously be some kind of disagreement between them.[87] He rounds off his discussion by submitting that an orator's aim should always be to identify 'what it is that comes into controversy', and to work out 'what our adversary's side and what our own side want to make of it'.[88]

To say that there is some matter in controversy is held to be equivalent to asserting that there is some *quaestio iudicii* or question for adjudication that the two parties need to resolve. This was known in turn as the *constitutio* of the case.[89] Cicero in his later years expresses some impatience with the theory of *constitutiones*, putting into Crassus's mouth the view that it is mainly a matter of common sense.[90] But in *De inventione* he is happy to put forward what became the standard definition of a *constitutio*: that it is 'the name we assign to the question out of which the cause is born'.[91] Quintilian alludes to Cicero's formula, slightly adapting it to suggest that the term should be taken to refer to 'the sort of question that arises out of the basic conflict' between two sides.[92] The general question in such legal arguments,

---

85. Quintilian 2001, 3. 10. 1, vol. 2, p. 154: 'Ceterum causa omnis in qua pars altera agendis est, altera recusantis, aut unius rei controversia constat aut plurium.'
86. *Rhetorica ad Herennium* 1954, I. II. 2, p. 4: 'Iudiciale est quod positum est in controversia, et quod habet accusationem aut petitionem cum defensione'; cf. also I. XVI. 26, p. 50.
87. Quintilian 2001, 3. 10. 1, vol. 2, p. 154.
88. Quintilian 2001, 3. 11. 23, vol. 2, p. 166: 'quid sit quod in controversiam veniat, quid in eo . . . velit efficere pars diversa, quid nostra'.
89. *Rhetorica ad Herennium* 1954, I. XI. 18, p. 32; Cicero 1949a, I. VIII. 10, p. 20. Quintilian 2001, 3. 6. 2, vol. 2, p. 48 prefers to speak of the *status* or state of the case, but concedes that the two words mean the same thing. The theory seems to have been developed by the Hellenistic rhetorician Hermagoras of Temnos. See Corbeill 2002, p. 29; Connolly 2007, pp. 69–70, 72–3.
90. Cicero 1949a, II. XXX. 132, vol. 1, p. 292.
91. Cicero 1949a, I. VIII. 10, p. 20: 'quaestionem ex qua causa nascitur constitutionem appellamus'.
92. Quintilian 2001, 3. 6. 5, vol. 2, p. 50: 'quod ex prima conflictione nascitur . . . genus quaestionis'.

he concludes, is therefore 'the point around which the matter chiefly turns, the most important point in the dispute'.[93]

We next need to know how many *constitutiones* need to be distinguished. Characteristically, Quintilian provides a full-scale historiography of the different answers furnished by the various schools of rhetorical thought, noting that according to some authorities there may be as few as two, and according to others as many as seven or eight.[94] His own answer is that there are only two basic types,[95] but he concedes that the most widely accepted conclusion is that there are three, and that the proper method of distinguishing them is to ask whether the question for adjudication is legal or conjectural or juridical in character.[96] He associates these commitments with Cicero's analysis in the *Orator*, but in fact Cicero refers only glancingly to the threefold classification in that work.[97] For the clearest exposition we need to return to the author of the *Ad Herennium*, who firmly insists that there are three and only three types, and that these can be labelled as the *constitutio legitima* or *legalis* (the legal), the *constitutio coniecturalis* (the conjectural), and the *constitutio iuridicalis* (the juridical).[98] The right way to discover which type you are dealing with is simply 'to put together the charge levelled by the accuser with the basic plea of the defence'.[99] When the *constitutio* is legal 'the controversy will arise out of a text or something stemming from a text'.[100] When the *constitutio* is conjectural 'the controversy will be about some matter of fact', and more specifically about some mystery surrounding a matter of fact that needs to be resolved.[101] When the *constitutio* is juridical the facts will not be in dispute, and the controversy will revolve entirely around 'whether something was justly or unjustly done'.[102]

93. Quintilian 2001, 3. 6. 21, vol. 2, p. 58: the *status* or *quaestio generalis* is 'quod esset in ea potentissimum et in quo maxime res verteretur'.
94. Quintilian 2001, 3. 6. 29, vol. 2, p. 62 and 3. 6. 55, vol. 2, p. 76.
95. Quintilian 2001, 3. 6. 86, vol. 2, p. 92.   96. Quintilian 2001, 3. 6. 45, vol. 2, p. 70.
97. Cicero 1962b, 45, p. 338.
98. See *Rhetorica ad Herennium* 1954, I. XI. 18, pp. 32–4, where the 'legal' issue is labelled *legitima*. Cicero 1949a, I. XI. 14, p. 30 prefers *negotialis*, while Quintilian 2001, 3. 6. 45, vol. 2, p. 70 prefers *legalis*. The vernacular writers generally pick up Quintilian's terminology, and I follow them.
99. *Rhetorica ad Herennium* 1954, I. XI. 18, p. 32: 'prima deprecatio defensoris cum accusatoris insimulatione coniuncta'.
100. *Rhetorica ad Herennium* 1954, I. XI. 18, p. 34: 'in scripto aut e scripto aliquid controversiae nascitur'.
101. *Rhetorica ad Herennium* 1954, I. XI. 18, p. 34: 'coniecturalis est cum de facto controversia est'.
102. *Rhetorica ad Herennium* 1954, I. XIV. 24, p. 42: 'iure an iniuria factum sit'.

Among these types, the *constitutio iuridicalis* is taken to be the most complicated, since it can arise in one of two contrasting ways. When something has been justly done, the *constitutio* will be *absoluta* or absolute, since the plaintiff will be able to contend that the act in question was absolutely right in and of itself.[103] But when something has been unjustly done, the *constitutio* will be *adsumptiva* or assumptive, since the plaintiff will be unable to defend his cause unless he can manage to add something (*assumere*) in the form of a *concessio* by way of justifying or exonerating himself.[104] It may be possible to present such a *concessio* in the form of a *purgatio*, a claim to the effect that you did not act *cum consulto*, with full intention and foresight, and hence deserve to be excused. But if you cannot hope to enter such a plea in mitigation, then your only recourse will be to offer a *concessio* in the form of a *deprecatio*, a straightforward admission of guilt accompanied by a plea for pardon.[105]

From Cicero's *Topica* and *De partitione oratoria* Quintilian takes up a further distinction between two different types of question that can arise.[106] Some can be *infinita*, wholly general in character, such as the question as to whether one should marry. But others can be *finita*, related to a particular person and place, such as the question as to whether Cato should marry.[107] Cicero seems willing in *De inventione* to concede that the first species of *quaestio*, in which one is said to put forward a *thesis*, arises more typically in philosophy. He agrees that the second species, in which one merely puts forward a *hypothesis*, is more characteristic of oratory.[108] Later, however, he makes a stronger claim for the philosophical significance of rhetoric, insisting that it can encompass questions of both types. It is this latter understanding that Quintilian picks up, arguing that in every 'special' question a more general one will always be implicit as well as prior to the specific hypothesis.[109] Reflecting on the scope of such arguments, Quintilian eventually concludes that 'the term *quaestio* can therefore be understood

103. *Rhetorica ad Herennium* 1954, I. XIV. 24, p. 44. Cf. Cicero 1949a, I. XI. 14–15, p. 30; Quintilian 2001, 7. 4. 4, vol. 3, p. 238.
104. *Rhetorica ad Herennium* 1954, I. XIV. 24, p. 44. Cf. Cicero 1949a, I. XI. 15, p. 30; Quintilian 2001, 7. 4. 7, vol. 3, p. 240.
105. *Rhetorica ad Herennium* 1954, I. XIV. 24, p. 44. Cf. Cicero 1949a, I. XI. 15, p. 30; Quintilian 2001, 7. 4. 17, vol. 3, pp. 244–6.
106. Cicero 1949b, XXI. 80, p. 444; Cicero 1942b, XVIII. 61, p. 356.
107. Quintilian 2001, 3. 5. 7, vol. 2, p. 40.
108. Cicero 1949a, I. IX. 12, pp. 24–6; cf. Heath 2009, p. 66.
109. Quintilian 2001, 3. 5. 9–10, vol. 2, p. 42.

in a broad sense as referring to anything that can plausibly be argued on either side of the case or even on various different sides'.[110]

If we return to Cicero's *De inventione*, we next find him arguing that, wherever there is a finite question to be resolved, we must be dealing with a *causa*, a legal case in which some hypothesis is submitted to judgement. 'It is from the question', as he summarizes, 'that the cause is born.'[111] As we have seen, however, what is said to distinguish the *genus iudiciale* is that there will always be some *res* or matter *in controversia* between two opposing sides. So it is not surprising to find that the term *causa* also came to be used to refer more specifically to whichever side an orator chooses to support. This is clearly the meaning that Cicero and the author of the *Ad Herennium* alike have in mind when they declare that the whole purpose of rhetorical invention is 'to work out what serves to render your cause probable'.[112] Following Cicero's *De partitione oratoria*, Quintilian goes so far as to assert that to speak of a definite question must be equivalent to speaking of such a *causa* or cause.[113] He quotes with apparent approval the *dictum* of Apollodorus to the effect that 'a cause is an affair where the outcome is a controversy'.[114] As a result, the summary view of judicial rhetoric at which these writers arrive is that an orator's principal aim should be that of working out how best to plead a cause in a matter in controversy—and hence in question—between two opposing sides.[115] It is around the concepts of *res, quaestio,* and *causa* that the whole discussion may be said to revolve.

The teaching of rhetoric in Tudor England

During the opening decades of the sixteenth century the theory I have been sketching succeeded to a remarkable degree in recovering the central position it had occupied in Roman educational practice.[116] To our more

---

110. Quintilian 2001, 3. 11. 1–2, vol. 2, p. 156: 'Quaestio latius intellegitur omnis de qua in utramque partem vel in plures dici credibiliter potest.' On *argumenta in utramque partem* see Peltonen 2013, esp. pp. 68–70.
111. Cicero 1949a, I. VIII. 10, p. 20: 'Eam igitur quaestionem ex qua causa nascitur.'
112. Cicero 1949a, I. VII. 9, p. 18; cf. *Rhetorica ad Herennium* 1954, I. II. 3, p. 6: 'Inventio est excogitatio rerum . . . quae causam probabilem reddant.'
113. Cicero 1942b, XVIII. 61, p. 356; cf. Quintilian 2001, 3. 5. 7, vol. 2, p. 40.
114. Quintilian 2001, 3. 5. 17, vol. 2, p. 46: 'causa est negotium cuius finis est controversia'.
115. On the meanings of legal *causae* in this period see Cormack 2007, pp. 19–21.
116. On the evolution of Renaissance rhetoric see Mack 2011; on the Renaissance reception of Cicero and Quintilian see Ward 1999.

historically minded age it is astonishing to see how far the English humanists of the Renaissance were prepared to treat the rhetorical and other texts of classical antiquity as if they were contemporary documents. This in turn means—an important point in relation to my present argument—that there is nothing unhistorical about yoking Cicero and Quintilian together with the vernacular rhetoricians of Tudor England and treating them as if they were contributing to a single argument. To do so is simply to reflect the extraordinarily strong sense of cultural continuity with which the humanists confronted their classical authorities.[117]

The specific syllabus reintroduced by the humanists had been known in antiquity as the *studia humanitatis*. Quintilian in Book 10 of his *Institutio oratoria* furnishes a celebrated summary of the scheme of instruction involved. As well as mastering the art of rhetoric,[118] aspiring orators are expected to immerse themselves in the study and appreciation of poetry, history, and moral philosophy.[119] Among the poets Quintilian gives pride of place to Homer and Virgil;[120] among the historians he singles out Thucydides and Herodotus, together with Sallust and Livy among the Romans;[121] and in moral philosophy he claims that 'Cicero stands out as a rival even to Plato himself'.[122] It was essentially this Roman vision of the distinctively 'humane' studies that the English educational theorists of the Renaissance revived.[123] One of the clearest statements of their resulting programme can be found in *The boke named the Governour*, which Thomas Elyot (*c.*1490–1546) published in 1531. After the study of grammar, the young student is introduced to classical poetry, and above all to Homer.[124] By the age of fourteen, the future 'governor' is ready for dialectic and rhetoric, and Quintilian's *Institutio oratoria* is recommended as a work from which the whole of the latter art can be learned.[125] Next the student is expected to turn to cosmography and (in much greater detail) to history, beginning with Livy and moving on to Caesar, Sallust, and Tacitus.[126] By

---

117. For this point and its ramifications see Skinner 1996, p. 40.
118. Quintilian 2001, 10. 1. 20–6, vol. 4, pp. 262–4.
119. Quintilian 2001, 10. 1. 27–36, vol. 4, pp. 166–70.
120. Quintilian 2001, 10. 1. 46 and 85, vol. 4, pp. 274, 296.
121. Quintilian 2001, 10. 1. 73 and 101, vol. 4, pp. 290, 306.
122. Quintilian 2001, 10. 1. 123, vol. 4, p. 318: 'M. Tullius...in hoc opere Platonis aemulus extitit.'
123. For a fuller account of this process, on which I draw in what follows, see Skinner 1996, pp. 19–40; see also Simon 1966, pp. 59–123, 299–332.
124. Elyot 1531, Sig. D, 7ᵛ–8ʳ; Sig. D, 8ᵛ to Sig E, 1ʳ.   125. Elyot 1531, Sig. E, 4ʳ.
126. Elyot 1531, Sig. E, 4ʳ–8ᵛ.

the time he reaches the age of seventeen, it is 'nedefull to rede unto hym some workes of philosophie: specially that parte that may enforme him unto vertuous maners'.[127] At this juncture he is exhorted to concentrate on Aristotle's *Ethics*, Cicero's *De Officiis*, and the works of Plato 'above all other'.[128]

As Elyot concedes, however, this road to wisdom is heavily barricaded. Most Greek and Roman authorities 'holde opinion that before the age of seven yeres, a chylde shulde not be instructed in letters'. However, these writers were able to take it for granted that 'all doctrine and sciences were in their maternall tonges' and were able to save their pupils 'all that longe tyme whiche at this dayes is spent in understandyng perfectly the greke or latyne'. By contrast, the infelicity of the present age is such that we have no alternative but to begin as early as possible to learn the classical languages. Without acquiring these preliminary skills, we can never hope to enter the house of humane learning and attain gravity and wisdom.[129]

As a consequence, the grammar-school curriculum that evolved in Tudor England was overwhelmingly linguistic in scope. For an indication of what was taught we can turn to *The Education of Children in Learning* by William Kempe, a graduate of Trinity College Cambridge who became Master of Plymouth Grammar School, and who published his handbook in 1588.[130] Kempe recommends that the first five years of schooling should be devoted to learning Latin, after which the pupil progresses to the sixth form, in which he can expect to spend three further years.[131] There he should be introduced to the study of logic and rhetoric, but with a continuing emphasis on the use of Latin to write 'themes' in proper rhetorical style. Apart from some mathematics in the final year, the study of Latin dominates the entire syllabus.[132]

The two-stage process of learning Latin that Kempe envisages was generally equated with the mastering of the two linguistic elements in the *studia humanitatis*, the *ars grammatica*, and the *ars rhetorica*.[133] Juan Luis Vives (1493–1540), who first arrived in England to teach the humanities at Oxford

---

127. Elyot 1531, Sig. F, 1ʳ.   128. Elyot 1531, Sig. F, 1ʳ.   129. Elyot 1531, Sig. C, 2ʳ.
130. On Kempe see Baldwin 1944, vol. 1, pp. 437–49; Howell 1956, pp. 258–61.
131. Kempe 1588, Sig. F, 3ᵛ to Sig. G, 1ʳ.
132. Kempe 1588, Sig. G, 2ᵛ to Sig. H, 1ʳ. See also Charlton 1965, pp. 105–6, 109–12. On the primacy of grammar in the curriculum see Percival 1983 and Crane 1993, pp. 79–86; on the place of rhetoric see Curtis 2002. On the teaching of the humanist disciplines see also Bushnell 1996.
133. For a full analysis of these stages see Green 2009, pp. 129–90.

in 1523, had already underlined the point in his *De tradendis disciplinis* of 1531.[134] As he notes, we begin to study grammar as soon as we start to learn Latin, and hence to memorize declensions, conjugations, and so forth.[135] We embark on the study of rhetoric as soon as we learn to identify figures and tropes, after which we are ready for what Vives describes as the greater rhetorical exercises.[136] These include the writing of themes and declamations, as well as speaking 'in controversy' on one side or the other in a given cause.[137] By the time a student arrives at the stage of writing themes of his own, he will have succeeded in putting together his initial understanding of grammar with his later studies of rhetoric and 'fineness of speach'.[138]

The principles of rhetoric were generally inculcated by studying one or other of the classical handbooks. Quintilian was sometimes rather ambitiously recommended, but by far the most popular manuals were the *Ad Herennium* and Cicero's introductory works, especially the *De inventione* and *De partitione oratoria*. When Vives lays out his curriculum in *De tradendis disciplinis* he refers to the *Ad Herennium* as one of the most useful introductions,[139] and this judgement was strongly endorsed by Johannes Sturm in his *De literarum ludis*. Sturm suggests that a child's education should begin at the age of five or six and thereafter continue for nine years.[140] The study of rhetoric should begin in the fifth year with the topic of *elocutio*, followed in the sixth year by *inventio*, and in each case the most suitable textbook to use is said to be the *Ad Herennium*.[141]

The surviving statutes of the Tudor grammar schools show that this advice was widely taken up. The 'laws' drawn up in 1550 for King Edward VI Grammar School at Bury St Edmunds state that, in the most senior form, 'the master should read Quintilian's *Institutio oratoria*, or else the precepts of Rhetoric contained in the *Ad Herennium*.'[142] The ordinances of 1556 for Norwich Grammar School likewise specify that Quintilian and the *Ad Herennium* should be read 'in the highest fourme'.[143] The 1574 statutes of the Free Grammar School at Leicester require that, after the rules of Latin grammar have been learned, the master should construe with his highest

---

134. Simon 1966, pp. 106–14.   135. Vives 1913 [1531], pp. 96–7.
136. Vives 1913 [1531], p. 98.   137. Vives 1913 [1531], p. 184.
138. Kempe 1588, Sig. G, 3ʳ.   139. Vives 1913 [1531], p. 183.
140. Sturm 1538, fo. 14ʳ.   141. Sturm 1538, fos. 19ᵛ, 20ʳ, 23ᵛ.
142. BL Lansdowne MS 119, fo. 14ʳ, item 25: 'Institutiones Oratorias Quintilliani, aut praeceptiones Rhetoricae eas quae sunt apud Herennium a ludimagistro audiunto.'
143. Saunders 1932, pp. 136, 147.

form 'some parte of Tullie ad Herennium' at least twice a week.[144] The 1576 statutes of Rivington School similarly state that, after the necessary grammatical exercises have been completed, the master should 'enter his Scholar into the rules of Rhetoric, in Tully's Books, (ad Herennium) to let him understand the divers kinds, and parts of an Oration', so that he may be able 'to declaim probably on any Questions propounded'.[145]

Due to the earlier triumph of humanist pedagogy in Italy,[146] these classical handbooks had for some time been widely available, and were indeed among the best-sellers of the earliest age of the printed book. Quintilian's *Institutio oratoria* was first published in Rome in 1470 and reissued at least six times before 1500, chiefly in Venice.[147] There were as many as twenty Paris printings in the first half of the sixteenth century,[148] while at Lyon Sébastian Gryphius began to produce the *Institutio* together with Quintilian's *Declamations* in 1531, reprinting this version more than half a dozen times over the next twenty years.[149] Still more popular were the elementary handbooks, especially the *Rhetorica ad Herennium* and Cicero's *De inventione*.[150] The latter was first published by Nicolas Jenson in Venice in 1470, and thereafter went through at least a dozen Italian printings before the end of the century.[151] It was the *Ad Herennium*, however, that was most widely disseminated.[152] After its initial publication by Jenson in 1470 there were at least ten Italian printings within the next twenty years.[153] A frequent arrangement—initiated by Jenson—took the form of putting the *Ad Herennium* together with the *De inventione* and issuing them as a single book.[154] Battista Torti followed this practice in his 1481 edition, which was reprinted several times within the next decade.[155] Like Jenson, Torti ascribed both works to Cicero, referring on his title-page to the *De inventione* as Cicero's 'old' rhetoric, and to the *Ad Herennium* as his 'new' and more systematic handling of the same themes.[156] Besides these joint

144. Cross 1953, p. 16.
145. Whitaker 1837, pp. 213–14. See also Kay 1966, pp. 53, 187 and for the date of the statutes see p. xvi. Note here, as in the Norwich and Leicester statutes, the mistaken attribution of the *Ad Herennium* to 'Tully', i.e. Cicero.
146. Grendler 1989, pp. 117–21, 133–41 dates this triumph to the mid-*quattrocento*.
147. Green and Murphy 2006, pp. 352–3. On its impact see Grendler 1989, pp. 120–1.
148. Green and Murphy 2006, pp. 352–3, 354–6.   149. Green and Murphy 2006, p. 355.
150. On the printing histories of these texts see Mack 2011, pp. 14–18.
151. Green and Murphy 2006, pp. 107, 109, 114.   152. Grendler 1989, pp. 208, 213–14.
153. Green and Murphy 2006, pp. 114, 125.   154. Green and Murphy 2006, p. 114.
155. Green and Murphy 2006, p. 114.
156. Cicero 1481. I have put together the separate title pages of the two texts (BL copy).

printings, the two works were also the subject of a large number of glosses and commentaries in the first years of the printed book.[157]

These arrangements were abruptly called in question when Raphael Regius (c.1440–1520) published his *Ducenta problemata* in 1490.[158] His concluding essay is entitled 'Whether the *Rhetorica ad Herennium* has been falsely attributed to Cicero', and he leaves no doubt that the attribution is indeed false.[159] His conclusion was quickly accepted by most of the leading educational writers, and Vives remarks in his *De tradendis disciplinis* that he cannot understand how it ever came to be supposed that Cicero wrote the book.[160] To the Italian booksellers, however, the uncoupling of the *Ad Herennium* from the magic name of Cicero was so unwelcome that Regius's critique was at first widely ignored. The ascription only seems to have been generally abandoned after Paolo Manuzio (1512–74) issued his collection of Cicero's rhetorical works in 1546, in which he accepted that the *Ad Herennium* was 'by an unknown author'.[161] Even after this, however, the French and German booksellers remained obdurate. The Cologne firm of Gymnich was still printing the *Ad Herennium* as an authentically Ciceronian text in the 1550s,[162] while Antoine Gryphius of Lyon gave up the ascription only in his edition of 1570, in which he finally left the work unattributed.[163]

By this time there was a growing interest in publishing these handbooks in England. Such an arrangement first became possible in 1569, when Henry Bynneman evidently received a patent to publish classical books for use in schools, some of which he printed himself while also licensing others to produce them.[164] One of the first London printers to take advantage of this arrangement was John Kingston, who had already published a number of rhetorical texts, including an edition of Erasmus's *De*

---

157. See Ward 1983, pp. 142–5. The earliest was a gloss on the *De inventione* published in 1474.
158. Green and Murphy 2006, p. 372. I refer to the BL copy, dated September 1492.
159. Regius 1492, Sig. F, 8ʳ: 'Utrum ars rhetorica ad Herennium Ciceroni falso inscribatur.' Regius's finding raises some questions that have never been resolved. If Cicero did not write the *Ad Herennium*, who did? And what could have prevented the authorship of such a widely influential work from becoming known? Regius pays no attention to such issues, limiting himself to demolishing the case in favour of Cicero's authorship in little more than three pages of withering analysis.
160. Vives 1913 [1531], p. 183.
161. See Cicero 1546 and cf. Green and Murphy 2006, p. 112.
162. See Cicero 1550, where *De inventione* is said to be 'by the same writer' (*eiusdem*) as the *Ad Herennium*.
163. Cicero 1570; cf. Green and Murphy 2006, p. 116.
164. Baldwin 1944, vol. I, pp. 494–502; Mack 2002, p. 16 and n.

copia in 1569.[165] In 1573 Kingston issued Cicero's *Brutus* and *De oratore*, and in the following year he published Cicero's *De inventione* together with the *Ad Herennium*, making use of the version originally printed by Gymnich in 1535.[166] But Kingston's edition was not altogether satisfactory. He continued to treat the *Ad Herennium* as an authentically Ciceronian work, which by the 1570s had become a mark of bibliographical ignorance, and his text was continually interrupted by a somewhat laboured commentary. The need for a more up-to-date and user-friendly edition accordingly remained, and this was duly met by the rival London printer Thomas Vautrollier, who made use of the version issued by Antoine Gryphius in 1570. Vautrollier abandoned any pretence that Cicero was the author of the *Ad Herennium*, while continuing to associate it closely with the undoubtedly authentic *De inventione*. The resulting volume, containing a complete and impressively accurate version of both works, was published in 1579 under the title *Rhetoricorum ad C. Herennium Libri Quattuor. M. T. Ciceronis De Inventione Libri Duo*.[167]

Thomas Vautrollier was a native of Troyes who had arrived in London in the late 1550s, acquiring the status of an English 'denizen' by 1562.[168] He first set up as a bookseller in 1567 in association with another French immigrant, Jean Deserrans,[169] but shortly afterwards he began to work in collaboration with Thomas Marsh, who obtained a patent in 1572 to publish Latin books for use in schools.[170] By the mid-1570s Vautrollier was running a print shop with six assistants,[171] and he further increased his staff in 1579 when he took on an apprentice named Richard Field.[172] Field had come to London from Stratford-upon-Avon, where his parents were acquainted with the family of William Shakespeare. When Field's father died in 1592, Shakespeare's father was one of a group of Stratford citizens called upon to

165. Green and Murphy 2006, p. 187. Green and Murphy 2006, pp. 362, 462 also record that Kingston took over the printing of Thomas Wilson's *Arte of Rhetorique* in 1560 and published Rainolde's *Foundacion of Rhetorike* in 1563.

166. See Cicero 1539 for Gymnich's title-page and Cicero 1574 for Kingston's virtually identical one.

167. Cicero 1579a. The sole difference between this title-page and Gryphius's of 1570 is that the latter has 'quatuor' instead of 'quattuor'.

168. McKerrow 1968, p. 272.   169. LeFanu 1959–64, p. 15.

170. LeFanu 1959–64, p. 18.   171. Arber, 1875–94, vol. 2, p. 746; cf. Nicholl 2007, p. 176.

172. Kirwood 1931, p. 1 notes that Field was baptized on 16 November 1561. Arber 1875–94, vol. 2, p. 30 records that he was apprenticed in September 1579 to George Bishop for seven years, the first six to be served with Thomas Vautrollier.

make an inventory of his goods.[173] Field was more than two years older than Shakespeare, but they must have overlapped as pupils at the King's New School in Stratford and, as we shall see, they undoubtedly kept in touch.

Shortly before Field began his apprenticeship, Vautrollier had embarked on the production of an impressive range of classical texts of rhetoric, poetry, history, and moral philosophy—the full gamut of the *studia humanitatis*. During 1579 he printed several works of classical rhetoric, including an edition of Cicero's orations as well as the *De inventione*.[174] He also printed one of the most celebrated translations of a work of classical history, Thomas North's version of Plutarch, which appeared as *The Lives of the Noble Grecians and Romanes*.[175] The same year saw him issue a collection of Cicero's works on moral philosophy,[176] and soon afterwards he branched out into classical poetry, printing Ovid's *Metamorphoses* in 1582 and two further collections of his verse in the following year.[177]

When Thomas Vautrollier died in 1587 his widow Jacqueline took over the running of the printing house,[178] facing down stiff opposition from the Stationers' Company.[179] Within a year she was issuing texts to be sold by her late husband's erstwhile apprentice, Richard Field,[180] who had meanwhile become a freeman of the Company.[181] By January 1589 Jacqueline Vautrollier and Richard Field were married, and thereafter Field seems to have assumed control of the business, which he ran with steady success until his death in 1624.[182] He continued to issue books in the *studia humanitatis*, and was much prized as an accurate printer of Latin texts.[183] But his preference seems to have been for contemporary rather than ancient works in the humanistic disciplines. He produced a number of best-selling

173. See Kirwood 1931, p. 1; McKerrow 1968, p. 102.   174. Cicero 1579b.
175. Plutarch 1579.
176. See Cicero 1579c, and cf. Cicero 1584, a collection of *sententiae* partly taken from Cicero.
177. Ovid 1582; Ovid 1583a; Ovid 1583b.
178. Kirwood, 1931, p. 5; LeFanu, 1959–64, pp. 21, 23.
179. Greg and Boswell 1930, p. 26 record that in March 1588 the Stationers' Company's court forbade her to 'prynte anye manner of Booke'. See also McKerrow 1968, pp. 271–2.
180. See *Copie of a Letter* 1588, 'imprinted by J. Vautrollier for Richard Field'.
181. Arber 1875–94, vol. 2, p. 332 records his admission in February 1587.
182. LeFanu 1959–64, p. 14; Nicholl 2007, p. 175. Duncan-Jones 2001, pp. 5, 114 suggests that it may have been Vautrollier's daughter whom Field married; but McKerrow 1968, p. 273 notes that Vautrollier had four sons but no daughter.
183. Kirwood 1931, p. 23. McKerrow 1968, p. 103 rates him as no more than 'creditable' as a printer, but it is surely significant that Harington, who cared deeply about the production of his *Orlando Furioso*, specifically chose Field to print it.

books on grammar, including John Brinsley's guide to the teaching of Latin,[184] as well as vernacular works on rhetoric, including George Puttenham's *Arte of English Poesie* in 1589 and Thomas Campion's *Observations* in 1602.[185] He printed several major works of history, including Fenton's translation of Guicciardini,[186] and he continued to issue North's translation of Plutarch's *Lives*, new versions of which appeared in 1595 and 1603. He also printed a number of works of moral philosophy, including Lipsius's *Sixe books* in 1594 and a Latin translation of Castiglione's *Cortegiano* in 1612.[187]

It was in contemporary poetry, however, that Field achieved his most spectacular success. He printed and published John Harington's translation of *Orlando Furioso* in 1591.[188] He printed some poems by George Chapman in 1594, as well as his translations of Homer in 1611 and 1614.[189] He produced the first complete edition of Edmund Spenser's *Faerie Queene* in 1596,[190] and was one of the earliest to print Sidney's *Arcadia* in 1598.[191] He also issued—as publisher as well as printer—the first work of Shakespeare's to be published, his *Venus and Adonis* of 1593.[192] A year later he printed— for the publisher John Harrison—Shakespeare's *Lucrece*.[193] Although Field ceased to issue Shakespeare's poems after 1596,[194] it was he who, with his edition of *Venus and Adonis*, enabled Shakespeare to present his patron, the Earl of Southampton, with what he described in his Dedication as 'the first heire of my invention'.[195]

The Tudor rhetoricians

While the classical manuals, especially the *Ad Herennium*, continued to dominate the teaching of rhetoric in English schools throughout the sixteenth century, a number of contemporary Latin works on the subject

---

184. Brinsley 1622.   185. Puttenham 1589; Campion 1602.
186. Guicciardini 1599.   187. Lipsius 1594; Castiglione 1612.
188. Harington 1591.   189. Chapman 1594; Chapman 1611; Chapman 1614.
190. Spenser 1596. No printer is credited, but the emblem inherited by Field from Vautrollier (the anchor of hope) appears identically here and in Chapman 1594. The publisher in both cases was William Ponsonby.
191. Sidney 1598.   192. Shakespeare 1593.   193. Shakespeare 1594.
194. Field printed only the 1594 edition of *Lucrece*, and no edition of *Venus and Adonis* after 1596. See Erne 2013, pp. 146–8.
195. Shakespeare 1986, *Venus and Adonis*, p. 254.

began to be widely published at around the same time. One of the most influential was Erasmus's *De copia* of 1512, which was reprinted at an average of three new editions every year throughout the half-century after its first appearance,[196] including a first London printing in 1528 and John Kingston's improved edition in 1569.[197] Scarcely less popular was Omer Talon's *Rhetorica* of 1545, which went through seventy-five printings before the end of the century,[198] including a Cambridge edition in 1592.[199] Still more widely used were Philipp Melanchthon's two handbooks on rhetoric, his *De rhetorica libri tres* of 1519,[200] and his *Rhetorices Elementa* of 1531.[201] Neither work was published in England, but both were widely available, and were issued in a total of well over a hundred editions before the end of the century.[202] By this time these texts had been supplemented by a new generation of Latin treatises, among the most popular being Cypriano Suarez's *De arte rhetoricae* of 1562 and the many rhetorical works of Ludovico Carbone.[203]

Of greater importance for my present argument is the fact that these Latin manuals began to be joined and even rivalled by a number of vernacular texts.[204] The earliest was *The Art or crafte of Rhetoryke* by Leonard Cox (*c.*1495–*c.*1550), first published in London in 1532.[205] An extensive traveller in his youth, Cox studied at Tübingen before becoming a schoolmaster in Poland and later in Hungary.[206] Returning to England in 1530, he became Master of the Grammar School at Reading, where he remained until shortly before his death.[207] Cox was the earliest English writer to propose that, once the rudiments of Latin have been mastered, the art of rhetoric should be

196. Mack 2011, pp. 31, 87.
197. Green and Murphy 2006, pp. 185–7. Erasmus's 1569 edition is the one from which I quote (BL copy).
198. Mack 2011, p. 31.
199. This version is lost, but a further Cambridge edition appeared in 1631. See Green and Murphy 2006, p. 425. This is the edition from which I quote. (CUL copy.)
200. Published in Basel as well as Wittenberg. See Meerhoff 1994, p. 46 and cf. Green and Murphy 2006, p. 296. The Basel edition is the one from which I quote. (BL copy.)
201. On the original edition, published in Wittenberg, see Meerhoff 1994, p. 49. The Lyon edition of 1539 is the one from which I quote (BL copy).
202. Green and Murphy 2006, pp. 296–8. According to Mack 2011, p. 31, 117 editions of Melanchthon's rhetorics were published between 1510 and 1600.
203. For a discussion of these texts, together with translations, see Moss and Wallace 2003.
204. For this literature see Skinner 1996, pp. 51–65; Mann 2012, pp. 1–3, 8–19.
205. On Cox see Howell 1956, pp. 90–5; Ryle 2003.   206. Dowling 1986, pp. 128, 152.
207. Cox 1532, Sig. A, 2ʳ. But cf. Dowling 1986, p. 128.

the chief subject taught in schools.[208] Following Melanchthon, from whose *Rhetorices Elementa* he translated much of his treatise, Cox added that among the elements of rhetoric 'the moost difficile or harde is to invent what thou must say', and he ends by explaining that this is why the topic of invention has been his exclusive concern.[209]

The next English guide to invention was *The Foundacion of Rhetorike* by Richard Rainolde (*c.*1530–1606),[210] who graduated from Cambridge in 1553 and served for most of his life as a clergyman in Essex.[211] First published in 1563, Rainolde's *Foundacion* is basically a translation of Aphthonius's *Progymnasmata*, a fourth-century Greek manual of writing exercises that Rudolph Agricola had already rendered into Latin for use in schools.[212] Although derivative, Rainolde's work was of value not merely for its adaptation of Aphthonius's examples to English life, but for offering many models of simple orations that, when taken together, show how to invent and organize suitable arguments in each of the main parts of an oration in which 'the cause shalbe in controversie'.[213] Rainolde illustrates how to assemble a narrative of facts,[214] how to confirm the statement of a case,[215] how to mount a 'destruccion' of one's adversaries,[216] and how to bring one's oration to an appropriately resounding close.[217] As he says himself, his aim is to guide our natural wisdom to produce 'wittie invencion' and 'goodlie disposicion', thereby enabling us 'to pleade with all facilitee, and copiouslie to dilate any matter or sentence'.[218]

By this time a boundary dispute had arisen between the disciplines of logic and rhetoric, one effect of which was to question the classical picture of rhetoric as a fivefold art in which invention constitutes the primary element. The challenge arose partly from the new view of dialectic first put forward by Lorenzo Valla and later developed by Rudolph Agricola in the early years of the sixteenth century. Both insist that *inventio* and *dispositio* must be treated as aspects of the *ars dialectica*, and thus that the *ars rhetorica*

---

208. Cox 1532, Sig. A, 3ᵛ.
209. Cox 1532, Sig A, 4ᵛ and Sig. F, 6ʳ. On Cox and Melanchthon see Eden 1997, pp. 79–89.
210. On Rainolde see Howell 1956, pp. 140–3; Williams 2001; Peltonen 2013, pp. 52–5.
211. Williams 2001, pp. 223, 230.
212. Mack 2002, pp. 27–8. On progymnasmata in sixteenth-century English schooling see also Weaver 2012, pp. 14–43.
213. Rainolde 1563, fo. iᵛ.　　214. Rainolde 1563, fos. xiiʳ to xviʳ.
215. Rainolde 1563, fos. xxxᵛ to xxxiiiʳ.　　216. Rainolde 1563, fos. xxivᵛ to xxxᵛ.
217. Rainolde 1563, fos. xxxiiiʳ⁻ᵛ.　　218. Rainolde 1563, fos.1ʳ⁻ᵛ.

must consist solely of *elocutio, memoria,* and *pronuntiatio*.[219] We already find
Thomas Elyot endorsing this new line of demarcation in *The Governor,* in
which he recommends Agricola as a logician 'whose worke prepareth
invention, tellynge the places from whence an argument for the profe of
any mater may be taken'.[220] Elyot accepts, that is, that the study of *inventio*
forms an aspect of dialectic, and advises schoolmasters to devote half a year
to it before turning to the separate art of rhetoric.[221]

A much stronger impetus in the same direction was provided by Petrus
Ramus (1515–72) and his associates through their efforts to reform the
teaching of the liberal arts.[222] Ramus's proposed reorganization was driven
by his perception that the traditional curriculum, and especially the teaching
of the trivium (grammar, rhetoric, logic), had become filled with redun-
dancies and overlapping categories. He mainly devoted himself to the
simplification of logic or dialectic, while the place of rhetoric in the new
scheme of things was clarified by his associate Omer Talon (1510–62).
Ramus announced his new approach in his *Dialecticae Partitiones* of
1543,[223] while Talon's *Rhetorica* first appeared in 1545.[224] Subsequently,
Ramus rounded off his exposition of the new programme by producing a
vernacular digest of his logic, the *Dialectique,* in 1555.

According to the *Dialectique,* 'the parts of logic are two in number,
Invention and Judgment'.[225] Invention seeks to discover 'reason, proof
and argument', while Judgment ('which is also called Disposition') 'shows
the ways and means of organising arguments'.[226] The art of memory forms
an aspect of Disposition or Judgment, because ease of recollection depends
in part on effective logical arrangement. But if Invention and Disposition
constitute the elements of a 'natural' logic, then neither can feature in a
separate art of rhetoric. Moreover, if the most effective method of strengthening the memory is simply to organize what needs to be recollected in the
most logical style, then Memory as a further element in the art of rhetoric
similarly drops away.[227] That these were the inferences that Ramus and his

---

219. Vasoli 1968, pp. 28–77; Mack 1993, pp. 120–1, 168–9.   220. Elyot 1531, Sig. E, 3ᵛ–4ʳ.
221. Elyot 1531, Sig. E, 4ʳ.   222. On Ramus and his followers see Mack 2011, pp. 136–59.
223. Green and Murphy 2006, p. 363.
224. Green and Murphy 2006, p. 424. Ong 1965, p. 228 suggests that Ramus may have had a hand
     in this text as well.
225. Ramus 1964, p. 63: 'Les parties de Dialectique sont deux, Invention et Jugement.'
226. Ramus 1964, pp. 53–4: Invention is concerned with 'raison, preuve, argument' while
     Judgment—'aussi nommé disposition'—'monstre les manières et espèces de les disposer.'
227. Howell 1956, p. 269.

followers wished to draw becomes clear as soon as we turn to Talon's *Rhetorica*. 'Rhetoric', he begins, 'is the art of speaking well.' This being so, 'the parts of rhetoric are two: *Elocutio* and *Pronunciatio*'.[228] As Ramus confirms, 'the tropes and figures of elocution, together with the graces of action, form the entirety of Rhetoric as a true art distinct from Dialectic'.[229]

This new approach affected the Tudor rhetorical manuals in two distinct ways.[230] Some writers actively embraced the Ramist programme, agreeing that rhetoric consists of little more than a study of figures and tropes. The pioneering English Ramist was Dudley Fenner (*c.*1558–87),[231] a graduate of Cambridge who became an uncompromising puritan and was forced into exile, ending his life as preacher in the Calvinist church at Middelburg.[232] There he wrote *The Artes of Logike and Rethorike,* first published anonymously in 1584 and reissued under his name in 1588.[233] Fenner begins with logic, describing it as an art of reasoning in two parts. The first, which 'doth helpe much to the finding out of reasons' is invention; the second, 'concerning the ordering of reasons', is disposition or judgement.[234] Having allocated invention and disposition to logic, Fenner duly infers that the art of rhetoric can only consist of two elements, 'garnishing of speech, called Eloquution' and 'garnishing of the maner of utterance, called Pronunciation'.[235] His ensuing discussion of *elocutio* basically follows Talon's *Rhetorica,* but when he turns to *pronuntiatio* he truncates the scope of rhetoric still further, suddenly announcing that this aspect of the art 'is not yet perfect' and that this part of Talon's text is not worth rendering into English.[236]

The later years of Elizabeth's reign saw the publication of two further manuals in the same Ramist mould. One was the work of Abraham Fraunce (*c.*1560–93),[237] a graduate of St John's College Cambridge who became a Fellow there in the early 1580s and subsequently trained as a lawyer at Gray's Inn.[238] In 1588 Fraunce published two related works, one entitled *The Arcadian Rhetorike* and the other *The Lawiers Logike.* The former is another adaptation of Talon's *Rhetorica,* which begins by repeating that the art 'hath

228. Talon 1631, pp. 1–2: 'Rhetorica est ars bene dicendi...Partes Rhetoricae duae sunt; Elocutio & Pronunciatio.'
229. Ramus 1964, p.152: 'tous les tropes et figures d'élocution, toutes les grâces d'action, qui est la Rhétorique entière, vraye et séparée de la Dialectique.'
230. On Ramist rhetoric in sixteenth-century England see Howell 1956, pp. 247–81.
231. On Fenner see Howell 1956, pp. 219–22; Collins 2001.
232. Collins 2001, pp. 118–19.
233. Collins 2001, p. 118.   234. [Fenner] 1584, Sig. B, 1ʳ and Sig. C, 1ʳ.
235. [Fenner] 1584, Sig. D, 1ᵛ.   236. [Fenner] 1584, Sig. E, 1ᵛ.
237. On Fraunce see Howell 1956, pp. 257–8; Barker 2001.   238. Barker 2001, pp. 141, 144.

two parts, Eloqution and Pronuntiation'.[239] Fraunce mainly concentrates on *elocutio*, following Talon's analysis while supplementing it with elegant illustrations from ancient and modern verse. Unlike Fenner, however, he also translates Talon's account of *pronuntiatio*, including his detailed assessment of how to intensify the cut and thrust of debate by means of appropriate gestures of the head, body, and hands, thereby creating a good 'show' and 'a fit delivering of the speach'.[240]

The last Ramist handbook of the Elizabethan era was the *Rhetoricae Libri Duo* of Charles Butler (*c.*1560–1647),[241] a graduate of Magdalen College Oxford who spent most of his life as a clergyman in Hampshire.[242] Butler's text was never translated, but it achieved a notable popularity, and after its first publication in 1598 was reprinted eight times before the author's death.[243] Reworking Talon's *Rhetorica* yet again, Butler begins by reiterating that 'there are two parts of rhetoric, Elocutio and Pronunciatio',[244] and accepts that the former element, to which he devotes most of his attention, 'can be equated with the exornation of speech' and thus 'with a trope or a figure'.[245] By contrast with Fenner, however, Butler agrees with Talon that voice and gesture can also help to create a persuasive 'show', and like Fraunce he concludes by translating Talon's section on *pronuntiatio*.[246]

The other way in which the Ramist programme exercised an influence in England was more indirect. A number of Tudor rhetoricians simply came to accept that the art of rhetoric can basically be equated with *elocutio*, the analysis of the figures and tropes of speech. This had already been the view of Antonio Mancinelli, whose *Carmen de Figuris* was first printed in Venice in 1493, and of Johann Susenbrotus, whose *Epitome Troporum ac Schematum* became perhaps the most widely used treatise on *elocutio* of the later sixteenth century. Richard Sherry (1506–*c.*1555), the headmaster of Magdalen College School, drew heavily on Susenbrotus for his *Treatise of Schemes and Tropes* of 1550.[247] So did Henry Peacham (1547–1634) in his *Garden of Eloquence*, first published in 1577 and reprinted in an expanded form in

---

239. Fraunce 1588a, Sig. A, 2ʳ.   240. Fraunce 1588a, Sig. I, 7ᵛ.
241. On Butler see Howell 1956, pp. 262–70; Cook 2001.   242. Cook 2001, p. 82.
243. Cook 2001, p. 83.
244. Butler 1598, Sig. A, 1ʳ: 'Partes Rhetoricae duae sunt, elocutio & pronunciatio.'
245. Butler 1598, Sig. A, 1ʳ: 'Elocutio est exornatio orationis ... elocutio est tropus aut figura.'
246. Butler 1598, Sig F, 4ʳ to Sig. G, 3ʳ.
247. On Sherry see Howell 1956, pp. 125–31; Sharon-Zisser 2001; Mack 2002, pp. 76–7, 87–90.
     Sherry's treatise is largely devoted to *elocutio*, but it ends (Sig. E, 6ᵛ to Sig. F, 8ᵛ) with a discussion of rhetorical proofs.

1593.[248] A further study of *elocutio*, partly dependent on Sherry and Peacham,[249] appeared in *The Arte of English Poesie* in 1589.[250] The *Arte* was published anonymously, but has generally been attributed to George Puttenham (1529–90), a nephew of Thomas Elyot.[251] Puttenham divides his text into three sections, the first of which considers the standing of poets and poetry, while the second applies the Ciceronian ideal of decorum to the writing of English verse. But the third and longest part, 'Of Ornament', is as much concerned with rhetoric as with poetics, and is largely given over to a yet further analysis of the figures and tropes of speech.[252] The last Elizabethan rhetorician to focus on *elocutio* was Angel Day (*c.*1550–99),[253] the compiler of a formulary of model letters, *The English Secretorie*, which first appeared in 1586. Day initially used a series of marginal glosses to draw attention to his use of the figures and tropes, but when he reissued his book in 1592 he included a separate manual on the subject, and in this format his work went on to enjoy a considerable vogue.[254]

It might seem that by this stage a generally Ramist understanding of the scope of rhetoric had largely conquered the field. But in fact there is little evidence that these reforms had much impact on the teaching of rhetoric in English schools. The *Ad Herennium* remained the most widely recommended manual throughout the Elizabethan period, and anyone opening that work would immediately have come upon the unambiguous assertion that 'there are five skills required of an orator, and these are invention, disposition, elocution, memory and delivery'.[255] Furthermore, this classical understanding of the scope of the art was weightily reaffirmed for English readers by Thomas Wilson in his *Arte of Rhetorique* in 1553. Wilson's treatise became by far the most popular vernacular rhetoric of the second half of the sixteenth century, and kept fully alive a pre-Ramist understanding of rhetoric as a fivefold art in which the theory of invention was held to constitute the most important part.

---

248. On Peacham see Howell 1956, pp. 132–7; Smith 2001; Mack 2002, pp. 76–8, 87–99.
249. See Appendix on sources in Willcock and Walker 1970, pp. 319–22.
250. See [Puttenham] 1589 and cf. Willcock and Walker 1970, pp. xliv–liii.
251. Willcock and Walker 1970, pp. xi–xliv. For biographical details see Willcock and Walker 1970, pp. xviii–xxxi.
252. [Puttenham] 1589, pp. 114–257.
253. On Day see Henderson 2001; Mack 2002, pp. 76–7, 81–4, 87–92.
254. Day 1592; cf. Green and Murphy, 2006, p. 159.
255. *Rhetorica ad Herennium* 1954, I. II. 3, p. 6: 'Oportet igitur esse in oratore inventionem, dispositionem, elocutionem, memoriam, pronuntiationem.'

Thomas Wilson (1524–81)[256] was educated in the humanities under John Cheke at Cambridge, where he took his MA in 1549.[257] A determined Protestant, he was forced to flee abroad in 1554, but returned to England in 1560, after which he served as Master of the Court of Requests and as secretary to the Privy Council from 1577 until his death.[258] Wilson's two most important works were both composed during a brief period of intensive study in the early 1550s.[259] The first was his pioneering work on logic, the earliest to be published in English, which appeared as *The Rule of Reason* in 1551.[260] The other was his *Arte of Rhetorique*, first published two years later and reprinted on at least seven occasions before the end of the century.[261]

If we compare the opening pages of Wilson's two treatises, we find him unrepentant in his acceptance of the overlap between logic and rhetoric that the Ramists had sought to eliminate.[262] Wilson begins his *Rule of Reason* by repeating Cicero's contention in the *Topica* that 'every systematic theory of argumentation contains two parts, invention and judgement'.[263] Reversing the usual order, Wilson begins by defining judgement, which 'standeth in framing of thinges aptlye together, in knitting woordes, for the purpose accordingly'.[264] He then discusses invention, which 'consisteth in finding out matter, and searching stuffe agreable to the cause'.[265] He appears, in other words, to assign the skills of invention and disposition to the art of logic. If we turn, however, to the opening of his *Arte of Rhetorique* we find him arguing that there are 'five thynges to be considered in an Oratour', the first two of which are 'Invencion of matter' and 'Disposicion of the same'. By invention, he repeats, he means 'the findyng out of apte matter', and by disposition 'the settelyng or orderyng of thynges invented'.[266] Both skills are now firmly associated with the art of rhetoric.

---

256. On Wilson see Howell 1956, pp. 98–110; Medine 1986; Mack 2002, pp. 76–8, 83–4, 96–9; Shrank 2004, pp. 182–219.
257. Medine 1986, pp. 6–12.
258. Medine 1986, pp. 75, 77–8, 96–105; Baumlin 2001, p. 283.
259. Medine 1986, pp. 15, 55; Baumlin 2001, p. 286.
260. Medine 1986, p. 30. See also Howell 1956, pp. 12–31; Crane 1993, pp. 26–30; Altman 2010, pp. 119–28.
261. Baumlin 2001, pp. 283, 289–90.
262. On the relations between the two works see Shrank 2004, pp. 183–6.
263. Cicero 1949b, II. 6, p. 386: 'omnis ratio diligens disserendi duas habet partes, unam inveniendi alteram iudicandi'.
264. Wilson 1551, Sig. B, 1ʳ.   265. Wilson 1551, Sig. B, 1ʳ.
266. Wilson 1553, Sig. A, 3ᵛ. Wilson's text is not paginated, and the foliation is erratic, so I give references by signature.

What, then, is the difference between the two disciplines? At first Wilson appears to regard it as little more than a question of style. As he puts it in *The Rule of Reason*, logic 'doeth playnly and nakedly set furthe with apt wordes the summe of thinges', whereas rhetoric 'useth gay painted Sentences, and setteth furth those matters with fresh colours and goodly ornamentes'.[267] It soon emerges, however, that there is a categorical distinction between logical and rhetorical invention. The former is capable of discovering general reasons and proofs, whereas the latter is largely restricted to finding out probable arguments.[268] It is true that this contrast is initially somewhat blurred, for Wilson's definition of logic speaks of it as 'an art to reason probably on both partes, of all matters that be put furth'.[269] Later, however, he lays much stress on the special power of logical invention to supply general proofs. By this method, he now tells us, we can find the means 'to prove every matter where upon question maie ryse'.[270]

By contrast, when Wilson turns to rhetorical invention at the start of *The Arte of Rhetorique*, he aligns himself with Cicero and the *Ad Herennium* in placing much more emphasis on plausibility and verisimilitude. He describes the process of invention as 'a searchyng out of thynges true, or thynges likely, the whiche maie reasonably sette furth a matter, and make it appere probable'.[271] When considering how to set about confirming a cause, he acknowledges yet more frankly that the most we can do is bring together a number of contentions that can be made to look plausible: 'Wee muste heape matter and finde out argumentes, . . . makyng firste the strongest reasons that wee can, and nexte after, gatheryng all probable causes together, that beeyng in one heape, thei maie seme strong, and of greate weighte.'[272] The implication that rhetorical invention must be adapted for specific audiences is explicitly brought out in his discussion of narrative. One way to 'make our saiynges appere lykely, and probable' is to 'frame our invencion accordyng as we shal thynke them most willyng to allowe it, that have the hearyng of it'.[273] We need to recall that we shall frequently be speaking before people with widely different opinions, and we need to adjust our arguments to fit their prejudices. As he somewhat brutally concludes, 'the multitude (as Horace doth say) is a beast, or rather a monster that hath many

267. Wilson 1551, Sig. B, 3^r.   268. Wilson 1551, Sig. J, 4^v.
269. Wilson 1551, Sig. B, 1^r.   270. Wilson 1551, Sig. J, 4^v.
271. Wilson 1553, Sig. A, 3^v.   272. Wilson 1553, Sig. Q, 1^v–2^r.
273. Wilson 1553, Sig. P, 3^r.

heades and therefore like unto the diversitie of natures, varietie of invencion must alwaies be used'.[274]

Wilson had already underlined these distinctions in his *Rule of Reason*, in which two contrasting species of proposition are discriminated. Those which belong to the realm of logic are said to amount to 'infallible reasons, or rather necessary Argumentes' which 'are assuredly true, and knowen so to be either by nature, or els by experience'.[275] But there are others that belong to the realm of enthymemes, and hence to the art of rhetoric, and only amount to what Wilson calls 'likelyhodes'. Here, although 'the conjecture have some probabilite with it, yet is it not for ever true'. 'Therfore in all communicacion', he concludes, 'good hede ought to bee taken, that likelyhodes of thynges, be not used for necessarie reasons'; otherwise we shall fail to appreciate the limited extent to which rhetorical arguments are genuinely susceptible of proof.[276]

Despite the noise made by the Ramists, there is little doubt that the impact of Wilson's *Arte of Rhetorique*, combined with the continued use of the *Rhetorica ad Herennium* as the basic school text-book, maintained the ascendancy of the classical theory of rhetoric throughout the Elizabethan period in a form that Cicero and Quintilian would readily have recognized. Drawing heavily on these authorities, Wilson summarizes the classical theory in a series of four lists that he sets out in the opening part of his book. The first informs us that rhetoric is unquestionably a fivefold art. The primary task is that of 'findyng out of apte matter, called otherwise Invencion'. Next comes Disposition, 'the settelyng or orderyng of thynges invented for this purpose'. Then we need 'to beautifie the cause', and accordingly stand in need of good Elocution, 'an appliyng of apte wordes and sentences to the matter, founde out to confirme the cause'. Finally, we need a powerful Memory, 'a fast holdyng, bothe of matter and woordes', together with an effective style of Delivery, 'a framyng of the voyce, countenaunce, and gesture' in such a way as to enforce our case. To make a perfect orator 'every one of these must go together'.[277]

Wilson's second list focuses on Disposition, and enlarges on his classical sources by insisting that 'there are vii partes in every Oracion'.[278] The first is

---

274. Wilson 1553, Sig. 2D, 1[v.]   275. Wilson 1551, Sig. F, 2[r]–3[v] and Sig. H, 4[v].
276. Wilson 1551, Sig. H, 4[v] and 5[v].   277. Wilson 1553, Sig A, 3[v]–4[r].
278. Wilson 1553, Sig. A, 4[r]. But see Mack 2002, pp. 36–7 and Hutson 2006, pp. 91–2, who note
    that school exercises in rhetoric in Tudor England tended to cleave to the simpler

the Entrance, when 'the will of the standers by, or of the Judge is sought for, and required to heare the matter'. Next comes the Narration, 'a plain and manifest poynctyng of the matter, and an evident settyng furthe of all thynges, that belong unto the same'. Then follows the Proposition, 'a pithie sentence, comprehendyng in a smale roume, the some of the whole matter'. After this comes the Division, 'an openyng of thynges, wherin we agree and rest upon, and wherein we sticke, and stande in traverse'. Then comes the Confirmation, which takes the form of 'a declaracion of our awne reasons with assured and constaunt profes'. This is closely associated with the Confutation, in which we attempt 'a dissolvyng or wipyng awaie, of all suche reasons as make against us'. And finally there is the Conclusion, 'a clarkely gatheryng of the matter, spoken before, and a lappyng up of it altogether'.[279]

Wilson's third list informs us that 'there are three kyndes of causes, or Oracions, whiche serve for every matter'.[280] First there is 'the Oracion demonstrative', which 'standeth either in praise, or dispraise of some one man, or of some one thyng, or of some one deede doen'.[281] Next comes the 'Oration deliberative', which is 'a meane, wherby we do perswade, or disswade, entreate, or rebuke, exhorte, or dehorte, commende, or comforte any man'.[282] Finally there is the 'Oration judicial', which Wilson regards as by far the most important, and which he proceeds to define in solemn terms:[283] 'Oration Judiciall is, an earnest debatyng in open assemblie of some weightie matter before a judge, where the complainaunt commenseth his action, & the defendaunt thereupon aunswereth at his peril to al suche thynges as are laied to his charge.'[284]

As Wilson observes at the outset of his discussion, he is deliberately circumscribing the art of rhetoric with his exclusive focus on these three *genera* of utterance, and in doing so is following the line of reasoning that Cicero had put into the mouth of Scaevola in his *De oratore*. Rhetoric is of no help, Wilson agrees, in disciplines such as astronomy or mathematics, which are capable of supplying demonstrations and proofs, and consequently have little need of 'greate utteraunce'. Rhetoric is only of value when what is required is 'a learned, or rather an artificiall declaracion of the

---

Aristotelian idea of a four-part oration. As we shall see, Shakespeare generally follows this arrangement too.

279. Wilson 1553, Sig. A, 4^{r-v}.   280. Wilson 1553, Sig. B, 2^r.
281. Wilson 1553, Sig B, 2^v.   282. Wilson 1553, Sig. D, 4^r.
283. Shrank 2004, pp. 196–7.   284. Wilson 1553, Sig. M, 3^r.

mynde, in the handelyng of any cause, called in contencion', and thus when the essential skill is that of knowing how to argue persuasively *in utramque partem*, on both sides of a case.[285]

This commitment is further underlined when Wilson turns to examine the classical distinction between the two different types of question, the infinite and the definite. Here he agrees with the *Ad Herennium* that infinite questions 'are more proper unto the Logician, who talketh of thynges universally', whereas 'the definite question (as the whiche concerneth some one persone) is moste agreyng to the purpose of an Orator'.[286] The reason why the orator will usually be concerned only with definite questions is that the most important task of oratory is 'consideryng particuler matters in the Lawe'.[287] These 'are ever debated betwixte certain persones' so that the orator will always find himself facing some 'particuler question' that 'is ever called in controversie'.[288]

Wilson's fourth and final list is exclusively concerned with judicial rhetoric, and itemizes what the classical writers had described as the different *constitutiones* that orators need to be able to discriminate. As we have seen, the *constitutio* is the name given to the central question in dispute between two opposed parties. To speak of such a question is accordingly to refer to what is basically at issue in a given case, and Wilson helpfully proposes that the word *constitutio* should therefore be translated as 'issue'. 'The State, or constitucion of the Cause', he explains, is 'the chief grounde of a matter, and the pryncipal poincte whereunto both he that speaketh shoulde referre his whole wit, & thei that heare should chefely marke.'[289] This being so, 'I cannot better terme it in Englishe than by the name of an issue', because there will always be some issue to be settled in any such debate, 'the whiche must wholly and onely be proved of the one side, and denied of the other.'[290] It is worth noting the alacrity with which this terminology was adopted by English legal writers concerned with the handling of pleas in common law. Thomas Smith, examining this topic in his *De Republica Anglorum* in the early 1560s, already speaks of 'the issue and state of some fact which is denied of the one partie and averred of the other', and proceeds

285. Wilson 1553, Sig. A, 1ʳ. For this cast of mind as well-suited to the nurturing of the drama see Altman 1978, where he speaks (p. 31) of 'the moral cultivation of ambivalence'. On arguing *pro et contra*, especially in deliberative rhetoric, see Palonen 2008.

286. Wilson 1553, Sig. A, 1ᵛ.   287. Wilson 1553, Sig. A, 1ᵛ.

288. Wilson 1553, Sig. A, 1ᵛ.   289. Wilson 1553, Sig. M, 3ᵛ–4ʳ.

290. Wilson 1553, Sig. M, 4ᵛ.

to explain how a plea is decided 'when it doth come to the question, state or issue of the deede or fact'.[291]

Quintilian had suggested that there may be as few as two or perhaps as many as eight distinct judicial issues.[292] Wilson prefers to endorse the typically forthright contention in the *Ad Herennium* that there are three and only three types,[293] and he trenchantly adds (in a rare criticism of Quintilian) that 'the wisest and best learned have agreed' that there are 'three only, and no lesse', and that they are most appropriately described as the conjectural, the legal, and the juridical.[294] Usefully, he adds a mnemonic for distinguishing between them. First he gives an example of a conjectural issue: 'Assertion. Thou hast killed this manne. The Aunswere. I have not killed him. The State or Issue. Whethcr he hath killed this man or no.' Next he gives an example of a legal issue: 'Assertion. Thou hast committed treason in this facte. Aunswere. I denye it to be treason. State or issue. Whether his offence done maye be called treason or no.' Finally, he gives an example of a juridical issue: 'Assertion. Thou hast kylled this manne. Aunswere. I graunte it, but I have doone it lawfullye.'[295]

As with the classical rhetoricians, Wilson's underlying aspiration is to fashion the figure of the perfect orator, and he agrees with Cicero that such a man must possess in the highest degree the quality of *ratio* or reason in combination with *oratio* or eloquent speech. Recalling the beginning of the *De inventione*, he reiterates Cicero's contention that, in the absence of powerful *oratio*, even the force of *ratio* would never have been sufficient to foster a sociable and civilized life. He cannot imagine, he says, how men 'coulde have bene broughte by anye other meanes to lyve together in felowshyppe of life, to mayntayne Cities, to deale trulye, and willyngelye to obeye one another, if menne at the firste hadde not by Art and eloquence perswaded that, which they ful oft found out by reason'.[296] The political leader who knows how to combine *ratio* with *oratio* is accordingly the hero of Wilson's book. He is 'most worthye fame' who 'dothe chiefelye, and above all other, excell menne, wherin men do excell beastes'.[297] As Philip

291. Smith 1982 [1583], p. 96. As Dewar 1982, pp. 1, 8 notes, Smith's treatise was written between 1562 and 1565 and first published in 1583.
292. Quintilian 2001, 3. 6. 32–55, vol. 2, pp. 64–76.
293. *Rhetorica ad Herennium* 1954, I. XI. 18, pp. 32–4.
294. Wilson, 1553, Sig. M, 4ᵛ, Sig. N, 4ʳ.   295. Wilson 1553, Sig. N, 1ᵛ.
296. Wilson 1553, Preface, Sig. A, 4ʳ.   297. Wilson 1553, Preface, Sig. A, 4ʳ.

Sidney was later to put it in his *Defence of Poesie*, '*Oratio*, next to *Ratio*, Speech next to Reason, be the greatest gift bestowed upon *Mortalitie*.'[298]

Wilson tells two stories by way of illustrating his point. The first concerns King Pyrrhus and how he waged war against Rome. One of his methods of winning towns and fortresses was to send the orator Cineas 'to perswade with the Capitaynes & people that were in them, that they shoulde yelde up the sayde holde or townes without fyght or resistaunce'.[299] Cineas was able to speak so 'winningly' and 'disarmingly' that the enemy frequently laid down their arms and the towns were won without battle ever being joined. The moral of the story, Wilson submits, is that anyone who can combine reason with eloquence is 'not onelye to be taken for a singuler manne, but rather to be counted for halfe a God'.[300] With his other story he makes clear which specific 'half a God' he has in mind:

> The Poetes do feyne that Hercules being a man of greate wisdome, had all men lincked together by the eares in a chaine, to draw them and leade them even as he lusted. For his witte was so greate, his tongue so eloquente, & his experience suche, that no one man was able to withstand his reason, but everye one was rather driven to do that whiche he woulde.[301]

The moral, as before, is that no one can withstand the force of *ratio* when combined with powerful *oratio*, for 'suche force hath the tongue, and such is the power of eloquence and reason, that most men are forced even to yelde in that, whiche most standeth againste their will'.[302]

Among the Elizabethan grammar-school boys who would have had this scale of values drilled into them at an impressionable age was William Shakespeare,[303] who attended the King's New School at Stratford-upon-Avon in the 1570s. Shakespeare not only imbibed these lessons in youth, but it is clear that he subsequently returned to them in the course of his professional life. As we shall see, he was closely acquainted with the arguments of the *De inventione* and the *Ad Herennium* about how to

---

298. Sidney 1595, Sig. F, 3[*recte* 4]ᵛ.
299. Wilson 1553, Epistle, Sig. A, 1ʳ. On the pen as mightier than the sword see also Churchyard 1579, Sig. M, 4ʳ⁻ᵛ; Peltonen 2013, p. 22.
300. Wilson 1553, Preface, Sig. A, 4ʳ.
301. Wilson 1553, Preface, Sig. A, 3ᵛ. On this image of *Hercules Gallicus*, taken from Lucian, see Rebhorn 1995, pp. 66–77; Skinner 1996, pp. 92–3, 389–90.
302. Wilson 1553, Preface, Sig. A, 3ᵛ.
303. On rhetoric in Shakespeare's education see Baldwin 1944; Jones 1977; Altman 1978.

construct forensic speeches, and he sometimes directly quotes them. He seems in addition to have studied a number of vernacular rhetorical texts, including Thomas Wilson's *Arte of Rhetorique*, to which he also makes explicit reference.[304] What effect did this reading have on his practice as a dramatist? This is the question to which I now turn.

304. Parrolles's speech in which he claims 'It is not politicke, in the Common-wealth of Nature, to preserve virginity' draws extensively on the translation of Erasmus's Epistle on marriage that Thomas Wilson had inserted into his *Arte of Rhetorique*, in which Wilson asks 'what thing could be invented more perilous to a commune weale then virginitie'. See *All's Well That Ends Well*, TLN 126–7, p. 970 (1. 1. 111–12) and cf. Wilson 1553, Sig. G, 4ᵛ.

2

Shakespeare's Forensic Plays

Towards the forensic plays

Shakespeare is interested at most stages of his literary career in the full range of distinctively rhetorical utterance. He writes a number of speeches in the *genus demonstrativum*, some of which are orations of praise and some of blame. The Archbishop of Canterbury pronounces a classical *laudatio* on the king in Act 1 of *The Life of Henry the Fift*,[1] and Claudius adopts the style of a *vituperatio* in his opening speech in Act 1 of *Hamlet*.[2] Shakespeare also composes numerous speeches in the *genus deliberativum*, in which a character reflects on possible courses of action and tries to decide between them. Brutus deliberates in soliloquy in Act 2 of *Julius Caesar* on whether the threat of tyranny posed by Caesar's rule is such that he deserves to die.[3] Hamlet similarly deliberates in Act 3 of *Hamlet* on whether it will be nobler to suffer the slings and arrows of outrageous fortune or to take arms against a sea of troubles.[4] More publicly, the princes of Greece deliberate at length in Act 1 of *Troilus and Cressida*—almost in a parody of 'politic' language—on how to bring the siege of Troy to an end.[5] Within the three *genera* of rhetorical utterance, however, Shakespeare is principally concerned with judicial rhetoric, and thus with the question of how to develop an argument in accusation or defence before a judge. As the *Ad Herennium* had particularly emphasized, such judicial causes are by far the most important and difficult to handle,[6] and this commitment is reflected in

1. *The Life of Henry the Fift*, TLN 59–72, 73–94, p. 639 (1. 1. 24–37, 38–59).
2. *Hamlet*, TLN 243–73, pp. 739–40 (1. 2. 87–117).
3. *Julius Caesar*, TLN 572–96, p. 681 (2. 1. 10–34).
4. *Hamlet*, TLN 1594–1628, p. 754 (3. 1. 56–90).
5. *Troilus and Cressida*, TLN 436–647, pp. 813–15 (1. 3. 1–213).
6. *Rhetorica ad Herennium* 1954, II. I. 1, p. 58.

the relative space allocated by the rhetorical theorists to judicial as opposed to demonstrative and deliberative speech. Shakespeare likewise concentrates on the *genus iudiciale*, and it is with his treatment of judicial causes that I shall exclusively be concerned.[7]

Shakespeare pays some attention to the technicalities of judicial rhetoric at almost every stage in his literary career. At first, however, he reveals only a generalized interest in the advice offered by the classical rhetoricians about how to speak in court. The earliest play in which he dramatizes a trial is *The First Part of the Contention (2 Henry VI)*, probably written in 1591,[8] in which the Duchess of Gloster is convicted on a charge of 'Dealing with Witches and with Conjurers'.[9] The accusation is put forward by the duke of Buckingham, and the king assures him that his cause will be heard and justice administered:

> To morrow toward London, back againe,
> To looke into this Businesse thorowly,
> And call these foule Offendors to their Answeres;
> And poyse the Cause in Justice equall Scales,
>
> TLN 875–8, p. 75 (2. 1. 199–202)

The king is promising that he will listen to questions and answers debated *in utramque partem* and will judge where the balance of justice lies. However, when he appears in state to conduct the trial he simply announces a sentence of banishment. No formal speech is made in prosecution, no answers are sought in defence, and after the delivery of the verdict the duchess merely welcomes it in defiance before being led away.

Something more elaborate is attempted in *Richard II*, a work that can be dated to the year 1595.[10] The play opens with a scene in which Bulling-brooke comes before the king with an accusation of treason against Thomas

---

7. I shall thus be focusing on speeches of accusation at least as much as defence. It is important to underline this point, if only because Kennedy in his classic study of orations in Shakespeare claims that 'forensic or judicial orations in Shakespeare come in each case in answer to charges brought forward against a defendant'. See Kennedy 1942, p. 74 and table p. 67. This is so far from being the case as to vitiate Kennedy's attempt to provide a complete list of forensic orations in Shakespeare's plays. It means, for example, that he is unable to find any in *Julius Caesar*, *Hamlet*, or *All's Well That Ends Well*.

8. Wells and Taylor 1987, pp. 111–12; Knowles 1999, p. 111. Hattaway 2012, p. 61 suggests between 1589 and 1591. Wiggins and Richardson 2013, p. 92 give 1591 as the best guess.

9. *The First Part of the Contention*, TLN 835, p. 75 (2. 1. 170). For a discussion see Keeton 1967, pp. 165–76.

10. Wells and Taylor 1987, pp. 117–18; Forker 2002, pp. 111, 120; Gurr 2003, pp. 1–3; Wiggins and Richardson 2013, p. 287.

Mowbray, duke of Norfolk. The king speaks of the 'cause' that has made them adversaries, and undertakes to hear both sides of the case:

> face to face,
> And frowning brow to brow our selves will heare,
> The accuser and the accused freely speake:
>
> TLN 15–17, p. 415 (I. I. 15–17)

The king appeals to the terminology of judicial rhetoric, but neither Mowbray nor Bullingbrooke pays the least attention to it. As we saw in Chapter 1, the classical rhetoricians had been particularly concerned with the importance of winning goodwill at the outset of a speech. They had argued that this requirement can most readily be met by a *prohoemium* in which 'we praise our service without arrogance',[11] and speak 'about the person of our adversaries, the person of our hearers and the facts of the case'.[12] Bullingbrooke shows some faint awareness of these considerations, but Mowbray none at all. He says nothing about the person of the king and nothing about the facts of the case. He speaks with unbridled arrogance about his own hot blood, mounts a violent tirade in which he hurls back the charge of treason, and ends by throwing down his gage in a demand for single combat. He and Bullingbrooke are living in a world far removed from the careful verbal calculations recommended by the classical theorists of eloquence.

Meanwhile, however, there had come a point when Shakespeare's artistic purposes required of him something more than these nods in the direction of the rhetorical handbooks he had studied in his youth. The moment came in 1594, the year in which he published *Lucrece*, his narrative poem in rhyme royal about Tarquin's rape of the virtuous Lucrece and her resulting suicide.[13] The outline of Lucrece's story would have been available to him in a number of different sources,[14] the most widely current being Ovid's telling of the tale in his *Fasti*,[15] and William Painter's translation of Livy's version in

---

11. *Rhetorica ad Herennium* 1954, I. IV. 8, p. 14: 'nostrum officium sine adrogantia laudabimus'. See also Cicero 1949a, I. XVI. 22, p. 44.
12. *Rhetorica ad Herennium* 1954, I. 4. 8, p. 14: 'ab adversariorum nostrorum, ab auditorum persona, et ab rebus ipsis'. See also Cicero 1949a, I. XVI. 22, p. 44.
13. In the running titles of the original quarto (1594) the poem is called *The Rape of Lucrece*. But on the title page it is simply called *Lucrece*, and this is the version I therefore adopt. The distinction is important, since one of the leading questions raised in the poem is whether Lucrece can hope to confirm that she was indeed raped.
14. On the history of the myth and its changing uses see Donaldson 1982.
15. Ovid 1996, II, 721–852, pp. 108–18.

his *Palace of Pleasure*, first published in 1566.[16] Both Ovid and Livy make much of the fact that Tarquin overcame Lucrece's modesty, as Livy puts it, by adding a threat of disgrace to the terror he induced.[17] As Painter renders the passage, Tarquin first warned Lucrece that 'if thou crie, I will kill thee', at which point she 'could not tell what to doe'.[18] Then he added that 'he would also kill his slave, and place hym by her, that it might be reported she was slain, beyng taken in adulterie'.[19] According to Livy's account it was Lucrece's horror at this further prospect that conquered her.[20] This was the fatal moment, in Painter's words, when Tarquin's 'fleshly and licencious enterprise overcame the puritie of her chast harte'.[21]

Lucrece's decision, although made under threat of death, was held to raise the issue—closely examined by Augustine in *The City of God*—as to whether she was to some extent complicit in Tarquin's crime. As Augustine puts the question (in John Healey's translation of 1610): was it 'no unchastenesse in her to suffer the rape unwillingly', or did she give a 'secret consent', perhaps even a 'lustfull consent' and thereby make herself 'privy to her owne sinne?'[22] It is evident from Shakespeare's poem that he became deeply interested in exploring these problems about guilt and responsibility, but neither in Ovid's nor in Livy's telling of the story are they made the subject of any scrutiny. Ovid has nothing to say, merely observing that when Lucrece explained her distress to her husband and his friends 'she told them what she could'.[23] Livy is more alive to her plight, but confines himself to reporting her insistence that (as Painter translates) 'it is my bodie onely that is violated, my minde God knoweth is giltles', while at the same time mentioning the assurance she had received from her husband and his friends that 'where consente was not, there the crime was absent'.[24]

While these sources would have been of no help to Shakespeare in considering the issue of complicity and guilt, he evidently remembered that the question of how to excuse oneself from a possible charge of being

---

16. Painter 1566, fos. 5ᵛ–7ᵛ. I am much indebted to the discussion of Shakespeare's sources for *Lucrece* in Burrow 2002, pp. 45–50.
17. Livy 1919, I. LVIII, p. 200: 'addit ad metum dedecus'. Cf. Ovid 1996, II. 810.
18. Painter 1566, fo. 5ᵛ. But Livy does not speak of any uncertainty.
19. Painter 1566, fo. 5ᵛ.
20. Livy 1919, I. LVIII, p. 200: 'Quo terrore cum vicisset obstinatam pudicitiam.'
21. Painter 1566, fo. 5ᵛ. Cf. Livy 1919, I. LVIII. 5, p. 200.
22. Augustine 1610, Bk. 1, ch. 18, p. 30.
23. Ovid 1996, II, 827: 'quaeque potest, narrat'. In translating I have changed the tense.
24. Painter 1566, fo. 6ʳ.

accessory to a crime was one that the classical writers on judicial rhetoric had taken very seriously and examined at length. Both the author of the *Ad Herennium* and Cicero in his *De inventione* had furnished detailed advice about how to articulate a speech of exoneration in such circumstances. If, as seems clear from the poem, Shakespeare decided at this juncture that he needed to renew his acquaintance with their advice, it is worth recalling that the relevant texts would have been very readily available to him. As we saw in Chapter 1, his schoolfellow Richard Field had by this time inherited the stock of the London printing house that had produced the only accurate version of both the *Ad Herennium* and the *De inventione* so far printed in England, publishing them as a single volume in 1579 under the title *Rhetoricorum ad C. Herennium Libri Quattuor. M. T. Ciceronis De Inventione Libri Duo.*[25] The likelihood that Field supplied Shakespeare with a copy is much increased by the fact that he and Field would have been in close contact with each other at the relevant time.[26] Field had already printed *Venus and Adonis* in 1593, and in 1594 it was he who printed *Lucrece*. But by whatever means Shakespeare gained access to the *Ad Herennium* and *De inventione*, there can be little doubt that they played a significant role in the writing of his poem. This emerges most clearly from the sequence of stanzas towards the end in which Lucrece relates what befell her and seeks to excuse herself. As we shall see, this section is basically organized around the prescriptions laid down in particular in the *Ad Herennium* about how to develop a speech of exoneration in a judicial cause.

The possibility that Shakespeare may at this stage have reacquainted himself with these classical manuals is reinforced by the fact that, in several of the plays he finished shortly after this time, he began to engage with the technicalities of judicial rhetoric at a new level of detail and complexity. The first play in which we encounter clear signs of this development is *Romeo and Juliet*, probably written in the second half of 1595.[27] Shakespeare's principal source is Arther Brooke's *Tragicall Historye of Romeus and Juliet*, which had originally been published in 1562 and had reached a third edition

---

25. Cicero 1579a.
26. On Shakespeare as a borrower of books from Field see Duncan-Jones 2001, p. 5.
27. Gibbons 1980, p. 26; Wells and Taylor 1987, pp. 117–18; Potter 2012, p. 183. Wiggins and Richardson 2013, p. 268 give 1595 as the best guess. The first quarto speaks of performances by '*the L. of Hunsdon his Servants*'. See Shakespeare 1597, title page. But this description was applicable to Shakespeare's company only between July 1596 and March 1597. See Blakemore Evans 2003, p. 1. The play must therefore have been finished at the latest by the middle of 1596.

by 1587. Brooke's version—a poem of over three thousand lines in poulter's measure[28]—culminates in a scene at the tomb of the Capulets. Friar Lawrence and Romeus's servant find the dead body of Romeus,[29] at which moment the watchmen of the town arrive, imprison them on suspicion of murder and arraign them before the prince the next day. The Friar thereupon launches into a long speech of exculpation, aided by a separate narrative from Romeus's servant, in the course of which they explain what happened and enable the prince to pronounce sentence, thereby drawing the tragedy to a close.

Shakespeare takes most of these details from Brooke, except that he evidently found Friar Lawrence's exculpatory oration wholly unusable. The Friar is defending himself on a capital charge, but in Brooke's version his speech is so far from following the rules for constructing a *refutatio* as to be almost rhapsodic in character.[30] Although he ends by providing a detailed assessment of what took place, he prefaces his explanation with numerous observations about the action of the poem, together with reflections on his advancing years, his previously innocent life, and how he plans to conduct himself on the day of judgement.[31] It appears from Shakespeare's version that he must have decided not merely to rework the scene, but to turn once more to the *Ad Herennium* and the *De inventione* for technical help. When drawing on these sources in *Lucrece* he had needed to know how to present and confirm a *purgatio* in a *constitutio iuridicalis*. Now he needed to remind himself how to mount a defence in a *constitutio coniecturalis*, the form of *constitutio* in which the *quaestio iudicii* or question for adjudication arises from a mystery about a matter of fact.[32] The mystery in the final scene of *Romeo and Juliet* surrounds the cause of the young lovers' deaths. The Chief Watchman in Shakespeare's version begins to develop a conjectural claim about this question in correct classical style.[33] Friar Lawrence then responds with a defence of himself in which he closely follows the classical rules about how to handle a *constitutio coniecturalis*,

---

28. The poulter's measure, first so labelled by George Gascoigne in the 1570s, takes the form of rhymed couplets with alternating lines of twelve and fourteen syllables.
29. But not of the County Paris, who in Brooke's version is not present at the tomb.
30. It is thus misleading for Kennedy 1942, p. 79 to claim that Friar Lawrence's oration 'in outline and detail' follows Brooke's poem.
31. Brooke 1562, fos. 79ᵛ–81ᵛ.   32. *Rhetorica ad Herennium* 1954, I. XI. 18, p. 34.
33. As noted in Baldwin 1944, vol. 2, pp. 76–80.

exhibiting (like Lucrece) a particularly exact knowledge of the directions offered by the author of the *Ad Herennium*.

The next play in which Shakespeare draws on the principles of judicial rhetoric is *The Merchant of Venice*, which he seems to have started in the second half of 1596 and completed in the following year.[34] The trial scene in Act 4, in which Shylocke lays his case before the duke of Venice, juxtaposes two different types of judicial cause, both of which are handled with close attention to the classical rules. Shylocke takes his case to be *absoluta*, an instance of an absolute form of a *constitutio iuridicalis* by contrast with the assumptive type of defence offered by Lucrece.[35] But the learned Dr Balthazer (Portia in disguise) is able to show that what the court has before it is not a *constitutio iuridicalis* at all, but rather an instance of a *constitutio legitima* or *legalis*, as a result of which Shylocke is forced to withdraw his plea and loses his case.[36]

Soon afterwards, in *Julius Caesar*, which can be securely dated to the year 1599,[37] Shakespeare once again dramatized a *constitutio iuridicalis*, this time on a grander scale. Like Shylocke, Brutus considers his cause to be *absoluta,* and in Act 3 he defends before the assembled plebeians the absolute rightfulness of his decision to assassinate Caesar. Antony in his reply at first appears to accept that his own case must be correspondingly assumptive, and

34. Shakespeare makes use of Lazarus Piot's translation of Alexander Silvayn's *The Orator*, which was not published until 1596. See Silvayn 1596, pp. 400–2. The play also mentions a Spanish vessel seized in the attack on Cadiz in June 1596. See Bullough 1957–75, vol. 1, p. 445 and cf. Mahood 2003, pp. 1–2, who notes that the same ship was even more in the news in October 1597. The play cannot, however, have been finished much later than the end of that year, for it appears in the list of Shakespeare's comedies published by Francis Meres in his *Palladis Tamia* in 1598. See Meres 1598, p. 282. The consensus is that the play must therefore have been written between 1596 and 1597. See Wells and Taylor 1987, pp. 119–20; Drakakis 2010, p. 31; Potter 2012, pp. 210–11 and Wiggins and Richardson 2013, p. 341, who give 1596 as the best guess. The play was entered by James Roberts in the Stationers' Register in July 1598 and first printed in 1600. See Shakespeare 1600 and cf. Arber 1875–94, vol. 3, p. 39; Bullough 1957–75, vol. 1, p. 445.

35. As we saw in Chapter 1, this is the type of *constitutio* in which the controversy is about whether something 'was rightfully or unjustly done'. See *Rhetorica ad Herennium* 1954, I. XIV. 24, p. 44.

36. As we saw in Chapter 1, this is the type of *constitutio* in which 'the controversy arises from a text or something stemming from a text'. See *Rhetorica ad Herennium* 1954, I. XI. 18, p. 34. Baldwin 1944, vol. 2, pp. 81–4 discusses this passage, but confuses the two different *constitutiones* involved.

37. The play is not mentioned in Francis Meres's list of Shakespeare's tragedies in his *Palladis Tamia* of 1598. See Meres 1598, p. 282; Spevack 2004, p. 1. But the Swiss traveller Thomas Platter saw it performed at the Globe theatre in September 1599. See Wells and Taylor 1987, p. 121; Shapiro 2005, p. 191. The play must therefore have been written in 1599, and Shapiro 2005, p. 132 argues that it was begun in March and completed by May. According to Daniell 1998, p. 3 and Shapiro 2005, p. 132, it was probably the first play performed at the Globe.

begins by speaking in an elaborately concessive style. But he then turns from *concessio* to *accusatio*, develops a rival *constitutio iuridicalis* and finally convinces the plebeians of the absolute justice of his own opposing cause.

Shakespeare next put his knowledge of judicial rhetoric to still more ambitious use in *Hamlet*, which he seems to have completed around the year 1600.[38] Here again he applies himself to the most intricate form of judicial oratory, the *constitutio coniecturalis*, in which the speaker's aim is to employ conjecture to uncover some hidden truth. He had already dramatized this type of case in *Romeo and Juliet*, but in *Hamlet* he engages with the principles of the *genus iudiciale* at a much higher level of complexity. During the first half of the play two distinct conjectural causes, and hence two separate questions for adjudication, are pursued in parallel until they are eventually made to meet. The ghost declares that there is a hidden truth to be made known about how he met his death, while at the same time Polonius attempts to contrive a means of uncovering the hidden cause of Hamlet's apparent insanity. The principles of judicial rhetoric are employed in each instance not merely to help organize a number of speeches but to lend structure to entire scenes.

Shakespeare also reveals in *Hamlet* a deeper preoccupation with the theory of forensic eloquence than in any of his earlier works, suffusing the language of the play with the technical vocabulary developed by the rhetoricians to distinguish the *genus iudiciale*. As we saw in Chapter 1, this vocabulary centred around three connected terms. First, the classical writers refer to the *res* or range of subjects on which judges are expected to pronounce. Picking up this terminology, the vernacular rhetoricians speak of the 'matters' that stand in need of investigation and judgement. Thomas Wilson, for example, declares that an orator must be capable of discoursing on 'all those questions, whiche by lawe and mannes ordinaunce are enacted', since they constitute 'the matter whereupon an Oratour must speake'.[39] Next, the classical writers observe that, in speaking of such

38. Hibbard 1987, pp. 4–5; Irace 1998, p. 5; Potter 2012, p. 284. But some critics suggest a completion date of 1601. See Wells and Taylor 1987, pp. 122–3; Edwards 2003, p. 31. Others believe that the play may have been fully drafted before the end of 1599. See Jenkins 1982, pp. 6, 13; Shapiro 2005, pp. 339, 341. The play must unquestionably have been completed and performed by 1601, for the printer James Roberts entered 'the Revenge of HAMLETT Prince Denmarke' in the Stationers' Register on 26 July 1602, adding that it had been 'latelie Acted by the Lord Chamberleyne his servantes'. See Arber 1875–94, vol. 3, p. 84.
39. Wilson 1553, Sig. A, 1ʳ. See also Cox 1532, Sig. B, 2ʳ; Rainolde 1563, fo. 1ʳ.

matters for adjudication, we are pointing to the fact that there must be some *quaestio in controversia* that needs to be argued on both sides of the case. Here again Wilson echoes their terminology, arguing that in judicial oratory some 'particuler question, is ever called in controversie' and debated on either side.[40] Finally, to speak of such questions is held to be equivalent to claiming that there must be two parties who have contracted to support rival *causae* in a dispute. Once again Wilson speaks in identical terms, agreeing that 'when tyme shalbe to talke of any matter', the orator must first 'consider the nature of the cause [it]self, that the rather he might frame his whole Oracion thereafter'.[41]

The same vocabulary reappears in each of the plays I have mentioned, but in *Hamlet* it spills out from the judicial passages to saturate the drama as a whole.[42] We are first introduced to the concept of a *quaestio in controversia* when Rosencrans explains to Hamlet why the troupe of players, who are about to arrive at Elsinore, have been forced to travel in search of an audience.[43] They are out of fashion in the city because of a vogue for child actors, who 'crye out on the top of question; and are most tyrannically

40. Wilson 1553, Sig. A, 1ᵛ. See also Rainolde 1563, fo.xiiiʳ.
41. Wilson 1553, Sig. A, 4ᵛ.
42. It might even be said that the play opens with a question that gives rise to a controversy. The sentinel Barnardo calls out 'Whose there?' Francisco responds 'Nay answere me. Stand and unfolde your selfe'. He is satisfied only when Barnardo offers what appears to be a password: 'Long live the King'. See *Hamlet*, TLN 1–3, p. 737 (1. 1. 1–3) and cf. Zurcher 2010, p. 231. Wilson 1995, p. 192 estimates that grammatically there are more than four hundred questions in the play.
43. I need, however, to insert a word of caution about this passage, which appears only in the First Folio text. As we have seen, Shakespeare completed a draft of the play *c.*1600, and critics are generally agreed that this manuscript reached print by two different routes. First, Shakespeare seems to have transcribed and revised his draft, probably in 1601, thereby producing the version eventually published in the First Folio in 1623. See Jenkins 1982, pp. 5, 18, 55; Hibbard 1987, pp. 3–5; Wells and Taylor 1987, pp. 400–1; Irace 1998, p. 5; Edwards 2003, pp. 4–5, 8, 31; Shapiro 2005, p. 356. But meanwhile his original and fuller manuscript of *c.*1600 was published as the second quarto in 1604, in which the title-page announces, correctly, that the text is almost twice as long as that of the quarto published in 1603. See Shakespeare 1603 and Shakespeare 1604. On the first quarto see Melchiori 1992; Irace 1998; Menzer 2008. On the provenance and production of the second quarto see Wilson 1934a, pp. 89, 92–3; Jenkins 1982, pp. 5, 18, 37; Hibbard 1987, p. 3; Wells and Taylor 1987, pp. 399, 401; Irace 1998, pp. 3, 5; Edwards 2003, p. 10; Shapiro 2005, p. 339. (Note, however, that of the seven surviving copies, four are dated 1605 rather than 1604. See Jenkins 1982, p. 14; Wells and Taylor 1987, p. 396.) It seems most probable, therefore, that the passage seemingly alluding to the 'war of the theatres' was added in 1601. Bednarz 2001, pp. 226–7, 230, 235–6 notes that the climax of the 'war' was reached when the Children of Queen Elizabeth's Chapel performed Ben Jonson's *Poetaster* at the Blackfriars Theatre in the winter of 1600–01, in which members of Shakespeare's company were parodied. It remains a possibility, however, that the passage may have been inserted at some later date.

clap't' for commending their own performances.[44] Hamlet wonders if their playwrights may be doing them a disservice in prompting them to criticize adult actors, and Rosencrans answers that such a *controversia* has indeed arisen, and that numerous arguments have been mounted *in utramque partem*:

> Faith there ha's bene much to do on both sides: and the Nation holds it no sinne, to tarre them to Controversie. There was for a while, no mony bid for argument, unlesse the Poet and the Player went to Cuffes in the Question.[45]

The question in controversy—whether child actors should be preferred— was for a time so hotly debated, Rosencrans is telling us, that no new plays could be staged unless the adult actors were ready to fight for them.[46]

Shakespeare is evidently referring to the so-called 'war of the theatres' sparked off in 1601 by the popularity of the children's acting companies.[47] When he speaks in *Hamlet* about questions in controversy, however, he chiefly does so in connection with the much darker suggestion that the conduct of genuine warfare can be figured as just such a question between two opposing sides. We first encounter this image in the opening scene, in which Horatio explains why so many military preparations are going forward in Denmark. Some time ago[48] Hamlet's father killed old Fortin- brasse in single combat, thereby gaining some territory that his son is planning to win back. Barnardo agrees that this explains the recent com- motions, to which he adds that it seems to him appropriate that a ghost resembling old Hamlet should have appeared to them at this time:

> Well may it sort that this portentous figure
> Comes armed through our watch so like the King
> That was and is the question of these warres.
>
> TLN 2–4, p. 775, col. 1 (1. 1. 109–11)

The question in controversy is about the ownership of the lands forfeited by old Fortinbrasse. The issue was settled by old Hamlet, but young Fortinbrasse

---

44. *Hamlet*, TLN 1270–1, p. 750 (2. 2. 315–16).
45. *Hamlet*, TLN 1282–6, p. 751 (2. 2. 326–9).
46. As we have seen, this passage occurs only in the First Folio. The text in Shakespeare 1986 is based on the second quarto (1604) but the passage is nevertheless included at TLN 1267–92, pp. 750–1. (2. 2. 313–33). Bednarz 2001, pp. 262–3 prints the parallel passages.
47. See Gurr 1992, pp. 49–55; Bednarz 2001, pp. 225–56; Munro 2005; Donaldson 2011, pp. 165, 168, 173–4.
48. We subsequently learn from the clown (the first gravedigger) that this happened thirty years ago, and on the very day when young Hamlet was born. See *Hamlet*, TLN 3115, 3129, p. 769 (5. 1. 123–4, 137–8).

has raised it anew. As a result, the figure of old Hamlet has again become 'the question of these warres'.

Later in the play, when Hamlet is about to set sail for England, he encounters the army of young Fortinbrasse marching towards Poland. He enquires whether they are planning to attack the main part of the country, and is answered by the Captain of the troops:

> Truly to speake, and with no addition,
> We goe to gaine a little patch of ground
> That hath in it no profit but the name
>
> TLN 8–10, p. 776, col. 2 (4. 4. 17–19)

Hamlet is shocked that so much treasure and so many lives are about to be expended to so little purpose:

> Two thousand soules, & twenty thousand duckets
> Will now debate the question of this straw,[49]

Once again the waging of warfare is imagined as a question in controversy, but in this case we are given to understand that the question should never have been raised, since it does not matter a straw.

Of all the uses of judicial terminology in *Hamlet*, the most significant arise from the fact that Hamlet is so insistent (if indecisive) in seeing himself as the protagonist of a cause. He agrees at the outset to make the ghost's cause his own, thereby leaving himself with a controversy to pursue on the ghost's behalf. The ghost asks Hamlet to remember him and his call for revenge, and Hamlet promises that this 'matter' will now occupy him to the exclusion of all else:

> And thy commandement all alone shall live,
> Within the booke and volume of my braine
> Unmixt with baser matter,
>
> TLN 719–21, p. 745 (1. 5. 102–4)

Hamlet is thinking of his brain as matter—we would say grey matter—with a certain volume or size. But there is also a judicial 'matter' that he not only needs to retain within his brain, but with the permanence that comes from being inscribed in a volume or book. When he begins to have his doubts, the question of how this matter should be pursued leaves him increasingly

---

49. This passage appears only in the First Folio, and is printed in Shakespeare 1986 in the 'Additional passages' included at pp. 775–8. See TLN 16–17, p. 776 col. 2 (4. 4. 25–6).

disturbed, as Claudius recognizes after eavesdropping on his meeting with Ophelia:

> This something setled matter in his hart,
> Whereon his braines still beating puts him thus
> From fashion of himselfe.
>
> TLN 1712–14, p. 755 (3. 1. 167–9)

Claudius thinks of the matter disturbing Hamlet as an infection, as peccant matter lodged in his heart. But he also perceives that Hamlet is beating his brains about a 'matter', that is, a judicial question, and that Hamlet is trying to settle the matter in his heart before deciding on what course of action to pursue.

Meanwhile Hamlet is berating himself for having failed to pursue his cause. He initially expresses his self-disgust after watching the First Player weep while recounting the story of Priam and Hecuba:

> what would he doe
> Had he the motive, and the Cue for passion
> That I have? . . .
>
> yet I,
> A dull and muddy metteld raskall peake,
> Like John-a-dreames, unpregnant of my cause,
> And can say nothing;
>
> TLN 1491–3, 1497–1500, pp. 752–3 (2. 2. 512–14, 518–21)

Hamlet meditates once again on his failure to pursue his cause after watching Fortinbrasse's army embark on its futile campaign:

> I doe not know
> Why yet I live to say this thing's to doe,
> Sith I have cause, and will, and strength, and meanes
> To doo't;
>
> TLN 34–7, p. 777, col. 1 (4. 4. 43–6)

Fortinbrasse's army is about to fight for a mere plot of land where 'the numbers cannot try the cause'.[50] But Hamlet cannot manage to bestir himself even in a cause to which he is attached by reason as well as blood.[51] When in the final scene he eventually manages to kill Claudius,

---

50. *Hamlet*, TLN 52–4, p. 777, col. 1 (4. 4. 61–3).
51. *Hamlet*, TLN 49, p. 777, col. 1 (4. 4. 58).

he does so only to learn from Laertes that he himself has already been poisoned. With his dying breath he calls on Horatio to speak on his behalf:

> *Horatio* I am dead,
> Thou liv'st, report me and my cause a right
> To the unsatisfied.

TLN 3558–60, p. 774 (5. 2. 317–19)

The cause is that of revenging his father's murder, but it will be left to Horatio to try to explain that old Hamlet was indeed murdered, and thus that his son's conduct can be explained and perhaps exonerated.

The early Jacobean plays

Despite the importance of the examples I have been considering, it would be misleading to imply that Shakespeare made any extensive use of judicial rhetoric in his late Elizabethan works. If he can be said to have had any overriding artistic preoccupation during this period, it was with the completion of his cycle of history plays and the writing of his festive comedies, and in neither of these bodies of work do we encounter any significant interest in the theories of *inventio* and *dispositio* in judicial causes. If we turn, however, to his early Jacobean plays, we find that for a brief period he became intensely absorbed by the possibilities of using the principles of judicial rhetoric as a dramaturgical technique. I next want to say a preliminary word about the three plays in which these possibilities are most fully realized: *Othello*, *Measure for Measure*, and *All's Well That Ends Well*.

While a number of terminal dates have been proposed for the completion of *Othello*, extending from 1601 to 1604,[52] the balance of evidence suggests that the play must have been written in the closing months of 1603.[53] It

---

52. Honigmann 1997, pp. 1, 349 suggests 1600–01; Neill 2006, pp. 403–4 suggests 1602–03. Bullough 1957–75, vol. 7, p. 194, Wells and Taylor 1987, p. 126, and Sanders 2003, p. 2 argue for dates between the end of 1603 and early 1604.

53. The play cannot have been completed much earlier than the end of 1603, for the opening scenes contain several allusions (although Honigmann 1993 seeks to cast doubt on some of them) to Knolles's *Generall Historie of the Turke*, which was not signed off until 'the last of September. 1603'. See Knolles 1603, Sig. A, 6ᵛ. This is noted in Bullough 1957–75, vol. 7, pp. 194, 262–5; Wells and Taylor 1987, p. 126; Sanders 2003, pp. 1, 10. For a full discussion see Vaughan 2011.

must certainly have been finished before the start of 1604,[54] and the first recorded performance took place at court in November of that year.[55] Here Shakespeare again dramatizes the most complex form of judicial rhetoric, the *constitutio coniecturalis*. In Act 1 Brabantio attempts but fails to confirm his conjecture that Othello must have practised witchcraft on Desdemona, while in Act 3 Iago succeeds in confirming to Othello's satisfaction his fabricated conjecture that Desdemona has been conducting an adulterous affair with Cassio. The classical precepts of judicial rhetoric are invoked in Act 1 to structure a series of major speeches, and in Act 3 to give shape to several successive scenes.

After *Othello*, Shakespeare's next play appears to have been *Measure for Measure*.[56] Critics have found a number of topical allusions suggesting a date of composition between May and August 1604, and the work was performed at court as part of the Christmas festivities of that year.[57] Here Shakespeare reverts to his earlier interest in dramatizing the *constitutio iuridicalis*, the juridical version of the judicial cause.[58] Two juridical issues are handled in the course of the play, both linked to the preternaturally eloquent figure of Isabella.[59] First she comes before Angelo to plead an assumptive case on behalf of her brother Claudio. She is not in a position to attempt a *purgatio*, and is obliged to content herself with a *confessio* in the

---

54. The reason is that, as Honigmann 1993, pp. 212–13 notes, at least one echo of *Othello* appears in the first quarto of *Hamlet* in 1603. See *Othello*, TLN 531, p. 934 (1. 3. 241) and cf. Shakespeare 1998, [5] 7–8, p. 48.

55. Stamp 1930 [Facsimiles of the Accounts Book of Edmund Tilney, Master of the Revels], Plate 3, headed '1604': 'By the Kings Ma[tis] plaiers/Hallamas Day being the first of Novembar a play in the Banketinge house att Whithall called The Moor of Venis'. Hamilton 1986, pp. 223–8 restates earlier doubts about this manuscript, but Stamp 1930, pp. 7–13 gives strong reasons for accepting its authenticity. See also Duncan-Jones 2001, pp. 170–2, where the page is reproduced.

56. Some critics posit a *terminus a quo* of as early as mid-1603, which would mean that *Measure for Measure* predates *Othello*. See, for example, Wells and Taylor 1987, p. 126, suggesting a date between summer 1603 and November 1604. I need to stress that, if such an early date could be established, this would not affect my own argument. I tend, however, to accept the general view that the play was probably written in the spring or summer of 1604. Stevenson 1959 examines an incident involving James I in March 1604 to which the play appears to allude. See also Goldberg 1983, p. 235. For summer 1604 as the main period of composition see Lever 1965, pp. xxxi–xxxv; Bawcutt 1991, pp. 2–4; Gibbons 1991, p. 23.

57. Stamp 1930, Plate 3, headed '1604': 'By his ma[tis] plaiers:/On S[t] Stivens night in the hall a play caled Mesur for Mesur:/Shaxberd:' The feast of St Stephen falls on 26 December.

58. On the rhetoric of the play see Bennett 2000. But Bennett does not speak of judicial rhetoric; his concern is to link the play to Erasmian aspirations to use drama in the cause of social reform.

59. On the play as a judicial debate see Newman 1985, pp. 14–19; on competing forms of rhetoric in the play see Roberts 2002.

form of a *deprecatio*, a straightforward plea for mercy and pardon in the face
of an admitted crime. Later, in the final Act, she presents the duke of Vienna
with what she claims by contrast to be an instance of an absolute juridical
cause. She begins to mount an accusation against Angelo for misuse of his
office, and attempts to establish the unqualified rightfulness of her charge.
But in this case she is cut off in the course of her *narratio*, and the confirmation of her accusation is supplied not by any further display of judicial
eloquence but rather by the revelation, at the climax of the closing scene,
that Angelo has been duped into revealing his villainy by the device of a bed
trick.

The last play in which Shakespeare makes systematic use of judicial
rhetoric is *All's Well That Ends Well*. The consensus used to be that *All's
Well* was written between 1603 and early 1605, but in an article of 2001
Jackson claimed that it 'cannot have been composed earlier than mid-
1606'.[60] This contention has since received extensive support, but Jackson's
reasoning is not persuasive, and the balance of evidence continues to point
to a date of completion between late 1604 and early 1605.[61] With *All's Well*
Shakespeare rounds off a group of plays—beginning with *The Merchant of
Venice* and continuing with *Measure for Measure*—that appear to belong
together, and stand in strong and perhaps deliberate contrast with his festive
comedies.[62] They all involve the breaking off of nuptials, and no prominent
scenes of revelry ever take place. They all have a predominantly urban
setting, and no one ever escapes to the forest. They all involve imposture
and deceit, and in *All's Well*, as in *Measure for Measure*, the plot pivots around
a bed trick, with the exposure and humiliation of the victim again occupying much of the closing scene. Still more significantly, they are all intensely
forensic plays, and all of them contain a trial scene that serves as the climax
and resolution of the work. The use of judicial rhetoric is similar in each
case, but in *All's Well* it is carried to unprecedented heights of complexity.
Rynaldo develops a *constitutio coniecturalis* in his confrontation with the
countess in Act 1, while Diana and her mother pursue an absolute form of
a *constitutio iuridicalis* in the presence of the king in Act 5, in the course of
which their accusations of wrongdoing against Count Bertram become

60. Jackson 2001, p. 299.   61. I present evidence for this claim in the Appendix.
62. See the analysis in Salingar 1974, esp. pp. 301–5, on which I am drawing here. Salingar
    focuses, as he says (p. 305), on 'broken nuptials and a legal crisis'. He traces the plots of these
    plays to the *novella* tradition, arguing (p. 303) that in using these sources Shakespeare 'was
    looking for such dramatic possibilities, not merely finding them'.

intertwined with two successive *constitutiones coniecturales* being investigated by the king himself.

The crescendo of *All's Well*, in which these three different strands of forensic argument are suddenly brought together, must count as Shakespeare's most spectacular use of judicial rhetoric for dramatic purposes. After the completion of this *tour de force*, however, his interest in the minutiae of judicial oratory seems to have fallen away. Why this should have happened is not clear, but it may be relevant that by this stage he had not only dramatized every known type of judicial cause but was beginning to repeat himself. Lucrece attempts to excuse herself with an assumptive plea in a juridical cause, and Isabella attempts to excuse her brother Claudio with exactly the same type of plea in *Measure for Measure*. Friar Lawrence defends himself in a *constitutio coniecturalis* in the presence of a hostile judge in the closing scene of *Romeo and Juliet*, and Othello defends himself in the same rhetorical predicament in Act 1 of *Othello*. The classical rhetoricians had served Shakespeare well, but he may have felt that he had exhausted the seam.

This is not to say that Shakespeare displays no interest in judicial rhetoric in his later works, for he went on to compose no fewer than three further plays in which he stages a trial scene. The first takes place in Act 3 of *Timon of Athens*, which he appears to have written jointly with Thomas Middleton,[63] probably between 1605 and 1607.[64] Alcibiades comes before the Athenian senators to plead for the life of a friend who has killed a man in a duel. Here, however, Shakespeare limits himself to presenting yet another assumptive plea in a juridical cause, and hence to dramatizing a petition for mercy rather than a full-scale forensic debate.[65] A further trial scene occurs

63. Klein 2001, p. 63 urges caution, but Wells and Taylor 1987, pp. 127–8 refer to several scholars (Jackson, Lake, and especially Holdsworth) whom they take to have proved beyond doubt that Middleton had a hand in the work. Vickers 2002, pp. 244–90 agrees, as does Jowett 2004 (title page). Dawson and Minton 2008, pp. 401–7 attribute each individual scene.

64. The sense-pause test reported in Fitch 1981, p. 300 places *Timon* closest to *All's Well*. I date the completion of *All's Well* to early 1605, which perhaps implies a date of 1605 for *Timon*, as proposed in Wells and Taylor 1987, pp. 127–8. However, more recent commentators have assigned *Timon* to a later period. Klein 2001, p. 1 tentatively opts for 1607–8; Jowett 2004, p. 4 suggests early 1606; Dawson and Minton 2008, p. 12 suggest 1607 or earlier. I should add that nothing in my own argument depends on who is right.

65. The scene is 3. 5 in the usual numbering, but appears as 3. 6 in Dawson and Minton 2008, which follows Shakespeare 1986, *Timon of Athens*, TLN 1094–1107, p. 1013 (3. 4. 97–111) in turning these lines, usually the conclusion of 3. 4, into a separate scene.

in *Henry VIII*, perhaps Shakespeare's final work,[66] on which he seems to have collaborated with John Fletcher.[67] But in this case there is even less engagement with the detailed prescriptions of judicial rhetoric. Arraigned in Act 2 before the king, Queen Katherine simply refuses the jurisdiction of the court, announces that she will appeal directly to the Pope and insists on taking her leave.[68]

The only late play of which Shakespeare is the sole author and that also contains a trial scene is *The Winters Tale*, usually said to have been written between 1609 and 1611.[69] Here Shakespeare returns to his earlier interest in the *constitutio coniecturalis*, which had last played a significant role in *All's Well That Ends Well*. King Leontes comes to believe that his queen, Hermione, has been guilty of adultery with his friend Polixenes. Leontes speaks in correct judicial terms about his wish to bring the 'matter' to court,[70] about his 'conjecture' relating to Hermione's faithlessness,[71] and about his willingness to offer a 'confirmation' of his cause.[72] But when he arrives to judge the case he simply commands that the accusation against his wife be read out, without making any attempt to develop a *narratio* or build up a *confirmatio* of his charge.[73] Hermione's predicament is thus that she finds herself falsely accused before a hostile judge. The classical rhetoricians have a great deal to say about how best to conduct oneself in such dangerous circumstances, but Hermione appears entirely ignorant of their advice. She mounts three speeches in her own defence, but she largely contents herself with making an appeal to heaven while adding swelling protestations about her loyalty and her willingness to die. The only effect of her intense but vague magniloquence is to illustrate its incapacity

---

66. *The Two Noble Kinsmen* may be later, but was not included in the First Folio. The first recorded performance of *All Is True* (*Henry VIII*) took place on 29 June 1613, when the Globe theatre burned down. See McMullan 2000, p. 9. There is general agreement that the play was written in late 1612 or early 1613. See Wells and Taylor 1987, p. 133; Margeson 1990, pp. 1–3; Potter 2012, pp. 393–5.

67. For details of the collaboration, in which the trial scene (2. 4) has usually been attributed to Shakespeare, see McMullan 2000, p. 449; Vickers 2002, pp. 339, 342, 356, 361, 375.

68. *All Is True* (*Henry VIII*), TLN 1188–1202, p. 1383 (2. 4. 116–31). For a discussion see Keeton 1967, pp. 158–64.

69. Pafford 1963, pp. xxii–xxiii favours 1610–11, as do Snyder and Curren-Aquino 2007, p. 63. Wells and Taylor 1987, p. 131 argue for 1609, while Orgel 1996, pp. 79–80 suggests 'before the end of 1610'.

70. *The Winters Tale*, TLN 784, p. 1275 (2. 3. 2).

71. *The Winters Tale*, TLN 690, p. 1274 (2. 1. 176).

72. *The Winters Tale*, TLN 694, p. 1274 (2. 1. 180).   73. As noted in Syme 2012, pp. 222–3.

to overcome the tyranny to which she is exposed. By this time Shakespeare's dramatic purposes had changed, and he may even have lost his earlier interest in how best to defend oneself in a judicial cause in a 'winning' and persuasive style.[74]

74. On vagueness and intensity in Shakespeare's late style see McDonald 2006, pp. 30–7.

3
The Open Beginning

Prohoemium

My aim in the chapters that follow is to show that, in the plays I have now singled out, there are numerous major speeches, as well as several complete scenes, that are basically constructed according to the classical rules governing the *inventio* and *dispositio* of judicial arguments. A word first about Shakespeare's reliance on the rules of *dispositio*. As we saw in Chapter 1, these specify that any oration must be laid out in five main parts: the *prohoemium*, the *narratio*, the *confirmatio*, the *confutatio*, and the *peroratio*. One of my aims will be to demonstrate that this is the pattern according to which Shakespeare's judicial speeches are invariably organized. Yet more important is his use of the precepts embodied in the underlying theory of *inventio*. As we also saw in Chapter 1, this theory lays down a number of guidelines about how to articulate each section of a judicial speech. First we need to understand how to construct a *prohoemium* in such a way as to establish our *ethos* and win the attention and goodwill of the judge. Then we need to know how to develop a *narratio* that will not only convey the facts of the case but will have the effect of getting the judge on our side. When it comes to the *confirmatio* and *confutatio* we need to have a full understanding of how to present 'non-artificial' as well as 'artificial' proofs, and finally we need to know how to fill our *peroratio* with 'amplifications' to arouse the emotions of the judge and move him to decide in favour of our case. The classical and Renaissance handbooks on the art of rhetoric are almost entirely devoted to offering detailed instructions under each of these headings, and Shakespeare follows them with a remarkable degree of tenacity and exactitude. This is the claim that—beginning with his handling of beginnings—I next want to illustrate, and my attempt to do so will occupy me for the rest of this book.

Two ways to begin

'A faulty *prohoemium*', Quintilian warns, 'looks as bad as a scarred face', to which he gnomically adds that 'the worst pilot is undoubtedly the one who runs his ship aground while leaving the harbour'.[1] Thomas Wilson also speaks in nautical terms when introducing his discussion of the *prohoemium* or 'enteraunce' in Book 2 of his *Arte of Rhetorique*:

> Before all thynges, this would be wel marked, that, whensoever we shal largely talke of any matter, wee alwaies so invent, and finde out our first enteraunce in the cause, that the same be for ever taken, even from the nature and bowelles therof, that al thynges, whiche shall first be spoken, maie seme to agree with the matter, and not made as a Shippe mannes hose, to serve for every legge.[2]

Wilson assumes that we shall be concerned with a matter in controversy and asks how we should enter into a discussion of the cause. His answer is that our first task must be to invent or find out the most suitable arguments to use at the outset of our speech. As Quintilian had already warned, 'there can be nothing worse than finding yourself destitute of the verbal power to continue at this stage'.[3]

This is not to say that a *prohoemium* will be essential in every case. Cicero in his *De inventione* allows that, 'when your cause is obviously praiseworthy, it may be better to omit a formal beginning and start with the *narratio* or facts of the case'.[4] Quintilian similarly argues that there may be circumstances in which a *prohoemium* is superfluous, noting that Aristotle goes so far as to assert that in front of good judges there is never any genuine need for one.[5] It was generally accepted, however, that a formal beginning will be indispensable whenever there is a need, as Cicero puts it, 'to prepare the mind of your audience to be in a suitable condition to hear the rest of your speech'.[6]

---

1. Quintilian 2001, 4. 1. 61, vol. 2, pp. 208–10: 'vitiosum prohoemium possit videri cicatricosa facies: et pessimus certe gubernator qui navem dum portu egreditur impegit'.
2. Wilson 1553, Sig. O, 3ᵛ.
3. Quintilian 2001, 4. 1. 61, vol. 2, p. 208: 'continuandi verba facultate destitui nusquam turpis'. See Benabu 2013 on the classical *prohoemium* and some of Shakespeare's opening scenes.
4. Cicero 1949a, I. XV. 21, p. 42: 'Cum autem erit honestum causa genus, vel praeteriri principium poterit vel... a narratione incipiemus.' Cf. *Rhetorica ad Herennium* 1954, I. IV. 6, p. 12.
5. Quintilian 2001, 4. 1. 72, vol. 2, p. 214.
6. Cicero 1949a, I. XV. 20, p. 40: 'animum auditoris idonee comparans ad reliquam dictionem [audire]'.

Quintilian agrees that you cannot do without one if there is any need for the judge to be *praeparatus*, that is, briefed and instructed, but also forewarned about what is to come.[7]

Given that a *prohoemium* will normally be necessary, what specific aims should we set ourselves in this opening part of our speech? The Roman rhetoricians answer with a single voice. The basic aim should be to speak in such a way that our audience is rendered attentive (*attentus*), responsive (*docilis*), and above all well-disposed (*benevolus*) towards our side of the case.[8] It is true that Cicero in his *De oratore* argues against his earlier assumption in the *De inventione* that the securing of goodwill should mainly be the work of the *prohoemium*, insisting that such emotional appeals ought not to be channelled into a single section of a speech, but ought instead to permeate it.[9] But Quintilian, more a stickler for tradition, reverts to the view that the distinctive as well as the principal aim of the *prohoemium* should be to do everything possible to win the benevolence of our audience.[10] We are basically engaged at this stage in what Cicero describes as a *captatio benevolentiae*, an attempt to win goodwill.[11]

The vernacular rhetoricians offer some helpful expansions of these somewhat laconic formulae. Leonard Cox begins by stressing the importance of ensuring that 'the herers shall be made attent or diligent' and that they 'give right good attendaunce',[12] while Thomas Wilson similarly speaks of the need to start by making our audience 'apte, to geve good eare out of hande, to that whiche shall folowe'.[13] Next Cox refers to the value of ensuring 'docilite',[14] which Wilson characterizes as a process of 'teachyng the hearers what the matter is', so that we 'make theim understande the matter easily'.[15] But our most important aspiration should be to create what Cox describes— again translating literally—as a feeling of benevolence on the part of our audience;[16] what Wilson speaks of as 'winnying their favour' and ensuring their 'good willes' from the start.[17]

---

7. Quintilian 2001, 4. 1. 72, vol. 2, p. 214.
8. Cicero 1949a, I. XV. 20, p. 40; *Rhetorica ad Herennium* 1954, I. IV. 6, p. 12 (and I. VII. 11, p. 20); Cicero 1942a, II. XIX. 80, vol. 1, pp. 256–8; Quintilian 2001, 4. 1. 5, vol. 2, p. 182.
9. Cicero 1942a, II. XIX. 81–3, vol. 1, pp. 258–60. Cf. Wisse 2002, p. 384; Heath 2009, pp. 67–8.
10. Quintilian 2001, 4. 1. 5, vol. 2, pp. 180–2.
11. See Cicero 1949a, I. XVI. 22, p. 44 on how the benevolence of our audience can be captured ('auditorum . . . benivolentia captabitur'). Cf. Cicero 1942a, II. XXVI. 115, vol. 1, p. 280 and Cicero 1949b, XXVI. 97, p. 456.
12. Cox 1532, Sig. B, 7ʳ.   13. Wilson 1553, Sig. O, 3ʳ.   14. Cox 1532, Sig. B, 7ʳ.
15. Wilson 1553, Sig. O, 3ᵛ.   16. Cox 1532, Sig. B, 2ᵛ.
17. Wilson 1553, Sig. O, 3ᵛ–4ʳ.

The rhetoricians next consider how to achieve these results. Before discussing this question, however, they have an important warning to announce. As Cicero expresses it, 'it is essential for anyone who wants to start speaking effectively to make himself carefully aware beforehand of the type of cause in which he is involved'.[18] The author of the *Ad Herennium* agrees that 'if we want to be able to make an appropriate beginning, the type of cause in which we are engaged must first be considered'.[19] Different causes call for different kinds of *prohoemium*, and it is vital to work out in advance which kind to use.

There is some disagreement about the number of causes that forensic orators need to be able to discriminate. The *Ad Herennium* thinks there are four;[20] Cicero thinks there are five;[21] Quintilian thinks there may be as many as six.[22] Some of these, however, are agreed to be of little significance. The *Ad Herennium* refers to the *causa humilis*, the mean or unimportant cause,[23] to which Cicero and Quintilian add the *causa obscura*, the obscure cause, but no one has much to say about either of these.[24] The general view is that there are just four types to be seriously discussed: the *causa honesta*, the *causa turpis*, the *causa admirabilis*, and the type that Cicero and Quintilian describe as *anceps*, that is, partly *turpis* and partly *honesta* in character.[25] Within this group, everyone agrees that the basic contrast is between the *causa honesta* and the cause that is wholly or partly *turpis*. These two pivotal terms are habitually treated as antonyms. As the *Ad Herennium* puts it, 'a cause is taken to be *turpis* when it involves an attack on some *res* or matter which is *honesta*'.[26] By contrast, a *causa honesta* is said to be one in which 'we either defend something that seems to everyone to be worthy of defence, or else oppose something that seems to everyone deserving of being opposed'.[27]

---

18. Cicero 1949a, I. XV. 20, p. 40: 'qui bene exordiri causam volet eum necesse est genus suae causae diligenter ante cognoscere'.
19. *Rhetorica ad Herennium* 1954, I. III. 5, p. 10: 'quo commodius exordiri possimus genus causae est considerandum'.
20. *Rhetorica ad Herennium* 1954, I. III. 5, p. 10.   21. Cicero 1949a, I. XV. 20, p. 40.
22. Quintilian 2001, 4. 1. 40, vol. 2, p. 198.   23. *Rhetorica ad Herennium* 1954, I. III. 5, p. 10.
24. Cicero 1949a, I. XV. 20, p. 40; Quintilian 2001, 4. 1. 40–1, vol. 2, p. 198.
25. Cicero 1949a, I. XV. 20, p. 40; Quintilian 2001, 4. 1. 40, vol. 2, p. 198. The author of the *Rhetorica ad Herennium*, who omits the *causa admirabilis*, prefers to speak not of *anceps* but of the *causa dubia*. See *Rhetorica ad Herennium* 1954, I. III, 5, p. 10.
26. *Rhetorica ad Herennium* 1954, I. III. 5, p. 10: 'turpe genus intelligitur cum...honesta res oppugnatur'. For *turpis* and *honestus* (and *turpitudo* and *honestas*) as antonyms see also Cicero 1949a, I. XV. 20 and 22, pp. 40, 42.
27. *Rhetorica ad Herennium* 1954, I. III. 5, p. 10: 'Honestum causae genus putatur cum aut id defendimus quod ab omnibus videtur oppugnari debere, aut oppugnabimus quod ab omnibus videtur oppugnari debere.'

To understand how these distinctions are put to use, we first need to know how these Latin terms were translated in Shakespeare's time. Here we need to pause for a moment to consider the availability of Latin–English dictionaries in Elizabethan England. The earliest was Thomas Cooper's *Thesaurus Linguae Romanae & Britannicae*, originally published in 1565.[28] The next was John Veron's *Dictionarie in Latine and English*, which first appeared in 1575 and was reprinted in 1584.[29] Thereafter these works seem to have been largely superseded by Thomas Thomas's *Dictionarium Linguae Latinae et Anglicanae*. Thomas's compilation is heavily dependent on Cooper, but was issued in a less unwieldy format and became a popular guide.[30] After its initial publication in 1587 it reappeared in a second edition in 1589 and a third in 1592,[31] after which it was reprinted at least four times before the end of the century.

If we consult any of these works under the adjectives *honestus* and *turpis* we encounter a strong measure of agreement. First, they all maintain that *turpis* means 'dishonest'.[32] More helpfully, they agree that one of its basic synonyms is 'foul', a usage that gave rise to the phrase 'foul play' to describe serious crimes, especially murder.[33] Hamlet speaks in these terms when Horatio first tells him about the appearance of the ghost:

> My fathers spirit (in armes) all is not well,
> I doubt some foule play,

TLN 410–11, p. 741 (1. 2. 254–5)

If *turpis* means foul or dishonest, then its antonym *honestus*, the lexicographers agree, must mean 'honest'.[34] This is not perhaps very illuminating, but they also propose an extensive catalogue of synonyms. Cooper suggests 'good: of good behaveour: of good reputation';[35] Veron adds 'laudable,

---

28. I use the first edition (BL copy). There were at least four reprints by 1587. On Cooper see Starnes 1954, pp. 85–110; Binns 1990, pp. 293–4; Green 2009, pp. 1–3, 245.
29. I use the edition of 1584 (CUL copy). On Veron see Binns 1990, p. 296.
30. On Thomas see Starnes 1954, pp. 114–38; Binns 1990, p. 295.
31. I use the edition of 1592 (BL copy).
32. Cooper 1565, Sig. 6K, 5ᵛ; Veron 1584, Sig. 2T, 1ʳ; Thomas 1592, Sig. 3C, 5ᵛ. Wilson 1553, Sig. A, 4ᵛ similarly refers to 'unhonest' causes while [Puttenham] 1589, p. 242 speaks yet more literally of 'turpitude'.
33. Cooper 1565, Sig. 6K, 5ᵛ: 'Turpis . . . foule: filthie'. See also Veron 1584, Sig. 2T, 1ʳ; Thomas 1592, Sig. 3C, 5ᵛ.
34. Cooper 1565, Sig. 3L, 3ᵛ: 'Honestus: honeste: good'. See also Veron 1584, Sig. T, 6ᵛ; Thomas 1592, Sig. Z, 1ʳ. The vernacular rhetoricians had already spoken in the same terms. See Cox 1532, Sig. B, 5ʳ; Wilson 1553, Sig. A, 4ᵛ.
35. Cooper 1565, Sig. 3L, 3ᵛ.

virtuous';[36] and Thomas more expansively offers 'good, kinde, noble, honourable, of good behaviour, well mannered'.[37]

The fundamental distinction between the *causa turpis* and the *causa honesta* is thus rendered in Elizabethan English as a contrast between 'foul' and 'honest' causes. These are agreed to be the basic cases, although it is important to note that Cicero and Quintilian both speak in addition of the *causa admirabilis*.[38] This is the type of cause that arises, in Cicero's words, 'when the minds of those who are about to hear a case are alienated from it'.[39] Quintilian puts forward a different definition, one that appears to embody an explanation of why the sympathies of an audience might have become alienated. A cause is described as *admirabilis*, he writes, 'when it is set up in a manner that is is out of line with the general opinion of men'.[40]

If we return to the Elizabethan lexicographers, we find them claiming that *admirabilis* means 'mervaylous' and 'to be woundered at',[41] but also 'straunge' and 'contrarie to the opinion of the most parte'.[42] Thomas Wilson agrees that to describe something as 'straunge' is to say that it is 'unlike to that, which men communely use to speake'.[43] Thomas Cooper adds in his entry on the underlying deponent verb *admiror* that it means 'to wonder: to mervayle at'.[44] To speak in Shakespeare's England of a *causa admirabilis* was thus to refer to a cause that was felt in some way to be strange or astonishing, a source of wonderment.

This type of *causa*, Quintilian notes, is treated by some authorities as a subspecies of the *causa turpis*.[45] This brings us back to the fundamental distinction between foul and honest causes, and to the importance of reflecting, before we begin to speak, on which of these basic types we have undertaken to support. This prior reflection is important, the *Ad Herennium* explains, because our judgement on whether the cause we have espoused is basically foul or basically honest will determine which of two contrasting styles of *prohoemium* we should use. Enlarging on these different ways of opening a judicial speech, he emphatically draws attention—for the first and only time—to the novelty of his own approach.

36. Veron 1584, Sig. T, 6ᵛ.   37. Thomas 1592, Sig. Z, 1ʳ.
38. Cicero 1949a, I. XV. 20, p. 40; Quintilian 2001, 4. 1. 40–1, vol. 2, p. 198.
39. Cicero 1949a. I. XV. 20, p. 40: 'alienatus animus eorum qui audituri sunt'.
40. Quintilian 2001, 4. 1. 41, vol. 2, p. 198: 'praeter opinionem hominum constitutum'.
41. Cooper 1565, Sig. D, 1ᵛ. See also Veron 1584, Sig. B, 2ᵛ–3ʳ; Thomas 1592, Sig. B, 4ʳ.
42. See Cooper 1565, Sig. 4T, 1ʳ, under *paradoxus* on that which is *admirabilis*.
43. Wilson 1553, Sig. Z, 2ʳ.   44. Cooper 1565, Sig. D, 1ʳ.
45. Quintilian 2001, 4. 1. 41, vol. 2, p. 198: 'turpe, quod alii ... admirabili subiciunt'.

'We alone', he declares, 'among all other writers, have made plainly available a perspicuous theory and a sure means of approaching the different types of opening', thereby establishing which particular style of *prohoemium* should be deployed in which particular circumstances.[46]

The central point to grasp, the *Ad Herennium* goes on, is that there are two distinct kinds of rhetorical opening, the *principium* and the *insinuatio*.[47] 'If your cause is honest it will be appropriate to use a *principium*',[48] but 'if your cause is foul then you must use an insinuative approach'.[49] The difference is that 'the *principium* ought to be of such a kind as to enable us instantly and by straightforward means to make our audience benevolent or attentive or responsive'.[50] By contrast, 'the *insinuatio* ought to be of such a kind as to enable us, by means of dissimulation, to achieve the same result in a more concealed way.'[51] Cicero speaks in almost identical terms, arguing that 'a *principium* is a clear and plain speech aiming to win from your hearers their goodwill, responsiveness and attention, whereas an *insinuatio* is a speech that manages by means of dissimulation and indirection to worm its way subtly into the mind of your audience'.[52]

Among the vernacular rhetoricians, Leonard Cox restates this contrast as a distinction between a 'preface' on the one hand and an 'insinuation' on the other.[53] A preface is appropriate to an honest cause, but when a cause is 'of litle honesty in it selfe', then the orator 'must use in stede of a preface an insinuacion' in which an attempt is made to 'find an excuse'.[54] Thomas Wilson helpfully redescribes Cox's 'preface' as an 'open' beginning, assuring us that 'if the matter bee honest, godly, and suche as of righte ought to bee

---

46. *Rhetorica ad Herennium* 1954, I. IX. 16, p. 28: 'soli nos praetor ceteros . . . plane certem viam et perspicuam rationem exordiorum haberemus.'
47. *Rhetorica ad Herennium* 1954, I. IV. 6, pp. 10–12.
48. *Rhetorica ad Herennium* 1954, I. IV. 6, p. 12: 'Sin honestum genus causa erit, licebit recte . . . uti principio'.
49. *Rhetorica ad Herennium* 1954, I. IV. 6, p. 12: 'Sin turpe causa genus est, insinuatione utendum est'.
50. *Rhetorica ad Herennium* 1954, I. VII. 11, p. 20: 'Principium eiusmodi debet esse ut statim apertis rationibus . . . aut benivolum aut adtentum aut docilem faciamus auditorem'.
51. *Rhetorica ad Herennium* 1954, I. VII. 11, p. 20: 'insinuatio eiusmodi debet esse ut occulte, per dissimulationem, eadem illa omnia conficiamus'.
52. Cicero 1949a, I. XV. 20, p. 42: 'Principium est oratio perspicue et protinus perficiens auditorem benivolum aut docilem aut attentum. Insinuatio est oratio quadam dissimulatione et circumitione obscure subiens auditoris animum'.
53. Cox 1532, Sig. B, 2^r discusses 'the Preamble or exorden' in the case of demonstrative speech, but later notes (Sig. D, 8^v) that the same rules apply in judicial oratory.
54. Cox 1532, Sig. B, 5^{r-v}.

well liked, we maie use an open beginnyng, and will the hearers to rejoyce, & so go through with our parte'. If, on the other hand, our cause is manifestly foul, we shall have to have recourse to an 'insinuacion', which Wilson describes as 'a privey twinyng, or close creping in, to win favor with muche circumstaunce'.[55]

Introducing an honest cause

Shakespeare was chiefly drawn to dramatizing judicial predicaments in which the speaker is constrained to accept that an insinuative beginning is required. But there are several plays in which a character puts forward a judicial accusation in what he or she considers to be a wholly honest and lawful cause, and duly starts with an 'open' beginning in the highest rhetorical style. The first to develop such a *prohoemium* is the ghost in *Hamlet*, who begins by addressing his son not merely as his audience but in the manner of a plaintiff appealing to a judge: 'lend thy serious hearing/ To what I shall unfold'. Hamlet responds in the manner of a judge acknowledging his duty to consider a case: 'Speake, I am bound to heare'.[56] Hamlet is one of several characters in the plays I am considering who are called upon to act as judges in a judicial cause. Few are judges in the strict legal sense of the word, but all of them, including Hamlet, have a judicial role to play in hearing, assessing, and delivering a verdict on the truth of what they are told.

Although the ghost signals his honesty by developing an open *prohoemium*, he reveals himself to be to be a figure of disquieting ambiguity. To Hamlet's invitation 'Speake, I am bound to heare', he immediately responds: 'So art thou to revenge, when thou shalt heare'.[57] Some critics have gone so far as to see in this demand a sufficient indication that, even if the ghost is telling the truth about how he met his death, he must be regarded as an evil spirit, an agent of the devil himself.[58] The exacting of private vengeance was undoubtedly frowned upon by the Church in Shakespeare's time, and St Paul's reference to God's command 'avenge

---

55. Wilson 1553, Sig. O, 3^r.   56. *Hamlet*, TLN 622–3, p. 744 (1. 5. 5–6).
57. *Hamlet*, TLN 624, p. 744 (1. 5. 7).
58. See, most notably, Prosser 1971, pp. 102–3, 111–12. For criticisms see Mercer 1987, pp. 136–7; Greenblatt 2001, pp. 237–44. See also Mercer 1987 and Miola 2000, esp. pp. 120–2 on the ghost in relation to Senecan stereotypes.

not yourselves...for it is written, Vengeance is mine' was frequently cited.[59] There is no reason, however, to suppose that Shakespeare's original audience would have instantly concluded that the ghost must be bent on Hamlet's destruction. The ghost is about to inform Hamlet that his brother not only murdered him but seduced his queen. According to the courtly code of the time, anyone facing such a deep affront to his honour was positively obliged to seek revenge. As the satirist Philibert de Vienne wryly observes in *The Philosopher of the Court* (translated by George North in 1575), the courtly world is one in which 'honor and reputation is the finall conclusion of our vertue'. When our honour is at stake it is not merely 'permitted lawfull and just to kill a man'; it is accepted that such acts of private vengeance are 'not only to be excused, but rather to be commended'.[60] This is even the view taken by Lucrece, whom Shakespeare describes in his poem as a figure of pure piety.[61] After her violation by Tarquin she does not hesitate to call for immediate vengeance, demanding of her husband and his attendant lords that they should 'Be sodainelie revenged on my Foe.'[62] One reason she gives is that 'sparing Justice feeds iniquitie', but more revealingly she adds that ''tis a meritorious faire designe,/ To chase injustice with revengeful armes'.[63]

More troubling is the account that the ghost gives of his present plight. Before embarking on his *prohoemium* he identifies himself to Hamlet:

> I am thy fathers spirit,
> Doomd for a certaine tearme to walke the night,
> And for the day confind to fast in fires,
> Till the foule crimes done in my dayes of nature
> Are burnt and purg'd away:
>
> TLN 626–30, p. 744 (I. 5. 9–13)

As many in Shakespeare's original audience would have known, the fires in which our foul crimes can purportedly be burnt away are those of Purgatory. But most would in addition have been aware that, according to the Thirty-Nine Articles of the Church of England, there is no such place as

---

59. See *Romans* 12: 19 and cf. Prosser 1971, pp. 5–13.
60. Philibert de Vienne 1575, pp. 49–50. On Philibert see Peltonen 2003, pp. 22–3, 45–6. Prosser 1971, pp. 13–16 attempts to dismiss the relevance of the code of honour, but Watson 1960, pp. 127–35 and Peltonen 2003, pp. 44–58 both speak of circumstances in which private revenge was seen as an aristocratic imperative.
61. *Lucrece*, TLN 542, p. 276 (p. 178).   62. *Lucrece*, TLN 1683, p. 288 (p. 230).
63. *Lucrece*, TLN 1687, 1692–3, p. 288 (p. 230).

Purgatory, which had been condemned by the Church as unscriptural and denounced for its association with priestly venality.[64] The ghost is claiming to come from a non-existent place. Should we not feel deeply suspicious as we wait to hear the rest of his case?

These are unsolved and perhaps insoluble puzzles, and nor do they bring us to the end of the ghost's rhetorical difficulties. No less serious is the fact that no one in Denmark appears to believe that he died as the result of a foul and most unnatural murder; everyone has been told a very different story about his death:

> Tis given out, that sleeping in mine Orchard,
> A Serpent stung me, so the whole eare of Denmarke
> Is by a forged processe of my death
> Ranckely abusde:

> TLN 652–5, p. 744 (1. 5. 35–8)

With his foul crime Claudius has succeeded in abusing not merely his brother's ear but the whole ear of Denmark. It is perhaps not surprising, however, that the story of a serpent in a garden should have proved so easy to impose, and Hamlet himself finds it hard to shake off. To begin with he is convinced by the ghost's shockingly different narrative, but he subsequently becomes more doubtful, fearing that 'The spirit that I have seene/ May be the deale [devil]', and confiding to Horatio that it may be 'a damned ghost that we have seene'.[65] We do not finally learn that the ghost has been telling the truth until Claudius in soliloquy confesses to 'a brothers murther' in Act 3.[66] Meanwhile the ghost's hard task is to persuade Hamlet, as judge of his cause, to accept that his extraordinary story of fratricide, although inherently improbable and currently believed by no one, is nevertheless the truth. How can he hope to speak winningly enough to persuade Hamlet to take up his cause and avenge his death?[67]

The first step, the rhetoricians agree, must be to ensure that we capture the undivided attention of our audience. We must do our utmost, in Thomas

---

64. Greenblatt 2001, p. 235.
65. *Hamlet*, TLN 1529–30, p. 753 (2. 2. 551–2) and TLN 1807, p. 756 (3. 2. 72). On Hamlet's concern with probability and evidence see Kerrigan 1996, pp. 77–9; Hutson 2007, pp. 137–44.
66. *Hamlet*, TLN 2152–4, p. 759 (3. 3. 36–8).
67. For an extended analysis of the ghost's speech (focusing on phonetic and syntactical elements) see Ratcliffe 2010, pp. 31–51.

Wilson's words, to make them 'attentive, and glad to heare us'.[68] The fullest account of how to bring off this effect is owed to the author of the *Ad Herennium*. One powerful method, he argues, is to invoke the figure of *exclamatio* and 'cry out to our hearers to listen attentively'.[69] Thomas Wilson and George Puttenham both translate *exclamatio* as 'outcry', explaining that we employ this device whenever we speak with 'extreme passion' and do so 'by way of exclamation'.[70] This is the figure on which the ghost duly relies to attract Hamlet's attention. After identifying himself as his father's spirit— doomed to walk the night but forbidden to disclose his secrets—he suddenly breaks off and cries out to his son:

> list *Hamlet* list, ô list:
> If thou did'st ever thy deare father love.
>
> TLN 639–40, p. 744 (I. 5. 22–3)

Hamlet's anguished cry in response—'O God'—shows that his attention has already been caught.[71]

According to the *Ad Herennium*, the next and principal means of winning attention is 'to promise that we shall speak about things that are important, or novel, or unusual, or about things that concern the public realm, or the worship of the immortal gods, or those who are listening to us'.[72] Cicero's *De inventione* offers a similar list,[73] to which Quintilian adds that 'it serves above all to make a judge attentive if the matter to be adjudicated can be shown to be unknown and important as well as heinous in character'.[74] As usual, the vernacular rhetoricians write in close agreement. Leonard Cox suggests that speakers should promise their audience to 'shew them new thynges or els necessary or profitable'.[75] Thomas Wilson agrees that 'wee shall make the people attentive' if we promise 'to speake of weightie

68. Wilson 1553, Sig. O, 4^r.
69. *Rhetorica ad Herennium* 1954, I. IV. 7, p. 14: 'rogabimus ut adtente audient'. See also IV. XV. 22, p. 282 on *exclamatio*.
70. [Puttenham] 1589, p. 157; cf. Wilson 1553, Sig. 2E, 1^v. On *exclamatio* see also Sherry 1550, Sig. D, 1^v; Fenner 1584, Sig. D, 4^r; Peacham 1593, p. 62. Fraunce 1588a, Sig. E, 5^r to Sig. F, 6^r offers the fullest analysis, with many illustrations from Virgil, Tasso, Sidney, and others.
71. *Hamlet*, TLN 641, p. 744 (I. 5. 24).
72. *Rhetorica ad Herennium* 1954, I. IV. 7, p. 14: 'Adtentos habebimus, si pollicebimur nos de rebus magnis, novis, inusitatis verba facturos, aut de iis quae ad rem publicam pertineant, aut ad eos ipsos qui audient, aut ad deorum immortalium religionem.'
73. Cicero 1949a, I. XVI. 23, p. 46.
74. Quintilian 2001, 4. 1. 33, vol. 2, p. 194: 'plerumque attentum iudicem facit si res agi videtur nova magna atrox'.
75. Cox 1532, Sig. B, 7^r.

matters, of wholsome doctrine' and 'tell them thynges, concernyng either their awne profite, or thadvauncement of their countrey'.[76]

Entering into conversation with his son, the ghost closely follows this advice:

> GHOST If thou did'st ever thy deare father love.
> HAMLET O God.
> GHOST Revenge his foule, and most unnaturall murther.
> HAMLET Murther.
> GHOST Murther most foule, as in the best it is,
> But this most foule, strange and unnaturall.
>
> TLN 640–5, p. 744 (I. 5. 23–8)

To win attention, the rhetoricians lay down, we must speak of new and unknown events. The ghost informs Hamlet about a murder of which he is entirely unaware, reducing him to murmuring incredulity. Next, we must concentrate on matters of importance to the public realm. The ghost reports his own killing as head of state, a matter of obvious public significance. We are also told to speak about things of concern to our specific audience. The ghost's audience consists of his son, who is audibly shocked to learn how his father met his death. Finally, we are told to speak if possible about strange and heinous events. Here the ghost explicitly points out that his murder was not only a foul crime but 'strange and unnaturall'. Just as the rhetoricians promise, Hamlet's attention is fully caught:

> Hast, hast me to know it, that with wings as swift
> As meditation, or the thoughts of love
> May sweepe to my revenge.
>
> TLN 646–8, p. 744 (I. 5. 29–31)

The ghost has successfully attained the first goal that any *prohoemium* must attempt to achieve. With the urgent tone of his response Hamlet even comes close to figuring himself as an avenging angel already prepared to strike.

Having captured the attention of our hearers, our next aim must be to render them responsive to our cause. If, however, we have succeeded in making them attentive, this battle will already be half-won. As the *Ad Herennium* explains, 'a responsive hearer is someone who is ready to listen

---

76. Wilson 1553, Sig. O, 4ʳ.

attentively'.[77] Beyond this consideration, the rhetoricians have one further piece of advice. As Cicero expresses it, 'we shall make our hearers responsive if we provide them with a clear and brief exposition of the essence of our cause, that is, of the nature of the controversy involved.'[78] Leonard Cox repeats that, if we are to encourage 'docilite', we must 'make the mater playne & easy to be perceyved',[79] while Thomas Wilson picks up Cicero's suggestion at greater length. We must begin by summarizing our cause, seeking 'to expounde it plainly, and in brief woordes'. We must recognize that 'by no meanes better, shall the standers by, knowe what we saie, and cary awaie that, whiche thei heare, then if at the firste, wee couche together the whole course of our tale, in as smale roume as we can'.[80]

As the ghost continues, he is at pains to follow this advice:

> now *Hamlet* heare,
> Tis given out, that sleeping in mine Orchard,
> A Serpent stung me, so the whole eare of Denmarke
> Is by a forged processe of my death
> Ranckely abusde: but knowe thou noble Youth,
> The Serpent that did sting thy fathers life
> Now weares his Crowne.

> TLN 651–7, p. 744 (1. 5. 34–40)

Beginning with self-conscious briskness, the ghost summarizes everything that Hamlet needs to know: that the commonly believed story of his death is false, and that he was in fact killed by the man who now occupies his throne. The solemn spondees with which he draws to a close underline the enormity of the usurpation involved. Hamlet immediately replies: 'O my propheticke soule! mine Uncle?'[81] With his exclamation he implies that he may have had some precognition of the truth, and with his question he further indicates his responsiveness, calling on the ghost to explain his accusation at greater length. The second goal of the *prohoemium* has been achieved.

Once our hearers are attentive and responsive, the next and most important task is to induce in them a feeling of goodwill towards our cause. Here

---

77. *Rhetorica ad Herennium* 1954, I. IV. 7, p. 14: 'docilis est qui adtente vult audire'. See also Cicero 1949a, I. XVI. 23, p. 46.
78. Cicero 1949a, I. XVI. 23, p. 46: 'dociles auditores faciemus si aperte et breviter summam causae exponemus, hoc est, in quo consistat controversia'. See also *Rhetorica ad Herennium* 1954, I. IV. 7, p. 12; Quintilian 2001, 4. 1. 34–5, vol. 2, p. 196.
79. Cox 1532, Sig. B, 7ʳ.   80. Wilson 1553, Sig. O, 3ᵛ.
81. *Hamlet*, TLN 658, p. 744 (1. 5. 40–1).

the rhetoricians warn us that our entire bearing is liable to have an influence on the outcome. There can be no *oratio* without *actio*, so that the element of *pronuntiatio*—what Wilson calls 'a framyng of the voyce, countenaunce, and gesture'—must be carefully controlled.[82] We must take great care, Wilson adds, to manage this framing 'after a comely maner' and avoid any indecorousness or excess.[83] The rhetoricians are more concerned, however, with what lines of reasoning we need to follow at this juncture, and their principal suggestion is that we should concentrate on saying something about the different persons involved in the case. As the *Ad Herennium* puts it, this is the moment to talk 'about our own person, about the person of our adversaries, and about the person of our hearers, as well as about the matters at issue themselves'.[84] Cicero and Quintilian speak in almost identical terms,[85] and Thomas Wilson agrees that 'we shall get the good willes of our hearers' if we 'speake of our selves, or els of our adversaries, or els of the people, and company present' in addition to speaking about 'the matter it self'.[86]

Cicero and the author of the *Ad Herennium* go on to describe in detail the attributes, and especially the vices and virtues, that we shall need to highlight if we are to induce in our hearers a feeling of hostility towards our adversaries and of benevolence towards our own side of the case. The accounts they furnish are very similar, but it will be most illuminating to focus on the *Ad Herennium*, partly because its discussion is the most extended, but also because it appears to have been the text with which Shakespeare was most closely acquainted. Discussing our adversaries, the *Ad Herennium* first tells us that we can hope to acquire goodwill if we speak of them 'in such a way that we succeed in bringing them into *odium*, *invidia* and *contemptio*, hatred, unpopularity and contempt'.[87] We can bring them into hatred 'if we are able to show that they have acted'—and here a flurry of adverbs follows—'*spurce* and *superbe* and *perfidiose* and *crudeliter* and *confidenter* and *malitiose* and *flagitiose*'.[88] Next, we can make them unpopular 'if we can

82. Wilson 1553, Sig. A, 4^r.
83. Wilson 1553, Sig. A, 4^r. Cf. [Puttenham] 1589, p. 221.
84. *Rhetorica ad Herennium* 1954, I. IV. 8, p. 14: 'ab nostra, ab adversariorum nostrorum, ab auditorum persona, et ab rebus ipsis'.
85. Cicero 1949a, I. XVI. 22, p. 44; Quintilian 2001, 4. 1. 6–32, vol. 2, pp. 182–94.
86. Wilson 1553, Sig. O, 4^{r-v}.
87. *Rhetorica ad Herennium* 1954, I. V. 8, p. 14: 'si eos in odium, in invidiam, in contemptionem adducemus.' For echoes among Tudor rhetoricians see Peltonen 2013, pp. 95–6.
88. *Rhetorica ad Herennium* 1954, I. V. 8, pp. 14–16: 'si quid eorum spurce, superbe, perfidiose, crudeliter, confidenter, malitiose, flagitiose factum proferemus.'

show that among their characteristics are *vis, potentia, factio* and *incontinentia*'.[89] Finally, we can bring them into contempt if we can show that among their bad qualities are such vices as *inertia, ignavia, desidia,* and *luxuria.*[90]

When the ghost responds to Hamlet's astonished question—'mine Uncle?'—he begins to speak of Claudius as his principal adversary. However, he is far from denouncing him in the gibbering manner common among ghosts on the Elizabethan stage.[91] He knows to comport himself with classical decorum and steadiness, although he makes it clear that his specific aim is indeed to bring Claudius into hatred, unpopularity, and contempt:

> I that incestuous, that adulterate beast,
> With witchcraft of his witt, with trayterous gifts,
> O wicked wit, and giftes that have the power
> So to seduce; wonne to his shamefull lust
> The will of my most seeming vertuous Queene;
> O *Hamlet*, what a falling off was there
>
> TLN 659–64, p. 744 (I. 5. 42–7)

To bring our adversaries into hatred, the *Ad Herennium* had proposed, we must first describe them as *spurcus,* a word usually translated in the Latin–English dictionaries of the time as unclean and filthy,[92] but with connotations of impurity, adulteration, and defilement.[93] The ghost duly begins by reviling Claudius as 'that incestuous, that adulterate beast'. We must also describe our adversaries as *perfidiosus,* a word generally rendered as treacherous or traitorous.[94] The ghost next denounces Claudius's 'trayterous gifts', which he attributes to his devilish power of witchcraft. Finally, we are told to protest that the conduct of our adversaries has been *malitiosus* and *flagitiosus*. Cooper, Veron, and Thomas all translate *malitiosus* as 'deceitful'

---

89. *Rhetorica ad Herennium* 1954, I. V. 8, p. 16: 'In invidiam trahemus si vim, si potentiam, si factionem . . . incontinentiam . . . adversariorum proferemus.'
90. *Rhetorica ad Herennium* 1954, I. V. 8, p. 16: 'In contemptionem adducemus si inertiam, ignaviam, desidiam, luxuriam adversariorum proferemus.'
91. On Shakespeare's innovations in his characterization of the ghost see Mercer 1987. See also Kerrigan 1996, pp. 181–9; Pincombe 2001, pp. 182–6; Pearlman 2002, pp. 76–8.
92. Cooper 1565, Sig. 6A, 2ᵛ: 'Spurcus . . . Uncleane: filthy: unpure'. See also Veron 1584, Sig. 2P, 8ᵛ; Thomas 1592, Sig. 2Y, 6ʳ.
93. See entries on the underlying verb *spurcare*. Cooper 1565, Sig. 6A, 2ᵛ has 'to defile, or make uncleane'. Thomas 1592, Sig. 2Y, 6ʳ has 'to defile, corrupt or make uncleane'.
94. On *perfidiosus* see Cooper 1565, Sig. 4Y, 2ᵛ: 'Ful of treacherie . . . trayterous, and false'. Cf. Veron 1584, Sig. 2G, 8ʳ: 'traiterous and false'; Thomas 1592, Sig. 2M, 6ᵛ: 'treacherous, traiterous'.

and 'wily',[95] and *flagitiosus* as 'sinful' and 'abominable'.[96] Thomas adds that to act *flagitiose* is to behave wickedly,[97] while Veron speaks of being lustful and 'full of whoredom'.[98] The ghost duly condemns Claudius not merely for his 'wicked wit' and the 'witchcraft of his witt' but also for his 'shamefull lust' and his deceitfully seductive gifts.

The *Ad Herennium* next suggests that we should seek to make our adversaries unpopular. This we can hope to do by pointing to such qualities as their *vis* or violence, their *potentia* or excessive power, and their *incontinentia*, which Cooper and Thomas both render as 'lacke of stay and moderation in lustes and affections'.[99] The ghost has nothing to say about Claudius's physical powers, because it is one of his aspirations to reveal him as a man of wretched feebleness. But he strongly emphasizes his *incontinentia*, speaking with wounded pride of his 'giftes that have the power/ So to seduce'.

We must finally seek to bring our adversaries into contempt, which requires us to accentuate their *inertia* and *ignavia*. To speak of *inertia*, according to Cooper, is to refer to slackness and idleness,[100] while to accuse someone of being *ignavus* is to say that he is 'unmanly' as well as 'cowardous and fainte harted'.[101] The ghost duly dismisses Claudius as nothing more than 'a wretch whose naturall gifts were poore'.[102] We are also told to refer to our enemies' *desidia*, to the fact that (in Cooper's translation) their manners are 'fallyng in decay',[103] and also to their *luxuria*, which is treated as a vice of some complexity. Cooper defines it as 'living in too much pleasure',[104] and Thomas speaks of 'excesse in carnall pleasure',[105] but

95. Cooper 1565, Sig. 4D, 4ʳ; Veron 1584, Sig. B, 6ᵛ; Thomas 1592, Sig. 2F, 3ʳ.
96. Cooper 1565, Sig. 3E, 2ʳ; Veron 1584, Sig. R, 6ᵛ; Thomas 1592, Sig. V, 5ᵛ.
97. Thomas 1592, Sig. V, 5ᵛ.
98. Veron 1584, Sig. R, 6ᵛ; Thomas 1592, Sig. V, 5ᵛ.
99. Cooper 1565, Sig. 3P, 5ᵛ; Thomas 1592, Sig. 2A, 6ʳ.
100. Cooper 1565, Sig. 3Q, 6ʳ; Veron 1584, Sig. X, 3ʳ.
101. Cooper 1565, Sig. 3M, 5ʳ; Veron 1584, Sig. V, 1ᵛ; Thomas 1592, Sig. Z, 5ʳ.
102. *Hamlet*, TLN 668, p. 744 (1. 5. 51).
103. The derivation of *desidia* is complicated, or perhaps merely confused. Cooper finds one root in *desideo* (infinitive *desidere*) 'to sitte still', thereby taking one meaning of *desidia* to be 'idlenes: slouthfulnes'. See Cooper 1565, Sig. 2M, 1ʳ. But he also finds a root in *desido* (infinitive again *desidere*) 'to sinke downe' or 'fall lower', thereby taking *desidia* to refer to a process of decline and translating the participle *desidens* as 'maners fallyng in decay'. See Cooper 1565, Sig. 2M, 1ʳ. The ghost's references to 'falling off' and 'decline' suggest that Shakespeare had the second meaning in mind.
104. Cooper 1565, Sig. 4C, 5ᵛ under *luxuriosus*.
105. Thomas 1592, Sig. 2E, 8ᵛ.

Cooper and Veron connect it more specifically with rankness,[106] wanton-ness,[107] and 'uncleanly lust'.[108]

The ghost ends by referring to all these failings, while making it clear that he thinks of himself as confronting not one but two adversaries who are guilty of them. When he exclaims 'O *Hamlet*, what a falling off was there', he is referring to the queen's contemptible *desidia*, or moral decline. And when he draws his *prohoemium* to a close with some disgusted references to lewdness and uncleanly lust, he links Gertrard with Claudius as equally subject to these contemptible vices:

> But vertue as it never will be mooved,
> Though lewdnesse court it in a shape of heaven
> So lust though to a radiant Angle linckt,
> Will sate it selfe in a celestiall bed
> And pray on garbage.

TLN 670–4, p. 744 (1. 5. 53–7)

Here the ghost reverts to his initial complaint that the whole ear of Denmark has been rankly abused. Behind his murder, he now explains, we find the kind of rankness that prefers vice to virtue, and Gertrard is scarcely less to blame than Claudius for the lewdness involved.

We are left in little doubt that the ghost is speaking of two distinct kinds of lewdness. Not only does he condemn Claudius as incestuous for having married his brother's wife; he also denounces him for having 'wonne to his shamefull lust/ The will of my most seeming vertuous Queene'.[109] The ghost cannot simply mean that Claudius wooed and won Gertrard after his death, for this is something that Hamlet already knows. He is telling Hamlet that, before his murder, the 'adulterate' Claudius had already seduced the queen.[110] Later Gertrard appears to confess as much when Hamlet confronts her with his passionate comparison between her present and former hus-band. The crime of adultery was commonly described in Shakespeare's England as the sin that leaves a woman's soul 'spotted with infamie',[111]

---

106. Cooper 1565, Sig. 4C, 5ᵛ and Veron 1584, Sig. 2B, 4ʳ⁻ᵛ both equate behaving *luxuriose* with acting 'riotously' and 'rankelie'.

107. Cooper 1565, Sig. 4C, 5ᵛ defines *luxuriare* as 'to be wanton'.

108. Cooper 1565, Sig. 2G, 5ᵛ under *cum*.   109. *Hamlet*, TLN 662–3, p. 744 (1. 5. 45–6).

110. Bradley 2007 [1904], p.122 already insists that these lines refer not merely to Gertrard's hasty remarriage but to her earlier adultery. On Gertrard's sexuality see de Grazia 2007, pp. 98–104.

111. For this phrase see, for example, Guazzo 1581, Bk 3, fo. 15ᵛ; Greene 1584, Sig. B, 1ᵛ.

and Gertrard speaks in just such terms in her shattered response to Hamlet's tirade:

> Thou turnst mine eyes into my very soule,
> And there I see such blacke and greined spots
> As will not leave their tin'ct.[112]

The queen may appear virtuous, as the ghost says, but there are hidden thorns 'that in her bosome lodge/ To prick and sting her', and among these is her faithlessness.[113]

The rhetoricians next argue that, in addition to condemning our adversaries, we must be sure to speak of our own person in such a way as to win goodwill. According to the *Ad Herennium*, there are two contrasting features of our situation of which our judges need to be particularly mindful: 'We must seek to praise, although without arrogance, the manner in which we have discharged our *officium* or duty, and we must reveal what we have done for the benefit of the public realm, or for our parents and friends, or for those who are listening to us.'[114] We must also draw attention to what the *Ad Herennium* in another flurry of evaluative terms describes as 'our *incommoda, inopia, solitudo* and *calamitas*'.[115] After making these claims, 'we must then plead for help to be given to us, and at the same time indicate that we have no wish to place our hope in anyone else'.[116]

The ghost begins to follow this advice even before making his outcry to Hamlet. He refers to his present state as *incommodus*, that is, as 'hurtful, troublous and noisome',[117] assuring Hamlet that it would 'harrow up thy soule, freeze thy young blood' if he were to speak of it.[118] He mentions his *solitudo* as someone 'Doomd for a certaine tearme to walke the night'[119] and he emphasizes the *calamitas*, the 'destruction, miserie and adversity'[120] of

---

112. *Hamlet*, TLN 2293–5, p. 761 (3. 4. 89–91). Zurcher 2010, p. 251 objects that the black spots could refer to the pupils of Gertrard's eyes, but without noting the significance of spots in the discourse about adultery.
113. *Hamlet*, TLN 704–5, p. 744 (1. 5. 87–8).
114. *Rhetorica ad Herennium* 1954, I. V. 8, p. 14: 'nostrum officium sine adrogantia laudabimus, atque in rem publicam quales fuerimus, aut in parentes, aut in amicos, aut in eos qui audiunt aperiemus'.
115. *Rhetorica ad Herennium* 1954, I. V. 8, p. 14: 'nostra incommode proferemus, inopiam, solitudinem, calamitatem'.
116. *Rhetorica ad Herennium* 1954, I. V. 8, p. 14: 'orabimus ut nobis sint auxilio, et simul ostendemus nos in aliis noluisse spem habere'.
117. Cooper 1565, Sig. 3P, 5ʳ; Veron 1584, Sig. V, 8ʳ; Thomas 1592, Sig. 2A, 5ᵛ.
118. *Hamlet*, TLN 633, p. 744 (1. 5. 16).   119. *Hamlet*, TLN 627, p. 744 (1. 5. 10).
120. Cooper 1565, Sig. P, 5ᵛ; Thomas 1592, Sig. H, 1ᵛ–2ʳ.

living amid 'sulphrus and tormenting flames' and being 'confind to fast in fires'.[121] Still following the *Ad Herennium*, he then pleads directly for Hamlet's help:

> If thou did'st ever thy deare father love. . . .
> Revenge his foule, and most unnaturall murther.
>
> TLN 640, 642, p. 744 (1. 5. 23, 25)

He might even be said to be indicating, as the *Ad Herennium* had additionally recommended, that he has no wish to place his hopes in anyone else.

The ghost is no less eager to follow the *Ad Herennium*'s contrasting advice and praise himself for discharging his duty and acting for the benefit of the public realm. He begins by drawing attention to his acceptance of his *officium* or duty of fidelity towards the queen in contrast to her adultery:

> O *Hamlet*, what a falling off was there
> From me whose love was of that dignitie
> That it went hand in hand even with the vowe
> I made to her in marriage,
>
> TLN 664–7, p. 744 (1. 5. 47–50)

When he swore his marriage vows, hand in hand with the queen, love and dignity were similarly joined together. Following this affirmation, he ends by hinting at his superior ability to serve the public realm by comparison with the new king, whose talents he dismisses as 'poore,/ To those of mine'.[122]

The author of the *Ad Herennium* rounds off by explaining 'how it is possible to acquire goodwill from discussing the person of your hearers'.[123] We are told that this can be done in two specific ways. One is to indicate— and here there is one final list of adverbs—that we believe them 'to have acted *fortiter, sapienter, mansuete* and *magnifice* in their judgements in the past'.[124] To adopt the translations proposed in the Latin–English dictionaries of the time, we need to claim that they have acted manfully,[125] wisely,[126] gently,[127] and nobly.[128] The other thing we must do is to 'make clear to our

121. *Hamlet*, TLN 620, 628, p. 744 (1. 5. 3, 11).
122. *Hamlet*, TLN 668–9, p. 744 (1. 5. 51–2).
123. *Rhetorica ad Herennium* 1954, I. V. 8, p. 16: 'Ab auditorum persona benivolentia colligitur'.
124. *Rhetorica ad Herennium* 1954, I. V. 8, p. 16: 'res eorum fortiter, sapienter, mansuete, magnifice iudicatas proferemus'.
125. Cooper 1565, Sig. 3F, 3^r; Thomas 1592, Sig. V, 8^v.
126. Cooper 1565, Sig. 5S, 6^v; Veron 1584, Sig. 2O, 1^r; Thomas 1592, Sig. 2V, 3^r.
127. Cooper 1565, Sig. 4D, 6^r; Veron 1584, Sig. B, 7^v; Thomas 1592, Sig. 2F, 4^v.
128. Cooper 1565, Sig. 4D, 2^r; Thomas 1592, Sig. 2F, 2^r.

hearers the extent of the *existimatio* they enjoy'.[129] Here the lexicographers agree that this important term of commendation refers to the possession of credit and esteem,[130] good reputation, and even renown.[131]

It is Hamlet who constitutes the ghost's audience and judge. So one would expect the ghost to try to enlist Hamlet's goodwill by assuring him that he esteems his judgement and admires the manner in which he has previously conducted himself. Those members of Shakespeare's audience who were well-versed in the art of rhetoric—and in the two universities, where *Hamlet* received some of its earliest performances, they would have been in a majority[132]—would have been waiting for the ghost to conclude his *prohoemium* in precisely these terms. But here he produces a stunning silence. He never tells Hamlet that he holds him in esteem, nor does he ever commend him for acting manfully or wisely or gently or nobly in the past. He limits himself to making some withering remarks about what he would think of Hamlet if he were to fail to exact revenge:

> And duller shouldst thou be then the fat weede
> That rots it selfe in ease on *Lethe* wharffe,
> Would'st thou not sturre in this;
>
> TLN 649–51, p. 744 (I. 5. 32–4)

To anyone trained in the *ars rhetorica,* the implications of what the ghost is saying—and especially what he is failing to say—would have been inescapable. The ghost is making it clear to Hamlet, and Shakespeare is making it clear to us, that there may be serious grounds for doubting whether Hamlet can be expected to act manfully or wisely or gently or nobly, even in matters of the highest public as well as personal significance.

★ ★ ★ ★ ★

Shakespeare later introduces a further judicial cause into the action of *Hamlet,* and in doing so contrives one of the many symmetries around which the plot is organized.[133] When the ghost levels his charge against Claudius at the end of Act 1, he asks for the truth about his death to be revealed, and hence for justice to be posthumously done to him. When

---

129. *Rhetorica ad Herennium* 1954, I. V. 8, p. 16: 'quae de iis existimatio ... aperiemus'.
130. Cooper 1565, Sig. 2Y, 5ᵛ.   131. Veron 1584, Sig. Q, 7ᵛ.
132. See Shakespeare 1603, title page, noting that the play 'hath beene diverse times acted ... in the two universities of Cambridge and Oxford'.
133. Brown 1979, p. 48 speaks of the extreme structural tidiness of *Hamlet*. Bradshaw 1993, pp. 76–7 and 145–7 speaks of dramatic 'rhyming' in his examination of such symmetries.

Hamlet himself is at the point of death at the end of Act 5, he makes a closely parallel request to Horatio:

> O god *Horatio*, what a wounded name
> Things standing thus unknowne, shall live behind me?
> If thou did'st ever hold me in thy hart,
> Absent thee from felicity a while,
> And in this harsh world drawe thy breath in paine
> To tell my story:

> TLN 3564–9, p. 774 (5. 2. 323–8)

Hamlet has just killed Claudius with a poisoned rapier—just as Claudius had earlier poisoned Hamlet's father.[134] But in doing so he has heard the assembled courtiers greet his action with a cry of 'Treason, treason'.[135] His dying concern is that his reputation will be wounded unless Horatio is willing to 'report me and my cause a right/ To the unsatisfied'.[136] Critics rightly describe Horatio as being invested with 'narrative responsibility' at this juncture,[137] but this falls short of explaining what Hamlet is asking of him. He is calling on Horatio not merely to tell his story, but to take up his cause and mount a judicial accusation against Claudius, just as the ghost at the beginning of the play had called upon him to do the same.

The parallels extend yet further, for Horatio is left in a comparable rhetorical dilemma.[138] Just as Hamlet only has the ghost's word that he was killed by his brother, so Horatio only knows that Hamlet believes that his uncle killed his father. Horatio already knows that Claudius has no scruples about asking for murder to be committed, for Hamlet has shown him the letter in which Claudius had called for Hamlet to be summarily assassinated on his arrival in England. Horatio has also learned that, according to Laertes, Claudius is capable of murder himself, for he has just heard Laertes accuse the king of envenoming the rapier to make certain of Hamlet's death. But Horatio does not know with the full assurance that we, the theatre audience, by this stage know that Claudius definitely killed his brother, and we may reflect that Horatio has a complex rhetorical task on his hands if he is to persuade Fortinbrasse to believe a story that Hamlet originally accepted on the mere testimony of a ghost.

---

134. A symmetry noted in Ratcliffe 2010, pp. 35–6.
135. *Hamlet*, TLN 3543, p. 774 (5. 2. 302).
136. *Hamlet*, TLN 3559–60, p. 774 (5. 2. 318–19).
137. See, for example, Lucking 1997, pp. 135, 136.
138. For discussions about this passage I am particularly indebted to John Kerrigan.

We may also reflect, however, that the dying Hamlet has placed the prosecution of his cause in good hands.[139] As we saw in Chapter 1, Cicero had laid it down at the beginning of his *De inventione* that there are two cardinal qualities that enable us to speak persuasively, and even to convince our hearers of truths they may be unwilling to believe.[140] They are *ratio* or reason in combination with *oratio* or powerful speech. Horatio's name incorporates both *ratio* and *oratio*, signalling his possession of both these attributes and perhaps explaining why Hamlet is so anxious that it should be Horatio who lives to tell his tale to the unsatisfied.

Responding to Hamlet's plea, Horatio shows that he is fully possessed of the required rhetorical powers. When Fortinbrasse and the English ambassadors arrive, he immediately takes control, boldly issuing them with instructions and announcing that he will mount a speech in the *genus iudiciale* at once:

> But since so jump upon this bloody question
> You from the *Pollack* warres, and you from *England*
> Are heere arriv'd, give order that these bodies
> High on a stage be placed to the view,
> And let me speake, to th'yet unknowing world
> How these things came about;

> TLN 3597–602, p. 775 (5. 2. 354–9)

There is a bloody question to be considered—a *quaestio* for adjudication, as the rhetoricians would say—and Horatio instantly turns to address it.

The speech that ensues is sometimes treated as a mere summary of the action,[141] but this is to overlook the precision of Horatio's rhetorical performance. Horatio is a scholar, and hence a student of rhetoric, and what he offers is an open *prohoemium*, serving at once to introduce Hamlet's cause and establish that he regards it as a wholly honest one:

> And let me speake, to th'yet unknowing world
> How these things came about; so shall you heare
> Of carnall, bloody and unnaturall acts,
> Of accidentall judgements, casuall slaughters,
> Of deaths put on by cunning, and forc'd cause
> And in this upshot, purposes mistooke,

139. Special thanks to Laura Adrian for alerting me to this point.
140. Cicero 1949a, I. II. 2, p. 6.
141. See, for example, Cox 1973, p. 149; Wilson 1995, p. 57.

> Falne on th'inventers heads: all this can I
> Truly deliver.
>
> TLN 3601–8, p. 775 (5. 2. 358–65)

Critics have sometimes expressed surprise and even indignation at this tendentious outline of what has taken place.[142] But Horatio is not offering an outline of what has taken place; he is introducing a conjectural issue in a judicial cause, and he knows exactly how to do it. He is aware that he must start by calling for attention, and begins by asking everyone present to let him speak and explain. He also knows that, in order to hold their attention, he must then promise to tell them things not merely unknown but unnatural and strange. He duly stresses that the present slaughter is the fruit of unnatural acts as yet unknown to the world, and makes emphatic use of *anaphora*, the figure of repetition, to underscore the number of tragic events that have taken place.[143] Next, he knows that, to make his audience responsive, he must provide a summary of Hamlet's side of the case. He accordingly reveals that in the course of his *narratio* he will not only speak ('so shall you heare') of accidents and misjudgements, but will vindicate Hamlet's cause by revealing that it is a story of mistaken purposes. Finally, he knows that, if he is to win his audience's goodwill, he must refer to the different persons involved in the case. When alluding to Hamlet's adversaries he must try to make them hated by referring to their impurity, treachery, cunning, and deceit. He duly speaks of carnal and bloody acts, and of deaths put on by cunning and forced cause. When alluding to his own person he must praise, without boasting, his capacity to perform his duty, and he ends by offering the crucial assurance that he is someone who can be trusted to deliver the truth.

Horatio's *prohoemium* fully succeeds in its essential task of winning responsiveness and goodwill, and Fortinbrasse invites him to proceed directly to his *narratio*: 'Let us hast to heare it,/ And call the noblest to the audience'.[144] Still speaking with the same assurance, Horatio proposes that the dead bodies should first be carried away, and Fortinbrasse gives the order that this should be done. We begin to return from a world of violence to

---

142. See, for example, Cox 1973, p. 149; Wilson 1995, p. 57.
143. On *anaphora* see Sherry 1550, Sig. C, 8ʳ; Wilson 1553, Sig. 2D, 3ᵛ; [Puttenham] 1589, p. 165; Day 1592, pp. 84–5; Peacham 1593, pp. 41–2.
144. *Hamlet*, TLN 3608–9, p. 775 (5. 2. 365–6).

one of negotiation and diplomacy.[145] The play draws to an end with Fortinbrasse's speech, but we are left with the partly redemptive promise that Horatio will shortly be able to present a *narratio* of Claudius's villainy, and to follow it with a *confirmatio* of his own version of events. Whether Horatio knows enough to give a recognizable account of Hamlet's tragedy may be doubted,[146] but at least his story will be brought to a fitting rhetorical close.

★ ★ ★ ★ ★

If we turn to the period when Shakespeare was most preoccupied with the *genus iudiciale*, we come upon three further characters who have an accusation to put forward in what they regard as a wholly honest and lawful cause, and who begin by developing an open *prohoemium* in the highest rhetorical style. The first is Isabella in *Measure for Measure*. When we initially encounter her, Isabella is about to enter a convent, and her name tells us that she is consecrated to God. But she is suddenly drawn into worldly entanglements as a result of the behaviour of her brother Claudio, whose betrothed has become pregnant in advance of their intended marriage. The laws against such acts of fornication have long been in disuse, but the duke, in announcing his departure from Vienna for a while, has left its government in the hands of Angelo, who has revived a decree requiring execution for such crimes and condemned Claudio to death. When Isabella pleads with Angelo for her brother's life, he informs her that he will pardon Claudio if she will agree, as he infamously puts it, to yield her body to his will.[147]

The duke has not in fact left the city, but has secretly adopted the *persona* of Friar Lodowick, and in this guise has learned from Isabella about Angelo's hidden vice. The duke's response is to contrive a plot that strangely echoes his decision to appoint Angelo as his deputy.[148] He proposes a bed trick that will cause Angelo to believe that he has succeeded in spending the night with Isabella. The means are conveniently to hand: Angelo was once betrothed to Mariana, but abandoned her when she lost her dowry, although she remains in love with him. The trick to be played on Angelo is that Isabella will appear to yield to his demands, but Mariana will take her

---

145. As noted in Hampton 2009, pp. 144–9.   146. As emphasized in Kerrigan 1996, p. 189.
147. *Measure for Measure*, TLN 1083, p. 906 (2. 4. 165). See Rackley 2008 for a discussion of hostile responses to Isabella's refusal to save her brother's life at the expense of her chastity.
148. The play's concern with substitution and deputation has been much discussed. See, for example, Goldberg 1983, pp. 234–5, 237–8; Leggatt 1988; Maus 1995, pp. 172–3.

place in his bed, thereby forcing him to keep his broken promise while revealing his corruption and falsehood.[149] Given that Isabella is a postulant nun, it is perhaps surprising that she responds with such ardent enthusiasm to the duke's scheme. The only condition she imposes is that she will not be party to a foul cause; she will only agree to the plan if it 'appeares not fowle in the truth of my spirit'.[150] But as soon as the duke reveals the details of his plot she immediately declares that 'The image of it gives me content already, and I trust it will grow to a most prosperous perfection.'[151]

Isabella has a grave charge of corruption to level against Angelo, and when the duke reassumes his powers at the beginning of Act 5 she prepares to confront him and put her case. She finds herself, however, in a serious rhetorical dilemma closely resembling that of the ghost in Act 1 of *Hamlet*. Although she plans to put forward what she describes as a true complaint, she cannot fail to admit that her accusation is liable to strike everyone as too improbable to be believed. While Angelo may be other than he seems (as the duke has cause to know)[152] he has managed to put on such a persuasive 'show' of austerity and judiciousness that any attempt to denounce him for injustice or impropriety will be almost certain to seem the merest calumny.

Here Shakespeare alludes to an aspect of the *ars rhetorica* that, as we saw in Chapter 1, the Ramists had particularly emphasized: the power of a confident rhetorical 'show', especially in the form of an imposing self-presentation, to mask and disguise the truth. We find an example very close to Shakespeare's interests in the *Triall of true Friendship* (1596), which mocks those who are so readily deceived by such shows that they 'wil choose a gilden boxe full of bones, before a leaden one ful of precious gems, for men judge onely by the outward appearance'.[153] That such 'seemings' can always be deceptive is what Bassanio, in Act 3 of *The Merchant of Venice*, similarly observes when he tries to choose between the three caskets laid before him. 'So may the outward showes be least themselves', he reflects, and he offers two examples:

---

149. See Briggs 1994, pp. 305–6 on the use of the trick to consummate a marriage. Desens 1994, pp. 80–1 comments that *Measure for Measure* may be the first play in which a bed trick is used to this effect.

150. *Measure for Measure*, TLN 1315–16, p. 909 (3. 1. 198).

151. *Measure for Measure*, TLN 1368–9, p. 909 (3. 1. 243–4).

152. See *Measure for Measure*, TLN 317, p. 898 (1. 3. 55), where he perceptively wonders 'what our Seemers be'. He also knows about Angelo's earlier breach of promise to Mariana (which ought perhaps to have led him to ask himself how far Angelo can be trusted).

153. *Triall of true Friendship* (1596), Sig. C, 2^r.

> In Law, what plea so tainted and corrupt,
> But being season'd with a gracious voyce,
> Obscures the show of evill. In religion
> What damned error but some sober brow
> Will blesse it, and approve it with a text,
> Hiding the grosnes with faire ornament:
>
> TLN 1353, 1355–60, p. 495 (3. 2. 73, 75–80)

Bassanio is acknowledging the potentially overwhelming power of *pronuntiatio*: a sober brow and a gracious delivery can make an impression so forceful as to cover up grossness and even make damnable errors sound like the truth.

Angelo ruthlessly relies on the deceiving power of such 'shows' in his confrontation with Isabella. As soon as he makes his infamous proposal, Isabella warns him that she will proclaim his false 'seeming' to the world:

> Seeming, seeming.
> I will proclaime thee *Angelo*, looke for't.
> Signe me a present pardon for my brother,
> Or with an out-stretcht throate Ile tell the world aloud
> What man thou art.
>
> TLN 1069–73, p. 906 (2. 4. 151–5)

But Angelo remains unmoved. He has no doubt that, if he responds by speaking out against Isabella, his high standing and reputation will be enough to cause his lies to be accepted by everyone:

> Who will beleeve thee *Isabell*?
> My unsoild name, th'austeerenesse of my life,
> My vouch against you, and my place i'th State,
> Will so your accusation over-weigh,
> That you shall stifle in your owne report, . . .
> Say what you can; my false, ore-weighs your true.
>
> TLN 1073–7, 1089, p. 906 (2. 4. 155–9, 171)

Isabella instantly recognizes that what Angelo says is all too probable: 'Did I tell this,/ Who would beleeve me?'[154] When spoken by the powerful, falsehoods can always outweigh and stifle the truth.

When Isabella appears before the duke at the beginning of Act 5 she is made acutely conscious of these difficulties.[155] No one seems to have any

---

154. *Measure for Measure*, TLN 1090–1, p. 906 (2. 4. 172–3).
155. For an outline of the structure of the ensuing scene see Brennan 1986, pp. 70–101.

doubts about the angelic character of Angelo, whom the duke on re-
entering the city fulsomely acknowledges with 'Many and harty thankings'
for 'Such goodnesse of your Justice'.[156] Yet more dauntingly, as soon as
Isabella begins to speak, Angelo moves instantly to silence her:

> My Lord, her wits I feare me are not firme:
> She hath bin a suitor to me, for her Brother
> Cut off by course of Justice....
> And she will speake most bitterly, and strange.
>
> TLN 2198–201, p. 917 (5. 1. 33–6)

Isabella reacts with outraged sarcasm—'By course of Justice!'[157] But while
she insists that she will speak 'most truely', she cannot fail to admit that what
she is about to allege will indeed sound 'Most strange'.[158]

Here we come upon a strong contrast with Shakespeare's principal
source, George Whetstone's verse drama *Promos and Cassandra* of 1578.[159]
Whetstone had already told the story of a corrupt judge, Promos, who
demands of a virtuous young woman, Cassandra, that she yield to his desires
as the price of saving her brother from execution. In Whetstone's version
Cassandra submits to Promos, and in Part 2 of the play denounces him in a
lengthy speech before the king in which she admits the humiliating truth.
But Whetstone shows no awareness of the rhetorical predicament in which
Cassandra finds herself, that of someone attempting to persuade a judge to
accept an inherently improbable story that he has every reason to disbelieve.
The rhetoricians have many specific words of advice to offer about how to
handle this dangerous type of situation, but Whetstone displays no knowledge of them. He simply supplies Cassandra with a brief *prohoemium* in
which she asks to be heard:

> Renowned King, I pardon crave, for this my bould attempt,
> In preasing thus so neare your grace, my sorrow to present:
> And least my foe, false *Promos* heare, doe interrupt my tale,
> Graunt gratious King, that uncontrould, I may report my bale.[160]

The king responds by warmly accepting the prospect of hearing her case:

---

156. *Measure for Measure*, TLN 2169, 2171, p. 917 (5. 1. 4, 6).
157. *Measure for Measure*, TLN 2200, p. 917 (5. 1. 35—from which I adopt the exclamation mark).
158. *Measure for Measure*, TLN 2202, p. 917 (5. 1. 37).
159. On Shakespeare's use of this source see Salingar 1974, pp. 71–2, 303–5.
160. Whetstone 1578, Sig. K, 1[v].

How now *Promos*? how lyke you, of this song?
Say on fayre dame, I long to heare thy wrong.[161]

With this encouragement Cassandra launches into her *narratio*, in which she explains how she was forced, as she contends, into ransoming her virginity.

By contrast, Isabella displays an intimate acquaintance with the rules for developing the kind of open *prohoemium* appropriate to her cause. Her expertise may seem surprising, but we have already been alerted by Claudio to the fact that, in spite of her youth and seeming unworldliness, she is a formidable rhetorician who 'hath prosperous Art/ When she will play with reason, and discourse,/ And well she can perswade'.[162] She is credited, no less than Horatio, with the two crucial attributes needed for speaking persuasively: *ratio* or reason in combination with *oratio*, artful discourse and speech.[163] As she prepares to mount her case, we wait to see how these talents will be displayed.

The classical rhetoricians had issued a preliminary warning about the moment when we first begin to speak. As the *Ad Herennium* emphasizes, this is when our entire bearing is most likely to have an impact on how our *prohoemium* is received. We must be sure to preserve decorum and above all keep a firm control over our voice. 'We need to deliver the opening of our speech in as calm and quiet a tone as possible',[164] for 'what could be more unpleasant than speaking stridently when starting to state our case?'[165] Thomas Wilson agrees that anyone who hopes 'to gette praise in tellying their minde in open audience must at the first beginnyng speake somwhat softely'.[166] For anyone aware of this advice, Shakespeare contrives a special moment of dramatic tension as Isabella steps forward. Her mentor, Friar Peter, has arranged for her to take up a position from which she can hope to attract the duke's attention:

Come I have found you out a stand most fit,
Where you may have such vantage on the *Duke*
He shall not passe you:

TLN 2160–2, p. 917 (4. 6. 10–12)

---

161. Whetstone 1578, Sig. K, 1ᵛ.
162. *Measure for Measure*, TLN 253–5, p. 897 (1. 2. 165–7). On Isabella as rhetorician see Crider 2009, pp. 127–44.
163. Cicero 1949a, I. II. 2, p. 6.
164. *Rhetorica ad Herennium* 1954, III. XII. 21, p. 192: 'maxime sedata et depressa voce principia dicemus'.
165. *Rhetorica ad Herennium* 1954, III. XII. 22, p. 194: 'Quid insuavius quam clamor in exordio causae?' See also Wilson 1553, Sig. 2G, 1ʳ.
166. Wilson 1553, Sig. 2G, 1ʳ.

When the duke appears, Friar Peter gives the signal: 'Now is your time. Speake loud, and kneele before him'.[167] Perhaps we are expected to understand that Isabella knows better than to follow the Friar's advice. But we are bound to wonder if things may be about to go badly wrong.

We quickly discover that we need not have worried, for as soon as Isabella begins to speak she reveals herself fully conversant with the rhetorical rules.[168] She knows that her first task is to make her judge attentive and responsive, and that the best way to make him responsive will be to offer a brief summary of her case:

> Justice, O royall *Duke*, vaile your regard
> Upon a wrong'd (I would faine have said a Maid)
>
> TLN 2185–6, p. 917 (5. 1. 20–1)

Isabella instantly makes the duke aware that an injustice has been done, and specifically that she has been sexually violated. (This is not true, of course, and secretly the duke knows it is not true, but Angelo believes it.) She also knows that, in order to make her judge attentive as well as responsive, she must cry out for his full attention, while urging that the matter on which she intends to speak is one that he cannot fail to regard as important:

> Oh worthy Prince, dishonor not your eye
> By throwing it on any other object,
> Till you have heard me, in my true complaint,
> And given me Justice, Justice, Justice, Justice.
>
> TLN 2187–90, p. 917 (5. 1. 22–5)

Having insisted on the overriding importance of her cause, she gives vent to her agonized 'outcry', as George Puttenham would call it, her repeated call to the duke to perform his duty and grant her justice.[169]

The duke is of course listening to Isabella's *prohoemium* from a position of secret knowledge. But in maintaining the fiction that he is learning about Anglelo's infamy for the first time, he concedes that she has indeed captured his attention and made him feel responsive:

---

167. *Measure for Measure*, TLN 2184, p. 917 (5. 1. 19).
168. Isabella's plea is analysed in Ross 1997, pp. 123–5, but without reference to its rhetorical character.
169. [Puttenham] 1589, p. 157.

> Relate your wrongs; In what, by whom? be briefe:
> Here is Lord *Angelo* shall give you Justice,
> Reveale your selfe to him.
>
> > TLN 2191–3, p. 917 (5. 1. 26–8)

As we know, however, the duke is merely playing with Isabella, who is driven to reiterate her plea that he alone must be her judge:

> Oh worthy *Duke*,
> You bid me seeke redemption of the divell,
> Heare me your selfe: . . .
> > Heare me: oh heare me, heare.[170]
> > > TLN 2193–5, 2197, p. 917 (5. 1. 28–30, 32)

This second *exclamatio* is a direct call for attention, rhythmically identical to that of the ghost and his cry of 'list *Hamlet* list, ô list'.[171]

While Isabella may have succeeded in capturing the duke's attention, his curt response ('be briefe') does nothing to suggest that she has made any headway with the main task of her *prohoemium*, that of winning his good-will. She knows, however, that according to the rhetoricians her best hope of doing so will be to refer to the different persons involved in the case. Speaking of herself, she follows the advice in the *Ad Herennium* that we should not only draw attention to our misfortunes—as she has already done—but make it clear that we have no hope of redress from anyone else:

> Heare me your selfe: for that which I must speake
> Must either punish me, not being beleev'd,
> Or wring redresse from you:
> > TLN 2195–7, p. 917 (5. 1. 30–2)

After this, perhaps recalling the advice that in referring to our own person we must speak as modestly as possible, Isabella proceeds directly to give her views about the person of Angelo, her adversary in the case.

Her specific aim, she knows, must be to bring Angelo into *odium, invidia*, and *contemptio*—hatred, unpopularity, and contempt.[172] She begins by describing the strange and unknown truth about his character:

---

170. Some editors—for example, Gibbons, following Keightley—read the final word as 'here'. Gibbons 1991, p. 173n comments that this conjecture produces 'a more conventional rhetorical plea'. The rhetoricians would not agree. For them the force of a rhetorical 'outcry' depends on repetition, as we have seen in the case of the ghost in *Hamlet*.

171. *Hamlet*, TLN 639, p. 744 (1. 5. 22).

172. *Rhetorica ad Herennium* 1954, I. V. 8, p. 14: 'si eos in odium, in invidiam, in contemptionem adducemus'.

> Most strange: but yet most truely wil I speake,
> That *Angelo's* forsworne, is it not strange?
> That *Angelo's* a murtherer, is't not strange?
> That *Angelo* is an adulterous thiefe,
>
> TLN 2202–5, pp. 917–18 (5. 1. 37–40)

To make someone unpopular, the *Ad Herennium* had suggested, one of the assertions we should make is that they enjoy *vis* and *potentia*, violence and excessive power. Isabella presses a vehement form of this accusation when she condemns Angelo as a murderer for having sentenced her brother to death. To cause someone to fall into contempt, the *Ad Herennium* had added, you must charge them with *luxuria*,[173] a vice associated with wantonness and 'uncleanly lust'.[174] Isabella duly impugns Angelo for precisely this vice when she denounces him as an adulterous thief.

Swiftly the duke responds with what Richard Rainolde would call a 'destruccion', repudiating her argument on the grounds that it is 'not agreyng to any likelihode', and is deserving of being reprehended.[175] He dismisses Isabella's charge as 'ten times strange', adding the reprehension that she must be speaking 'in th'infirmity of sence'.[176] But Isabella recognizes his rhetorical move and directly challenges it. She has already proclaimed Angelo to be 'An hypocrite, a virgin violator'[177] and now she pursues her attack, prefacing it with a rejection of the duke's 'destruccion':

> make not impossible
> That which but seemes unlike, 'tis not impossible
> But one, the wickedst caitiffe on the ground
> May seeme as shie, as grave, as just, as absolute:
> As *Angelo*, even so may *Angelo*
> In all his dressings, caracts, titles, formes,
> Be an arch-villaine:
>
> TLN, 2216–22, p. 918 (5. 1. 51–7)

Angelo may appear in his outward form to be 'absolute', to have right and justice entirely on his side. But as Isabella specifically attempts to show, he deserves to be an object of hatred. Denouncing him as a hypocrite, she refers to one of the qualities that the rhetoricians had judged particularly hateful,

---

173. *Rhetorica ad Herennium* 1954, I. V. 8, p. 16: 'In contemptionem adducemus si . . . luxuriam adversariorum proferemus.'
174. Cooper 1565, Sig. 2G, 5ᵛ, Sig. 4C, 5ᵛ.   175. Rainolde 1563, fo. xxivᵛ.
176. *Measure for Measure*, TLN 2207, 2212, p. 918 (5. 1. 42, 47).
177. *Measure for Measure*, TLN 2206, p. 918 (5. 1. 41).

that of being *malitiosus*, or filled with deceitfulness.[178] Reviling him as a virgin violator, she alludes to a further vice they had treated as detestable, that of being *spurcus*, or filthy and given to corruption and defilement.[179] Finally, in condemning him as an arch villain she speaks of yet another hateful quality, that of being *superbus*, or wicked and unjust.[180]

Having completed her *prohoemium*, Isabella ends with a further direct appeal to her judge, this time asking him to recognize his duty to use his *ratio*, or powers of reasoning, to penetrate beneath the surface of mere 'shows':

> let your reason serve
> To make the truth appeare, where it seemes hid,
> And hide the false seemes true.[181]
>
> TLN 2230–2, p. 918 (5. 1. 65–7)

To this the duke replies in the manner of someone whose feelings of goodwill have at last been aroused. To speak more accurately, Shakespeare next shows the duke permitting himself the judgement that, were he not already in possession of the facts, he would consider the opening of Isabella's speech to be sufficiently persuasive to grant her permission to narrate her case. While insisting that she must be mad, he now makes clear his benevolence and his willingness to hear her cause:

> Many that are not mad
> Have sure more lacke of reason: What would you say?
>
> TLN 2232–3, p. 918 (5. 1. 67–8)

With his question he invites Isabella to proceed to her *narratio*, thereby acknowledging that the goal of her *prohoemium* has been successfully achieved.

★ ★ ★ ★ ★

The two other characters who have an open *prohoemium* to present in a judicial cause both make their appearance in *All's Well That Ends Well*. One is Rynaldo, the countess of Rossillion's steward, who has an accusation to put forward in Act 1 about Hellen, the countess's ward. The other is Diana,

---

178. For these translations see Cooper 1565, Sig. 4D, 4ʳ; Veron 1584, Sig. B, 6ᵛ; Thomas 1592, Sig. 2F, 3ʳ.
179. For these translations see Cooper 1565, Sig. 6A, 2ᵛ; Thomas 1592, Sig. 2Y, 6ʳ.
180. For these translations see Cooper 1565, Sig. 6D, 2ᵛ; Thomas 1592, Sig. 3A, 1ʳ.
181. Isabella's main task (like the ghost in *Hamlet*) is to persuade her judge that the truth has been deliberately obscured. On being and seeming in *Hamlet* see Cox 1973 and Kerrigan 1996, pp. 191–2; in *Measure for Measure* see Hillman 1993, pp. 113–14, 121, 125.

a young Florentine, who has a legal case to mount in Act 5 against Bertram, the countess's son. The moving force in both episodes is Hellen, although initially she appears to be far from energetic or active. When we first encounter her she is silent and tearful, and it seems appropriate (although it is in fact ironic) that her name should recall Helen of Troy.[182] The reason for her melancholy, she has allowed it to be understood, is her continuing grief at her father's recent death. As the countess explains to Lord Lafew: 'The remembrance of her father never approches her heart, but the tirrany of her sorrowes takes all livelihood from her cheeke.'[183] Later in the scene, however, Hellen admits in soliloquy that she has been engaged in a deception and confesses the truth:

> I thinke not on my father, . . .
> I have forgott him. My imagination
> Carries no favour in't but *Bertrams*.
> I am undone, there is no living, none,
> If *Bertram* be away.
>
> TLN 79, 82–5, p. 969 (1. 1. 67, 70–3)

The true reason for her unhappiness is that she has fallen in love with the young count Bertram, who is about to leave Rossillion for Paris to join the court of the king of France.

Soon afterwards we are introduced to Rynaldo, who appears before the countess to inform her about a 'matter' concerning Hellen.[184] No one supposes that there is any mystery about the cause of Hellen's melancholy, but Rynaldo has accidentally discovered the hidden truth, and considers it his duty to acquaint the countess with the facts.[185] The scene opens with the countess addressing him in the manner of a judge undertaking to listen to a case: 'I will now heare, what say you of this gentlewoman'.[186] Rynaldo's response makes it clear that he regards himself as having a wholly honest case to present, and he answers with an appropriately open *prohoemium*. He knows that his principal aim must be to win the countess's benevolence,

---

182. See Snyder 1992, pp. 271–2; Parker 1996, pp. 205–6, 341; Maguire 2007, pp. 104–9.
183. *All's Well That Ends Well*, TLN 47–9, p. 969 (1. 1. 37–9).
184. *All's Well That Ends Well*, TLN 411, p. 972 (1. 3. 86).
185. Shakespeare takes the story of Hellen's secret love from his principal source, William Painter's *Palace of Pleasure* (1566). But Rynaldo makes no appearance in Painter's telling of the tale. The scene in which Rynaldo puts his case to the countess owes nothing to Shakespeare's narrative sources and everything to his own knowledge of judicial rhetoric.
186. *All's Well That Ends Well*, TLN 305–6, p. 972 (1. 3. 1).

and he also knows that the most promising way of doing so will be to speak fittingly about the different persons involved in the matter at issue. The vernacular rhetoricians had particularly stressed the importance of referring appropriately to oneself. As Leonard Cox had put it, 'the easyest and moost used place of benevolence consysteth in the office or duety of the person whan we shew that it is our duety to do that we be about.'[187] When we speak of ourselves, Thomas Wilson agrees, we must 'modestly set furthe our bounden dueties, and declare our service doen, without all suspicion of vauntyng', reminding our hearers 'without all ostentacion' how much we have 'doen for theim in tymes paste, to the outermoste of our power'.[188]

Rynaldo's *prohoemium* is brief, but he manages to follow these instructions with impressive exactitude:

> Maddam the care I have had to even your content, I wish might be found in the Kalender of my past endevours, for then we wound our Modestie, and make foule the clearnesse of our deservings, when of our selves we publish them.
>
> TLN 307–11, p. 972 (1. 3. 2–5)

Rynaldo firmly reminds the countess how much he has done for her in the past. He also draws attention to his modesty, and by addressing his patron in prose he follows Wilson's further admonition to avoid ostentatious speech. Most important, he makes it clear that he regards the cause he is about to lay before the countess as an honest one, and not of such a kind as to 'make foule' his previously deserving behaviour.

It cannot be said that the countess responds with any great warmth, and Rynaldo is in any case interrupted by the antics of Lavatch. Perhaps we are to think of the steward's attempted eloquence as too close to the book, and consequently too mechanical in style, as it certainly sounds to a modern ear. After Lavatch is dispatched, however, Rynaldo is rewarded with a terse but benevolent nod from the countess: 'Well now'.[189] Mechanical or not, his *prohoemium* has achieved its purpose, securing him sufficient attention and goodwill to enable him to proceed to his *narratio*, the next stage in the presentation of his case.

If we turn from the opening to the closing Act of *All's Well* we come upon a parallel accusation in a judicial cause. Here Shakespeare closely

---

187. Cox 1532, Sig. B, 2ᵛ.   188. Wilson 1553, Sig. O, 4ᵛ.
189. *All's Well That Ends Well*, TLN 399, p. 972 (1. 3. 77).

follows his main source, William Painter's collection *The Palace of Pleasure* of 1566. Painter's thirty-eighth novell, one of ten that he translated from Boccaccio's *Decameron*, tells the story of Giletta and Count Beltramo, who in Shakespeare's version become Hellen and Count Bertram. Hellen uses the arts of her late father, a celebrated physician, to cure the ailing king of France of a fistula that had brought him close to death.[190] As a reward the king allows her to choose a husband from among the nobles at his court. These now include Bertram, who has arrived in Paris, and Hellen duly picks him out, telling the king that 'This is the man'.[191] But Bertram scornfully rejects her, and although the king insists on the marriage Bertram immediately leaves for military service in Florence. There he meets Diana, the daughter of an impoverished gentlewoman, whom he pursues and plans to seduce. Following him to Italy, Hellen sees in this imbroglio a means to win Bertram back. She prompts Diana to agree to an assignation with Bertram at which she will substitute herself for Diana in a bed trick, after which she will exchange rings with Bertram in a mutual pledge of love. If she can make the stratagem work, she can hope to meet the conditions laid down in the dreadful letter, as she calls it, that Bertram left for her when he made his escape: '*When thou canst get the Ring upon my finger, which never shall come off, and shew mee a childe begotten of thy bodie, that I am father too, then call me husband: but in such a (then) I write a Never.*'[192]

Shakespeare takes almost all these details from Painter, including the terms of the dreadful letter, which he repeats almost word for word.[193] Like Painter, he also follows Boccaccio's audacious reversal of the folk-tale convention according to which a young man is expected to perform impossible deeds to win a fair maiden's love. Hellen, like Giletta, adopts the masculine role, showing herself resourceful and determined in the pursuit of her desires.[194] Whereas Isabella in *Measure for Measure* had merely been an accomplice in the bed trick, in *All's Well* it is Hellen who takes the

---

190. See Painter 1566, fos. 95ʳ–100ᵛ. The story is reprinted in Bullough 1957–75, vol. 2, pp. 389–96. The fistula is mentioned in Painter 1566, fo. 95ᵛ and in *All's Well That Ends Well*, TLN 33, p. 969 (1. 1. 25).
191. *Alls's Well That Ends Well*, TLN 943, p. 978 (2. 3. 96).
192. *All's Well That Ends Well*, TLN 1365–8, p. 982 (3. 2. 50–3).
193. As noted in Bullough 1957–75, vol. 2, p. 392. Cole 1981, pp. 33–89, investigates other versions of the story on which Shakespeare may have drawn.
194. As Snyder 1993, p. 31, remarks, 'no other heroine in Shakespearean comedy goes after the man she wants without some prior attachment initiated by the man'. On Hellen's active agency see also Hanson 1998; Belton 2007. McCandless 1997 underlines Hellen's adoption of a masculine role.

sexual initiative.[195] Nor is she disappointed, for her stratagem works exactly as she had hoped, and she is left pregnant with Bertram's child, although she subsequently gives it out (and Bertram believes) that on leaving France she went on a pilgrimage and died.

In Painter's *Palace of Pleasure* the two women with whom Giletta contrives the bed trick make no further appearance in the tale. But in *All's Well* they reappear with a vengeance in the closing scene to prosecute a *constitutio iuridicalis* against Bertram, in the presence of the king of France, on the grounds of his seduction and abandonment of Diana. As the audience knows, this charge is in fact groundless, which might be thought to raise some doubts about the honesty of their cause. But Hellen at the time of the bed trick had offered them a careful reassurance:

> Let us assay our plot, which if it speed,
> Is wicked meaning in a lawfull deede;
> And lawfull meaning in a wicked act,
> Where both not sinne, and yet a sinfull fact.
>
> TLN 1758–61, p. 987 (3. 7. 44–7)

The sinful fact is that Bertram will believe that he is committing adultery, while Hellen will know that she is deceiving him.[196] The excuse is contained in the proverb to which Hellen alludes: 'it is no deceit to deceave the deceaver'.[197] Diana is readily persuaded, and agrees that it is 'no sinne,/ To cosen him that would unjustly winne'.[198] When she appears with her mother before the king, they accordingly consider themselves to have an honest cause to plead, and begin by presenting an open *prohoemium* in which they seek to win the king's benevolence as judge of their case.

Like Rynaldo in Act 1, they know that their best chance is to start by speaking in winning terms about themselves. The rhetoricians had recommended that in doing so we must be sure to impress on the judge the value of our past services and attempt to excite pity for our current plight. The

---

195. On Hellen as initiator of the bed trick see Parker 1996, pp. 206–9. Desens 1994, pp. 80–2, assuming *All's Well* to be the earlier play, argues that Shakespeare portrays a woman who takes the initiative in a sexual encounter and then responds to the fears this might have aroused by limiting Isabella's role to that of accomplice. See also Adelman 1989, p. 173, who speaks of *Measure for Measure* as 'an undoing' of *All's Well*.

196. As noted in Bullough 1957–75, vol. 2, p. 382; Donaldson 1977, p. 48; Haley 1993, p. 127.

197. [Ling] 1598, fo. 256ᵛ. This proverbial wisdom is recorded from the mid-sixteenth century according to Dent 1981, p. 89.

198. *All's Well That Ends Well*, TLN 1936–7, p. 989 (4. 2. 75–6).

vernacular writers place their main stress on the former strategy, but the classical theorists insist that the latter is no less important. 'You must emphasise,' Cicero urges, 'the sufferings you have endured, or the difficulties you continue to face, and you must make use of prayer and entreaty in a humble and supplicating way.'[199]

These are the suggestions on which Diana and her mother both seize. Diana first steps forward to petition the king:

> I am my Lord a wretched Florentine,
> Derived from the ancient Capilet,
> My suite as I do understand you know,
> And therefore know how farre I may be pittied.
>
> TLN 2678–81, p. 996 (5. 3. 156–9)

Diana's mother next speaks in similar vein:

> I am her Mother sir, whose age and honour
> Both suffer under this complaint we bring,
> And both shall cease, without your remedie.
>
> TLN 2682–4, p. 996 (5. 3. 160–2)

Diana and her mother both speak in a humble and supplicating way; they both refer to the sufferings they have endured; and they both entreat the king's pity for their plight. Finally, Diana's mother follows a further piece of advice added by the author of the *Ad Herennium*. He had proposed that 'as well as pleading for help to be given to us, we should declare at the same time that we have no wish to place our hope in anyone else'.[200] This is the anguished note on which Diana's mother brings the opening of her speech to an end. 'Without your remedie', she assures the king, both her life and her honour will be lost.

The king immediately indicates that these appeals have achieved their goal. Not only have they succeeded in winning his benevolent attention, but they have prompted him to recognize that there is a legal case for Bertram to answer. 'Come hether Count', he now commands, 'do you know these Women?'[201] Bertram guiltily acknowledges that he is committed to taking

---

199. Cicero 1949a, I. XVI. 22, p. 44: 'quae incommoda acciderint aut quae instent difficultates, proferemus . . . prece et obsecratione humili ac supplici utemur'.
200. *Rhetorica ad Herennium* 1954, I. V. 8, p. 14: 'orabimus ut nobis sint auxilio, et simul ostendemus nos in aliis noluisse spem habere'.
201. *All's Well That Ends Well*, TLN 2685, p. 996 (5. 3. 163).

part in a judicial proceeding in which he may have to answer further accusations:

> My Lord, I neither can nor will denie,
> But that I know them, do they charge me further?
>
> TLN 2686–7, p. 996 (5. 3. 164–5)

The *prohoemium* has succeeded, and the way is now clear for Diana and her mother to develop their case.

4

The Insinuative Beginning

The need for insinuation

When pleading in a judicial cause it may not be possible to begin with an open *prohoemium*; it may instead be necessary to adopt a more insinuating approach. This is not to say that the aim of our *prohoemium* will have changed. We shall still be trying to render our audience attentive, responsive, and above all benevolent towards our cause. We may find, however, that our circumstances are such that, in the words of the *Ad Herennium*, 'we can only hope to arrive at the same position of advantage if we speak in a surreptitious manner and employ dissimulation or concealment'.[1]

The basic situation in which an insinuative opening will be required, Cicero explains, is 'when the mind of your audience is hostile' towards your side of the case.[2] Translating Cicero's words, but at the same time intensifying them, Thomas Wilson confirms that it is 'when the judge is greaved with us', or when our cause is 'hated of the hearers', that 'a privy begynnyng, or crepying in, otherwyse called Insinuacion must then, and not els, be used'.[3] Cicero goes on to single out three possible reasons for such hostility.[4] The first and most obvious is that there may be something strange or, still worse, something foul about your cause. 'If you are pleading in a *causa admirabilis* or strange cause', he first advises, 'and if as a result your hearers are vehemently alienated, then it will be necessary for you to take refuge in an *insinuatio*.'[5] Likewise, 'if there is any element of *turpitudo* or foulness about

1. *Rhetorica ad Herennium* 1954, I. VII. 11, p. 20: 'occulte, per dissimulationem...ad eandem commoditatem in dicendi opera venire possimus'.
2. Cicero 1949a, I. XVII. 23, p. 46: 'cum animus auditoris infestus est'.
3. Wilson 1553, Sig. P, 1ʳ.
4. Cicero 1949a, I. XVII. 23, p. 46: 'id autem tribus ex causis fit maxime'.
5. Cicero 1949a, I. XV. 21, p. 42: 'In admirabili genere causae...Sin [auditores] erunt vehementer abalienati, confugere necesse erit ad insinuationem.'

your cause an *insinuatio* will again have to be used.'[6] The vernacular rhetoricians have nothing to say about strange causes, but they fully agree about what needs to be done if your cause is inherently lacking in honesty. Leonard Cox lays it down that 'insinuacion' will always be needed if the matter we are handling is 'of litle honesty in it selfe'.[7] Thomas Wilson agrees that the primary case in which 'a close, or privie gettyng of favour' will be necessary is when 'the matter [it]selfe be unhonest, and not meete to be utterd before an audience'.[8]

Sometimes the rhetoricians give the impression that it is only if a cause is *admirabilis* or *turpis* that an insinuative *prohoemium* will be required. The author of the *Ad Herennium* goes so far as to say that 'if the cause be honest, it will be appropriate to use an open beginning'.[9] But this is not his considered view. Rather he agrees with Cicero that, even if a cause is unquestionably honest, there are two further situations in which an *insinuatio* will be indispensable. One is when, as Cicero puts it, 'those who have already spoken may appear to have persuaded our audience', thereby leaving us confronting a sceptical or hostile judge.[10] As Wilson translates, we may find that 'the judge hymselfe by a former tale' has been 'perswaded to take part against us'.[11] The other possibility is that 'the opportunity may be given to us to speak at a time when those who ought to be listening to us have already become tired and irritated with the case'.[12] Wilson likewise refers to the danger of being 'forced to speake, when the judge is weried with hearyng of other'.[13] Even if your cause is honest, an exhausted or preoccupied judge is liable to be alienated or even hostile, and will certainly be 'muche more greeved if any thyng be spoken either overmuche, or els against his likyng'.[14] As Wilson summarizes, we are trying to ensure that 'nothyng shoulde bee spoken at the firste, but that whiche might please the

---

6. Cicero 1949a, I. XVII. 23, p. 46: 'Insinuatione igitur utendum est . . . si aut inest in ipsa causa quaedam turpitudo.'
7. Cox 1532, Sig. B, 5^{r-v}.   8. Wilson 1553, Sig. P, 1^r.
9. *Rhetorica ad Herennium* 1954, I. IV. 6, p. 12: 'Sin honestum genus causa erit, licebit recte . . . uti principio.'
10. Cicero 1949a, I. XVII. 23, p. 46: 'ab eis qui ante dixerunt iam quiddam auditori persuasum videtur'. Cf. *Rhetorica ad Herennium* 1954, I. VI. 9, p. 16.
11. Wilson 1553, Sig. P, 1^r.
12. Cicero 1949a, I. XVII. 23, p. 46: 'eo tempore locus dicendi datur cum iam illi quos audire oportet defessi sunt audiendo'. Cf. *Rhetorica ad Herennium* 1954, I. VI. 9, p. 16; Quintilian 2001, 4. 1. 48, vol. 2, p. 202.
13. Wilson 1553, Sig. P, 1^r.
14. Wilson 1553, Sig. P, 1^r. This insight has been confirmed by modern research. See Kahneman 2011, pp. 43–4.

judge', but under any of these circumstances the judge will easily be displeased, which is why a 'privy' beginning ('otherwise called Insinuacion') will in all these cases be required.[15]

Facing a hostile judge

Shakespeare is particularly interested in dramatizing situations in which a defendant who firmly believes in the honesty of his cause nevertheless finds himself confronting a judge who is hostile or suspicious because, in the words of the *Ad Herennium*, 'he has been persuaded by those who have already spoken on the other side', and consequently takes himself to be dealing with a foul cause.[16] The first character to face this dangerous problem is Friar Lawrence in the closing scene of *Romeo and Juliet*. He and Romeo's servant Balthazer have been discovered near the tomb of the Capulets, where Romeo, Juliet, and Paris all lie dead. The Chief Watchman declares this to be a matter of 'great suspition' and begins to assemble a case against them.[17] When the prince arrives he agrees that the Friar and Balthazer must be regarded as 'the parties of suspition',[18] and the Friar is left with the task of persuading the prince that, although he may appear to have behaved foully, he is innocent of anyone's death.[19]

How can the Friar hope to defend himself? We may reflect that he faces a task of unusual difficulty, not merely because the facts appear to tell against him, but also because he would have been likely to appear an inherently doubtful character to Shakespeare's original audience. As Arther Brooke had warned in the opening epistle of his *Romeus and Juliet*, 'superstitious friers' are 'the naturally fitte instrumentes of unchastitie'.[20] If we turn with these difficulties in mind to the usually reliable Quintilian, we find him surprisingly uninterested in offering specific directions and advice to persons unlucky enough to find themselves in this type of situation. He has one or two suggestions to make, but he complains in a rare moment of asperity that

---

15. Wilson 1553, Sig. P, 1ʳ.
16. *Rhetorica ad Herennium* 1954, I. VI. 9, p. 16: 'persuasus esse . . . ab iis qui ante contra dixerunt'.
17. *Romeo and Juliet*, TLN 2876, p. 411 (5. 3. 187).
18. *Romeo and Juliet*, TLN 2911, p. 411 (5. 3. 222).
19. Baldwin 1944, vol. 2, pp. 76–80 discusses this passage, arguing (p. 80) that Shakespeare makes Friar Lawrence 'serve both as accuser and defendant'. But the accusation is put forward by the Chief Watchman, and Friar Lawrence is called upon to respond.
20. Brooke 1562, Sig. A, 2ᵛ–3ʳ.

earlier authorities have written with excessive verbosity about the problem, and contents himself with proposing that 'we should take refuge in anything that redounds to our advantage'.[21] If, however, we turn back to the authorities whom Quintilian criticizes—and especially to Cicero's *De inventione*—we come upon a number of resourceful ideas about how to develop the kind of insinuative opening that, as Cicero explains, will be indispensable if we find ourselves facing a judge who believes that we may be pleading in a foul cause.

The first step according to Cicero is to try to bring it about 'that your audience becomes somewhat more moderate'.[22] He has several suggestions to make about how to achieve this effect. He first mentions some devices for calming the judge, after which he suggests that one thing to say is that 'what appears to your adversary to be shameful appears to you to be shameful as well'.[23] 'Once you have placated the judge in this fashion', he goes on, you should then directly challenge your adversaries 'by showing that nothing of the kind pertains to the present case'.[24] As Thomas Wilson crisply translates, 'when the hearers are thus wonne, we may saie, that all, whiche was saied, nothyng toucheth us'.[25]

Friar Lawrence evidently has this advice in mind, although he follows it only in a generalized way:

> I am the greatest able to do least,
> Yet most suspected as the time and place
> Doth make against me of this direfull murther:
> And heere I stand both to impeach and purge
> My selfe condemned, and my selfe excusde.
>
> TLN 2912–16, p. 411 (5. 3. 223–7)

He begins, as recommended, by striking a mollifying note, admitting that he is the leading suspect and conceding that appearances are against him, since he was undoubtedly present at the relevant time and place. But he then makes it clear, as the rhetoricians had advised, that the murder characterized

---

21. Quintilian 2001, 4. 1. 44, vol. 2, p. 200: 'ad ea quae prosunt refugiamus'.
22. Cicero 1949a, I. XVII. 24, p. 48: 'iam mitior factus erit auditor'.
23. Cicero 1949a, I. XVII. 24, p. 48: 'dicere ea quae indignentur adversarii tibi quoque indigna videri'. For *indignus* as 'shameful' and *nefarius* as 'detestable' see Cooper 1565, Sig. 3Q, 3ʳ and Sig. 4K, 6ʳ.
24. Cicero 1949a, I. XVII. 24, p. 48: 'deinde, cum lenieris eum qui audiet, demonstrare nihil eorum ad te pertinet'. Cf. *Rhetorica ad Herennium* 1954, I. VI. 9, p. 18.
25. Wilson 1553, Sig. P, 1ʳ⁻ᵛ.

by the prince as a foul offence appears no less direful to him. Finally, and again following their advice, he indicates that he has not in fact perpetrated any such crime, using the figure of *antithesis* to emphasize that he can hope at once to purge the impeachment and to excuse himself from blame.[26] His *insinuatio* is brief and formal, but it proves more than adequate to achieve its goal, that of securing sufficient goodwill from his judge to enable him to move on to his *narratio*. The prince immediately responds: 'Then say at once what thou dost know in this?'[27] The way is open for the Friar to lay out his own version of events.

★ ★ ★ ★ ★

If we turn from *Romeo and Juliet* to *Julius Caesar*, we find Antony at the climactic moment in Act 3 confronting the same rhetorical predicament. Brutus and the conspirators have assassinated Caesar, and Brutus next delivers his oration in their defence. He is wholly convinced of his honourable motives, and hence of the honest character of his cause. He accordingly begins with the briefest possible open *prohoemium*, conveying a strong sense that he thinks of his action as standing in little need of justification,[28] and underscoring his confidence by avoiding what Quintilian had called the grand style and speaking instead in prose.[29] This refusal of rhetoric, however, is part of the rhetoric of his performance. For all his seemingly offhand assurance, he takes great care to follow the advice given by the rhetoricians about how to attain the specific goal of a *prohoemium*, that of winning the attention, the responsiveness, and above all the goodwill of his audience.[30]

The *Ad Herennium* had emphasized that you will obtain responsive hearers if you begin by making them attentive, and that the quickest way of doing so will be to cry out to them to listen with care.[31] Brutus begins with just such an *exclamatio*:

---

26. On the figure of *antithesis* (or *contentio*) see *Rhetorica ad Herennium* 1954, IV. XV. 21, p. 282; Quintilian 2001, 9. 3. 81–6, vol. 4, pp. 150–2. See also Sherry 1550, Sig. D, 4ᵛ; Peacham 1577, Sig. R, 1ʳ⁻ᵛ; Day 1592, p. 92; Peacham 1593, pp. 160–1.
27. *Romeo and Juliet*, TLN 2917, p. 411 (5. 3. 228).
28. As noted in Serpieri 2002, p. 132; for a contrasting view of Brutus's brevity see Crider 2009, pp. 58–9.
29. Vickers 1968, pp. 241–5; McDonald 2001, pp. 132–3. For Quintilian on the *genus grande* see Quintilian 2001, 12. 10, 58–62, vol. 5, pp. 312–14.
30. On the rhetorical structure of Brutus's speech see Vickers 1968, pp. 241–2. Wills 2011, pp. 37–61 analyses Brutus's use of figures, especially *chiasmus* and *partitio*.
31. *Rhetorica ad Herennium* 1954, I. IV. 7, p. 14. See also Wilson 1553, Sig. 2E, 1ᵛ; [Puttenham] 1589, p. 157.

> Romans, Countrey-men, and Lovers, heare mee for my cause, and
> be silent, that you may heare.
>
> TLN 1400–1, p. 690 (3. 2. 13–14)

Brutus then moves directly to his principal task, that of winning the
goodwill of his audience. He knows that the surest means will be to focus
on the different persons involved in the case.[32] He begins by referring to his
own person, drawing attention to himself as a man of honour who can be
trusted to tell the truth: 'Beleeve me for mine Honor, and have respect to
mine Honor, that you may beleeve'.[33] He then praises his judges, making
particular reference (as the rhetoricians had recommended)[34] to the *sapientia*
or wisdom that can be expected of them: 'Censure me in your Wisedom,
and awake your Senses, that you may the better Judge.'[35]

With this request, Brutus indicates that he is ready to shift from his
prohoemium to the main body of his speech. The oration he then delivers
against Caesarism and in favour of Roman liberty scores a resounding
rhetorical success. As he steps down from the public chair, the first plebeian
immediately calls for a celebration: 'Bring him with Triumph home unto
his house.'[36] The second expresses equal enthusiasm: 'Give him a Statue
with his Ancestors.' The third is yet more excited, although he has evidently
failed to follow Brutus's reasoning, and cries out: 'Let him be *Caesar*'.
Correcting this ominous proposal, the fourth plebeian more soberly suggests
that '*Caesars* better parts,/ Shall be Crown'd in *Brutus*'. The first plebeian
then commands once more that they should 'bring him to his House, with
Showts and Clamors'. Brutus's speech has won him universal acclaim.

When Antony ascends the public chair he accordingly finds himself in a
serious rhetorical difficulty.[37] He intends to speak on the other side of the
case, and he believes no less firmly in the honesty of his cause. But he is
confronting an adversary who has just won the warm approbation of his
hearers, and is consequently facing a hostile body of judges. 'This *Caesar* was

---

32. *Rhetorica ad Herennium* 1954, I. IV. 8, p. 14; Cicero 1949a, I. XVI. 22, p. 44; Quintilian 2001,
    4. 1. 6–32, vol. 2, pp. 182–94.
33. *Julius Caesar*, TLN 1401–3, p. 690 (3. 2. 14–15).
34. *Rhetorica ad Herennium* 1954, I. V. 8, p. 16; Cicero 1949a, I. XVI. 22, p. 44.
35. *Julius Caesar*, TLN 1403–4, p. 690 (3. 2. 15–16).
36. For the ensuing quotations in this paragraph see *Julius Caesar*, TLN 1436–40, p. 691 (3. 2.
    41–5). I have preserved the First Folio numbering of the plebeians. See Shakespeare 1996,
    Julius Caesar, TLN 1579–85, p. 729.
37. Serpieri 2002, pp. 134–6 and Wills 2011, pp. 79–111 analyse the rhetoric of Antony's speech,
    but focus exclusively on his use of figures and tropes.

a Tyrant', the first plebeian declares, to which the third adds, 'Nay that's certaine:/ We are blest that Rome is rid of him.'[38] Referring darkly to Antony, the fourth plebeian sums up the general mood of suspicion when he puts it to the others that: ''Twere best he speake no harme of *Brutus* heere?'[39] Antony's first task is to persuade them to reconsider their current belief that he is pleading in a foul cause.

Although Shakespeare draws on Plutarch's lives of Antony, Brutus, and Caesar,[40] there is no record in any of these sources of the verbal battle between Antony and Brutus, and almost no information about how they might have spoken. We know from Plutarch that Brutus's letters 'were honored for their briefenes',[41] and we know from his life of Antony that, when addressing the people at Caesar's burial, 'he mingled his oration with lamentable wordes, and by amplifying of matters did greatly move their harts and affections unto pitie & compassion.'[42] But when Shakespeare turns to the task of showing how Antony succeeded in achieving these effects he has no models on which to fall back; he has to compose the scene entirely on the basis of his own understanding of the principles of forensic eloquence.

While Antony is in a difficult position, he is not without openings and opportunities. There are several weaknesses in Brutus's speech that Antony can hope to exploit.[43] Quintilian had highlighted some of the many ways in which a *prohoemium* can go wrong, beginning by fixing on two main pitfalls to avoid. One is that, even when a speaker is convinced that his cause is beyond reproach, 'he ought not to make an excessive display of self-confidence'.[44] The other is that, however much care and attention he may have lavished on his *prohoemium*, 'this preparation should be revealed as little as possible'.[45] The opening of a speech 'should not always appear

---

38. *Julius Caesar*, TLN 1456–7, p. 691 (3. 2. 61–2).
39. Here again I preserve the First Folio numbering. See Shakespeare 1996, *Julius Caesar*, TLN 1603–6, p. 729.
40. Bullough 1957–75, vol. 5, p. 36 thinks it likely 'that he wrote with North's Plutarch by his side'. Miola 2000, pp. 98–107 traces Shakespeare's adaptation of Plutarch's account. On Shakespeare's use of classical sources in the play see also Thomas 2005; Burrow 2013, pp. 215–26.
41. Plutarch 1579, p. 976. But as Vickers 1968, p. 241 notes, Shakespeare gives Brutus a speech of 'expansive Ciceronian symmetries'.
42. Plutarch 1579, p. 1056.
43. On the faults in Brutus's speech see Vickers 1968, pp. 243–5; Hatfield 2005, pp. 181–2.
44. Quintilian 2001, 4. 1. 55, vol. 2, p. 206: 'fiducia se ipsa nimium exerere non debeat'. On the need to avoid any suspicion of boasting see also Quintilian 2001, 11. 1. 15, vol. 5, p. 16.
45. Quintilian 2001, 4. 1. 56, vol. 2, p. 206: 'minime ostentari debet . . . cura'.

finely woven or carefully decorated, but should generally be simple rather than elaborate'.[46] As he later adds, the danger to be avoided is obvious, for 'when there is a contention about something terrible, or something worthy of hatred or pity, who can endure a speaker whose raging, weeping and pleading simply take the form of antitheses, poised cadences and verbal similarities'.[47]

Antony is quick to profit from the fact that Brutus's *prohoemium* manifestly fails these tests. After his opening call for attention, Brutus had continued in a studiously artificial style:

> heare mee for my cause, and be silent, that you may heare. Beleeve me for mine Honor, and have respect to mine Honor, that you may beleeve.
>
> TLN 1400–3, p. 690 (3. 2. 13–15)

Here Brutus indulges in precisely the kind of diction that the rhetoricians warn us to avoid.[48] He begins with an *antithesis* contrasting silent/ hear, after which he painfully constructs a series of poised cadences of the type that Quintilian had particularly condemned. The specific device he uses is *epanodos*, a figure of speech in which, as Dudley Fenner explains, 'the same sounde is repeated in the beginning and the middle, in the middle and the ende' of a sentence.[49] Brutus makes the two halves of his second sentence mirror each other, giving rise to the laboured pattern of believe/ honour; honour/believe. A more serious fault is that he fails to heed Quintilian's other warning and refers to his own *ethos*—and especially his honourable character—with what might seem to be an incautious degree of assurance and self-confidence.

Despite these weaknesses, the fact remains that Brutus's speech wins him a warm reception, so that Antony is left facing a hostile audience. He does not fail to recognize that this requires him to tread a carefully insinuating path.[50] He begins, as Friar Lawrence had done, by following Cicero's advice

46. Quintilian 2001, 4. 1. 60, vol. 2, p. 208: 'neque tamen deducta semper atque circumlita, sed saepe simplici atque inlaboratae'.
47. Quintilian 2001, 9. 3. 102, vol. 4, p. 162: 'Ubi vero atrocitate invidia miseratione pugnandum, quis ferat contrapositis et pariter cadentibus et consimilibus irascentem flentem rogantem.' Vickers 1968, p. 245 quotes this passage.
48. See Cicero 1949a, I. XVIII. 25, p. 52 on diction that is excessively *artificiosa*.
49. Fenner 1584, Sig. D, 3ʳ. Fenner's definition is repeated almost word-for-word by later Ramist rhetoricians. See Fraunce 1588a, Sig. D, 4ʳ–5ʳ; Butler 1598, Sig. C, 6ᵛ. For a discussion see Skinner 1996, pp. 416–17. On *epanodos* see also Peacham 1577, Sig. S, 1ʳ⁻ᵛ; [Puttenham] 1589, p. 184; Day 1592, p. 92; Peacham 1593, p. 129.
50. Joseph 1947, pp. 283–6 notes Antony's need to establish his *ethos*.

and acknowledging that what appears evil and grievous to his adversaries appears no less evil and grievous to him:[51]

> Friends, Romans, Countrymen, lend me your ears:
> I come to bury *Caesar*, not to praise him:
> The evill that men do, lives after them,
> The good is oft enterred with their bones,
> So let it be with *Caesar*. The Noble *Brutus*,
> Hath told you *Caesar* was Ambitious:
> If it were so, it was a greevous Fault,
> And greevously hath Caesar answer'd it.
>
> TLN 1460–7, p. 691 (3. 2. 65–72)

After his bold 'outcry' addressing his judges as friends and calling for their attention, Antony sets about the process of attempting to pacify them. He manages to insinuate a hint of criticism with his cunning *anaphora*, admitting that Caesar may have grievously erred while insisting that he paid grievously for his fault. But he basically recognizes the need to argue as concessively as possible. He promises that he will make no attempt to speak in the *genus demonstrativum* and offer up a *laudatio* to Caesar, as might be expected on the occasion of a funeral. He concedes that Caesar did evil in his life, and he agrees that if Caesar suffered from ambition then this failing was indeed what Cicero would describe as *indignus*, a grievous fault.

The next step according to the rhetoricians is to submit that 'no such fault pertains to the present case'.[52] But they have a further and closely related piece of advice to offer at this stage. Cicero proposes that 'you should now promise that you will begin by examining the argument that has not only commended itself most firmly to your audience, but that your adversaries regard as constituting their firmest defence'.[53] Thomas Wilson emphatically agrees that this is the right way to proceed. You must first attempt 'to weaken that, whiche the adversarie hath made moste strong for hym selfe, and confute that parte whiche the hearers didde most esteme, and best of all lyke'.[54] He then adds one further suggestion that Antony follows to especially

51. Cicero 1949a, I. XVII. 24, p. 48. Cf. *Rhetorica ad Herennium* 1954, I. VI. 9, p. 18.
52. Cicero 1949a, I. XVII. 24, p. 48: 'nihil eorum ad te pertinere'. Cf. *Rhetorica ad Herennium* 1954, I. VI. 9, pp. 16–18.
53. Cicero 1949a, I. XVII. 25, p. 48: 'oportet aut de eo quod adversarii firmissimum sibi putarint et maxime ei qui audient probarint, primum te dicturum polliceri'. Cf. *Rhetorica ad Herennium* 1954, I. VI. 10, p 18.
54. Wilson 1553, Sig. P, 1[v].

telling effect. You should 'take advauntage of some part of our adversaries tale' and do your utmost to turn it against them.[55]

Brutus had left the plebeians in no doubt as to what he took to be the strongest defence of his decision to assassinate Caesar. Caesar had been ambitious at the expense of the people's liberty. Should anyone ask, he had told them, 'why *Brutus* rose against *Caesar*, this is my answer: Not that I lov'd *Caesar* lesse, but that I lov'd Rome more.'[56] Next he had allowed himself a *percontatio*, a rhetorical question: 'Had you rather *Caesar* were living, and dye all Slaves; then that *Caesar* were dead, to live all Freemen?'[57] The answer being obvious, his defence had followed at once: 'As *Caesar* lov'd mee, I weepe for him…But, as he was Ambitious, I slew him.'[58] Caesar's death is figured as a sacrifice necessary to uphold the freedom of Rome.

This is the accusation—and the justification—that Antony next takes up. 'The Noble *Brutus*,/ Hath told you *Caesar* was Ambitious', he reminds the plebeians,[59] and he turns to consider the charge:

> He was my Friend, faithfull, and just to me;
> But *Brutus* sayes, he was Ambitious,
> And *Brutus* is an Honourable man.
> He hath brought many Captives home to Rome,
> Whose Ransomes, did the generall Coffers fill:
> Did this in *Caesar* seeme Ambitious?
> When that the poore have cry'de, *Caesar* hath wept:
> Ambition should be made of sterner stuffe,
> Yet *Brutus* sayes, he was Ambitious:
> And *Brutus* is an Honourable man.
> You all did see, that on the *Lupercall*,
> I thrice presented him a Kingly Crowne,
> Which he did thrice refuse. Was this Ambition?
> Yet *Brutus* sayes, he was Ambitious:
> And sure he is an Honourable man.
>
> TLN 1472–86, p. 691 (3. 2. 77–91)

---

55. Wilson 1553, Sig. P, 1ᵛ.   56. *Julius Caesar*, TLN 1407–9, p. 690 (3. 2. 18–20).
57. *Julius Caesar*, TLN 1409–11, p. 690 (3. 2. 20–1). On *percontatio* see Quintilian 2001, 9. 2. 6–7, vol. 4, pp. 36–8. See also Sherry 1550, Sig. D, 2ʳ⁻ᵛ; Wilson 1553, Sig. 2B, 2ʳ; Peacham 1577, Sig. L, 3ʳ⁻ᵛ; [Puttenham] 1589, p. 176; Day 1592, p. 87; Peacham 1593, pp. 105–6.
58. *Julius Caesar*, TLN 1411–14, p. 690. (3. 2. 21–3).
59. *Julius Caesar*, TLN 1464–5, p. 691 (3. 2. 69–70).

Antony seeks directly to rebut the accusation that Caesar was ambitious, but at the same time he introduces two further and more insinuating arguments. He begins covertly to develop the kind of funeral *laudatio* that he had promised to eschew, and he manages to raise some awkward questions about Brutus's elevated view of his own character. The *Ad Herennium* had warned that 'the opening of your speech will be seriously at fault if it is possible for your adversary to make use of it against you in a contrary sense'.[60] Brutus's opening had revolved around his sense of himself as an honourable man, and Antony now begins to turn Brutus's overweening words against him. One of the main techniques he uses is an elaborate form of *anaphora*. He repeats not individual words but whole sentences, harping on Brutus's sense of honour until his protestations are made to sound not merely self-serving but absurd. He also manages to introduce an *insinuatio* about Brutus's motives for his act. It is Brutus's basic contention that, as a man of honour, he had a duty to curb Caesar's ambitiousness. But is it obvious that Caesar was ambitious? If he was not, can Brutus really be an honourable man? These are the questions about Brutus's *ethos* that Antony is able, as Quintilian would put it, 'to insinuate as much as possible into the minds of his audience'.[61]

Antony next alludes to the opening words of Brutus's speech and casts doubt on them in the same way. Brutus's initial *exclamatio* had been 'heare mee for my cause'.[62] Antony echoes his choice of phrase, punning on it and turning it against him:

> You all did love him once, not without cause,
> What cause with-holds you then, to mourne for him?
>
> TLN 1489–90, p. 691 (3. 2. 94–5)

Antony assures the plebeians that they had cause (that is, good reason) to love Caesar, while demanding with his rhetorical question to know why Brutus's statement of his cause (that is, his side of the quarrel) should be sufficient to withhold them from mourning for Caesar's death.

Antony is still far from having completed his *prohoemium*, but we next discover that he has already attained two of the goals that the opening section of any speech needs to achieve. First, he has definitely managed to

---

60. *Rhetorica ad Herennium* 1954, I. VII. 11–12, pp. 20–2: 'Vitiosum exordium est... quo adversarius ex contrario poterit uti'.
61. Quintilian 2001, 4. 1. 42, vol. 2, p. 200: 'subrepat insinuatio animis maxime'.
62. *Julius Caesar*, TLN 1400–1, p. 690 (3. 2. 13).

capture the attention of his audience. The leading plebeian now comments admiringly on how he has combined *ratio* with *oratio*, observing that 'Me thinkes there is much reason in his sayings'.[63] Antony has also succeeded in winning a measure of responsiveness towards his cause. The second plebeian, who had earlier proposed that Brutus should be given a statue with his ancestors, now sees the legal 'matter' very differently. 'If thou consider rightly of the matter', he reflects, '*Caesar* ha's had great wrong.'[64] Having earlier agreed that Brutus should be crowned, the fourth plebeian now praises Caesar for having refused that honour and concludes that, 'Therefore 'tis certaine, he was not Ambitious'.[65] Antony has already begun to swing his judges round, as Cicero would say, to see things from his point of view.[66]

The rhetoricians have several additional pieces of advice to offer those whose cause may at first seem *turpis* or foul. One is that, in Cicero's words, 'you should deny that you will say anything about your opponents, whether on one side or the other, but you should act imperceptibly so far as possible in such a way as to alienate the goodwill of your hearers from their cause'. [67] Thomas Wilson agrees that we must be sure to leave the impression 'that wee mynde to speake nothyng at al against our adversaries', while addressing our hearers in such a way as 'to aulter their hartes'.[68] Enlarging on this suggestion, he mentions a consideration that Antony appears specifically to recall. It is never wise 'openly to speake against theim, whiche are generally well estemed and taken for honest menne'.[69] If you wish to discredit them, you must somehow manage to question their honesty while seeming to speak in their praise.

The specific technique by which this effect can be created was known to the rhetoricians as *paralepsis* or *occultatio*. This is the figure we invoke, according to the *Ad Herennium*, whenever we claim 'that we do not wish

63. *Julius Caesar*, TLN 1495, p. 691 (3. 2. 100).
64. Here and in the next note I again preserve First Folio numbering. See Shakespeare 1996, *Julius Caesar*, TLN 1646–7, p. 729.
65. Shakespeare 1996, *Julius Caesar*, TLN 1650, p. 730.
66. Cicero 1942a, II. XVII. 72, vol. 1, p. 252. On the inability of the plebeians to reach a reasoned verdict see Colclough 2009.
67. Cicero 1949a, I. XVII. 24, p. 48: 'negare quicquam de adversariis esse dicturum, neque hoc neque illud . . . tamen id obscure faciens, quoad possis, alienes ab eis auditorum voluntatem'. Cf. *Rhetorica ad Herennium* 1954, I. VI. 9, p. 18.
68. Wilson 1553, Sig. P, 1ᵛ.   69. Wilson 1553, Sig. P, 1ᵛ.

to say something when in fact we very much want to say it'.[70] The device is particularly useful, he goes on, 'as a method of indirectly arousing suspicion instead of directly making a speech that might be susceptible of disproof'.[71] George Puttenham agrees that it is 'a good pollicie in pleading or perswasion' to pretend that we are passing over a matter when in fact 'we do then intend most effectually and despightfully if it be invective to remember it'.[72] Henry Peacham adds that, when an orator makes use of this technique, arguing 'as though he would say nothing in some matter, when notwithstanding he speaketh most of all', the effect will be 'most fit to accuse and reprehend, and most usually in a negative forme'.[73]

This is just the kind of insinuating accusation that Antony begins to mount as he embarks on the second part of his *prohoemium*:

> But yesterday, the word of *Caesar* might
> Have stood against the World: Now lies he there,
> And none so poore to do him reverence.
> O Maisters! If I were dispos'd to stirre
> Your hearts and mindes to Mutiny and Rage,
> I should do *Brutus* wrong, and *Cassius* wrong:
> Who (you all know) are Honourable men.
> I will not do them wrong: I rather choose
> To wrong the dead, to wrong my selfe and you,
> Then I will wrong such Honourable men.
>
> TLN 1505–14, pp. 691–2 (3. 2. 110–19)

Antony promises that he will say nothing against his adversaries and do nothing to incite anyone to mutiny or rage. But his ringing *apostrophe* ('O Maisters!') is designed to flatter as well as engage the attention of his audience, and he manages at the same time to insinuate that Brutus and Cassius can hardly be the honourable men that they claim to be, for he maintains that in refusing to do them wrong he is wronging both the plebeians and himself.

---

70. *Rhetorica ad Herennium* 1954, IV. XXVII. 37, p. 320: 'nolle dicere id quod nunc maxime dicimus'. See also Quintilian 2001, 9. 3. 98, vol. 4, p. 158. Wills 2011 examines this aspect of Antony's speech under the heading of *praeteritio*.
71. *Rhetorica ad Herennium* 1954, IV. XXVII. 37, p. 320: 'utilius sit occulte fecisse suspicionem quam eiusmodi intendisse orationem quae redarguatur'. See also Quintilian 2001, 9. 3. 98, vol. 4, p. 158.
72. [Puttenham] 1589, p. 194.
73. Peacham 1593, pp. 130–1. See also Sherry 1550, Sig. D, 6ʳ; Day 1592, p. 95.

Antony rounds off his *prohoemium* at this juncture and launches directly into his *narratio* ('I remember . . . ').[74] By this stage it is clear that he has fully attained the principal goal of any *prohoemium*, that of winning the goodwill of his audience. Brutus had staked everything on his standing as a man of honour, not a mere murderer. As he had earlier confided to the conspirators, his highest hope was that their cause would strike 'the common eyes' in such a way that 'We shall be call'd Purgers, not Murderers'.[75] As Antony draws to a close, he is able to overturn this hope and the goodwill it had initially elicited. He ends by returning yet again to his repeated insinuation, strengthening it with a further *anaphora*:

> I feare I wrong the Honourable men,
> Whose Daggers have stabb'd *Caesar.* I do feare it.
>
> TLN 1538–9, p. 692 (3. 2. 143–4)

At this moment the fourth plebeian, picking up Antony's tone of sarcasm, bursts out: 'They were Traitors: Honourable men?'[76] The second plebeian echoes him, delivering the new verdict that Brutus had above all hoped to avoid: 'They were Villaines, Murderers'.[77] As Antony descends from the public chair to commence his *narratio*, the goodwill towards him is palpable. 'Roome for *Antony*, most Noble *Antony*', demands the second plebeian as he prepares to throw himself into the next and yet more inflammatory section of his speech.[78]

★ ★ ★ ★ ★

If we turn from *Julius Caesar* to *Othello*, the last tragedy I am considering, we find ourselves back in the commonwealth of Venice. The city, however, is far from being the *Serenissima*, the serene republic of self-congratulating myth. As in *The Merchant of Venice*, we are again introduced to a site of anxiety and violent disagreement, in this case with Othello at the heart of it.[79] There is a grave political crisis, and the republic stands in urgent need of Othello's generalship. As even Iago is willing to admit, 'Another of his fathome, they have none/ To leade their businesse'.[80] News has just

---

74. *Julius Caesar*, TLN 1554, p. 692 (3. 2. 161).
75. *Julius Caesar*, TLN 741–2, p. 683 (2. 1. 179–80). For Brutus's deployment here of the figure of *paradiastole* see Skinner 2007.
76. Here and in the next two notes I again preserve First Folio numbering. See Shakespeare 1996, *Julius Caesar*, TLN 1690, p. 730.
77. Shakespeare 1996, *Julius Caesar*, TLN 1692, p. 730.
78. Shakespeare 1996, *Julius Caesar*, TLN 1703, p. 730.
79. On Shakespeare's seemingly disenchanted view of Venice see Platt 2009, esp. pp. 57–93 and Holderness 2010.
80. *Othello*, TLN 155–6, p. 930 (1. 1. 151–2).

reached Venice of a Turkish fleet bearing down on Cyprus, and Othello is summoned to an emergency meeting of the Senate, where the duke immediately informs him that 'we must straite imploy you,/ Against the generall enemy *Ottaman*'.[81] But at the same time Othello has become embroiled in a violent domestic dispute. As we learn in the opening scene, he has eloped with Desdemona, the daughter of Senator Brabantio, and has secretly married her. Confronting Othello on his way to the Senate, Brabantio furiously accuses him of being a foul thief,[82] who has used magical powers to steal his daughter away:

> Judge me the world, if 'tis not grosse in sense,
> That thou hast practis'd on her with foule Charmes,
>
> TLN 259–60, p. 931 (1. 2. 72–3)

Calling for judgement, Brabantio voices his confidence that the duke and Senate will support his cause:

> Mine's not an idle cause, the Duke himselfe,
> Or any of my Brothers of the State,
> Cannot but feele this wrong, as twere their owne.
>
> TLN 282–4, p. 932 (1. 2. 95–7)

When Brabantio arrives with Othello at the meeting of the Senate he immediately reiterates that his daughter has been 'abus'd, stolne from me and corrupted', and stands awaiting the verdict of the duke and the assembled senators.[83]

Othello has little doubt that, in a judicial dispute with Brabantio, he will be able to gain the upper hand. As he has already confided to Iago, in an unflattering reflection on Venetian justice, 'My services which I have done the Seigniorie,/ Shall out tongue his complaints'.[84] Despite his confidence, however, Othello finds himself in what the rhetoricians would regard as a serious judicial predicament, and Iago is likewise of the opinion that Brabantio may well be able to 'gaule him with some checke'.[85] One of his problems is that, as soon as Brabantio repeats before the Senate his accusation that Othello has behaved foully, the duke immediately takes Brabantio's side, without even asking whom he is accusing of the alleged crime. This is one of the moments when Shakespeare closely follows his

---

81. *Othello*, TLN 334–5, p. 932 (1. 3. 48–9).   82. *Othello*, TLN 249, p. 931 (1. 2. 62).
83. *Othello*, TLN 346, p. 933 (1. 3. 60).   84. *Othello*, TLN 204–5, p. 931 (1. 2. 18–19).
85. *Othello*, TLN 151, p. 930 (1. 1. 147).

main source for the scene, the story of Silvanus and Valeria from Barnabe Rich's *Farewell* of 1581.[86] Valeria's father denounces Silvanus for abducting his daughter, and the judge promises that 'hee should have such justice on Silvanus, as himself would require'.[87] The duke, assuming that he is dealing with a similarly foul offence, addresses Brabantio in no less impulsive terms:

> Who ere he be, that in this foule proceeding
> Hath thus beguild your daughter of her selfe,
> And you of her, the bloody booke of Law,
> You shall your selfe, read in the bitter letter,
> After your owne sense, yea, tho our proper sonne
> Stood in your action.
>
> TLN 351–60, p. 933 (1. 3. 65–70)

The rhetorical situation in which Othello finds himself is thus that he is facing a judge who, in the words of the *Ad Herennium*, 'has already been persuaded by those who have spoken on the other side'.[88] Othello may be convinced of the honesty of his cause, and he may also be confident that, once the duke and senators learn who is accused, they will be anxious to acquit him. But for the moment he faces the danger that, in Thomas Wilson's words, 'the adversarie have so tolde his tale that the judge is wholy bent to give sentence with hym'.[89]

There is a yet further dimension to Othello's difficulties. The emergency meeting called by the duke is taking place in the middle of the night, an event so exceptional that Brabantio learns of it with amazement. 'How? The Duke in Councell?/ In this time of the night?'[90] Othello is committed to defending himself on a criminal charge at a moment when the senators, summoned from their beds to deal with an immediate and threatening crisis, are sure to be tired, anxious, and preoccupied. But as the rhetoricians warn, such judges are scarcely less likely to be impatient or even hostile than those who have already been convinced by your adversaries.[91] 'Who seeth

86. For details see Rich 1959, esp. pp. l–lii.   87. Rich 1959, p. 54.
88. *Rhetorica ad Herennium* 1954, I. VI. 9, p. 16: 'persuasus esse . . . ab iis qui ante contra dixerunt'.
89. Wilson 1553, Sig. P, 1ᵛ. Othello's situation is thus comparable to that of Silius in Ben Jonson's *Sejanus*, in which Shakespeare had recently acted (Donaldson 2011, p. 186). Silius is likewise falsely accused before a hostile judge who is also head of state. But whereas Othello responds by showing himself a master of *insinuatio*, Silius refuses any rhetorical help. He simply dismisses his accuser as a liar, denounces Tiberius as an enslaving tyrant and stabs himself to death. See Jonson 1605, Sig. F, 2ʳ–4ʳ.
90. *Othello*, TLN 280–1, p. 932 (1. 2. 93–4).
91. Cicero 1949a, I. XVII. 23, p. 46; *Rhetorica ad Herennium* 1954, I. VI. 9, p. 16; Quintilian 2001, 4. 1. 48, vol. 2, p. 202.

not', as Thomas Wilson says, 'that a weried man will soone mislike a right good matter?'[92]

Othello is thus doubly in need of an insinuative *prohoemium* when he is called upon to explain himself. The moment arrives when Brabantio informs the duke that 'this Moore' is the man whom he is accusing of acting foully.[93] The duke turns at once to Othello—no doubt with considerable shock—and asks: 'What in your owne part can you say to this?'[94] Thus prompted, Othello steps forward to embark on his defence. He knows that, as Quintilian had emphasized, it is important to start 'by addressing yourself above all to those whom you are trying to conciliate',[95] and he duly begins by apostrophizing the duke and senators in flattering and placatory terms:

> Most potent, grave, and reverend Seigniors,
> My very noble and approov'd good maisters:
>
> TLN 362–3, p. 933 (1. 3. 76–7)

Othello thereupon develops an insinuative *prohoemium* in which he follows the classical rules with exemplary care.[96] He is aware that, if your judges have any reason to regard your cause as foul, one way to produce an ingratiating response will be to start by seeming to admit your adversary's charge. He begins by adopting this advice:

> That I have tane away this old mans daughter,
> It is most true:
>
> TLN 364–5, p. 933 (1. 3. 78–9)

Here Shakespeare is again following Rich's story, in which we read that 'the day now being come Silvanus was brought to his answere, hee coulde not deny the fact wherewith he was charged, but that he had stolen Valeria from her father'.[97] Rich, however, simply adds that 'by which confession the lawe

---

92. Wilson 1553, Sig. P, 1^r.   93. *Othello*, TLN 357, p. 933 (1. 3. 71).
94. *Othello*, TLN 360, p. 933 (1. 3. 74).
95. Quintilian 2001, 4. 1. 63, vol. 2, p. 210: 'eos adloquamur potissimum quos conciliare nobis studemus'.
96. For a contrasting analysis of the rhetorical structure of Othello's speech see Plett 2004, pp. 422, 471, and note. Baldwin 1944, vol. 2, p. 199 also discusses the speech, although he mistakenly claims that Othello 'does not need to use an insinuating exordium'. Kennedy 1942, p. 81 (followed by Miola 2000, p. 155) states that Othello's defence is 'from beginning to end, Shakespeare's invention', failing to register that it is organized along classical rhetorical lines. On Shakespeare's debt to classical rhetoric in the scene see Moschovakis 2002, pp. 303–8.
97. Rich 1959, p. 59.

condemned him to die'.[98] Shakespeare by contrast knows that this kind of concession should be made only with a view to showing that, in Cicero's words, 'nothing of the kind pertains to the present case'.[99] Moving beyond Rich's simple narrative, Shakespeare makes Othello continue in just this vein:

> That I have tane away this old mans daughter,
> It is most true: true, I have married her,
> The very head and front of my offending,
> Hath this extent no more.

> TLN 364–7, p. 933 (I. 3. 78–81)

Brabantio's charge is that Othello has bewitched and thereby stolen his daughter. Othello admits that he has taken her away, but denies that this is a case of stealing, since she consented to marry him. Brabantio in his deposition had never mentioned marriage, so that Othello's declaration is the first news that the duke and senators have had of it.[100] His cause already begins to look much less foul than Brabantio has alleged, especially as Othello manages to allude to a well-known formula for describing a *causa turpis* while simultaneously distancing himself from it. Quintilian had characterized a foul cause as one in which the *frons* (translated by Cooper as 'the foreheade: the front'[101]) is not *honesta*.[102] Othello quotes Quintilian's formula (as Claudius had already done in *Hamlet*),[103] referring to the 'head and front of my offending' while adding that his sole offence has been to marry Desdemona, a course of action that can hardly be characterized as lacking in *honestum*.

The rhetoricians have several additional words of advice to offer those whose adversaries may appear to have succeeded in turning the judge against them. One is that they should seek to contrive a general air of doubt and bewilderment. The *Ad Herennium* proposes that 'we should make use of the figure of *dubitatio*, expressing uncertainty about what we can say that will be of the greatest force, or about what point we should first

---

98. Rich 1959, p. 59.
99. Cicero 1949a, I. XVII. 24, p. 48: 'nihil eorum ad te pertinet'. Cf. *Rhetorica ad Herennium* 1954, I. VI. 9, p. 18.
100. Although Brabantio already knows from Roderigo that they are in fact married. See *Othello*, TLN 170–1, p. 930 (I. 1. 166–7).
101. Cooper 1565, Sig. 3G, 1ʳ.   102. Quintilian 2001, 4. 1. 42, vol. 2, p. 200.
103. See *Hamlet*, TLN 2179, p. 759 (3. 3. 63), where he speaks of the 'forhead of our faults'.

attempt to take up, while indicating perplexity and surprise'.[104] Thomas
Wilson strongly agrees about the value of this kind of self-deprecating
approach: 'Begynne so, as though wee doubted what were best firste to
speake, or to what parte it were moste reason firste of all to aunswere,
wonderyng, and takyng GOD to wittenesse at the straungenesse of his
reporte, and confirmacion of his cause.'[105] As Othello continues, he takes
these admonitions very much to heart:

> Rude am I in my speech,
> And little blest with the soft phrase of peace, . . .
> And little of this great world can I speake,
> More then pertaines to feates of broyles, and battaile,
> And therefore little shall I grace my cause,
> In speaking for my selfe;
>
> TLN 367–8, 372–5, p. 933 (1. 3. 81–2, 86–9)

Othello specifically picks up the suggestion that we should use expressions
both of perplexity and uncertainty 'about what we can say that will be of the
greatest force'.[106] He conveys a professed sense of bewilderment as someone
who knows only about military life, and subtly reinforces his claim by the
use of *anaphora*, the figure of repetition, stressing how little is the force with
which he can hope to speak, how little he is blessed with soft phrases, how
little he can hope to grace his cause.

The rhetoricians have some further words of advice for those who, like
Othello, have reason to fear that their judges may in addition be too wearied
and preoccupied to give proper consideration to their case. Perhaps it may
be possible, Cicero suggests, to strike a note of levity; but if that seems out of
place then we should simply speak as briefly as possible.[107] Wilson agrees
that, if our judges 'be almost weried to heare any more', then 'we must
make promise at the first to be very shorte'.[108] The *Ad Herennium* adds that
it will be helpful 'if we also promise to speak in an unprepared style and give

104. *Rhetorica ad Herennium* 1954, I. VI. 10, p. 18: 'dubitatione utemur quid potissimum dicamus
aut cui loco primum respondeamus, cum admiratione'. Cf. Cicero 1949a, I. XVII. 25,
pp. 48–50; Quintilian 2001, 9. 2. 19, vol. 4, p. 44. For the vernacular rhetoricians on *dubitatio*
(or *aporia*) see Sherry 1550, Sig. D, 3ᵛ; Day 1592, p. 89; Peacham 1593, p. 109.
105. Wilson 1553, Sig. P, 1ᵛ.
106. *Rhetorica ad Herennium* 1954, I. VI. 10, p. 18: 'dubitatione utemur quid potissimum dicamus'.
107. Cicero 1949a, I. XVII. 25, p. 50. Cf. Quintilian 2001, 4. 1. 48, vol. 2, p. 202.
108. Wilson 1553, Sig. P, 1ᵛ.

a brief outline of what we plan to say next'.[109] Othello rounds off his *prohoemium* by closely following this advice:

> by your gracious patience,
> I will a round unvarnish'd tale deliver,
> Of my whole course of love, what drugs, what charmes,
> What conjuration, and what mighty Magicke,
> (For such proceeding I am charg'd withal:)
> I wonne his daughter.
>
> TLN 375–80, p. 933 (1. 3. 89–94)

Acknowledging that his judges may be tired, Othello begins by calling on their gracious patience. He then promises to be 'round'—that is, to speak briefly. He also promises an unvarnished tale—that is, to speak in an unprepared style. Finally, he furnishes them with an outline of what he plans to say next. Having started by professing to be rude in his speech, he ends by producing a faultless rhetorical performance.

The principal aim of any *prohoemium* is to win goodwill. How far does Othello succeed? Brabantio remains unmoved, and as soon as Othello finishes he simply repeats his accusation:

> I therefore vouch againe,
> That with some mixtures powerfull ore the blood,
> Or with some dram conjur'd to this effect,
> He wrought upon her.
>
> TLN 389–92, p. 933 (1. 3. 103–6)

Brabantio slightly softens his earlier stance, arguing that Desdemona must have been wrought upon by drugs even if not by witchcraft, but he continues to insist with undiminished vehemence that Othello has behaved foully.

By contrast, the duke now feels able—no doubt with great relief—to take a very different view. Whereas he had previously been ready to accept Brabantio's accusation on trust, he now responds with a stinging rebuke:

> To vouch this is no proofe,
> Without more wider and more overt test,
> Then these thin habits, and poore likelihoods,
> Of moderne seeming, do preferre against him.
>
> TLN 392–5, p. 933 (1. 3. 106–9)

---

109. *Rhetorica ad Herennium* 1954, I. VI. 10, p. 20: 'si promiserimus aliter ac parati fuerimus nos esse dicturos... quid nos facturi simus breviter exponemus'.

Having irritably reprimanded Brabantio for producing no proof, the duke goes on to indicate that Othello's *prohoemium* has succeeded in winning his goodwill. He is now prepared to hear his side of the case, attending to whatever overt tests of his innocence Othello may be able to provide. When Othello declares that he is ready to explain 'How I did thrive in this faire Ladyes love',[110] the duke commands 'Say it *Othello*', formally calling on him to proceed to the *narratio* of his cause.[111]

Introducing a foul cause

The other principal reason for resorting to an insinuative *prohoemium* is that, in the words of the *Ad Herennium*, 'we may have an inherently foul cause to plead, that is, one in which the mind of our audience is rendered hostile to us by the substance of the matter itself.'[112] For example, we may have been party to a crime, or we may have committed a crime ourselves, or we may have agreed to defend an action that is legally or morally reprehensible. If we cannot fail to admit that our cause lacks *honestum* in one of these basic ways, then it will be essential to begin by deploying an insinuative approach. Among the vernacular rhetoricians, Thomas Wilson particularly emphasizes the point. A 'privy begynnyng' is indispensable if we are attempting to introduce a cause in which 'the matter [it]selfe be unhonest, and not meete to be utterd before an audience', or in which 'the matter be so hainouse that it cannot be hearde without offence'.[113]

The earliest work in which Shakespeare places one of his characters in this exigency is his narrative poem *Lucrece*, first published in 1594.[114] Lucrece's husband Collatine has unwisely boasted in Tarquin's hearing about Lucrece's priceless qualities, thereby inflaming the young prince's lust.[115] The narrative that ensues lacks a formal *prohoemium* and begins *in medias res*. (Shakespeare

---

110. *Othello*, TLN 411, p. 933 (1. 3. 125).   111. *Othello*, TLN 412, p. 933 (1. 3. 126).
112. *Rhetorica ad Herennium* 1954, I. VI. 9, p. 16: 'turpem causam habemus, hoc est, cum ipsa res animum auditoris a nobis alienat'.
113. Wilson 1553, Sig. P, 1ʳ.   114. See Shakespeare 1594.
115. On Collatine's boast see Kerrigan 2001, pp. 43–8. Collatine's fatally proprietorial attitude towards Lucrece has sparked feminist readings of the poem. For a discussion and bibliography see Roe 2006, pp. 32–4.

himself speaks of the poem as 'without beginning'.)[116] Tarquin rides to Collatium, where Lucrece welcomes him unsuspectingly as her husband's friend. They converse for a long while, after which Lucrece retires to her rest. When midnight comes, Tarquin seeks out her chamber, threatens her with instant death if she will not yield to his desires, violently rapes her, and steals away unseen.

As he contemplates his deed, even Tarquin cannot fail to acknowledge that it is a foul crime:

> O shame to knighthood, and to shining Armes,
> O foule dishonor to my houshoulds grave:
> O impious act including all foule harmes.
>
> TLN 197–9, p. 273 (p. 161)

The narrator of the poem likewise excoriates the foulness of Tarquin's deed. He is said to have foul thoughts, a foul appetite, and his behaviour is compared with that of a foul usurper.[117] He is finally dismissed as no better than a 'fowle night-waking Cat'.[118]

In one of Lucrece's most rhetorically charged passages she similarly berates Tarquin for his foulness. When he enters her chamber and makes his violent intentions clear, she responds by warning him of the dangerous consequences he will suffer in his future position as king of Rome if he acts so foully:

> This deede will make thee only lov'd for feare,
> But happie Monarchs still are feard for love:
> With fowle offendors thou perforce must beare,
> When they in thee the like offences prove; . . .
>
> Thy Princelie office how canst thou fulfill?
>   When patternd by thy fault fowle sin may say,
>   He learnd to sin, and thou didst teach the way.
>
> TLN 610–13, 628–30, p. 277 (pp. 181, 182)

Here Lucrece speaks, with her habitual soaring eloquence, in the *genus deliberativum*, and in doing so appropriates the distinctively male voice of a royal counsellor advising a prince.[119] But even her authoritatively masculine tone is of no avail in saving her from Tarquin's violence.[120]

---

116. *Lucrece*, Dedication, p. 270 (p. 148).
117. *Lucrece*, TLN 346, 412, 546, pp. 274, 275, 276 (pp. 168, 172, 178).
118. *Lucrece*, TLN 554, p. 276 (p. 178).
119. See Burrow 2002, pp. 50–3, a discussion to which I am much indebted.
120. On the ambiguities of Lucrece's masculine language see Berry 1992.

While Tarquin's deed is unquestionably foul, this very characterization creates for Lucrece a grave moral difficulty, since she feels so deeply implicated in it. Neither Lucrece nor Shakespeare seems altogether sure about the extent to which she can justly be accused of complicity,[121] but Lucrece is frequently made to speak in tragically unequivocal terms. She refers to her trespass, her infamy, and her cureless crime,[122] and when thinking of its consequences for Collatine she pronounces herself 'guiltie of thy Honors wracke' and reflects on her 'violated troth'.[123] When she resolves to tell him what has happened, she goes on to speak of her fault and her sin:

> I will not poyson thee with my attaint,
> Nor fold my fault in cleanly coin'd excuses,
> My sable ground of sinne I will not paint,
> To hide the truth of this false nights abuses.
>
> TLN 1072–5, p. 282 (pp. 202–3)

Lucrece's rhetorical dilemma is thus that, in seeking to defend herself, she feels that she will be speaking as a disloyal and unworthy wife, and hence in a foul cause.[124]

Lucrece is thus committed, as the rhetoricians would say, to putting forward a merely assumptive argument in a juridical cause.[125] The question at issue is undoubtedly a juridical one.[126] To cite Thomas Wilson, it is a 'state Juridicall' when 'a deede is well knowen to be doen' and when we ask 'whether it be right, or wrong'.[127] There is no dispute about what has been done. As Lucrece prepares to deliver the *prohoemium* of her confession, the narrator presents us with an unambiguous summary of her case. We are told that what she is about 'to let them know' is that 'Her Honor is tane prisoner by the Foe'.[128] But this in turn means that her cause is merely assumptive. We are dealing with 'the state assumptive', as Thomas Wilson explains, when it is agreed that something has been 'wrongfully doen'.[129] The evil in

121. On the problem of consent in *Lucrece* see Burrow 2002, pp. 66–73; Roe 2006, pp. 23–31.
122. *Lucrece*, TLN 772, 1025, 1070, pp. 278, 281 (pp. 188, 200, 202).
123. *Lucrece*, TLN 841, 1059, pp. 279, 281 (pp. 192, 202).
124. *Lucrece*, TLN 1048–9, 1304, pp. 281, 284 (pp. 201, 213).
125. On Lucrece's rhetorical situation see Dubrow 1987, Weaver 2008, and Weaver 2012. Although my reading differs from Weaver's, I am greatly indebted to both his accounts.
126. *Rhetorica ad Herennium* 1954, I. XIV. 24, p. 42. Cf. Cicero 1949a, I. XI. 14–15, p. 30; Quintilian 2001, 7. 4. 4 and 7, vol. 3, pp. 238–40.
127. Wilson 1553, Sig. O, 1ᵛ.   128. *Lucrece*, TLN 1607–8, p. 287 (p. 227).
129. Wilson 1553, Sig. O, 1ᵛ.

this case is not merely that a stranger has lain on Lucrece's bed and that 'what wrong else may be imagined' has taken place.[130] Lucrece additionally fears that she may have done wrong herself, and in one of her recurrent moments of desperate ambiguity she refers to 'this wrong of mine'.[131]

If you admit that you have perpetrated or abetted a crime, and thus that your cause is merely assumptive, you will be left with no firm legal defence.[132] Your only hope will be to try to add some extraneous considerations that may somehow lend substance to your case. From the moment of her violation Lucrece recognizes this difficulty. She rails against the impossibility of entering a legal plea, and hence against the uselessness of words to furnish her with help:

> Out idle wordes, servants to shallow fooles,
> Unprofitable sounds, weake arbitrators,
> Busie your selves in skill contending schooles,
> Debate where leysure serves with dull debators:
> To trembling Clients be you mediators,
>   For me, I force not argument a straw,
>   Since that my case is past the helpe of law.
>
> TLN 1016–22, p. 281 (p. 200)

Here Lucrece explicitly accepts that her cause is merely assumptive. She has no hope of appealing to the law, no chance of enforcing a legally persuasive argument.

According to the rhetoricians, there is only one course of action to adopt in such circumstances. You must open your speech with an explicit acknowledgement of your offence.[133] As Thomas Wilson puts it, you must start with a 'grauntyng of the faulte committed'.[134] The *prohoemium* of Lucrece's oration to Collatine and his attendant lords accordingly takes the form of just such a self-consciously brief *concessio* in which she describes what happened and laments the trespass at the same time:

> Few words (quoth shee) shall fit the trespasse best,
> Where no excuse can give the fault amending.
> In me moe woes then words are now depending,

---

130. *Lucrece*, TLN 1620–22, p. 287 (p. 227).   131. *Lucrece*, TLN 1691, p. 288 (p. 230).
132. See *Rhetorica ad Herennium* 1954, I. XIV. 24, p. 44 on how your defence will be *infirma* in such a case. See also Cicero 1949a, I. XI. 15, p. 30.
133. On the *concessio* see *Rhetorica ad Herennium* 1954, I. XIV. 24, p. 44; Cicero 1949a, I. XI. 15, p. 30.
134. Wilson 1553, Sig. O, 2ʳ.

> And my laments would be drawn out too long,
> To tell them all with one poore tired tong.
>
> Then be this all the taske it hath to say,
> Deare husband in the interest of thy bed
> A stranger came, and on that pillow lay,
> Where thou wast wont to rest thy wearie head,
>
> TLN 1613–21, p. 287 (p. 227)

Using the same terminology as Thomas Wilson, Lucrece explicitly speaks of her fault and accepts that no excuse can amend it.

Lucrece's predicament is a grave one, but the rhetoricians are by no means willing to concede that there is nothing further to be said. As we saw in Chapter 1, some comfort may be gained from the fact that you can hope to develop a *concessio* in one of two ways. It is true that, in the worst case, you may be obliged to present it in the form of a *deprecatio*, a straightforward plea for compassion and clemency.[135] Such an entreaty will be your only option if you are forced to admit not merely that you have been involved in a crime, but that you acted *cum consulto*, with full intention and foresight of the consequences.[136] As the rhetoricians acknowledge, however, this is in effect to concede that your cause is legally hopeless. Cicero warns that such petitions almost never have any prospect of success, to which the *Ad Herennium* adds that generally it is not even possible to gain a hearing for them in court.[137] More encouragingly, however, they advise that sometimes you may instead be able to enter your *concessio* in the form of a *purgatio*. To speak of a *purgatio*, according to Thomas Cooper's *Thesaurus*, is to refer at once to an excuse and an act of cleansing,[138] and hence to wiping away the stain of a crime. When you enter such a plea, you will be contending that, although you were party to a foul offence, you did not act *cum consulto*, with any deliberate intent, in consequence of which the stain can be purged and wiped away.[139] As

---

135. On pity or compassion (*misericordia*) see *Rhetorica ad Herennium* 1954, I. XIV. 24, p. 46; on *misericordia* and the resulting possibility of clemency (*clementia*) see Quintilian 2001, 7. 4. 18–19, vol. 3, p. 246. See also Wilson 1553, Sig. O, 2^r.
136. *Rhetorica ad Herennium* 1954, I. XIV. 24, p. 46; Cicero 1949a, I. XI. 15, p. 30.
137. Cicero 1949a, I. XI. 15, p. 30; *Rhetorica ad Herennium* 1954, I. XIV. 24, p. 46 and II. XVII. 26, p. 104. Writing under the Empire rather than under the Republic, Quintilian is more sanguine, noting that such pleas for clemency can always be addressed to the emperor himself. See Quintilian 2001, 7. 4. 18, vol. 3, p. 246.
138. Cooper 1565, Sig. 5K, 5^r.
139. *Rhetorica ad Herennium* 1954, I. XIV. 24, p. 44: 'Purgatio est cum consulto negat se reus fecisse.'

Cicero summarizes, 'it is an act of purgation when the fact is admitted but culpability is denied'.[140]

There are three different ways in which you may be able to argue that you did not act *cum consulto*, and hence that you deserve to be excused. As the *Ad Herennium* puts it, you can plead that you acted out of necessity, or out of ignorance, or that the crime occurred by chance.[141] Cicero adds that, if you enter a plea of *necessitudo*, you will need to assert that 'the accused can be defended on the grounds that what they did was done in consequence of some external force'.[142] This is the defence that Lucrece proceeds to mount:

> Deare husband in the interest of thy bed
> A stranger came, and on that pillow lay,
> Where thou wast wont to rest thy wearie head,
> And what wrong else may be imagined,
>   By foule inforcement might be done to me,
>   From that (alas) thy LUCRECE is not free.
>
> TLN 1619–24, p. 287 (p. 227)

While acknowledging that an offence took place, Lucrece insists that she was compelled by external force and thus by foul enforcement to act against her will.

With the presentation of this *purgatio* Lucrece opens up for herself a further line of defence. After entering such a plea of duress, she can hope to offer a *confirmatio* of her allegation and fully purge the stain of her crime. She cries out for the necessary rhetorical powers: 'O teach me how to make mine owne excuse'.[143] She also pleads to be shown how to mount such a defence: 'How may this forced staine be wip'd from me?'[144] As she contemplates her answer, she has no need of a formal *narratio*, since the facts are not in dispute. She is ready to proceed directly to her attempted *confirmatio* of her cause. Like Collatine and his attendant lords, who 'With sad attention long to heare her words',[145] we wait to see how persuasive a case she can hope to produce.

★ ★ ★ ★ ★

The other Shakespearean heroine who finds herself committed to presenting an assumptive plea in a juridical cause is Isabella in Act 2 of *Measure*

---

140. Cicero 1949a, I. XI. 15, p. 30: 'Purgatio est cum factum conceditur, culpa removetur.'
141. *Rhetorica ad Herennium* 1954, I. XIV. 24, p. 44 and II. XVI. 23, p. 100. See also Cicero 1949a, I. XI. 15, p. 30, and II. XXXI. 94, p. 260; Quintilian 2001, 7. 4. 14–15, vol. 3, p. 244.
142. Cicero 1949a, II. XXXII. 98, p. 264: 'vi quadam reus id quod fecerit fecisse defenditur'.
143. *Lucrece*, TLN 1653, p. 287 (p. 229).   144. *Lucrece*, TLN 1701, p. 288 (p. 231).
145. *Lucrece*, TLN 1610, p. 287 (p. 227).

for Measure. Again the salient facts are not in doubt. Juliet, betrothed to Isabella's brother Claudio, has become pregnant in advance of their intended marriage. Nor is the evaluation of the facts in dispute. According to Angelo, in whose hands the evaluation lies, they point to a capital offence. Escalus pleads for mercy, but Angelo's final judgement is that Claudio has committed a 'foule wrong' and that in the name of justice 'he must dye'.[146] When Isabella accedes to her brother's request that she intercede with Angelo, she accordingly finds herself speaking in a foul cause. Still worse, as she confesses to Angelo, she finds herself attempting to win pardon for a crime that stems from 'a vice that most I doe abhorre'.[147]

Isabella's situation resembles that of Lucrece, but rhetorically she is in even graver difficulties. Unlike Lucrece, she has no prospect of being able to develop a *purgatio*, admitting her brother's crime while arguing that he did not act *cum consulto* and therefore deserves to be excused. Claudio and Juliet are both ready to admit that they acted willingly. When Claudio informs Lucio that he has been condemned, he emphasizes that his relationship with Juliet is grounded on 'most mutuall entertainment'.[148] When Juliet makes her confession to Friar Lodowick (the duke in disguise), and when he asks her whether 'your most offence full act/ Was mutually committed', she simply replies 'Mutually', thereby endorsing Claudio's account.[149]

This is the point at which the rhetoricians sometimes seem ready to give up. If your cause is so unambiguously foul, Quintilian warns, then any direct attempt to solicit the attention and goodwill of your judge will be impossible.[150] Thomas Wilson draws the inference that this may be the moment at which the art of rhetoric ceases to be of any use. If, as he says, you find yourself attempting to defend someone whose conduct is 'so hainouse that it cannot be hearde without offence', then your wisest decision may simply be 'to lette hym go'. The same applies in the case of a cause that is 'thought not honest'. The right course of action may be 'to take some other in stede therof which were better lyked', whatever may be the truth of the matter involved.[151]

146. *Measure for Measure*, TLN 437, 788, pp. 899, 903 (2. 1. 31, 2. 2. 106).
147. *Measure for Measure*, TLN 712, p. 902 (2. 2. 30).
148. *Measure for Measure*, TLN 197, 223, p. 897. (1. 2. 107, 135).
149. *Measure for Measure*, TLN 903–4, p. 904 (2. 3. 26–7).
150. Quintilian 2001, 4. 1. 42, vol. 2, p. 200: 'in turpi causae genere non possit'.
151. Wilson 1553, Sig. P, 1ʳ.

There is only one piece of advice that these writers feel able to give. If you have no hope of developing a *purgatio*, then you must simply plead for mercy with as much eloquence as you can summon up. As Quintilian puts it, 'the judge's mind needs to be agitated with expressions of hope and fear, with entreaty and prayers, and even with falsehoods if you believe they will be of any help.'[152] Thomas Wilson strongly underlines the point:

> If the cause be lothsome, or suche as will not be well borne withall, but nedeth muche helpe, and favour of the hearers: it shalbe the speakers parte, prively to get favour, and by humble talke, to wynne their good willes. Firste, requiryng theim to geve him the hearing, and next, not streightly to geve judgement, but with mercie to mitigate, all rigor of the Lawe.[153]

More circumstantial than Quintilian, Wilson envisages a *prohoemium* in which we begin with a humble demand for a hearing and end by begging for mercy in place of the strict letter of the law.

The figure of Cassandra in George Whetsone's *Promos and Cassandra* closely follows this advice, and in pleading for the life of her brother Promos she limits herself to just such a *deprecatio*.[154] Shakespeare, by contrast, follows the less pessimistic assessment that the earlier Roman rhetoricians had given of this type of predicament, and draws on two resourceful suggestions that Cicero and the author of the *Ad Herennium* had made about how to cope with it. First they had advised that, after a modest and humble opening, we should begin by assuring our judge 'that we do not in the least find acceptable what has been done, and that we too find it shameful and detestable'.[155] This is how Isabella introduces her case, speaking so forcefully that Shakespeare's original audience would have been likely to experience her reaction as unnecessarily severe:[156]

> ISABELLA   I am a wofull Sutor to your Honour,
> 'Please but your Honor heare me.

---

152. Quintilian 2001, 4. 1. 33, vol. 2, p. 194: 'cuius animus spe metu admonitione precibus, vanitate denique, si id profuturum credimus agitandus est'.
153. Wilson 1553, Sig. O, 3^{r-v}.
154. See Whetstone 1578, Sig B, 6^v to Sig. C, 1^r.
155. *Rhetorica ad Herennium* 1954, I. VI. 9, pp. 16–18: 'non placere nobis ipsis quae facta . . . et esse indigna aut nefaria.' Cf. Cicero 1949a, I. XVII. 24, p. 48.
156. Helmholz 1987, pp. 145–55 notes that the long-standing practice of the English church courts in cases of admitted fornication was simply to require the parties either to abjure one another or to contract a conditional marriage. Isabella's expression of abhorrence would therefore have sounded harsh.

ANGELO   Well: what's your suite.
ISABELLA   There is a vice that most I doe abhorre,
And most desire should meet the blow of Justice;
For which I would not plead, but that I must,
For which I must not plead, but that I am
At warre, twixt will, and will not.

> TLN 710–16, p. 902 (2. 2. 28–34)

Critics have sometimes dismissed this speech as 'an awkward preamble' that is 'hesitant and diffident' and amounts to little more than a 'labyrinth of contradictions'.[157] Isabella's words have even been taken to indicate that she 'has not yet learned to use the tools of rhetoric'.[158] But in fact she is using the relevant tools with exemplary skill and a mere pretence of diffidence. She knows to acknowledge the seeming contradiction, admitting that she intends to speak in favour of what she regards as an abhorrent cause. But at the same time she adopts the advice of the *Ad Herennium* and makes it as clear as possible—by her use of *anaphora*, the figure of repetition—that she is far from condoning her brother's sin. Not only does she assure Angelo that she desires the axe of justice to fall, but she goes much further than the *Ad Herennium* had recommended and berates herself for supporting a cause that she ought not to have espoused.

As we have seen, Cicero proposes a second line of argument to which we can also appeal if, as he puts it, 'the foulness of our cause gives rise to offence'.[159] 'We should try to substitute a consideration of the person who committed the crime for the crime itself, or the crime itself in place of the person who committed it', depending on which alternative seems to furnish the better chance of 'shifting the minds of our hearers away from what they dislike and in the direction of what they approve'.[160] This is how Isabella continues:

I have a brother is condemn'd to die,
I doe beseech you let it be his fault,
And not my brother.

> TLN 717–19, p. 902 (2. 2. 35–7)

---

157. Ross 1997, p. 60; McNeely 2004, p. 213; Kamaralli 2005, p. 53.
158. Kliman 1982, p. 137.
159. Cicero 1949a, I. XVII. 24, p. 48: 'Si causae turpitudo contrahit offensionem.'
160. Cicero 1949a, I. XVII. 24, p. 48: 'interponi oportet . . . aut pro re hominem aut pro homine rem, ut ab eo quod odit ad id quod diligit auditoris animus traducatur'. Compare *Rhetorica ad Herennium* 1954, I. VI. 9, p. 16. There is also a hint of this argument in Quintilian 2001, 4. 1. 44, vol. 2, p. 200.

Here the critics have tended to see in Isabella's request a simple appeal for mercy,[161] but rhetorically her plea is at once more precise and more complicated. She is following Cicero's advice to the letter, asking Angelo to focus on the crime itself, not on her brother, with the implication that her brother can perhaps be excused even if the crime be condemned.

The figure of the Provost, who is present at Isabella's interview, now urges her to pursue her advantage: 'Heaven give thee moving graces'.[162] Angelo, however, is wholly unmoved and responds indignantly:

> Condemne the fault, and not the actor of it,
> Why every fault's condemnd ere it be done:
> Mine were the verie Cipher of a Function
> To fine the faults, whose fine stands in record,
> And let goe by the Actor.
>
> TLN 720–4, p. 902 (2. 2. 38–42)

On receiving this rebuff Isabella simply decides to abandon her case. 'Oh just, but severe Law', she replies, adding 'I had a brother then; heaven keepe your honour'.[163] And with these words she prepares to take her leave.

Isabella may be ready to give up, but Claudio's friend Lucio, who has accompanied her to the interview, forcefully reminds her that she can still hope to develop a *deprecatio*. She can still attempt, in Quintilian's words, to mount a heated emotional appeal to the judge, 'whose mind needs to be agitated with prayers and entreaties and with expressions of hope and fear'.[164] This is the course of action that Lucio now vigorously recommends, and in almost explicitly sexualized terms:

> Give 't not ore so: to him againe, entreat him,
> Kneele downe before him, hang upon his gowne,
> You are too cold:
>
> TLN 726–8, p. 902 (2. 2. 44–6)

Despite the suggestiveness of Lucio's language, Isabella is quick to adopt his advice.[165] Not only does she begin to plead passionately with Angelo, but she takes up Thomas Wilson's specific suggestion that we should petition

161. See, for example, Crider 2009, pp. 129–30.
162. *Measure for Measure*, TLN 719, p. 902 (2. 2. 37).
163. *Measure for Measure*, TLN 724–5, p. 902 (2. 2. 42–3).
164. Quintilian 2001, 4. 1. 33, vol. 2, p. 194: 'cuius animus spe metu admonitione precibus... agitandus est'.
165. Hillman 1993, pp. 100–1 examines how Lucio lends this passage an erotic tone.

our judge 'not streightly to geve iudgement, but with mercie to mitigate, all rigor of the Lawe'.[166]

> ISABELLA (*to Angelo*) Must he needs die?
> ANGELO Maiden, no remedie.
> ISABELLA Yes: I doe thinke that you might pardon him,
> And neither heaven, nor man grieve at the mercy.
> ANGELO I will not doe't.
> ISABELLA   But can you if you would?
> ANGELO Looke what I will not, that I cannot doe.
> ISABELLA But might you doe't & do the world no wrong
> If so your heart were touch'd with that remorse,
> As mine is to him?
> ANGELO Hee's sentenc'd, tis too late.
>
>   TLN 731–40, p. 902 (2. 2. 49–56)

Isabella knows to make repeated entreaties for mercy, but Angelo remains unmoved, and at the end of their exchange Lucio feels driven to exclaim again 'You are too cold'.[167]

It is hard for Isabella to go further. She has already made use of all the arguments put forward by the rhetoricians, reinforcing them in highly ornamented verse that stands in stark contrast to the prose of the previous scene. Nor can she hope to proceed to a *narratio* in which she articulates Claudio's side of the case, since everyone accepts that he is guilty as charged. According to the rhetoricians, this leaves her with only one possibility. She must continue, as Quintilian had recommended, to plead with her judge in a still more extended and still more passionate *deprecatio*. She must do all she can to move and agitate his mind in the hope of eventually prompting him to show mercy instead of imposing the full rigour of the law.

This is accordingly how Isabella proceeds throughout the rest of the scene, making four speeches of mounting intensity about the quality of mercy, culminating in her denunciation of proud men dressed in a little brief authority whose lack of compassion makes the angels weep.[168] There is a sense in which this exceptionally elaborate *deprecatio*, together with the *prohoemium* from which it flows, prove to be a complete rhetorical success.

---

166. Wilson 1553, Sig. Q, 3[r–v].   167. *Measure for Measure*, TLN 741, p. 902 (2. 2. 57).
168. For an analysis of Isabella's *deprecatio*, seen as embodying eight stages, see Joseph 1947, pp. 232–3. On its theological orientation see Gless 1979, pp. 106–14.

Isabella finally succeeds in winning Angelo's attention and responsiveness, and
he ends by promising to see her again on the following day and meanwhile
to give further consideration to her case. But there is a sense in which
Isabella's eloquence succeeds only too well. She ends by attracting not
merely Angelo's goodwill but his instant infatuation, which declares itself
at their next meeting in the form of his proposal that he will spare Claudio's
life if, as he demands, she will yield her body to his will. As so often,
Shakespeare leaves us to ponder the symmetry he has contrived. The
scene opens with Isabella pleading in a foul cause, and closes with Angelo
asking himself in soliloquy: 'Dost thou desire her fowly?'[169]

By way of rounding off, it is worth recalling the one other moment in the
plays I am considering when a character puts forward what he describes as a
suit, while freely admitting that he has no legal case to argue and can only
offer a *deprecatio*.[170] The play is *All's Well That Ends Well*, and the moment
arrives when the king makes his closing speech to Hellen and the play comes
to an end. The king then steps forward—now out of character, as he assures
us—to pronounce an Epilogue:[171]

> *The Kings a Beggar, now the Play is done,*
> *All is well ended, if this suite be wonne,*
> *That you expresse Content: which we will pay,*
> *With strift to please you, day exceeding day:*
> *Ours be your patience then, and yours our parts,*
> *Your gentle hands lend us, and take our hearts.*
>
> TLN 2855–60, p. 998 (Epilogue, 1–6)

With the conclusion of the play, the king is reduced to a beggar in more
senses than one. He is no longer a rich monarch but a poor player, but he is
also a supplicant with something to beg from the playgoers. Speaking on
behalf of the company, he has no argument to expound in support of
their suit, save for a promise that they will daily strive to win the goodwill
of their audience.[172] Meanwhile he simply throws himself on their mercy,

---

169. *Measure for Measure*, TLN 862, p. 904 (2. 2. 178).
170. But if we count the play within the play in *Hamlet*, then there is one other example, that of
the *deprecatio* pronounced by the Prologue at the outset: 'For us and for our Tragedie,/ Heere
stooping to your clemencie,/ We begge your hearing patiently.' See *Hamlet*, TLN 1870–2,
p. 756 (3. 2. 130–2).
171. On the function of such epilogues see Munro 2005, p. 164.
172. Shakespeare is echoing the closing Chorus of *Twelfe Night*: '*But that's all one, our Play is done,/
And wee'l strive to please you every day*'. See *Twelfe Night*, TLN 2502–3, p. 805. (5. 1. 384–5).

begging that they will show their contentment by exchanging roles. The company will take their turn to listen patiently while the members of the audience play the parts of men and women sufficiently happy to express their appreciation with applause.

★ ★ ★ ★ ★

Of all Shakespeare's forensic plays, *Othello* is the one in which the pivotal categories of 'foul' and 'honest' are given their greatest prominence. Iago repeatedly commends himself to Othello as someone who is 'direct and honest' and motivated by 'honesty and love'.[173] Othello in turn commends Iago's honesty to everyone: to the duke of Venice as a man 'of honesty and trust', to Cassio as 'most honest' and to Desdemona as 'honest *Iago*'.[174] But as Iago confesses to Roderigo, his outward demeanour stands in terrible contrast with the figure of his heart.[175] He is in fact engaged in what he himself admits to be a plot of black sinfulness.[176] He plans to present Othello with a *narratio* in which he will claim that Desdemona has been having an adulterous affair with Cassio, after which he will provide Othello with a purported *confirmatio* of his alleged conjecture, thereby making a net, as he says, that will enmesh them all.[177] First he moves to ensnare Desdemona, assuring Othello that he sees in her conduct 'Foule disproportions: thoughts unnaturall'.[178] Next he persuades Othello that Desdemona has indeed behaved foully, thereby swinging him around, as Cicero would say, to share his point of view:

> OTHELLO I will chop her into messes—Cuckold me!
> IAGO O tis foule in her.
> OTHELLO With mine Officer.
> IAGO That's fouler.
>
> *Othello*, TLN 2323–6, p. 954 (4. 1. 188–91)

Othello is finally left echoing Iago's slanders, exclaiming 'O she was foule' even at the moment when Iago's wife Emilia is laying before him the evidence that he has been fatally deceived.[179]

---

173. *Othello*, TLN 1830, 1864, pp. 948, 949 (3. 3. 379, 413).
174. *Othello*, TLN 570, 1011, 2976, pp. 935, 939, 962 (1. 3. 280; 2. 3. 6; 5. 2. 73). On Iago's 'honesty' (a claim repeated fifteen times in the play) see Keller 2009, p. 170. Empson 1979, pp. 218–49 surveys the uses of 'honest' in the play, although without noting the rhetorical apposition of honest/foul.
175. *Othello*, TLN 61–2, p. 929 (1. 1. 62–3).   176. *Othello*, TLN 1351, p. 943 (2. 3. 318).
177. *Othello*, TLN 1361–2, p. 943 (2. 3. 328–9).
178. *Othello*, TLN 1686, p. 947 (3. 3. 235).
179. *Othello*, TLN 3104, p. 964 (5. 2. 199).

To initiate his plot, Iago is doubly committed to beginning with the most oblique and cunning *prohoemium* he can contrive. One reason why he needs such an *insinuatio* is that his cause is inherently as foul as possible, based as it is on a claim that he knows to be both cruel and false. He almost confesses the foulness to Othello: 'Utter my thoughts? Why, say they are vile and false:/ As where's that pallace, whereinto foule things/ Sometimes intrude not?'[180] But a further reason for starting with an *insinuatio* is that—as Iago rightly anticipates—as soon as he offers Othello any hint of his accusation that Desdemona may have been unfaithful, he will find himself facing a hostile judge. As he acknowledges in soliloquy, Othello is so much enslaved by his passion for Desdemona that he will be reluctant, at least initially, to believe any ill of her.[181] Iago's first task is therefore to introduce his accusation in such a way as to offset any anger and resistance that he may at first arouse, gradually attempting to win Othello's attention, responsiveness, and good-will before turning to his wholly mendacious narrative.[182]

Shakespeare's handling of the scene in which Iago begins to unveil his plot diverges markedly from his principal source. He relies for the outline of his story on the seventh novella in the third decade of Giraldi Cinthio's *Gli Hecatommithi*, first published in Venice in 1565 and translated into French by Gabriel Chappuys in 1584.[183] The villain in Cinthio's novella is an ensign in the service of a Moorish captain employed by the republic of Venice.[184] The ensign makes advances to the general's wife, Disdemona, but she is entirely devoted to the Moor and gives no thought 'to the Ensign or anybody else'.[185] He decides in revenge to accuse her of committing adultery with the Moor's corporal, 'who was very dear to the Moor'.[186] When the corporal is deprived of his rank for a misdemeanour, Disdemona petitions her husband to reinstate him. Cinthio tells us that the ensign 'saw in this a hint for setting in train the deceit he had planned'. Perhaps, he puts it to the Moor, Disdemona 'has good cause to look on him so favourably'. When the Moor asks why this might be so, the ensign replies that 'if you keep your eyes open you will see for yourself'.[187]

---

180. *Othello*, TLN 1589–91, p. 946 (3. 3. 137–9).
181. *Othello*, TLN 1345–6, p. 943 (2. 3. 312–13).
182. For a contrasting analysis of the ensuing scene see Plett 2004, pp. 464–70.
183. Bullough 1957–75, vol. 7, p. 194.
184. On Giraldi's version of the Moor's character see Attar 2011.
185. Bullough 1957–75, vol. 7, p. 244. I quote from the translation of Cinthio's story (made from the Italian edition of 1566) in Bullough 1957–75, vol. 7, pp. 239–52.
186. Bullough 1957–75, vol. 7, p. 243.   187. Bullough 1957–75, vol. 7, p. 244.

By contrast with this blunt and straightforward dialogue, Shakespeare closely follows the advice given by the classical rhetoricians about how to develop an insinuative *prohoemium*, and makes Iago broach the subject of Desdemona's possible infatuation with Cassio in a much more involuted and circuitous style. Iago begins, ironically enough, by deploying the technique that Othello had put to such effective use in responding to Brabantio. Othello had adopted the suggestion that, in constructing an *insinuatio*, it may be helpful to invoke the figure of *dubitatio*, expressing uncertainty and contriving an air of surprise.[188] As soon as Iago enters at the start of the fatal scene in Act 3, he begins to speak in just such a style of feigned perplexity and doubt.

When Iago appears, Cassio has been pleading with Desdemona to intercede for him with Othello. Seeing Othello with Iago, Cassio feels too uneasy to meet him after his recent dismissal and immediately takes his leave. As he slips away, Iago sees his chance:

> IAGO Ha, I like not that.
> OTHELLO What doest thou say?
> IAGO Nothing my Lord, or if, I know not what.[189]
>
> *Othello*, TLN 1481–3, p. 944 (3. 3. 35–6)

With his 'or if . . . ' and his failure to complete the sentence, Iago calls on the figure of *aposeopesis* to convey the recommended tone of stammering doubt.[190] According to Dudley Fenner, 'aposeopesis is when the course of the sentence begun is so stayed, as thereby some part of the sentence not being uttered, may be understood'.[191] The power of the device, George Puttenham explains, stems from giving the impression, when we 'breake off in the middle way' that 'we were ashamed, or afraide to speake it out'.[192] We can even hope, Henry Peacham adds, to leave 'the venome of some false suspicion behind'.[193]

---

188. *Rhetorica ad Herennium* 1954, I. VI. 10, p. 18. Cf. Cicero 1949a, I. XVII. 25, pp. 48–50.
189. For a contrasting reading see Altman 2010, pp. 217–18.
190. For the classical rhetoricians on *aposeopesis*, see *Rhetorica ad Herennium* 1954, IV. XXX. 41, p. 330 (where it is labelled *praecisio*) and Quintilian 2001, 9. 2. 54–5, vol. 4, pp. 64–6.
191. Fenner 1584, Sig. D, 4ᵛ.   192. [Puttenham] 1589, p. 139.
193. Peacham 1593, p. 118. On *aposeopesis* see also Peacham 1577, Sig. N, 1ᵛ; Fraunce 1588a, Sig. F, 6ᵛ; Day 1592, p. 81.

So successful is Iago at implanting a false suspicion that some critics have seen in his 'if' the fulcrum of the play.[194] As he continues with his conversation the venom begins to take effect:

> OTHELLO Was not that *Cassio* parted from my wife?
> IAGO *Cassio* my Lord?—no sure, I cannot thinke it,
> That he would steale away so guilty-like,
> Seeing your comming.

> TLN 1484–7, p. 944 (3. 3. 37–40)

Reacting to Othello's air of suspicion, Iago seeks to intensify it by his use of *paralepsis*, the technique by which a speaker (in Henry Peacham's words) 'maketh as though he would say nothing in some matter, when notwithstanding he speaketh most of all'.[195] Iago seems to reassure Othello, but contrives to insinuate that Cassio was indeed stealing away, and was doing so with guilt rather than embarrassment.

Iago is interrupted at this juncture by Desdemona, who pleads with Othello to call Cassio back and offer him some reconciling words. Othello asks her to leave, at which point Iago recaptures Othello's attention and resumes his *prohoemium*.[196] He now deploys a technique particularly recommended by the author of the *Ad Herennium* for use when we need to proceed insinuatingly. 'We should deny', he advises, 'that we shall say anything against our adversaries or anything else, but we should make use of an interjection of words in such a way as to manage to do so surreptitiously.'[197] Iago proceeds to follow this advice:

> IAGO Did *Michael Cassio* when you wooed my Lady,
> Know of your love?
> OTHELLO He did from first to last:—Why doest thou aske?
> IAGO But for a satisfaction of my thought.
> No further harme.

> TLN 1544–8, p. 945 (3. 3. 93–7)

---

194. See, for example, Doran 1976, pp. 63–4, 79–81; Melchiori 1981, p. 64; Serpieri 2002, pp. 143–4.
195. Peacham 1593, p. 130.
196. On the elocutionary devices in this passage see Plett 2004, p. 459.
197. *Rhetorica ad Herennium* 1954, I. VI. 9, p. 18: 'negabimus nos de adversariis aut de aliqua re dicturos, et tamen occulte dicemus interiectione verborum'.

Iago insists that he means no harm, but with his admission that Cassio's relationship with Desdemona has provoked him to thought he makes a further use of *paralepsis* to insinuate that there may be more to be said.

Othello's attention is immediately caught: 'Why of thy thought *Iago*?'[198] By way of reply, Iago makes a series of surreptitious interjections of just the kind that the *Ad Herennium* had recommended:

> IAGO I did not thinke he had beene acquainted with her.
> OTHELLO O yes, and went betweene us very oft.
> IAGO Indeed?
> OTHELLO Indeed? I indeed, disern'st thou ought in that?
> Is he not honest?
> IAGO Honest my Lord?
> OTHELLO Honest? I honest.
> IAGO My Lord, for ought I know.
> OTHELLO   What doest thou thinke?
> IAGO Thinke my Lord?
>
> TLN 1549–57, p. 945 (3. 3. 98–106)

To emphasize his interjections Iago deploys the figure of *mimesis*, which Richard Sherry had defined as a form of imitation in which we repeat the exact words of another person.[199] Henry Peacham likewise writes of 'immitating every thing as it was',[200] and notes that the use of the device 'causeth great attention'.[201] Iago's *mimesis* undoubtedly captures Othello's attention, and also serves to meet the second requirement of a successful *prohoemium*, that of making one's hearer responsive to one's cause. Replying to Iago's final interjection ('Thinke my Lord?') Othello bursts out:

> Thinke my Lord? By heaven thou ecchos't me,
> As if there were some monster in thy thought:
> Too hideous to be shewne: thou dost meane something;
> I heard thee say even now, thou lik'st not that,
> When *Cassio* left my wife: what didst not like?
>
> TLN 1558–62, p. 945 (3. 3. 107–11)

---

198. *Othello*, TLN 1548, p. 945 (3. 3. 97).
199. Sherry 1550, Sig. E, 3ʳ.   200. Peacham 1577, Sig. O, 4ʳ.
201. See Peacham 1593, pp. 138–9, and cf. Plett 2004, p. 460. On the rhetoric of the passage see Keller 2009, pp. 168–9.

Here Iago meets the expected element of anger and resistance, but at the same time Othello reacts to his seeming suspicion with shocking alacrity and suddenness.

Iago's main goal, as with any *prohoemium*, is to win sufficient goodwill to be able to proceed to the *narratio* and *confirmatio* of his charge. Othello next makes it clear that Iago has succeeded:

> And for I know, thou'rt full of love and honesty,
> And weigh'st thy words, before thou giv'st them breath,
> Therefore these stops of thine fright me the more:
> For such things in a false disloyall knave,
> Are trickes of custome; but in a man that's just,
> They're close dilations working from the heart,
> That passion cannot rule.
>
> TLN 1571–7, p. 945 (3. 3. 119–25)

As Othello indicates, what has chiefly captured his attention is Iago's use of *aposeopesis*. This is the figure that, in Angel Day's definition, we deploy whenever 'we stop our speech on a sudden' while implying that there is more to be said.[202] It is Iago's 'stops', as Othello also calls them, that chiefly worry him. He knows that they could amount to nothing more than a rhetorical trick, but he continues to think of Iago as full of love and honesty, and accordingly believes that his hesitations must come, as he says, directly from the heart. Specifically, Othello senses the presence of a 'close dilation', an expansive working of Iago's heart and at the same time a paradoxical form of rhetorical utterance. To speak of a rhetorical 'dilation', as we know from Thomas Wilson, is a way of describing how 'matters are amplified'.[203] Richard Rainolde agrees that we may say of a rhetorician that he 'dilateth' when he speaks 'in moste ample and large maner'.[204] But Iago produces an oxymoronic 'close dilation', enlarging on what he is saying by closing off his speech.[205] The effect is to leave Othello in a state of deepening anxiety, but also of warm goodwill towards Iago and his apparent largeness of heart. With this encouragement Iago is ready to set to work, and as the scene unfolds he begins to move in the direction of claiming that he can hope to supply Othello with a *confirmatio* of Cassio's guilt and Desdemona's faithlessness.

---

202. Day 1592, p. 81.   203. Wilson 1553, Sig. Z, 2ᵛ.   204. Rainolde 1563, fo. 1ᵛ.
205. For a contrasting interpretation see Parker 1987, pp. 8–26, 82–5 on delation and dilation (and hence fat ladies). See also Parker 1996, pp. 232, 235, arguing that such dilations 'convey the sense of partial opening and partial glimpses of something closed or hid', and hence 'the discovery of a secret female place'. She takes this (p. 235) to be an example of 'the easy movement between rhetorical and sexual opening'.

5

The Failed Beginning

Defying the rules

When the duke of Venice makes his entrance at the start of Act 4 of *The Merchant of Venice*, he is arriving to try the case brought by Shylocke against the merchant Anthonio. Shylocke has entered into a bond with Anthonio with a penalty for non-payment of a pound of flesh. Anthonio's losses at sea have left him unable to meet his debt and Shylocke is now demanding the forfeit. When Shylocke appears before the court, the duke begins by pointing out that he is pursuing a *causa admirabilis*, a 'strange' suit or cause. As we saw in Chapter 3, to classify a cause as *admirabilis* is to say, in Quintilian's words, 'that it has been set up in a manner out of line with the general opinion of men'.[1] That this applies to Shylocke is immediately made clear to him. The strangeness of his suit, the duke declares, lies in the fact that he is maliciously demanding the letter of the law in circumstances in which the general opinion—indeed, the opinion of the whole world—would be that he ought instead to be offering mercy and remorse:

> *Shylocke* the world thinks, and I thinke so to
> That thou but leadst this fashion of thy mallice
> To the last houre of act, and then tis thought
> Thowlt shew thy mercy and remorse more strange,
> Than is thy strange apparant cruelty;
>
> TLN 1825–9, p. 500 (4. 1. 17–21)

What is strange about Shylocke's cause is that, although he is within his legal rights, he is behaving with unnatural cruelty.

---

1. Quintilian 2001, 4. 1. 41, vol. 2, p. 198: 'praeter opinionem hominum constitutum'.

Later in the scene, when the duke asks the young doctor Balthazer (Portia in disguise) to determine the case, she begins by invoking the same rhetorical terminology:

> Of a strange nature is the sute you follow,
> Yet in such rule, that the Venetian law
> Cannot impugne you as you doe proceed.
>
> TLN 1983–5, p. 501 (4. 1. 173–5)

While refusing to admit that Shylocke's cause is honest, Portia is careful not to imply that it can be dismissed as foul, since it is in no way contrary to the law. As she correctly attests, it is neither *turpis* nor *honesta*; rather it is *admirabilis*, 'of a strange nature'. The duke concludes his opening address in similar terms, arguing that Shylocke's demand is so much out of line with general opinion as to be inadmissible. Anthonio's losses should be sufficient to win commiseration even 'From stubborne Turkes, and Tarters never traind/ To offices of tender curtesie'.[2]

Cicero had warned that, if you are bent on pursuing a strange cause, you will find that 'the mind of those about to hear you will be alienated from your case'.[3] You will find, that is, that you will be treated as *alienus*. To describe someone in these terms, Thomas Cooper's *Thesaurus* explains, is to object that they are 'of an other sorte' and 'none of ours'; that they are foreign or alien to humankind.[4] This is how the duke reacts to Shylocke at the outset of the scene, describing him to Anthonio as a mere force of nature, 'an inhumaine wretch,/ Uncapable of pitty'.[5] When Bassanio attempts to reason with Shylocke, Anthonio reiterates the duke's view that Shylocke is no better than a natural or at best a brutish force:

> I pray you think you question with the Jewe,
> You may as well goe stand upon the Beach
> And bid the maine flood bate his usuall height,
> You may as well use question with the Woolfe,
> Why he hath made the Ewe bleate for the Lambe:
>
> TLN 1878–82, p. 500 (4. 1. 70–4)

As Anthonio observes, there is undoubtedly a *quaestio iudicii* or question for adjudication to be raised with Shylocke. But it makes no sense, he insists, to

---

2. *The Merchant of Venice*, TLN 1840–1, p. 500 (4. 1. 32–3).
3. Cicero 1949a. I. XV. 20, p. 40: 'alienatus animus eorum qui audituri sunt'.
4. Cooper 1565, Sig. G, 1ᵛ.   5. *The Merchant of Venice*, TLN 1812–13, p. 499 (4. 1. 4–5).

try to raise it with someone no better than a destructive animal. Gratiano later recurs to the same image of Shylocke as a wild beast wholly alien—and lethally hostile—to humankind:

> Thy currish spirit
> Governd a Woolfe, who hangd for humaine slaughter
> Even from the gallowes did his fell soule fleete,
> And whilest thou layest in thy unhallowed dam;
> Infusd it selfe in thee: for thy desires
> Are wolvish, bloody, starv'd, and ravenous.
>
> TLN 1941–6, p. 501 (4. 1. 133–8)

Shylocke's immediate penalty for demanding that his strange cause be heard is that everyone regards him, in Cooper's words, as 'none of ours'.[6]

As Cicero warns, and as these reactions attest, it is very difficult for anyone pursuing a *causa admirabilis* to win the goodwill of a court. But Cicero refuses to admit that this is impossible, and as we know he has several words of counsel to offer plaintiffs in this predicament. His basic suggestion is that 'when your cause is strange, it is essential to make use of an *insinuatio*'.[7] Quintilian agrees that, even if your cause is not inherently *turpis*, it will be essential to adopt a tone of insinuation 'when the matter at issue is approved by scarcely anyone'.[8] More specifically, the author of the *Ad Herennium* adds, you must make sure that you avoid the first fault in any kind of *prohoemium*, that of failing to speak in a manner that is sufficiently *lenis*.[9] If we return to Thomas Cooper's *Thesaurus*, we find that *lenis* was understood to mean 'full of sufferance . . . gentill'.[10] Drawing his speech to a close, the duke appears to refer specifically to this advice when he reminds Shylocke what is required of him: 'We all expect a gentle aunswere Jewe'.[11]

Many in Shakespeare's original audience would have been sufficiently well-versed in the rhetorical conventions to know exactly what to expect from Shylocke in response. If your cause is agreed to be honest, you can use an open *prohoemium*, calling attention to your person, speaking of your standing and duties, and declaring that your case raises issues of special

---

6. Cooper 1565, Sig. G, 1ᵛ. Leimberg 2011, p. 162 argues that Anthonio and Shylocke are 'bound . . . by their common humanity', but this is what Bassanio and Anthonio deny.
7. Cicero 1949a, I. XVII. 23, p. 46: 'Insinuatione igitur utendum est cum admirabile genus causae est'.
8. Quintilian 2001, 4. 1. 42, vol. 2, p. 200: 'quia res . . . hominibus parum probetur'.
9. *Rhetorica ad Herennium* 1954, I. VII. 11, p. 20.   10. Cooper 1565, Sig. 4A, 1ᵛ.
11. *The Merchant of Venice*, TLN 1842, p. 500 (4. 1. 34).

significance to the state. But otherwise you must begin with an *insinuatio*, speaking concessively and apologetically before trying to establish that, in spite of appearances, your cause may be susceptible of defence. Far more than for a modern audience, the opening of Shylocke's *prohoemium* would thus have come as a considerable shock:[12]

> I have possest your grace of what I purpose,
> And by our holy Sabaoth have I sworne
> To have the due and forfet of my bond,
> If you deny it, let the danger light
> Upon your charter and your Citties freedome.
> Youle aske me why I rather choose to have
> A weight of carrion flesh, then to receave
> Three thousand ducats: Ile not aunswer that.
> But say it is my humour, is it aunswerd?

> TLN 1843–51, p. 500 (4. 1. 35–43)

Here Shylocke speaks in defiance of all the rules. He not only refuses to offer anything in the nature of an apologetic or even a concessive tone, but he begins to develop an open *prohoemium* in which he calls attention to his person, speaks of his standing and duties, and declares that his case raises issues of special significance to the state. He seems bent on doing exactly what plaintiffs in his situation are warned to avoid.

Cicero had made one further suggestion about the most suitable tone to adopt at the outset of any kind of judicial speech. 'Your opening', he had advised, 'should exhibit sententiousness and gravity in the highest degree, and should contain everything that conduces to a tone of dignity.'[13] 'What is most appropriate in a *prohoemium*', Quintilian agrees, 'is that it should exhibit a certain sententiousness, together with a modesty and restraint of voice and gesture as well as of literary style.'[14] Here Shylocke exhibits a yet more scornful contempt. He devotes the rest of his *prohoemium* to explaining why he chooses not to accept three thousand ducats but rather to insist on his bond. The source on which Shakespeare draws for this part of the scene is Alexander Silvayn's account in *The Orator* (translated by Lazarus Piot in

---

12. Holmer 1995, pp. 186–93 analyses Shylocke's opening dispute with the duke, but without noting Shylocke's attitude to the rhetorical rules.
13. Cicero 1949a, I. XVIII. 25, p. 50: 'Exordium sententiarum et gravitatis plurimum debet habere et omnino quae pertinent ad dignitatem in se continere.'
14. Quintilian 2001, 4. 1. 55, vol. 2, p. 206: 'Frequentissime vero prohoemium decebit et sententiarum et compositionis et vocis et vultus modestia.'

1596)[15] of 'a Jew, who would for his debt have a pound of the flesh of a Christian'—a cause that Silvayn had already classified as 'strange'.[16] Despite its strangeness, Silvayn is careful to allow that there could be several reasons why the Jew might, as he phrases it, prefer to take the man's flesh rather than his silver, including the possibility that his credit might be damaged if he failed to enforce his bond.[17] But Shylocke speaks in altogether different terms. There is no particular reason for his preference, he declares, and he is under no obligation to supply one. He presses home his point with a series of comparisons:

> Some men there are love not a gaping pigge.
> Some that are mad if they behold a Cat.
> And others when the bagpipe sings ith nose,
> Cannot containe their urine.

> TLN 1855–8, p. 500 (4. 1. 47–50)

There is no clear reason why any of these things should be so, and the same applies to his own failure to give a reason for wishing to have the terms of his bond enforced.

The point is a legally valid one, but what is notable is the scorn with which Shylocke expresses it. Cicero calls for a sententious tone and the greatest possible dignity of utterance, while Quintilian warns us to avoid any indecency or unseemliness.[18] Shylocke talks about pigs, cats, bagpipes, and an irrepressible urge to urinate. He is deploying the satirical figure of *tapinosis*, the figure in play when someone decides (in George Puttenham's words) to 'diminish and abbase the matter he would seeme to set forth, by imparing the dignitie, height, vigour or majestie of the cause he takes in hand'.[19] Shylocke's treatment of the 'matter' at issue reflects a determined desire to abase the dignity of the cause before the court. It is as if he has asked himself what the rhetorical rules require in order to make sure of flouting them, offering the most undignified examples he can think of, the examples most lacking in gravity or sententiousness.

---

15. See the Epistle in Silvayn 1596, Sig. A, 3ʳ⁻ᵛ signed by Lazarus Piot. On the sources of the scene see Melchiori 1994, pp. 332–5. As Rhodes 2004, p. 102 notes, Alexander Silvayn was the pseudonym of Alexander van den Busche and Lazarus Piot ('the magpie') was the pseudonym of Anthony Munday.

16. Silvayn 1596, pp. 400, 401.   17. Silvayn 1596, p. 402.

18. Cicero 1949a, I. XVIII. 25, p. 50; Quintilian 2001, 11. 1. 30, vol. 5, p. 24. See also Quintilian 2001, 4. 1. 55, vol. 2, p. 206.

19. [Puttenham] 1589, p. 216. For earlier discussions of *tapinosis* see Quintilian 2001, 8. 3. 48, vol. 3, p. 366; Sherry 1550, Sig. C, 1ᵛ; Peacham 1577, Sig. G, 2ʳ.

Having mocked the conventions, Shylocke is left facing a court in which there is no longer any vestige of goodwill towards his cause. The duke had indicated in his opening *captatio benevolentiae* that he was willing to be mollified if Shylocke would withdraw his suit. He was hoping, as he said, to find that Shylocke was 'toucht with humaine gentlenes and love'.[20] But when Shylocke continues to declare that 'I would have my bond',[21] the duke is reduced to exchanging verbal blows with him:

> DUKE How shalt thou hope for mercy rendring none?
> SHYLOCKE What judgment shall I dread doing no wrong?[22]
>
> TLN 1896–7, p. 500 (4. 1. 88–9)

After listening to Shylocke's *prohoemium* the duke is more hostile than ever, and draws this part of the scene to an end by reminding Shylocke of his power to dismiss the court and with it his suit.[23]

To conclude, however, that Shylocke's *prohoemium* is a failure would be to imply that he makes some attempt to win the goodwill of his audience. But he never does. One reason for his refusal, as he makes clear, is that he takes himself to be pleading in an absolute form of a *constitutio iuridicalis*, a cause in which his request to the court is so evidently in line with law and justice that he stands in no need of an ingratiating tone. As he reminds the duke, what he is demanding is simply what has legally become his property:

> The pound of flesh which I demaund of him
> Is deerely bought, tis mine and I will have it:
> If you deny me, fie upon your Law,
>
> TLN 1907–9, p. 500 (4. 1. 99–101)

He also draws attention to the fact that in making this demand he is in no way acting contrary to the dictates of Venetian justice. He is merely asking for what is his due, and in asking for it he is 'doing no wrong'.

There seems, however, to be a further and deeper reason for Shylocke's defiance. He has a powerful disdain for flattery and ingratiating speech, as we already know from his response to Anthonio's request for a loan:

---

20. *The Merchant of Venice*, TLN 1833, p. 500 (4. 1. 25).
21. *The Merchant of Venice*, TLN 1895, p. 500 (4. 1. 87).
22. As noted by Elam 1984, p. 203, the duke assumes that it is for him to ask the questions, but Shylocke insists on answers from the duke.
23. *The Merchant of Venice*, TLN 1912, p. 500 (4. 1. 104).

> Shall I bend low, and in a bond-mans key
> With bated breath, and whispring humblenes
> Say this: Faire sir, you spet on me on Wednesday last,
> You spurnd me such a day, another time
> You called me dogge: and for these curtesies
> Ile lend you thus much moneyes.
>
> TLN 439–44, p. 485 (1. 3. 115–21)

Shylocke sees no reason to bend the knee or crave the goodwill of anyone. He is simply asking for his rights, and as he explicitly points out to Bassanio, 'I am not bound to please thee with my answers'.[24] More remarkably, his way of showing that he has no time for the rhetorical courtesies is not merely to ignore them but to invoke and satirize their requirements. Uniquely among the characters whom Shakespeare shows presenting a formal *prohoemium* in a judicial cause, Shylocke not only refuses to play the game but exhibits scorn for its rules.

Mishandling the rules

Polonius makes it clear in his conversations with the king and queen in Act 2 of *Hamlet* that he takes much pride in the fact that he has been well-trained in the art of rhetoric. Unfortunately he is no longer able to remember what he learned, and succeeds in engineering two successive rhetorical catastrophes. He first appears as the protagonist of a judicial cause at the start of Act 2, when he lays before Claudius and Gertrard the outcome of his enquiry into the cause of Hamlet's seeming insanity. For the background to his investigation we need to return to the end of Act 1, when Hamlet tells Horatio and Marcellus, after his encounter with the ghost, that he plans to adopt the stratagem of pretending to be mad. This would have been known to many in Shakespeare's original audience as a well-tried method of putting one's adversaries off their guard. Plutarch records that Solon 'fayned him selfe to be out of his wittes' in order to persuade the Athenians to attack Megara,[25] while Livy tells us that Junius Brutus used similar means to disarm the suspicions of the Tarquins.[26] After listening to the ghost's narrative Hamlet likewise decides, as he tells his friends, that he will 'put an Anticke

---

24. *The Merchant of Venice*, TLN 1873, p. 500 (4. 1. 65).   25. Plutarch 1579, p. 90.
26. Livy 1919, I. LVI. 8, p. 194; cf. Ovid 1996, II, 717, p. 108.

disposition on', and warns them that his demeanour may henceforth strike them as 'strange or odde'.[27]

Some two months pass, in the course of which Hamlet succeeds in persuading everyone that he has indeed become strange and odd.[28] Claudius becomes so concerned that he invites Rosencrans and Guyldensterne to Elsinore to see if they can discover what ails him. Welcoming them to court, Claudius speaks of Hamlet's almost unrecognizable state:

> something have you heard
> Of *Hamlets* transformation, so I call it,
> Since not th'exterior, nor the inward man
> Resembles that it was,
>
> TLN 932–5, p. 747 (2. 2. 4–7)

Gertrard similarly speaks of 'My too much changed sonne', while Polonius refers more brutally to Hamlet's lunacy.[29]

Hamlet always insists that he is fully in control of his pretence of insanity, and later assures his mother that 'I essentially am not in madnesse,/ But mad in craft'.[30] We have earlier been shown, however, that his mastery is less than complete. Soon after his encounter with the ghost we learn that he has for some time been paying court to Ophelia, much to the consternation of Polonius, who dismisses Hamlet's protestations of love as mere attempts at seduction and orders Ophelia to stop receiving him.[31] Now, more than two months later, Ophelia confesses that he has just made a sudden and alarming reappearance in her life:

> Pale as his shirt, his knees knocking each other,
> And with a looke so pittious in purport
> As if he had been loosed out of hell
> To speake of horrors,[32]

---

27. *Hamlet*, TLN 788, 790, p. 746 (1. 5. 170, 172).
28. Hamlet at the beginning of Act I states that his father has been dead for less than two months. See *Hamlet*, TLN 294, p. 740 (1. 2. 138). Ophelia during the play scene reminds Hamlet that his father has been dead for four months. See *Hamlet*, TLN 1850, p. 756 (3. 2. 114). But the play scene takes place only one night after the events of Act 2. See *Hamlet*, TLN 1471, p. 752 (2. 2. 493). So it would appear that there must be a gap of more than two months between the end of Act 1 and the beginning of Act 2. For a discussion of Hamlet's delay, linking it to the corruption of the court, see Fitzmaurice 2009.
29. *Hamlet*, TLN 964, 977, pp. 747–8 (2. 2. 36, 49).
30. *Hamlet*, TLN 2385–6, p. 762 (3. 4. 188–9). 31. *Hamlet*, TLN 547, p. 743 (1. 3. 134).
32. *Hamlet*, TLN 890–3, p. 747 (2. 1. 79–82). Hutson 2007, p. 141 describes the passage as 'a vividly enargeitic narration'.

Polonius at once diagnoses a case of love-madness, and Ophelia tremulously agrees with him:

> POLONIUS   Mad for thy love?
> OPHELIA   My lord I doe not know,
> But truly I doe feare it.[33]

TLN 894–5, p. 747 (2. 1. 83–4)

After listening to Ophelia's narrative Polonius interrogates her further:

> POLONIUS   What, have you given him any hard words of late?
> OPHELIA   No my good Lord, but as you did command
> I did repell his letters, and denied
> His accesse to me.

TLN 916–19, p. 747 (2. 1. 105–8)

Ophelia's response confirms Polonius in his diagnosis. 'That hath made him mad', he declares, and he proposes that they wait upon the king to tell him that the mystery of Hamlet's lunacy has been solved.[34]

The conjecture that Polonius plans to announce is a straightforward one, so that strictly speaking there is nothing more for him to do, as the *Ad Herennium* puts it, than 'briefly lay out what matters are going to be explained'.[35] But he cannot resist the opportunity to impress the king and queen with a formal *prohoemium*.[36] As we have seen, several precepts need to be observed if such an opening is to be successfully carried off. You must begin by focusing on the *personae* involved, calling attention to your discharge of your duties and emphasizing the standing of your auditors and the high respect in which they are held.[37] You must take care to speak in a distinctive style, introducing your argument *protinus*, immediately and without waste of time,[38] and stating your case *statim*, briskly and without preamble.[39] You must also speak *perspicue*, clearly and plainly,[40] taking particular pains, as Cicero puts it, not to incur 'any suspicion of excessive preparation and artificial carefulness'.[41] This is the advice that Brutus failed to heed when he used the figure of *epanodos*, the figure that consists (in Dudley

---

33. On the concept of love-madness in the Renaissance see Gowland 2006, pp. 65–70.
34. *Hamlet*, TLN 919, 926–7, p. 747 (2. 1. 108, 115–16).
35. *Rhetorica ad Herennium* 1954, I. IV. 6, p. 12: 'breviter quibus de rebus simus dicturi exponere'.
36. For a contrasting analysis of Polonius's speech see Baldwin 1944, vol. 2, pp. 374–7.
37. Cicero 1949a, I. XVI. 22, p. 44.   38. Cicero 1949a, I. XV. 20, p. 42.
39. *Rhetorica ad Herennium* 1954, I. IV. 6, p. 12.   40. Cicero 1949a, I. XV. 20, p. 42.
41. Cicero 1949a, I. XVIII. 25, p. 52: 'suspicio quaedam apparationis atque artificiosae diligentiae'. See also Quintilian 2001, 4. 1. 54–6, vol. 2, pp. 206–8.

Fenner's definition) of using the same words 'in the beginning and the middle, in the middle and the ende' of a sentence.[42] The effect can be striking, but it is all too easy, as Henry Peacham remarks, to produce nothing more than 'tedious and wearisome repetition'.[43] One additional caution, Cicero adds, is that you must never lapse into jocularity or make any attempt at brilliance or wit.[44] There may be moments in a speech when it is appropriate to try to raise a laugh,[45] but a *prohoemium* 'must exhibit sententiousness and gravity in the highest degree'.[46]

Polonius launches into his oration as soon as the ambassadors returning from Norway have given their report:

> This busines is very well ended.
> My Liege and Maddam, to expostulate
>
> TLN 1014–15, p. 748 (2. 2. 85–6)

There is already something inept about Polonius's sudden change of register from diplomatic self-congratulation to rhetorical apostrophe, and Shakespeare underlines the comedy with a strong hint that Polonius next begins to perform the rhetorical act of *expostulatio*. As we saw in Chapter 1, the Ramist rhetoricians had placed special emphasis on the correct use of voice and gesture in the successful invention of arguments. Among Elizabethan Ramists, Abraham Fraunce had most fully addressed the topic, and in the course of his analysis had defined the act of expostulation in detailed terms:

> The middle finger meeting with the thumb and the other three stretched out, is an urgent and instant gesture. The former finger stretched out doth point at or showe, when the other three are closed and kept in with the thumb. In expostulating or declaring of anie thing, this former finger dooth affirme and assevere, when it is somewhat inclined and bowed downe, the whole hand now and then somewhat lifted up, and tending towards the shoulders.[47]

When Polonius a few moments later condemns as tedious 'the lymmes and outward florishes' of rhetoric,[48] we are to think of him as doing so while pointing his middle finger downwards and lifting his hands upwards towards his shoulders in just such an outward flourish.

---

42. Fenner 1584, Sig. D, 3^r.
43. Peacham is here discussing the closely related figure of *traductio*. See Peacham 1593, p. 49.
44. Cicero's words are *splendor* and *festivitas*. See Cicero 1949a, I. XVIII. 25, p. 52.
45. See, for example, Cicero 1949a, I. XVII. 25, p. 50.
46. Cicero 1949a, I. XVIII. 25, p. 50: 'Exordium sententiarum et gravitatis plurimum debet habere.'
47. Fraunce 1588a, Sig. K, 4^r.   48. *Hamlet*, TLN 1020, p. 748 (2. 2. 91).

While expostulating, Polonius explains that he does not plan to
expostulate:

> My Liege and Maddam, to expostulate
> What majestie should be, what dutie is,
> Why day is day, night, night, and time is time,
> Were nothing but to wast night, day, and time,
> Therefore since brevitie is the soule of wit,
> And tediousnes the lymmes and outward florishes,
> I will be briefe,
>
> TLN 1015–21, p. 748 (2. 2. 86–92)

Polonius knows that he must be brief, but he cannot resist inserting some
remarks about the persons of his hearers—with an allusion to their elevated
status—and his own person and duties. He also knows that he must avoid
'artificial' flourishes, but he allows himself a carefully prepared and
unusually complex *epanodos* centred on the sequence day/night/time;
night/day/time, just the kind of wearisome repetition that Peacham had
warned us to avoid.[49]

Next Polonius recalls that the principal aim of an open *prohoemium* is
supposed to be that of briefly laying out the basic claim one wishes to put
forward:

> I will be briefe, your noble sonne is mad:
> Mad call I it, for to define true madnes,
> What ist but to be nothing els but mad,
> But let that goe.
>
> TLN 1021–4, p. 748 (2. 2. 92–5)

Here Polonius contrives to forget the whole point of his speech. He had
promised to tell Claudius the cause of Hamlet's madness, but he merely tells
him that Hamlet is mad—something that Claudius already believes, as
Polonius knows. Yet worse, and in defiance of all advice, he thinks that
this is the moment to introduce a little joke.[50] He believes that Hamlet is
mad, he says, but he does not wish to specify what he means, because to try
to define true madness would itself be mad. Still worse, the joke misfires,
leaving him not merely with a definition of madness after all (and a
definition according to which it is simply the state of being mad) but an
apparent confession that he must be mad himself. Worst of all, it is not even

49. Peacham 1593, p. 49.   50. For a discussion see Edwards 2003, p. 135n.

clear that he notices how badly things have gone wrong. His closing phrase ('But let that goe') may sound apologetic, but he may equally be delighted by his neat turns of phrase. He is almost, at times, the Fool.

Polonius's *prohoemium* not only fails to win the goodwill of the king and queen but leaves them visibly annoyed. Claudius is reduced to silence, and Gertrard's sole response is a remarkably tart command: 'More matter with lesse art'.[51] She wants less of what Cicero would call 'artificial' speech, and more about the *res* or 'matter' of Hamlet's insanity. Polonius is prone to sudden agitation, and the queen's rebuke leaves him floundering and at a loss:

> Maddam, I sweare I use no art at all,
> That he is mad tis true, tis true, tis pitty,
> And pitty tis tis true, a foolish figure,
> But farewell it, for I will use no art.
>
> TLN 1025–8, p. 748 (2. 2. 96–9)

He has indeed made no use of art; he has flouted every rule in the book. While disavowing any artifice, however, he cannot resist drawing once more on the 'artificial' figure of *epanodos* with his pattern of mad/true/true; pity/pity/true. 'A foolish figure', as he rightly admits, although as usual he sounds rather pleased with himself.[52]

Polonius rounds off by circling back to his original promise to address 'The very cause of *Hamlets* lunacie':[53]

> Mad let us graunt him then, and now remaines
> That we find out the cause of this effect,
> Or rather say, the cause of this defect,
> For this effect defective comes by cause:
> Thus it remaines, and the remainder thus.
> Perpend,
>
> TLN 1029–34, p. 748 (2. 2. 100–5)

Although he has promised to employ no further artifice, he succumbs once again to the lure of the figures and tropes, beginning with the painful assonance

---

51. *Hamlet*, TLN 1024, p. 748 (2. 2. 95).
52. This classification of Polonius's figure might be disputed. Horvei 1984, p. 128 thinks of it as a *chiasmus*; Keller 2009, p. 162 takes it to be a case of *antimetabole*. On *epanodos* see Peacham 1577, Sig. S, 1^{r-v}; Fenner 1584, Sig. D, 3^r; Fraunce 1588a, Sig. D, 4^r–5^r; Day 1592, p. 92; Peacham 1593, p. 129; Butler 1598, Sig. C, 6^v.
53. *Hamlet*, TLN 977, p. 748 (2. 2. 49).

of effect/defect and adding two further instances of *epanodos*: cause/defect; defective/cause, followed by thus/remains; remainder/thus. With these additional examples of wearisome repetition he finally brings his disastrous *prohoemium* to a close.

The limits of rhetoric

As the case of Polonius reminds us, the rhetoricians believe that there are many precepts we must be sure to follow if we are to make a good impression at the outset of a speech. But suppose we follow them all—are we guaranteed success? Or could we obey every rule for winning goodwill but nevertheless fail to win it? The rhetoricians themselves are anxious to acknowledge the possibility of defeat. Quintilian in particular insists that the art of rhetoric should never be defined by reference to its power to persuade.[54] It is a mistake, he argues, 'to subject the orator to the sway of fortune to such an extent that, if he fails to persuade, he cannot retain the name of an orator'.[55] He objects to the definition in part because it is possible to convince people by means other than rhetoric, but chiefly because he dislikes any definition that has the effect, as he puts it, 'of tying the art to results'.[56] We have to recognize that it is possible to speak with genuine eloquence and nevertheless fail to gain the goodwill of our audience. He concludes that we should go no further than saying that 'rhetoric is the science of speaking well'.[57] Unless we master its principles we can never hope to succeed, but even with complete mastery we can never guarantee success.[58]

Shakespeare agrees, of course, that we can be persuaded by methods other than the use of rhetorical techniques. We may be swayed by mere threats, which as Lucrece discovers to her fatal cost are capable of having an overwhelmingly coercive effect. We may also find ourselves compelled even in the absence of any intentionally persuasive force. This is the

54. See Quintilian 2001, 2. 15. 3, vol. 1, p. 350, citing 'rhetoricen esse vim persuadendi' as the most usual definition of the art.
55. Quintilian 2001, 2. 15. 12, vol. 1, p. 356: 'oratorem fortunae subicit, ut, si non persuaserit, nomen suum retinere non possit'.
56. Quintilian 2001, 2. 15. 35, vol. 1, p. 366: 'artem ad exitum alligat'.
57. Quintilian 2001, 2. 15. 38, vol. 1, p. 368: 'rhetoricen esse bene dicendi scientiam'.
58. As modern theorists of rhetoric would say (following J. L. Austin), Quintilian is arguing that the art should not be defined in terms of its capacity to bring about perlocutionary effects.

power of which Longavill complains in the Sonnet he recites in Act 4 of *Loves Labors Lost*:

> Did not the heavenly Rethorique of thine eye,
>   Gainst whom the world cannot holde argument,
> Perswade my hart to this false perjurie?[59]

The power of beauty to overcome argument, and hence to make us act against our will, is here treated as equivalent to the compelling force of eloquence.

What of the converse possibility—that we may employ every device of rhetoric and nevertheless fail to speak 'winningly'? Shakespeare is chiefly interested in illuminating the power and efficacy of the *ars rhetorica*, but his attitude is sometimes ambiguous, and in one scene he fully explores the limitations of the art. This is when Alcibiades comes forward in Act 3 of *Timon of Athens* to address a judicial plea to the senators of Athens on behalf of a condemned friend.[60] There is nothing in Shakespeare's sources resembling a model for the *prohoemium* that Alcibiades goes on to present. Although Plutarch reports that Timon and Alcibiades were acquainted, and that Timon once accosted Alcibiades after he had delivered a speech in the Assembly, he gives no report of what Alcibiades said.[61] Shakespeare's scene appears to be fashioned entirely out of his own knowledge of the principles of forensic eloquence.

Like Isabella in Act 2 of *Measure for Measure*, Alcibiades is in the worst possible rhetorical predicament. As the rhetoricians would say, his task is that of speaking in favour of a purely assumptive issue in a juridical cause. The facts of the case are not in dispute. The friend on whose behalf he wishes to plead has killed a man in a duel. Nor is there any doubt about the

---

59. *Loves Labors Lost*, TLN 1299–1301, p. 331 (4. 3. 52–4). The play most probably dates from 1595 or 1596. See Carroll 2009, p. 29; Wiggins and Richardson 2013, p. 320.
60. As we saw in Chapter 2, it is now regarded as beyond doubt that Shakespeare wrote *Timon of Athens* in collaboration with Thomas Middleton. So it might be wondered if Shakespeare wrote this particular scene. The consensus used to be that it was written by Middleton. See Vickers 2002, pp. 256–7, 266, 270, 286. But Dawson and Minton 2008, p. 405 find it 'a bit surprising that Middleton would have been charged with this central moment'. Further reasons for believing that the scene may have been written by Shakespeare include its rhetorical construction and its close echoes of *Measure for Measure*. For the purposes of my argument, however, it is sufficient that Shakespeare should have negotiated the production of the text with Middleton (as he evidently did) and been willing to accept the line of argument in this particular scene.
61. Plutarch 1579, p. 219.

evaluation of the facts. His friend's crime is a capital one, and he has already been condemned to death. The scene opens with the First Senator confirming his verdict:

> My Lords, you have my voyce too't, the faults Bloody:
> 'Tis necessary he should dye:
>
> TLN 1108–9, p. 1013 (3. 5. 1–2)

The Second Senator concurs, saying of all such malefactors that 'the Law shall bruise'em'.[62]

Alcibiades has committed himself, in other words, to speaking in favour of an unambiguously foul cause. Nor can he hope to enter a *purgatio* on behalf of his friend, claiming that he did not act *cum consulto* and ought therefore to be excused. As he is forced to concede, his friend believed that his reputation had been 'touch'd to death' by his adversary, and deliberately decided to 'oppose his Foe' in order to clear his name.[63] Like Isabella pleading for the life of her brother Claudio, he therefore has no option but to enter a *deprecatio*, a straightforward admission of his friend's guilt and a plea for mercy and pardon. Isabella had begun with a direct appeal to Angelo as her judge:

> I am a wofull Sutor to your Honour,
>
> TLN 710, p. 902 (2. 2. 28)

Alcibiades opens by addressing the senators with a rhythmically identical feminine-ended line:

> I am an humble Sutor to your Vertues;[64]
>
> TLN 1114, p. 1013 (3. 5. 7)

Like Isabella, Alcibiades emphasizes that his plea is simply for compassion, a recognition that pity is greater than justice. Before turning to his *prohoemium* he hails the senators by wishing them 'Honor, health, and compassion', and he begins by reminding them that 'pitty is the vertue of the Law'.[65]

---

62. *Timon of Athens*, TLN 1111, p. 1013 (3. 5. 4).
63. *Timon of Athens*, TLN 1126–7, p. 1013 (3. 5. 19–20).
64. Alcibiades echoes Isabella so closely as to suggest not merely that Shakespeare wrote this scene, but that its date may be close to that of *Measure for Measure*. The similarity in general theme between *Timon* and *King Lear* might also incline one to accept such a date. As we have seen, however, Klein 2001, p. 1, Jowett 2004, p. 4, and Dawson and Minton 2008, p. 12 all argue that *Timon* was written between 1606–8.
65. *Timon of Athens*, TLN 1112, 1115, p. 1013 (3. 5. 5, 8).

Although Alcibiades can only offer a *deprecatio*, he nevertheless starts by attempting to claim that his friend did not genuinely act *cum consulto* and should therefore be excused. As we saw in Chapter 4, there are three possible ways of defending such a claim: you can plead that the crime was unavoidable, or that it arose out of ignorance, or that it occurred by misfortune and chance.[66] Alcibiades tries to press the third excuse, arguing that his friend's fault lies in his stars rather than in himself:

> It pleases time and Fortune to lye heavie
> Upon a Friend of mine, who in hot blood
> Hath stept into the Law: which is past depth
> To those that (without heede) do plundge intoo't.
>
> TLN 1117–20, p. 1013 (3. 5. 10–13)

As Alcibiades quickly sees, however, he has no hope of being able to develop such a *purgatio*, and he almost immediately contradicts himself and admits that his friend behaved soberly, and hence with foresight of the consequences.[67]

How then can he hope to proceed? As we saw in the case of Isabella, the rhetoricians have some encouraging words to offer even in these most adverse circumstances. One strategy, Cicero suggests, is that you should try to substitute a consideration of the person who committed the crime in place of the crime itself.[68] More specifically, the *Ad Herennium* adds, you should try to claim 'that there was virtue or nobility in the supplicant'.[69] This is how Alcibiades continues:

> He is a Man (setting his Fate aside)
> Of comely Vertues,
> Nor did he soyle the fact with Cowardice.
> (An Honour in him, which buyes out his fault)
>
> TLN 1121–4, p. 1013 (3. 5. 14–17)

Alcibiades attempts to shift attention away from the crime and towards the person who committed it, implying that as soon as his friend's virtues are recognized they will prompt a reconsideration of his act.

---

66. *Rhetorica ad Herennium* 1954, I. XIV. 24, p. 44 and II. XVI. 23, p. 100. See also Cicero 1949a, I. XI. 15, p. 30 and II. XXXI. 94, p. 260; Quintilian 2001, 7. 4. 14–15, vol. 3, p. 244.
67. *Timon of Athens*, TLN 1128, p. 1013 (3. 5. 21).
68. Cicero 1949a, I. XVII. 24, p. 48. Cf. *Rhetorica ad Herennium* 1954, I. VI. 9, p. 16.
69. *Rhetorica ad Herennium* 1954, II. XVII. 25, p. 102: 'virtus aut nobilitas erit in eo qui supplicabit'.

You must also attempt to show, Cicero goes on, that the charge does not really pertain to the act performed.[70] As the author of the *Ad Herennium* more revealingly puts it, you must try to argue that the act performed was not really an instance of the crime alleged, that it was 'not at all similar' to the condemnatory description that has been given of it.[71] Rather you must attempt to show that the suppliant 'committed his offence out of a sense of duty and a right understanding of things'.[72] Alcibiades closely follows this advice:

> But with a Noble Fury, and faire spirit,
> Seeing his Reputation touch'd to death,
> He did oppose his Foe:
> And with such sober and unnoted passion
> He did behave his anger ere 'twas spent,
> As if he had but prov'd an Argument.
>
> TLN 1125–30, p. 1013 (3. 5. 18–23)

Here Alcibiades attempts to redescribe his friend's behaviour in such a way as to prompt a re-evaluation of its worth. He does so by deploying the figure known to the rhetoricians as *paradiastole*, the figure we employ when, as Quintilian says, 'we call someone wise rather than cunning, or courageous rather than overconfident, or careful instead of avaricious'.[73] Quintilian's discussion was extensively taken up by the Tudor rhetoricians, several of whom contribute their own examples.[74] We are employing *paradiastole*, Henry Peacham tells us, when we 'call him that is craftye, wyse; a covetous man, a good husband; murder, a manly deede'.[75] We are using the same figure, according to Angel Day, 'when we call a subtill person, wise: a bold fellow, courageous: a prodigall man liberall: a man furious or rash, valiant'.[76] Alcibiades almost seems to have these specific examples in mind. The claim that his friend acted out of noble fury implies that a furious man can be

---

70. Cicero 1949a, I. XVII. 24, p. 48: 'demonstrare nihil eorum ad te pertinere'.
71. *Rhetorica ad Herennium* 1954, I. VI. 9, p. 18. 'nihil simile . . . factum'.
72. *Rhetorica ad Herennium* 1954, II. XVII. 25, p. 102: 'officio et recto studio commotus fecit'.
73. Quintilian 2001, 9. 3. 65, vol. 4, p. 138: 'cum te pro astuto sapientem appelles, pro confidente fortem, pro illiberali diligentem'.
74. See, for instance, Peacham 1577, Sig. N, 4ᵛ; [Puttenham] 1589, p. 154; Day 1592, p. 84; Peacham 1593, p. 168. For two important intermediary sources see Castiglione 1994 [1528], pp. 37–8 and Susenbrotus 1562, p. 46. For discussions see Javitch 1972; Whigham 1984, pp. 40–2 and examples at pp. 204–5; Skinner 1996, pp. 142–53, 156–72, 174–80; Skinner 2007.
75. Peacham 1577, Sig. N, 4ᵛ.
76. Day 1592, p. 84. For similar examples see [Puttenham] 1589, p. 154.

valiant, while the claim that his friend was a man of fair spirit who avoided cowardice suggests that murder can be a manly deed. These are the means, as Peacham had confided, by which we can hope to 'excuse our own vices, or other mens whom we doe defend'.[77]

By this time Alcibiades has made use of both the arguments that give us the best chance, according to the rhetoricians, of winning over our audience while pleading in a foul cause. But in spite of all his efforts Alcibiades's *prohoemium* proves a humiliating failure. Far from engendering any feelings of goodwill, he prompts the First Senator to react in tones of high indignation to what he perceives as an attempt to play a rhetorical trick:

> You undergo too strict a Paradox,
> Striving to make an ugly deed looke faire:
> Your words have tooke such paines, as if they labour'd
> To bring Man-slaughter into forme, and set Quarrelling
> Upon the head of Valour; which indeede
> Is Valour mis-begot, and came into the world,
> When Sects, and Factions were newly borne.
>
> TLN 1131–7, pp. 1013–14 (3. 5. 24–30)

The laboured character of Alcibiades's oratory conveys to the First Senator the thought that his words themselves are in labour, painfully bringing to birth a misbegotten and paradoxical conception of valour, a quality not to be found among those who duel to the death.

Having uncovered this attempted deception, the First Senator proceeds to explain the true concept of valour, which resides not in action but in magnanimous endurance:

> Hee's truly Valiant, that can wisely suffer
> The worst that man can breath, and make his Wrongs, his Outsides,
> To weare them like his Rayment, carelessely,
> And ne're preferre his injuries to his heart,
> To bring it into danger.
>
> TLN 1138–42, p. 1014 (3. 5. 31–6)

When Alcibiades tries to protest, the First Senator tells him once again that he is merely trying 'to make an ugly deed looke faire':

---

77. Peacham 1577, Sig. N, 4ᵛ.

> You cannot make grosse sinnes looke cleare,
> To revenge is no Valour, but to beare.
>
> TLN 1145–6, p. 1014 (3. 5. 39–40)

With his rhyming couplet the senator signals an end to the argument and Alcibiades's case is dismissed.[78]

Like Isabella in her interview with Angelo, Alcibiades is left with only one rhetorical possibility. As Quintilian had expressed it, you should try to move your audience's mind 'with prayers and entreaties, with expressions of hope and fear'.[79] This is what Alcibiades now attempts to do, amplifying his plea by rising from blank to rhymed verse:

> Oh my Lords,
> As you are great, be pittifully Good,
> Who cannot condemne rashnesse in cold blood?
> To kill, I grant, is sinnes extreamest Gust,
> But in defence, by Mercy, 'tis most just.
>
> TLN 1158–62, p. 1014 (3. 5. 52–6)

Besides pleading with gathering intensity, Alcibiades tries to introduce a further claim designed to induce pity, now arguing that his friend merely acted out of self-defence. But the senators have heard more than enough, and the Second Senator speaks for them all when he scornfully retorts, 'You breath in vaine'.[80] No one is prepared to accept Alcibiades's elevation of mercy above justice, and the First Senator concludes, 'We are for Law, he dyes, urge it no more'.[81] When Alcibiades continues to protest, the senators summarily banish him. He brings the scene to an end with an enraged speech in which he abandons all thought of persuasion and swears vengeance on them all.

---

78. Graham 1994, pp. 186–8 notes the tendency for disputation in the play to turn into a mere struggle of wills.
79. Quintilian 2001, 4. 1. 33, vol. 2, p. 194: 'spe metu admonitione precibus'.
80. *Timon of Athens*, TLN 1165, p. 1014 (3. 5. 60).
81. *Timon of Athens*, TLN 1192, p. 1014 (3. 5. 87).

6

The Judicial Narrative

Constructing a judicial narrative

After the *prohoemium* comes the *narratio*, in which we lay out the facts of the case, seeking to do so in such a way as to persuade our audience to accept our version of events.[1] It is perhaps surprising that Shakespeare never speaks of narratives or the act of narrating, in spite of his evident familiarity with a number of rhetorical texts in which these were standard terms.[2] Whenever his characters mount narratives in judicial causes they invariably refer more informally to the act of saying or relating something. When the duke in Act 5 of *Measure for Measure* invites Isabella to describe Angelo's alleged misconduct, his request is 'Relate your wrongs'.[3] When he subsequently asks her to deliver her narrative, he simply enquires 'What would you say?'[4] The same vocabulary recurs even in the more complicated cases in which someone is asked to present a narrative in response to a judicial charge. When Friar Lawrence is ordered to explain the deaths of the lovers in *Romeo and Juliet*, the prince's command is 'say at once what thou dost know in this'.[5] When the duke in Act 1 of *Othello* responds to Othello's request to narrate the history of his love, his yet simpler command is 'Say it Othello'.[6]

---

1. Quintilian 2001, 4. 2. 24–5, vol. 2, pp. 228–30 cautions that, although it will almost always be right to follow this sequence, it should not be regarded as a rigid rule. On rhetorical *narratio* in Shakespeare see Hutson 2013; more generally see Hardy 1997. For a survey of views about Shakespeare's handling of narrative see Meek 2009a. On Shakespeare's narrative techniques see Mack 2010, pp. 74–88, 100–5.
2. It is the ready availability of concordances, not my perfect recollection of Shakespeare's vocabulary, that enables me to speak in such categorical terms.
3. *Measure for Measure*, TLN 2191, p. 917 (5. 1. 26).
4. *Measure for Measure*, TLN 2233, p. 918 (5. 1. 68).
5. *Romeo and Juliet*, TLN 2917, p. 411 (5. 3. 228).
6. *Othello*, TLN 412, p. 933 (1. 3. 126).

If we turn instead to the vernacular rhetoricians, we find them speaking freely about acts of narration and the construction of narratives. Leonard Cox refers to the place of the 'narracion or tale' in judicial rhetoric, defining it as 'the shewynge of the dede in maner of an historye'.[7] Richard Rainolde similarly describes 'narracion' as 'an exposicion, or declaration of any thing dooen in deede',[8] while Thomas Wilson equates the act of narrating with 'reportyng of our tale'.[9] But as these passages reveal, the rhetoricians also like to speak of telling a tale, and Shakespeare generally prefers this homely diction too. When Polonius begins to narrate the story of Hamlet's apparent descent into madness he promises Claudius and Gertrard that he will tell 'a short tale'.[10] When Lucio interrupts Isabella's account of her mistreatment by Angelo she informs the duke that Lucio has now 'told somewhat of my Tale'.[11] As before, Shakespeare retains this straightforward vocabulary even when dramatizing the more complex cases in which a narrative forms part of a judicial defence. When Friar Lawrence is ordered to give an account of himself, he promises not to tell 'a tedious tale'.[12] When Othello is asked to recount the story of his love, he begins by assuring his audience that he will deliver 'a round unvarnish'd tale'.[13]

The tellers of these tales disclose an impressively firm grasp of the classical rules about how to mount a narrative in a judicial cause.[14] For a general statement of the relevant principles we can hardly do better than return to Book 4 of Quintilian's *Institutio oratoria*.[15] There he begins by laying it down that our aim should be to speak in such a way 'that it becomes easier for the judge to understand, to remember and to believe what we say',[16] to which he adds the warning that, if we fail in any of these respects, 'we shall undertake the whole of the rest of our labours in vain'.[17] He then considers how we can hope to meet these exacting requirements. With a nod at Aristotle's partly contrasting analysis, he chooses at this juncture to follow the authority of Isocrates.[18] To be readily understood, Isocrates had laid

---

7. Cox 1532, Sig. D, 8[r].　　　　8. Rainolde 1563, fo. xii[r].　　　　9. Wilson 1553, Sig. P, 2[v]–3[r].
10. *Hamlet*, TLN 1075, p. 749 (2. 2. 144).
11. *Measure for Measure*, TLN 2249, p. 918 (5. 1. 84).
12. *Romeo and Juliet*, TLN 2919, p. 411 (5. 3. 230).　　　　13. *Othello*, TLN 376, p. 933 (1. 3. 90).
14. For a full account of the rhetorical theory of judicial narrative and its applications in late Elizabethan drama see Hutson 2007, pp. 121–45.
15. As noted in Hutson 2007, pp. 121–8.
16. Quintilian 2001, 4. 2. 33, vol. 2, p. 236: 'quo facilius iudex intellegat meminerit credit'.
17. Quintilian 2001, 4. 2. 35, vol. 2, p. 236: 'frustra in reliquis laborabimus'.
18. For Quintilian on Isocrates see Quintilian 2001, 4. 2. 31, vol. 2, p. 234 and 12. 10. 22, vol. 5, p. 292.

down, we must above all be lucid; to be memorable we must be brief; and to be credible we must ensure that what we say has the appearance of truth.[19] Drawing on this assessment almost word-for-word, Thomas Wilson agrees that our purpose is to make our hearers 'remember, understande, & beleve', and that this requires us to learn three lessons, 'whereof the firste is to be shorte, the next to be plaine, and the thirde is, to speake likely'.[20]

As usual, Quintilian is less interested than his predecessors in offering specific directions about how to ensure that our orations embody these qualities. He even inserts some dark remarks about the stupidity of textbook writers on the subject and their superstitious attachment to rhetorical rules.[21] He does of course provide some guidance, but he has fewer precepts to offer, chiefly because he appears not to share the anxiety continually expressed by earlier rhetoricians about the pitfalls to be circumvented if we are to tell a successful tale. For a survey of these pitfalls, and the positive guidelines to be followed if we wish to steer around them, we need to return once more to the *Ad Herennium* and Cicero's *De inventione*.

First of all, how can we ensure that our narrative is winningly brief? Cicero and the author of the *Ad Herennium* agree that, as the latter puts it, 'we should narrate the facts in summary fashion, without entering into too many particulars'.[22] 'It will frequently be sufficient,' Cicero concurs, 'to offer a summary, without going into specific elements of the story, for often it is enough to say what happened without recounting how and why it happened.'[23] They likewise agree that it is important to know how to unfold a story in such a way that you do not have to describe the complete sequence of events for it to be grasped.[24] For example, as the *Ad Herennium* observes with a glimpse of the obvious, 'if I say that I have returned from a province, it will be understood that I travelled to that province', so that there is no need for the latter claim to be expressed.[25]

19. On the need for the *narratio* to be *lucida*, *brevis*, and *veri similis* see Quintilian 2001, 4. 2. 31, vol. 2, p. 234.
20. Wilson 1553, Sig. P, 2ᵛ. See also Rainolde 1563, fo. xiiiᵛ.
21. Quintilian 2001, 4. 2. 60, vol. 2, p. 248 and 4. 2. 86, vol. 2, p. 262.
22. *Rhetorica ad Herennium* 1954, I. IX. 14, pp. 24–6: 'summatim, non particulatim narrabimus'.
23. Cicero 1949a, I. XX. 28, p. 56: 'satis erit summam dixisse, eius partes non dicentur—nam saepe satis est quid factum sit dicere, ut ne narres quemadmodum sit factum'.
24. Cicero 1949a, I. XX. 28, p. 58; *Rhetorica ad Herennium* 1954, I. IX. 14, p. 26. Cf. Quintilian 2001, 4. 2. 41–2, vol. 2, p. 240.
25. *Rhetorica ad Herennium* 1954, I. IX. 14, p. 26: 'si dicam me ex provincia redisse, profectum quoque in provinciam intellegatur'.

Apart from these observations, both writers concentrate on the dangers to be avoided if we are to speak with brevity. Here the *Ad Herennium* provides the fullest treatment. We must take care 'that we begin our story only where it is necessary to do so, without going back to the ultimate starting-point or carrying it forward to its uttermost end'.[26] As Thomas Wilson graphically translates, we must avoid raising it from the bottom.[27] We must then make sure 'that we make no use of digressions, and that we do not wander from the point we have started to expound'.[28] Finally, 'we must be careful not to say the same thing twice or more often, and above all avoid immediately repeating something we have just said'.[29]

Next, how can we hope to tell our story as clearly as possible? According to the author of the *Ad Herennium*, one key to lucidity is brevity: 'The shorter our narrative, the clearer it will be and the easier to follow.'[30] But his main advice is that we must always be sure to respect chronology. This may seem a somewhat unsophisticated recommendation, especially when one thinks of the many classical narratives (reaching as far back as the *Iliad*) that begin *in medias res*. Quintilian seems alert to this criticism, and explicitly allows that the requirement of chronology, although usually sensible, should never be treated as a rigid principle.[31] But the author of the *Ad Herennium* is unrepentant in his insistence that 'if we wish to present a lucid story, we must start by offering an exposition of what happened first, and thereafter preserve the order of events and times exactly as they took place'.[32] Strongly agreeing, Thomas Wilson reiterates that 'to make our matter plaine' it will always be wisest 'first and formest to tell every thyng in

---

26. *Rhetorica ad Herennium* 1954, I. IX. 14, p. 24: 'inde incipiemus narrare unde necesse est; et si non ab ultimo initio . . . et si non ad extremum . . . persequemur'. Cf. Cicero 1949a, I. XX. 28, p. 56; Quintilian 2001, 4. 2. 40, vol. 2, p. 240.
27. Wilson 1553, Sig. P, 2^v.
28. *Rhetorica ad Herennium* 1954, I. IX. 14, p. 26: 'transitionibus nullis utemur, et . . . non deerrabimus ab eo quod coeperimus exponere'.
29. *Rhetorica ad Herennium* 1954, I. IX. 14, p. 26: 'ne bis aut saepius idem dicamus cavendum est; etiam ne quid novissime quod diximus deinceps dicamus'. Cf. Cicero 1949a, I. XX. 28, p. 58.
30. *Rhetorica ad Herennium* 1954, I. IX. 15, p. 26: 'quo brevior, dilucidior et cognitu facilior narratio fiet'. Cf. Cicero 1949a, I. XX. 29, pp. 58–60.
31. Quintilian 2001, 4. 2. 83 and 87, vol. 2, pp. 260–2.
32. *Rhetorica ad Herennium* 1954, I. IX. 15, p. 26: 'Rem dilucide narrabimus si ut quicquid primum gestum erit ita primum exponemus, et rerum ac temporum ordinem conservabimus ut gestae res erunt.' Cf. Cicero 1949a, I. XX. 29, p. 58.

order' and make sure that we avoid any risk of 'tumblyng one tale in anothers necke'.[33]

After this basic admonition the *Ad Herennium* chiefly concentrates, as before, on the pitfalls to be avoided. These are said to be similar to the dangers standing in the way of brevity, including the error of 'shifting to another subject' and of 'starting out from the remotest point'.[34] But there are two additional warnings that relate specifically to the need for lucidity. One is that 'we must not speak in a perturbed or agitated style';[35] the other is that 'we must not to fail to mention anything pertinent to our case'.[36] As Thomas Wilson summarizes, we must never 'suffer our tongue to runne before our witte, but with much warenesse sette forthe our matter, and speake our mynde evermore with judgement'.[37]

The third and most important requirement is that a judicial narrative must possess verisimilitude. When we narrate the facts of a case, we are hoping to be permitted to move on to establish that our version of events can be corroborated and confirmed. So we need to persuade our judge that, as Rainolde puts it, our initial assessment is 'not unlike to be true'.[38] How, then, can we do our best to sound plausible? Cicero in his *De inventione* offers the most detailed answer:

> A narrative will sound plausible if it seems to embody qualities that commonly appear in actual fact; if the standing and dignities of the persons involved are noted; if the motives for what was done are manifest; if it appears that there were sufficient means and resources to perform the deed; if it can be shown that the time was suitable, that there was sufficient space, and that the place was an opportune one for the events about to be narrated to have occurred; and if the matter narrated fits with the known nature of those who take part in it, with the outlook of ordinary people and with the attitude of the audience. By respecting these principles it will be possible for verisimilitude to be achieved.[39]

33. Wilson 1553, Sig. P, 3[r]. As Fowler 2003, pp. 34–6 notes, Renaissance writers inherited a distinction between the 'natural' or chronological order expected of historians and the more fluid forms allowed to poets.
34. *Rhetorica ad Herennium* 1954, I. IX. 15, p. 26: 'ne quam in aliam rem transeamus, ne ab ultimo repetamus'.
35. *Rhetorica ad Herennium* 1954, I. IX. 15, p. 26: 'ne quid perturbate ... dicamus'. Cf. Cicero 1949a, I. XX. 29, p. 58.
36. *Rhetorica ad Herennium* 1954, I. IX. 15, p. 26: 'ne quid quod ad rem pertineat praetereamus'. Cf. Cicero 1949a, I. XX. 29, p. 58.
37. Wilson 1553, Sig. P, 3[r].   38. Rainolde 1563, fo. xiii[v].
39. Cicero 1949a, I. XXI. 29, p. 60: 'Probabilis erit narratio, si in ea videbuntur inesse ea quae solent apparere in veritate; si personarum dignitates servabuntur; si causae factorum exstabunt;

The author of the *Ad Herennium* offers a similar account, although he is even more exacting in his demand that our narrative should embody those qualities, which, in Cicero's phrase, 'commonly appear in actual fact'. If our narrative is to be *veri similis*, we must make sure 'that what we say is in line with custom, with common opinion and with nature'.[40] As usual, Thomas Wilson writes in close agreement. To win our case, we must ensure that 'our conjectures, tookens, reasons, & argumentes be suche that neither in them there appere any fablyng, nor yet that any thyng was spoken whiche might of right otherwyse be taken'. It is essential, in other words, for our narrative to 'appere lykely, and probable', for otherwise we cannot hope for an attentive hearing when we turn to confirm what we have alleged.[41]

There is one further consideration that is held to be of overriding importance. As the *Ad Herennium* expresses it, when we assemble our account of the facts, 'we must not only furnish an exposition of what happened, but pull it in the direction of our own advantage in order to win a victory for our cause'.[42] Cicero speaks even more emphatically, arguing that one aim of our *narratio* must always be 'to twist everything to the benefit of our cause, passing over any contrary evidence that can be passed over, and touching lightly on anything that has to be conceded'.[43] We must remember, as Quintilian summarizes, that the goal of a judicial narrative 'is not merely that the judge should be informed, but far more that he should side with us'.[44]

Quintilian goes on to explain at some length how we can hope to produce this kind of 'winning' effect. The key to success, he argues, lies in recognizing that we must be prepared not merely to regale the judge with

si fuisse facultates faciendi videbuntur; si tempus idoneum, si spati satis, si locus opportunus ad eandem rem qua de re narrabitur fuisse ostendetur; si res et ad eorum qui agent naturam et ad vulgi morem et ad eorum qui audient opinionem accommodabitur. Ac veri quidem similis ex his rationibus esse poterit.' Cf. *Rhetorica ad Herennium* 1954, I. IX. 16, p. 28; Quintilian 2001, 4. 2. 52, vol. 2, pp. 244–6.

40. *Rhetorica ad Herennium* 1954, I. IX. 16, p. 28: 'veri similis narratio erit si ut mos, ut opinio, ut natura postulat dicemus'.
41. Wilson 1553, Sig. P, 3^{r-v}.
42. *Rhetorica ad Herennium* 1954, I. VIII. 12, p. 22: 'exponimus rem gestam et unum quidque trahimus ad utilitatem nostrum vincendi causa'.
43. Cicero 1949a, I. XXI. 30, p. 62: 'omnia torquenda sunt ad commodum suae causae, contraria quae praeteriri poterunt praetereundo, quae dicenda erunt levitur attingendo'. Cf. Quintilian 2001, 4. 2. 26 and 4. 2. 80, vol. 2, pp. 230–2, 258.
44. Quintilian 2001, 4. 2. 21, vol. 2, p. 228: 'Neque . . . ut tantum cognoscat iudex, sed aliquanto magis ut consentiat'.

relevant information, but to inflame his passions at the same time. As he rhetorically asks, 'why should I not excite the judge's feelings while instructing him?'[45] One of Cicero's greatest qualities, he reminds us, was that even when simply outlining a case 'he was also able to move every emotion with the utmost quickness'.[46] Here Quintilian introduces a play on the verb *movere* that lies at the heart of his argument. The fundamental aim of a narrative should be to shift (*movere*) the judge to see things from our point of view, and one powerful means of doing so will always be to arouse (*movere*) his passions, thereby leaving him 'greatly moved'.

Thomas Wilson puts the point in even more manipulative terms. We must never lose sight of the fact that 'we purpose alwaies to have the victorie'.[47] We must therefore 'use whatsoever can bee saied, to wynne the chief hearers good willes, and perswade theim to our purpose'. If this can be done by means of reasoning, so much the better. But 'if the cause go by favour, and that reason cannot so muche availe', and 'if movyng affeccions can do more good, then bryngyng in of good reasons', then we must not hesitate to do everything in our power to arouse the passions of the judge, seeking to turn him against our adversaries and in favour of our own cause. As he levelly concludes, 'it is meete alwaies to use that waie, whereby we maie by good helpe, get the over hand'.[48] The most effective way of doing so may not be to offer reasons but rather to produce 'a stirryng, or forcyng of the mynde'.[49]

How, then, can we hope to force the mind of a judge? Quintilian gives his answer in Book 6, beginning with the arresting suggestion that 'the feelings we wish to have power over the judge must first of all have power over us; before trying to move others, we must move ourselves'.[50] This in turn leads him to ask which specific emotions we should be attempting to arouse. Alluding to the Aristotelian distinction between *ethos* and *pathos*, he argues that the art of rhetoric is largely concerned with *pathos*, with passions of the more violent kind.[51] When he itemizes them in Book 6 he speaks of rage, hatred, fear, envy and pity,[52] but in his earlier discussion he

---

45. Quintilian 2001, 4. 2. 111–12, vol. 2, p. 274: 'cur ego iudicem nolim dum doceo etiam movere?'
46. Quintilian 2001, 4. 2. 113, vol. 2, p. 274: 'omnis brevissime movit adfectus'.
47. Wilson 1553, Sig. B, 1ᵛ.   48. Wilson 1553, Sig. B, 1ʳ.
49. Wilson 1553, Sig. S, 3ᵛ.
50. Quintilian 2001, 6. 2. 28, vol. 3, p. 58: 'Primum est igitur ut apud nos valeant ea quae valere apud iudicium volumus, adficiamurque antequam adficere conemur.'
51. Quintilian 2001, 6. 2. 9, vol. 3, p. 48.   52. Quintilian 2001, 6. 2. 20, vol. 3, p. 54.

concentrates more specifically on *miseratio* and *ira*, pity and rage.[53] As he declares in summary, we need above all to know 'how to speak of crimes with hostility and of sorrow with grief'.[54]

Quintilian agrees with his predecessors that our efforts to arouse pity and rage should be pursued not merely in the *narratio* but still more in the *peroratio*,[55] and it is in connection with his analysis of the *peroratio* in Book 6 that he offers his principal examples. Certain figures and tropes, he first notes, are especially well-adapted to inducing compassion and distress. The *Ad Herennium* had already cited as an example the figure of *conduplicatio*, describing it as a particularly useful means of arousing pity or amplifying our utterances.[56] Quintilian adds the figure of *prosopopoeia*, which we employ when we pretend that the victims on whose behalf we are pleading are speaking for themselves. The impression 'of hearing the voice of those in misery' can excite the feelings of a judge so powerfully that 'their mute presence can move him to tears'.[57]

More interesting to Quintilian is the fact that we can also hope to arouse pity not merely by what we say but also by certain actions we may be able to perform in court:

> Hence the practice of bringing the accused into court dirty and unkempt, and their children and parents with them, while we see the prosecution displaying the bloody sword, the bits of bone taken from the wound, the blood-bespattered clothing, the unbandaging of the wound, the stripped bodies with the marks of the scourge. These things commonly make an enormous impression, because they confront people's minds directly with the facts. This is how Caesar's toga, carried in his funeral, covered in blood, drove the Roman people to fury. It was known that he had been killed; his body lay on the bier; but it was the clothing, wet with blood, that made the image of the crime so vivid that Caesar seemed not to have been murdered, but to be being murdered there and then.[58]

---

53. Quintilian 2001, 4. 2. 112, vol. 2. p. 274. Cf. also 4. 2. 128, vol. 2, p. 282.
54. Quintilian 2001, 4. 2. 120, vol. 2, p. 278: 'atrocia invidiose et tristia miserabiliter dicere'.
55. *Rhetorica ad Herennium* 1954, II. XXX. 47, p. 146; Cicero 1949a, I. LII. 98, p. 146.
56. *Rhetorica ad Herennium* 1954, IV. XXVIII. 38, p. 324.
57. Quintilian 2001, 6. 1. 26, vol. 3, p. 30: 'vocem auribus accipere miserorum, quorum etiam mutus aspectus lacrimas movet'. On *prosopopoeia* see also Erasmus 1569, fos. 107ʳ, 109ʳ⁻ᵛ, Peacham 1577, Sig. O, 3ʳ⁻ᵛ; [Puttenham] 1589, p. 200; Day 1592, pp. 90–1; Peacham 1593, pp. 136–7 and for a discussion see Alexander 2007.
58. Quintilian 2001, 6. 1. 30–1, vol. 3, p. 32: 'Unde et producere ipsos qui periclitentur squalidos atque deformes et liberos eorum ac parentis institutum, et ab accusatoribus cruentum gladium ostendi et lecta e vulneribus ossa et vestes sanguine perfusas videmus, et vulnera resolvi, verberata corpora nudari. Quarum rerum ingens plerumque vis est velut in rem praesentem

By introducing such elements of *pronuntiatio*, Quintilian concludes, the highest peaks of *pathos* can readily be scaled.[59]

Although Quintilian includes these suggestions in his discussion of the *peroratio*, he warns that 'it will be too late to arouse emotion if we have already spoken with complete calmness about the same matters in the course of narrating the facts'.[60] We must be sure, in other words, to make use of these techniques in our *narratio* as well as our *peroratio* if our speech is to have maximum persuasive force. There is thus a sense in which the last three elements in a judicial oration may be said to run into one another. When we state the facts we are already trenching upon the *confirmatio*, and when we state them in such a way as to excite the feelings of our judge we are already reaching out towards the culminating *peroratio* of our speech.

Narratives of accusation

When Shakespeare composes narratives in judicial causes, he usually takes some pains to follow the principles that the theorists of rhetoric prescribe. We can see this most clearly in the straightforward cases in which a character puts forward a judicial accusation in what is claimed to be an honest cause. The first to mount such a charge is the ghost in *Hamlet*, who moves uninterruptedly from his *prohoemium* to the *narratio* in which he describes how he met his death. To be fully understood, the rhetoricians had argued, a narrative must be as clear as possible, and must therefore follow the correct sequence of events. The ghost is meticulous about supplying a chronological account of how he was murdered. He tells us that he was sleeping, that his brother stole up on him, that he poured poison into his ears, that this had the effect of curdling his blood and that this brought about his instant death.[61] Thomas Wilson's injunction that we must 'tell every thyng in order'

---

animos hominum ducentium, ut populum Romanum egit in furorem praetexta C. Caesaris praelata in funere cruenta. Sciebatur interfectum eum, corpus denique ipsum impositum lecto erat, vestis tamen illa sanguine madens ita repraesentavit imaginem sceleris ut non occisus esse Caesar sed tum maxime occidi videretur.' Here I avail myself of Donald Russell's fine translation.

59. Quintilian 2001, 6. 1. 29, vol. 3, p. 32. The passage is quoted and discussed in Vickers 1988, pp. 78–9.
60. Quintilian 2001, 4. 2. 115, vol. 2, p. 276: 'Serum est enim advocare iis rebus adfectum in peroratione quas secures narraveris.'
61. *Hamlet*, TLN 676–97, p. 744 (1. 5. 59–80).

is carefully observed.[62] Next, the rhetoricians had argued, if our narrative is to be easily remembered it must be as brief as a full statement of the facts will allow. The ghost begins by referring to this second rule:

> But soft, me thinkes I sent the mornings ayre,
> Briefe let me be;

TLN 675–6, p. 744 (I. 5. 58–9)

He proceeds to pay close attention to the rhetoricians' precepts about brevity. He knows to unfold his story in such a way that he does not have to describe the complete sequence of events. Given that he was murdered while sleeping in his orchard, he must have gone into his orchard, found somewhere to rest and lain down to sleep. But this is too obvious to need saying, and the ghost (not being Polonius) does not say it. More important, he also knows the rules about the right juncture at which to begin and end a narrative. He goes no further back than the moment at which the crime was committed, nor does he carry his story further forward than the moment of the crime itself.

Of all the requirements that a narrative must satisfy, everyone agreed that the most important is verisimilitude. Here again the ghost does his best to follow the rules. One of his difficulties, however, is that he cannot hope to meet one of the main conditions laid down by the rhetoricians about how to sound plausible. 'The matter narrated', Cicero had warned, must be sure to fit 'with the outlook of ordinary people and the opinions of the audience'.[63] The ghost has no hope of being able to satisfy this requirement. As he admits himself, his narrative runs directly counter to the outlook and opinions of ordinary people, for no one in Denmark appears to believe that Claudius murdered him.

Perhaps because of this difficulty, Shakespeare makes the ghost follow with particular care the other guidelines about verisimilitude. You must show, Cicero had laid down, 'that the time was suitable, the space sufficient and the place opportune' for the perpetration of the crime.[64] Your aim, the *Ad Herennium* had added, must be to rebut any suggestion 'that there may

62. Wilson 1553, Sig. P, 3ʳ.
63. Cicero 1949a, I. XXI. 29, p. 60: 'res . . . ad vulgi morem et ad eorum qui audient opinionem accommodabitur'. Cf. *Rhetorica ad Herennium* 1954, I. IX. 16, p. 28; Quintilian 2001, 4. 2. 52, vol. 2, pp. 244–6.
64. Cicero 1949a. I. XXI. 29, p. 60: 'tempus idoneum, . . . spati satis, . . . locus opportunus'.

not have been enough time, or that the place may not have been suitable'.[65]
The ghost closely follows this advice:

> sleeping within mine Orchard,
> My custome alwayes in the afternoone,
> Upon my secure houre, thy Uncle stole
> With juyce of cursed Hebonon in a viall,
>
> TLN 676-9, p. 744 (1. 5. 59-62)

He was sleeping out of doors, so there was undoubtedly sufficient space for
the murder to be committed. He liked to sleep for an hour, so there was
ample time to administer the hebonon and escape. He always slept in the
same place, so Claudius would have known exactly where to look for him.
Space, time, and place were perfectly attuned, so that when Claudius stole
upon the king, what he was able to steal was his life.

You must next make it clear, Cicero continues, 'that there were sufficient
means and resources to perform the deed'.[66] The ghost alleges that Claudius
managed to possess himself of means that were not merely sufficient but
overwhelmingly effective:

> thy Uncle stole
> With juyce of cursed Hebonon in a viall,
> And in the porches of mine eares did poure
> The leaperous distilment, whose effect
> Holds such an enmitie with blood of man,
> That swift as quicksilver it courses through
> The naturall gates and allies of the body,
>
> TLN 678–84, p. 744 (1. 5. 61–7)

It was a simple matter for Claudius to keep the poison hidden, because he
was able to carry it in a vial; it was quick and easy to administer, because
he was able to pour it into the ears; it had so much enmity with the blood
that it took effect at once; and the enmity was so great that the body's
natural allies (as well as alleys) were overwhelmed, a hint that Claudius may
have succeeded in poisoning the body politic as well. There was no outcry,
no murder weapon, and Claudius was able to steal away unseen. The means
and resources were all to hand.

---

65. *Rhetorica ad Herennium* 1954, I. IX. 16, p. 28: 'aut temporis parum fuisse, . . . aut locum idoneum non fuisse'.
66. Cicero 1949a, I. XXI. 29, p. 60: 'fuisse facultates faciendi'.

You must also show, Cicero goes on, that 'the reasons for what was done are manifest'.[67] 'You must be able to refuse any suggestion,' the *Ad Herennium* explains, 'that there may have been no motive for the crime.'[68] The ghost rounds off his narrative by itemizing Claudius's motives for desiring his death:

> Thus was I sleeping by a brothers hand,
> Of life, of Crowne, of Queene at once dispatcht,
>
> TLN 691–2, p. 744 (I. 5. 74–5)

Claudius wanted his queen, and he also wanted his throne. With his overweening ambition and his overpowering lust he had a dual motive for his crime.

As we have seen, a narrative should not simply inform; it should aim to arouse the emotions of our judge, and in particular to induce tears of pity for our plight.[69] At first the ghost insists that he does not want to be pitied:

> GHOST   My houre is almost come
> When I to sulphrus and tormenting flames
> Must render up my selfe.
> HAMLET   Alas poore Ghost.
> GHOST Pitty me not,
>
> TLN 619–22, p. 744 (I. 5. 2–5)

He speaks very differently, however, when he goes on to explain how he met his death:

> Cut off even in the blossomes of my sinne,
> Unhuzled, disappointed, unanneld,
> No reckning made, but sent to my account
> With all my imperfections on my head,
>
> TLN 693–6, p. 744 (I. 5. 76–9)

Here he takes to heart Quintilian's advice that, if we want to arouse violent feelings in others, we must first arouse them in ourselves. Evoking his own shock and horror at dying unhuzled and disappointed—without taking the eucharist, without preparing for death[70]—he attempts to awaken in Hamlet a corresponding measure of pity and horror at the sufferings he has endured.

---

67. Cicero 1949a, I. XXI. 29, p. 60: 'causae factorum exstabunt'.
68. *Rhetorica ad Herennium* 1954, I. IX. 16, p. 28: 'refelli possit . . . causam nullam'.
69. Quintilian 2001, 4. 2. 111–12, vol. 2, p. 274.
70. On the ghost's unpreparedness see de Grazia 2007, pp. 142–3.

The ghost knows that one further means of arousing pity is to make use of certain powerfully emotive figures of speech. As we have seen, the *Ad Herennium* had particularly recommended *conduplicatio*, 'the reiteration of one or more words either for purposes of amplification or to arouse pity'.[71] Reflecting on his narrative, the ghost brings it to an end by deploying this specific device, suddenly bursting out 'O horrible, ô horrible, most horrible.'[72] Thomas Wilson similarly notes that 'the ofte repeatyng of one worde doth muche stirre the hearer', and his explanation of how this emotional effect is produced applies very well to the ghost's harrowing line. As he says, it is as if 'a sworde were ofte digged & thrust twise, or thrise in one place of the bodie'.[73]

The principal goal of a narrative is to establish that our accusation is probable, thereby gaining permission to move on to the *confirmatio* of our case and the *confutatio* of our adversaries. The ghost, however, is obviously in no position to enter into such a dialogue, and must leave it to Hamlet to take up his cause and pursue it on his behalf. As he takes leave of his son he lays this obligation upon him:

> If thou hast nature in thee beare it not,
> Let not the royall bed of Denmarke be
> A couch for luxury and damned incest.
> But howsoever thou pursuest this act,
> Tain't not thy minde, nor let thy soule contrive
> Against thy mother ought,
>
> TLN 698–703, p. 744 (I. 5. 81–6)

The act that Hamlet is enjoined to pursue is that of purifying the royal bed. As before, it appears to be as much Gertrard's adultery as Claudius's fratricide by which the ghost is preoccupied. Hamlet is being asked not merely to confirm the ghost's narrative, but to exact vengeance for both these crimes.

As in his *prohoemium*, the ghost allows himself a moment of doubt as to whether Hamlet has the necessary ability to undertake this task: 'If thou hast nature in thee beare it not'. Of course Hamlet has nature in him, but the ghost is not sure if his nature extends to taking arms against a sea of troubles. He also feels the need, as he takes his farewell, to adjure Hamlet to

---

71. *Rhetorica ad Herennium* 1954, IV. XXVIII. 39, p. 324: 'Conduplicatio est cum ratione amplificationis aut commiserationis eiusdem unius aut plurium verborum iteratio.'
72. *Hamlet*, TLN 697, p. 744 (I. 5. 80).   73. Wilson 1553, Sig. 2D, 3ʳ.

remember him,[74] as if Hamlet might forget an encounter even of such a traumatic kind.[75] As before, the ghost's doubts turn out to be well-grounded. Hamlet never explicitly promises revenge, and proves to be more concerned with memory than with action.[76] For the moment, however, his sense of pity has indeed been aroused. He now refers to 'thou poore Ghost',[77] and responds with a solemn pledge:

> thy commandement all alone shall live,
> Within the booke and volume of my braine
> Unmixt with baser matter,
>
> TLN 719–21, p. 745 (1. 5. 102–4)

The judicial 'matter' of Claudius's crime, Hamlet promises, will now occupy his mind to the exclusion of all else. He may not have promised vengeance, but he has certainly committed himself to producing a *confirmatio* of what the ghost has alleged.

★ ★ ★ ★ ★

The two other characters who have narratives of accusation to put forward in an honest cause are Rynaldo and Diana in *All's Well That Ends Well*. Rynaldo has discovered the true cause of Hellen's melancholy, and waits upon the countess to tell her what he has found out. After his brief and formulaic *prohoemium* he is about to launch into his *narratio* when he is interrupted by the clownish figure of Lavatch. As part of the comedy—but also as Shakespeare's way of breaking up what would otherwise be too long and undramatic a piece of expository prose—Lavatch is made to enter into a bantering dialogue with the countess.[78] His topic is his wish to get married,[79] and it is only after he becomes tedious and foul-mouthed on the

---

74. *Hamlet*, TLN 708, p. 745 (1. 5. 91).   75. Lewis 2012b, p. 614.

76. Kerrigan 1996, pp. 182, 186–7.   77. *Hamlet*, TLN 713, p. 745 (1. 5. 96).

78. Of all Shakespeare's strategies for avoiding prolixity in the presentation of judicial speeches, his favourite is to engineer this kind of interruption between the *prohoemium* and the *narratio*. After the *prohoemium* of Antony's answer to Brutus, the plebeians stop the flow by commenting on what he has said. After the *prohoemium* in which Isabella introduces her charge against Angelo, Angelo interrupts in an effort to have her testimony discounted. After the *prohoemium* of Othello's response to Brabantio, Brabantio intervenes in an attempt to discredit him before he can embark on his *narratio*. Nowadays we are rightly urged to see the production and 'owning' of Shakespeare's texts as a complex and partly communal matter. See, for example, Greenblatt 1988; Munro 2005, pp. 53, 164–5; Weimann and Bruster 2008; Marino 2011; van Es 2013. It is certainly plausible to imagine that Shakespeare may have worked out these kinds of details while his texts were being rehearsed for performance.

79. Lavatch appears to draw on Erasmus's letter on marriage, as Parrolles had earlier done in his debate with Hellen about virginity. Wilson 1553, Sig. F, 1^v to Sig. I, 2^v provides a translation of Erasmus's letter as a model of deliberative rhetoric.

subject, as the countess complains, that she dismisses him and Rynaldo is able to turn to his *narratio* of the facts.

Having assured the countess that he is fully aware of her fondness for Hellen, Rynaldo proceeds to tell his tale:

> Madam, I was verie late more neere her then I thinke shee wisht mee, alone shee was, and did communicate to her selfe her owne words to her owne eares, shee thought, I dare vowe for her, they toucht not anie stranger sence, her matter was, shee loved your Sonne; Fortune shee said was no goddesse, that had put such differ-ence betwixt their two estates: Love no god, that would not extend his might onelie, where qualities were levell, *Dian* no Queene of Virgins, that would suffer her poore Knight surpris'd without rescue in the first assault or ransome afterward: This shee deliver'd in the most bitter touch of sorrow that ere I heard Virgin exclaime in, which I held my dutie speedily to acquaint you withall, sithence in the losse that may happen, it concernes you something to know it.[80]

Although Rynaldo is mainly imparting information, he again reveals himself to be an almost painfully conscientious student of judicial oratory. He knows that he must state his case as lucidly as possible, and that this requires him (in Thomas Wilson's words) 'to tell every thyng in order so muche as is nedeful, observyng bothe the tyme, the place, the maner of doyng'.[81] He sticks closely to chronology, as well as taking note of the time when he came upon Hellen (very recently); the place where he saw and heard her (which she supposed to be private); and her manner of speaking (bitterly sorrowful). He also knows that he must speak concisely, and that this requires, in Wilson's phrase, 'tellyng the whole in a grosse summe'.[82] His reaction is to begin by stating the 'matter' he wishes to lay before the countess in a style that is summary to the point of abruptness: 'her matter was, shee loved your Sonne'.

While clarity and brevity are important, the basic aim is to achieve verisimilitude, and one way of doing so is to make sure that our narrative captures 'the known nature of those who appear in it'.[83] Here Rynaldo excels himself. Hellen's nature is ardent and poetical, as we already know from the Sonnet she spontaneously composes when confessing her love in soliloquy at the end of the opening scene. Rynaldo by contrast always speaks

---

80. *All's Well That Ends Well*, TLN 407–21, pp. 972–3 (I. 3. 83–94). With the insertion of '*Dian* no', the editors adopt a conjectural emendation originally proposed by Lewis Theobald.
81. Wilson 1553, Sig. P, 3ʳ.   82. Wilson 1553, Sig. P, 2ᵛ.
83. Cicero 1949a, I. XXI. 29, p. 60: 'res et ad eorum qui agent naturam . . . accommodabitur'.

with grave precision and in prose. Nevertheless, he makes a brave attempt to introduce Hellen's tone of voice into his otherwise businesslike narrative, managing to imitate her disposition to speak of love, fate, fortune, and her own sorrowful plight.

The countess immediately indicates that she regards Rynaldo's narrative as 'likely', as possessing the crucial attribute of verisimilitude. She assures him that 'manie likelihoods inform'd mee of this before, which hung so tottring in the ballance, that I could neither beleeve nor misdoubt'.[84] Thus encouraged, one might expect Rynaldo to proceed to his *confirmatio* at once. But the countess next explains that she proposes to take up the cause herself. She dismisses Rynaldo, thanking him for putting forward his honest cause but commanding that he say nothing further on the subject: 'praie you leave mee, stall this in your bosome, and I thanke you for your honest care'.[85] Rynaldo thereupon makes his exit, at which moment Hellen enters, and the countess turns to the task of finding out if Rynaldo's narrative can be confirmed.

★ ★ ★ ★ ★

The other character in *All's Well* who puts forward a narrative of accusation in an honest cause is Diana, abetted by her mother, who presents her case in the closing scene of the play. Together with her mother and Hellen, Diana has left Florence and followed the king of France to Marseilles, only to learn that he has suddenly left for Rossillion. Hellen is anxious that the king should receive as soon as possible an account of what she and Diana claim to have happened in Florence. Fortunately she encounters a 'gentle Astringer' on the road, a gentleman falconer with some attachment to the court.[86] To him she gives a letter for the king, purporting to come from Diana, which recounts the story of her alleged seduction and abandonment by Bertram.[87] This is read out by the king himself in advance of Diana's appearance

---

84. *All's Well That End's Well*, TLN 423–5, p. 973 (1. 3. 95–7).
85. *All's Well That Ends Well*, TLN 425–7, p. 973 (1. 3. 97–9).
86. The SD in *All's Well That Ends Well*, TLN 2429, p. 993 (5. 1. 6) reads: '*Enter a gentle Astringer*'. This has occasioned much editorial comment, and Hunter 1959, p. 125 follows the later Folios, as does Snyder 1993, p. 194, in changing the SD to 'Enter a Gentleman, a stranger'. But as Fraser 1985 argues, there is no reason to reject the First Folio reading that he is an 'Astringer' (or 'ostreger'), that is, a keeper of falcons, and specifically of goshawks, although admittedly it is unclear why his occupation should be specified. On the special qualities (patience, equability) needed of 'a good Falconer or Ostreger' see Turberville 1575, p. 207. They sound like good qualities for a carrier of messages, and this may be Shakespeare's point.
87. I assume in what follows that the letter is Diana's work.

(thereby reversing the usual order of *prohoemium* and *narratio*) and provides him with a summary of what Bertram mistakenly believes to have taken place at the time of the bed trick:

> *Upon his many protestations to marrie mee when his wife was dead, I blush to say it, he wonne me. Now is the Count Rossillion a Widdower, his vowes are forfeited to mee, and my honors payed to him. Hee stole from Florence, taking no leave, and I follow him to his Countrey for Justice: Grant it me, O King, in you it best lies, otherwise a seducer flourishes, and a poore Maid is undone.*
> Diana Capilet.

TLN 2659–67, p. 995 (5. 3. 139–45)

Diana knows that her narrative must be brief, and duly confines herself to admitting that she yielded to Bertram after he promised marriage. She also knows that she must be clear, and that this requires a respect for chronology. She accordingly lays out a step-by-step account: first Bertram seduced her, then he stole away, then she followed him, now she is calling for justice. Above all she knows that she must aim for verisimilitude (especially as her story is not in fact true) and again she closely follows the rhetorical rules. She refers to the dignity and standing of the persons involved, speaking of Bertram as the Count Rossillion and of herself as a poor maid, although she takes care to sign her letter with her noble name. She makes clear her reasons for writing to the king, explaining that she is not only seeking redress for a wrong but attempting to ensure that injustice does not flourish. Lastly, she invokes the attitudes of ordinary people, confessing to her shame and admitting to her blushes at allowing herself to be seduced. She draws to a close, as Quintilian had particularly advised, with a direct emotional appeal, calling on the king to grant her justice and declaring that she wishes to place her faith in no one else.

Diana's narrative scores a resounding rhetorical success. Lord Lafew, who had been in the process of marrying his daughter to Bertram (Hellen being supposed dead), for a moment displays the fire promised by his name and withdraws his plan in outraged disgust: 'I will buy me a sonne in Law in a faire, and toule for this. Ile none of him.'[88] The king immediately sees that there is a judicial case to answer, and while congratulating Lafew on a lucky escape he commands that the suitors be sought out. Bertram ignobly attempts—like Angelo when confronted by Isabella—to discredit her as 'a fond and desp'rate creature',[89] and asks the king not to think that he would so

88. *All's Well That Ends Well*, TLN 2668–9, p. 995 (5. 3. 146–7).
89. *All's Well That Ends Well*, TLN 2698, p. 996 (5. 3. 176).

much dishonour himself. But the king shockingly responds by questioning Bertram's honour and refusing to accept his word:

> Sir for my thoughts, you have them il to friend,
> Till your deeds gaine them: fairer prove your honor,
> Then in my thought it lies.
>
>   TLN 2702–4, p. 996 (5. 3. 180–2)

As the king indicates, he regards the accusation against Bertram as having reached the stage at which it will now be necessary for him to provide a *refutatio*, thereby rescuing his honour, or else for Diana to produce a *confirmatio* of her charge.

Narratives of justification

Besides presenting narratives of accusation, Shakespeare is no less interested in the contrasting type of case in which someone is obliged to tell a story in defence and justification of their cause against an accusation that they may have committed a crime or attempted to defend something indefensible. This is Friar Lawrence's predicament in the closing scene of *Romeo and Juliet*, in which he is charged with being one of the parties of suspicion in the case of a foul murder.[90] As we have seen, he responds with an insinuative *prohoemium* that wins him sufficient goodwill for the prince to prompt him to relate his version of events: 'Then say at once what thou doth know in this?'[91] It is now up to the Friar to develop a *narratio* exonerating himself from having been the cause of anyone's death.

Friar Lawrence knows that he must be brief, and begins by assuring the prince that he has taken this lesson to heart:

> I will be briefe, for my short date of breath
> Is not so long as is a tedious tale.
>
>   TLN 2918–19, p. 411 (5. 3. 229–30)

As his narrative unfolds, however, it becomes clear that he will not be able to keep his promise. *Romeo and Juliet* is a play in which several characters run on at such length that they have to be forcibly stopped. When the Nurse

---

90. *Romeo and Juliet*, TLN 2887, 2911, p. 411 (5. 3. 198, 222).
91. *Romeo and Juliet*, TLN 2917, p. 411 (5. 3. 228).

garrulously reminisces about Juliet's childhood, Lady Capulet irritably intervenes: 'Inough of this, I pray thee hold thy peace'.[92] When Mercutio unleashes his hurtling and even longer speech about Queen Mab, Romeo reacts with mock despair: 'Peace, peace, *Mercutio* peace,/ Thou talkst of nothing.'[93] The Friar is permitted to finish his narrative without interruption, but his speech is a match even for Mercutio's in length.

Although the Friar is not brief, it is arguable that he manages, as Quintilian would say, to speak as concisely as his story will allow.[94] Certainly he is careful to follow the guidelines about how to achieve brevity. There is a strong contrast here with Arthur Brooke's *Tragicall Historye of Romeus and Juliet*. The *Ad Herennium* had warned that 'we need to begin our story only where necessary, not at the ultimate starting-point',[95] but in Brooke's poem the Friar is very far from following this advice:

> And then the auncient frier
>   began to make dyscourse,
> Even from the first of Romeus,
>   And Juliets amours.
> How first by sodayn sight,
>   the one the other chose,
> And twixt them selfe dyd knitte the knotte.
>   which onely death might lose.[96]

By contrast, Shakespeare's Friar is careful to go no further back than is necessary for an understanding of what subsequently happened:

> *Romeo* there dead, was husband to that *Juliet*,
> And she there dead, that *Romeos* faithfull wife:
> I married them,
>
> TLN 2920–2, p. 411 (5. 3. 231–3)

We also need to remember, Cicero had added, that 'it is sufficient to say what happened without going into the details about how and why it happened'.[97] Again, the Friar in Brooke's poem shows no awareness of

---

92. *Romeo and Juliet*, TLN 403, p. 383 (1. 3. 50).
93. *Romeo and Juliet*, TLN 554–5, p. 385 (1. 4. 95–6).
94. Quintilian 2001, 4. 2. 47, vol. 2, p. 242.
95. *Rhetorica ad Herennium* 1954, I. IX. 14, p. 24: 'inde incipiemus narrare unde necesse est; et si non ab ultimo initio'.
96. Brooke 1562, fos. 81ᵛ–82ʳ.
97. Cicero 1949a, I. XX. 28, p. 56: 'satis est quid factum sit dicere, ut ne narres quemadmodum sit factum'.

this rule. He gives a long account of why he chose to marry the young lovers, explaining that he regarded them as well-suited and hoped that one outcome might be an end to the strife between their families. By contrast, Shakespeare's Friar is alive to the fact that none of this is relevant, and contents himself with acquainting the prince with the mere fact of the marriage itself.

Brooke's Friar next proceeds to explain how Romeo killed Tybalt and had to flee, how a marriage was arranged between Juliet and Paris, how Juliet threatened to kill herself unless the Friar found a means to prevent the match, and how he gave her a powder to simulate death. Here Shakespeare closely follows his source:

> I married them, and their stolne marriage day
> Was *Tibalts* doomesday, whose untimely death
> Banisht the new-made Bridegroome from this Citie,
> For whome, and not for *Tibalt, Juliet* pinde.
> You to remove that siege of griefe from her
> Betrothd and would have married her perforce
> To Countie *Paris*. Then comes she to me,
> And with wild lookes bid me devise some meane
> To rid her from this second mariage:
> Or in my Cell there would she kill her selfe.
> Then gave I her (so tuterd by my art)
> A sleeping potion, which so tooke effect
> As I intended, for it wrought on her
> The forme of death
>
> TLN 2922–35, pp. 411–12 (5. 3. 233–46)

To this story, however, Brooke's Friar joins a lengthy account of why he resolved to administer the sleeping potion. During his youth he had practised the occult arts, and when Juliet sought his help he decided to return to them, fearing that she might otherwise keep her promise and kill herself. Shakespeare's Friar knows that, as Cicero would put it, none of this is relevant, since our narrative only need state what actions we undertook, not why we undertook them, and again Friar Lawrence carefully follows his advice.[98]

The most important feature of any narrative is verisimilitude, but here Friar Lawrence faces an insuperable difficulty. The first rule about how to make a story sound plausible is to avoid saying anything inconsistent with

---

98. Cicero 1949a, I. XX. 28, p. 56.

the known nature of the persons involved. But the Friar has no hope of fulfilling this requirement. He is careful to make no explicit reference to the fact that his tale will appear almost incredible, but his story of clandestine marriage, magically efficacious potions, and sudden deaths is as far as possible from satisfying the condition laid down by the author of the *Ad Herennium* that no narrative should include anything contrary to nature, custom, or common belief.[99]

As with the ghost in *Hamlet*, however, this may help to explain why Shakespeare thereafter makes the Friar follow so closely the other guidelines for establishing verisimilitude:

> meane time I writ to *Romeo*
> That he should hither come as this dire night
> To help to take her from her borrowed grave,
> Being the time the potions force should cease.
> But he which bore my letter, Frier *John*,
> Was stayed by accident, and yesternight
> Returnd my letter back, then all alone
> At the prefixed hower of her waking,
> Came I to take her from her kindreds Vault,
> Meaning to keepe her closely at my Cell,
> Till I conveniently could send to *Romeo*.
> But when I came, some minute ere the time
> Of her awakening, here untimely lay,
> The Noble *Paris*, and true *Romeo* dead.
> She wakes, and I entreated her come forth
> And beare this worke of heaven with patience:
> But then a noyse did scare me from the Tombe,
> And she too desperate would not go with me:
> But as it seemes, did violence on her selfe.
> Al this I know,
>
> TLN 2935–54, p. 412 (5. 3. 246–65)

Here again there is a strong contrast with Brooke's *Romeus and Juliet,* in which the Friar's narrative is brought to a close in a style largely innocent of the rhetorical rules:

> and how that frier John
> With letters sent to Romeus,
> to Mantua is gone,

99. *Rhetorica ad Herennium* 1954, I. IX. 16, p. 28.

Of whom he knoweth not
    as yet, what is becomme,
And how that dead he found his frend
    within her kindreds tombe.
He thinkes with poyson strong,
    for care the yong man sterved,
Supposing Juliet dead, and how,
    that Juliet hath carved
With Romeus dagger drawne
    her hart and yelded breath,
Desyrous to accompany
    her lover after death.
And how they could not save
    her, so they were afeard,
And hidde them selfe, dreding the noyse
    of watchmen that they heard.[100]

Brooke sticks to chronology, but he shows no awareness of the other suggestions about how to make a narrative clear and plausible, whereas Friar Lawrence follows them meticulously. First of all, he knows that he must supply a coherent account of the time at which the tragic events took place. He duly speaks of asking Romeo to come to the tomb 'this dire night' and of how he arrived 'at the prefixed hour', or rather, as he adds with yet more precision, 'some minute ere the time'. He knows that he must establish that the place was opportune, and accordingly notes that, after giving Juliet a potion that imitated death, he needed a borrowed grave in which she could wait. He knows that he must refer to the standing of the persons involved, and speaks of the noble Paris and of Juliet as Romeo's faithful wife. Finally, he knows that he must explain the reasons for his actions, and duly tells us that he summoned Romeo to inform him where to go, and that he went to the tomb himself because, after his letter was returned, he decided to take Juliet to his cell until she and Romeo could be reunited.

    Friar Lawrence's telling of his story proves a complete rhetorical success. When he draws to a close by declaring 'Al this I know', the prince responds by assuring him 'We still have knowne thee for a holy man'.[101] As his respectful tone intimates, the prince has already been sufficiently persuaded by Friar Lawrence's narrative to be willing to permit him to present the rest

---

100. Brooke 1562, fo. 83ʳ.
101. *Romeo and Juliet*, TLN 2959, p. 412 (5. 3. 270).

of his case. It only remains for the Friar and Balthazer to provide a convincing *refutatio* of the suspicions voiced by the Chief Watchman in order to vindicate their innocence.

★ ★ ★ ★ ★

Antony in Act 3 of *Julius Caesar* likewise needs to develop a narrative in defence and justification of his cause. He has already aroused the rage of the plebeians against Brutus's contention that the death of Caesar was necessary for the preservation of Roman liberty, but he still needs to rebut the charge that he may be speaking in defence of an indefensible cause. He opens his narrative with a powerfully symbolic *pronuntiatio* or rhetorical gesture, descending from the public chair from which Brutus had harangued the plebeians in order to mingle with them as he delivers his contrasting account of the circumstances surrounding Caesar's death:[102]

> If you have teares, prepare to shed them now.
> You all do know this Mantle, I remember
> The first time ever *Caesar* put it on,
> 'Twas on a Summers Evening in his Tent,
> That day he overcame the *Nervii*.
> Looke, in this place ran *Cassius* Dagger through:
> See what a rent the envious *Caska* made:
> Through this, the wel-beloved *Brutus* stabb'd,
> And as he pluck'd his cursed Steele away:
> Marke how the blood of *Caesar* followed it,
> As rushing out of doores, to be resolv'd
> If *Brutus* so unkindely knock'd, or no:
> For *Brutus*, as you know, was *Caesars* Angel.
> Judge, O you Gods, how deerely *Caesar* lov'd him:
> This was the most unkindest cut of all.
> For when the Noble *Caesar* saw him stab,
> Ingratitude, more strong then Traitors armes,
> Quite vanquish'd him: then burst his Mighty heart,
> And in his Mantle, muffling up his face,
> Even at the Base of *Pompeyes* Statue
> (Which all the while ran blood) great *Caesar* fell.
> O what a fall was there, my Countrymen?
> Then I, and you, and all of us fell downe,
> Whil'st bloody Treason flourish'd over us.
>
> TLN 1553–76, p. 692 (3. 2. 160–83)

---

102. As noted in Wills 2011, pp. 97–8, who sees it as a movement 'from head to heart'.

Here Antony shows a full awareness of the precepts for making a narrative sound plausible. He is careful in the first place to take note of the stature and character of the persons involved. We hear about Caesar's nobility and greatness, his successful generalship, his mighty and loving heart, and on the other hand about the well-beloved Brutus's unkindness and ingratitude. He also takes care to underline what he sees as the motives for the conspiracy. Caska was envious, Brutus was ungrateful, and everyone was driven by a treasonous desire to bring their country down. He also knows to speak of the means by which their treason was accomplished. We are told about Caska's rending of Caesar's mantle, about Cassius running him through with a dagger, about Brutus stabbing him with cursed steel. Finally, we learn the details about the time and place of Caesar's death. The moment at which he was vanquished was when Brutus stabbed him, and the place where he fell was, by a terrible irony, at the base of the statue of Pompey, the mighty rival whom Caesar had overcome.

As Quintilian emphasizes, as well as outlining the facts our *narratio* must aim to excite the pity of our audience.[103] Antony rounds off by gratefully acknowledging that this is the effect he has achieved:

> O now you weepe, and I perceive you feele
> The dint of pitty: These are gracious droppes.
>
> TLN 1577–8, p. 692 (3. 2. 184–5)

Quintilian had spoken of one further means of arousing anger as well as pity in an audience. We can do so by exhibiting not merely the bloodstained clothing but the mutilated body of the victim whose cause we have espoused.[104] Plutarch in his life of Antony makes a similar point, telling us that Antony 'unfolded before the whole assembly the bloudy garments of the dead, thrust through in many places with their swords, & called the malefactors, cruell & cursed murtherers'.[105] Here Shakespeare closely follows his sources, making Antony lift Caesar's toga to reveal to the people his mangled corpse:

> Kinde Soules, what weepe you, when you but behold
> Our *Caesars* Vesture wounded? Looke you heere,
> Heere is Himselfe, marr'd as you see with Traitors.
>
> TLN 1579–81, p. 692 (3. 2. 186–8)

---

103. Quintilian 2001, 4. 2. 111–12, vol. 2, p. 274.
104. Vickers 1988, pp. 78–9 notes Antony's adoption of Quintilian's advice. See also Enders 1992, pp. 61–4.
105. Plutarch 1579, p. 976.

With his exhibiting of Caesar's marred body, and his final condemnation of the conspirators as traitors, Antony draws his story to a close.

Antony's *narratio* is an overwhelming success. As the plebeians stare at Caesar's corpse their compassion is further aroused: 'O pitteous spectacle!', 'O Noble *Caesar!*', 'O wofull day!'[106] But Antony has also succeeded in arousing in them a violent desire for vengeance. 'O Traitors, Villaines', shouts one of them, while another responds 'We will be reveng'd'.[107] The scene is set for Antony to supply the *confirmatio* of his charge that Caesar was unjustly killed, and the plebeians now make clear that they are very ready to hear him. 'Peace there, heare the Noble *Antony*', demands the first plebeian, as Antony prepares to complete the statement of his case.[108]

★ ★ ★ ★ ★

The other character in the tragedies I am considering who is forced to produce a narrative of rebuttal and justification is Othello in the scene from Act 1 in which Brabantio arraigns him on a charge of witchcraft.[109] As we saw in Chapter 4, Othello responds with an insinuative *prohoemium* that wins him so much goodwill that the duke and senators become positively eager to hear his version of events. The duke thereupon formally invites him to present his *narratio*. 'Say it *Othello*' he commands, and Othello launches into the story of his love.[110] He proceeds to offer two interconnected narratives, a central one about the tale of his life and a framing one about the telling of this tale.[111] The central story is one of wild adventure, and includes some astounding and barely credible episodes. By contrast, the framing story pays close attention to ensuring that what he says sounds as much as possible like the truth. First of all, Othello knows that he needs to refer to the standing and dignity of the persons involved. He begins by drawing attention to the fact that Desdemona's father acted as his host:

> Her Father lov'd me, oft invited me,
> Still question'd me the story of my life,
>
> TLN 413–14, p. 933 (1. 3. 127–8)

---

106. *Julius Caesar*, TLN 1582–3, p. 692 (3. 2. 189–91).
107. *Julius Caesar*, TLN 1584–5, p. 692. (3. 2. 192, 194).
108. *Julius Caesar*, TLN 1588, p. 692 (3. 2. 198).
109. Adamson 1980, p. 127 emphasizes Othello's 'story telling', but without noting that he is engaged in a forensic *narratio*.
110. *Othello*, TLN 412, p. 933 (1. 3. 126).
111. On Othello's narrative and metanarrative see Wilson 1995, pp. 102–7.

Later he emphasizes Desdemona's role as dutiful daughter and manager of the house:

> these things to heare,
> Would *Desdemona* seriously incline;
> But still the house affaires would draw her thence,
> Which ever as she could with hast dispatch,
> Shee'd come againe,
>
> TLN 430–4, p. 933 (1. 3. 144–8)

He also knows that he must establish, in Cicero's words, 'that the time was suitable, the space sufficient and the place opportune' for the alleged events to have occurred.[112] There was certainly enough time for him to tell his tale. Brabantio 'oft invited me', and Desdemona was able to listen whenever she could dispatch her house affairs. There was also sufficient space to take advantage of a pliant hour to converse with her in private.[113] Finally, the place was altogether opportune, because all their meetings happened at Desdemona's house. Othello is likewise mindful that (to quote Cicero again) he must 'make manifest the reasons for what was done'.[114] His initial reason for telling his tale was that Brabantio 'Still question'd me the story of my life'. But later he acquired a further reason for recounting it anew after noticing how much Desdemona loved to devour his discourse:

> which I observing,
> Tooke once a plyant houre, and found good meanes
> To draw from her a prayer of earnest heart,
> That I would all my pilgrimage dilate,
> Whereof by parcells she had something heard,
> But not intentively,
>
> TLN 435–40, p. 933 (1. 3. 149–54)

He was finally rewarded with her assurance that, 'if I had a friend that lov'd her,/ I should but teach him how to tell my story,/ And that would wooe her.'[115]

Othello is unable to express himself briefly, but in other respects his *narratio* follows all the classical principles, and the duke feels able to salute its rhetorical power. As we saw in Chapter 1, the metaphors generally used to

---

112. Cicero 1949a. I. XXI. 29, p. 60: 'tempus idoneum, . . . spati satis, . . . locus opportunus'.
113. *Othello*, TLN 435–9, p. 933 (1. 3. 149–53).
114. Cicero 1949a, I. XXI. 29, p. 60: 'causae factorum exstabunt'.
115. *Othello*, TLN 449–51, p. 934 (1. 3. 163–5).

portray the force of eloquence refer to conquering one's adversaries by means of 'winning' and 'disarming' speech. The duke now brings both images into play. After confiding that 'I thinke this tale would win my daughter to', he adds that Brabantio appears to have been disarmed, left with nothing but 'broken weapons' and 'bare hands'.[116] This is not to say that the duke commits himself to accepting the truth of what Othello has alleged. Othello has just been talking about men whose heads do grow beneath their shoulders, and the duke may well be reflecting, like Iago, that Othello appears to have won Desdemona by telling her fantastical lies.[117] Othello has also insisted that it was by means of his eloquence that he bewitched Desdemona, and the duke may also be wondering if the story of how exactly she was entranced may have been sanitized for public consumption. But he is willing to allow that, although Othello has yet to frame a *refutatio* of Brabantio's charge, his *narratio* already embodies the crucial quality of verisimilitude, and he already puts it to Brabantio that he will be well-advised to give up his case and 'Take up this mangled matter at the best'.[118]

Failed narratives

After the disastrous *prohoemium* of Polonius's speech about Hamlet's madness, he is again the butt of Shakespeare's satire as he turns with a self-conscious flourish to introduce the *narratio* of his case. 'Perpend', he somewhat insolently demands, calling on the king and queen to ponder the story he is about to relate.[119] As he begins, he remembers that brevity is the soul of wit, but he contrives to forget everything the rhetoricians tell us about how to avoid long-windedness.[120] The first rule is to avoid going back to the ultimate starting-point.[121] But this is what Polonius does. Convinced that Hamlet's madness stems from unrequited love for Ophelia, he begins by informing Claudius and Gertrard that 'I have a daughter, have whil'st she is mine'.[122] Starting so far back, he merely succeeds in telling them something they already know. Next, we must be careful not to digress or wander from

---

116. *Othello*, TLN 456, 458–9, p. 934 (1. 3. 170, 172–3).
117. *Othello*, TLN 905, p. 938 (2. 1. 214). On Othello's 'bombast' see Honigmann 1980.
118. *Othello*, TLN 458, p. 934 (1. 3. 171).   119. *Hamlet*, TLN 1034, p. 748 (2. 2. 105).
120. *Hamlet*, TLN 1019, p. 748 (2. 2. 90).
121. *Rhetorica ad Herennium* 1954, I. IX. 14, p. 24.
122. *Hamlet*, TLN 1035, p. 748 (2. 2. 106).

the point.[123] But again this is what Polonius does. The proof of Hamlet's love-madness, he believes, can be found in a letter that Ophelia has handed to him, and he now begins to read it out: '*To the Celestiall and my soules Idoll, the most beautified* Ophelia.'[124] But he immediately digresses: 'that's an ill phrase, a vile phrase, beautified is a vile phrase'.[125] Finally, we must be careful not to say the same thing twice.[126] But again this is what Polonius does. Before starting to read the letter, he informs Claudius and Gertrard that Ophelia 'in her dutie and obedience' has shown it to him, and as soon as he finishes he tells them again that, 'This in obedience hath my daughter shew'd me'.[127]

Polonius is no better at avoiding the pitfalls standing in the way of lucidity. The first rule is not to omit anything relevant to your case.[128] But this is what he does as he ploughs on with reading the letter: 'but you shall heare: *these in her excellent white bosome, these*'. The queen can contain herself no longer: 'Came this from *Hamlet* to her?'[129] Polonius has forgotten to mention the most pertinent fact of all. The other rule is to avoid speaking in a perturbed or agitated style.[130] As Polonius warms to his story, however, he becomes increasingly agitated, especially when he reflects that he might seem to have been pushing his daughter in the direction of a royal match. When Claudius asks how Ophelia received Hamlet's love, he suddenly bursts out: 'What doe you thinke of me?' Mollifyingly the king responds 'As of a man faithfull and honorable',[131] but Polonius becomes even more overwrought:

> I would faine prove so, but what might you thinke
> When I had seene this hote love on the wing,
> As I perceiv'd it (I must tell you that)
> Before my daughter told me, what might you,

---

123. *Rhetorica ad Herennium* 1954, I. IX. 14, p. 26.
124. *Hamlet*, TLN 1038–9, p. 748 (2. 2. 109).
125. *Hamlet*, TLN 1040–1, p. 748 (2. 2. 110). With interesting touchiness, Shakespeare appears to be settling an old score here. Robert Greene had spoken of 'an up-start Crow, beautified with our feathers', an apparent reference to the young Shakespeare. See Greene 1592, Sig. F, 1ᵛ and cf. Edwards 2003, p. 135n.; Potter 2012, pp. 98–9.
126. *Rhetorica ad Herennium* 1954, I. IX. 14, p. 26. See Edwards 2003, p. 135n., and cf. Potter 2012, pp. 98–9.
127. *Hamlet*, TLN 1036, 1054, p. 748 (2. 2. 107, 123).
128. *Rhetorica ad Herennium* 1954, I. IX. 15, p. 26.
129. *Hamlet*, TLN 1041–3, p. 748 (2. 2. 110–13).
130. *Rhetorica ad Herennium* 1954, I. IX. 15, p. 26.
131. *Hamlet*, TLN 1058–9, p. 748 (2. 2. 127–8).

> Or my deere Majestie your Queene heere thinke,
> If I had playd the Deske, or Table booke, . . .
> What might you thinke?
>
> TLN 1060–5, 1068, pp. 748–9 (2. 2. 129–34, 137)

Polonius would like to prove that he is 'honest', but he fears that appearances may be against him, and he may indeed be harbouring a desire to marry his daughter to a prince. Anxious as well as flustered, he asks the king and queen no less than four times what they think of him.

The best way to attain lucidity, everyone agrees, is simply to lay out your narrative as briefly as possible.[132] Polonius manages to round off his story by breaking this rule as well. He knows to promise 'a short tale', and indeed he has nothing to report other than his instruction to Ophelia to refuse Hamlet's advances and his belief that this drove Hamlet mad. But shortness is what he cannot manage:

> then I precepts gave her
> That she should locke her selfe from his resort,
> Admit no messengers, receive no tokens,
> Which done, she tooke the fruites of my advise:
> And he repulsed, a short tale to make,
> Fell into a sadnes, then into a fast,
> Thence to a watch, thence into a weakenes,
> Thence to a lightnes, and by this declension,
> Into the madnes wherein now he raves,
> And all we waile for.
>
> TLN 1071–80, p. 749 (2. 2. 140–9)

The decline that Polonius wants to chart is simply from sadness to madness, but he cannot resist a detour through fasting, watching, weakness, and lightness, nor the echoing figure of *anaphora* with his then, thence, thence, thence.[133] His *narratio* comes to a halt on another rambling and repetitive note.

Polonius's narrative is a model of technical incompetence, but the main question is whether it succeeds in conveying a sense of verisimilitude. The somewhat surprising answer is that in this respect it succeeds. Before hearing it, Claudius had informed Gertrard that Polonius believed himself to have uncovered 'The head and source of all your sonnes distemper'.[134] Gertrard

---

132. *Rhetorica ad Herennium* 1954, I. IX. 15, p. 26.
133. As noted in Keller 2009, p. 150.
134. *Hamlet*, TLN 983, p. 748 (2. 2. 55).

had shrewdly replied: 'I doubt it is no other but the maine/ His fathers death, and our o're-hastie marriage'.[135] After listening to Polonius, however, she changes her mind. Of Polonius's tale of rejected love Claudius now asks her: 'Doe you thinke 'tis this?' To which she replies: 'It may be very likely'.[136] Polonius's narrative strikes her as embodying the crucial quality of likelihood. Claudius immediately sees the further question that this judgement provokes: 'How may we try it further?'[137] As he recognizes, what they now need is a *confirmatio* of what Polonius has alleged.

★ ★ ★ ★ ★

The other character who presents a judicial narrative that is even more unequivocally a failure is Isabella in Act 5 of *Measure for Measure*. This passage has been little discussed,[138] and it may be that Isabella's inability to tell a convincing tale is one reason for this neglect. When she appears before the duke to mount her 'true complaint' against Angelo, her prospects at first look promising. The duke declares himself sufficiently impressed by her *prohoemium* to encourage her to continue. 'What would you say?' he asks, inviting her to proceed to the *narratio* of her case.[139] Isabella at once throws herself into her story with self-conscious concision and forcefulness:

> I am the Sister of one *Claudio*,
> Condemnd upon the Act of Fornication
> To loose his head, condemn'd by *Angelo*,
> I, (in probation of a Sisterhood)
> Was sent to by my Brother; one *Lucio*
> As then the Messenger.
>
> TLN 2234–9, p. 918 (5. 1. 69–74)

The irrepressible Lucio, hearing his name, cannot forbear from taking up the story himself:

> That's I, and't like your Grace:
> I came to her from *Claudio*, and desir'd her,
> To try her gracious fortune with Lord *Angelo*,
> For her poore Brothers pardon.
>
> TLN 2239–42, p. 918 (5. 1.74–7)

135. *Hamlet*, TLN 984–5, p. 748 (2. 2. 56–7).
136. *Hamlet*, TLN 1081–2, p. 749 (2. 2. 149–50).
137. *Hamlet*, TLN 1089, p. 749 (2. 2. 157).
138. This applies even to Wheeler 1981, Hawkins 1987, and Shuger 2001.
139. *Measure for Measure*, TLN 2233, p. 918 (5. 1. 68).

Isabella acknowledges that Lucio has now 'told somewhat of my Tale',[140] after which she completes it herself:

> In briefe, to set the needlesse processe by:
> How I perswaded, how I praid, and kneel'd,
> How he refeld me, and how I replide
> (For this was of much length) the vild conclusion
> I now begin with griefe, and shame to utter.
> He would not, but by gift of my chaste body
> To his concupiscible intemperate lust
> Release my brother; and after much debatement,
> My sisterly remorse, confutes mine honour,
> And I did yeeld to him: But the next morne betimes,
> His purpose surfetting, he sends a warrant
> For my poore brothers head.
>
> TLN 2257–68, p. 918 (5. 1. 92–103)

With her strict adherence to chronology Isabella carefully observes the basic precept about how to achieve lucidity, and at the same time follows the rhetoricians' more complex advice about how to speak with as much brevity as possible. She starts by promising to be brief; she begins her story no further back than is necessary to explain her presence before the duke; and she carries it no further forward than Angelo's broken promise, and hence her present charge. She speaks in summary style, explaining what happened but without adding any extraneous information about when and where it happened, and she narrates the outcome in such a way that various details can be inferred. Still more important, she does her best to follow the rules about how to create an air of likelihood. She begins by referring to her status and dignity, explaining that she is a postulant nun as well as the sister of the man condemned. She enlarges on Angelo's motives, claiming that he agreed to pardon Claudio only if she yielded to his lust. She indicates the opportunities afforded by the scene of the crime, emphasizing that she and Angelo met alone and spoke at length. Finally, she makes it clear that there was ample time and space for the crime to be committed, since she appears to imply that she and Angelo remained together all night.

As Isabella immediately discovers, however, she faces an insuperable difficulty in attempting to persuade her audience that her narrative embodies the crucial attribute of verisimilitude. This is not because her story is untrue,

---

140. *Measure for Measure*, TLN 2249, p. 918 (5. 1. 84).

although as we have seen it does contain one massive falsehood. (She claims to have slept with Angelo, but he has been deceived into spending the night with Mariana.) As the rhetoricians agree, however, there is no reason why such fabrications should not be made to sound entirely plausible. Isabella's problem is rather that she cannot manage to meet the two tests of plausibility on which the rhetoricians always insist: that 'the matter narrated must fit with the known nature of those who appear in it' and that what is alleged must appear inherently natural and reasonable.[141]

Shakespeare's treatment strongly contrasts at this juncture with the handling of the corresponding scene in George Whetstone's *Promos and Cassandra*. Bypassing the rhetorical complexities, Whetstone simply makes Promos confess at once to his crime.[142] Shakespeare instead makes the duke point out that Isabella's accusation fails the standard tests of plausibility. Her story is not only at variance with the known facts about Angelo's nature but inherently unreasonable:

> first his Integritie
> Stands without blemish: next it imports no reason,
> That with such vehemency he should pursue
> Faults proper to himselfe: if he had so offended
> He would have waigh'd thy brother by himselfe,
>
> TLN 2272–6, p. 918 (5. 1. 107–11)

Isabella's narrative lacks any verisimitude, and the duke dismisses it with deepest sarcasm: 'This is most likely!'[143] She is left to bewail the unbridgeable gulf between the essential truth of her story and its lack of likelihood: 'Oh that it were as like as it is true.'[144] As always, her own oratory is soaring, but she finds herself in a dilemma in which the maxims and prescriptions so beloved of the rhetoricians have no power to help.

Fortunately for Isabella, her story is subsequently confirmed by the testimony of Mariana and the truth about Angelo is finally revealed. Meanwhile, however, she is made painfully aware that her narrative has failed:[145]

---

141. Cicero 1949a, I. XXI. 29, p. 60: 'res et ad eorum qui agent...accommodabitur.' Cf. *Rhetorica ad Herennium* 1954, I. IX. 16, p. 28: 'veri similis narratio erit si ut...natura postulat dicemus'.

142. Whetstone 1578, Sig. K, 2^r.

143. *Measure for Measure*, TLN 2268, p. 918 (5. 1. 103—from which I adopt the exclamation mark).

144. *Measure for Measure*, TLN 2269, p. 918 (5. 1. 104).

145. For a discussion see Greenblatt 1988, pp. 138–42.

> And is this all?
> Then oh you blessed Ministers above
> Keepe me in patience, and with ripned time
> Unfold the evill, which is heere wrapt up
> In countenance: heaven shield your Grace from woe,
> As I thus wrong'd, hence unbeleeved goe.
>
> TLN 2279–84, p. 918 (5. 1. 114–19)

With her final rhyming couplet Isabella signals that she is about to take her leave, but as she does so the duke violently intervenes:

> I know you'ld faine be gone: An Officer:
> To prison with her:
>
> TLN 2285–6, p. 918 (5. 1. 120–1)

Isabella's attempt to develop her accusation against Angelo is brought to a sudden and shocking stop. There is no question of being allowed to attempt a *confirmatio*; she is permitted no further speech and is led away under guard.

7

Confirmation

Juridical and Legal Issues

Two methods of confirmation

Aristotle distinguishes in Book 1 of his *Art of Rhetoric* between two different types of rhetorical confirmation and proof.[1] Some are said to be *atechnoi*, not dependent for their effectiveness on rhetorical techniques, and these are subsequently classified by Quintilian as 'non-artificial' proofs. But most methods of confirmation are said to be *entechnoi*, wholly dependent on the successful application of rhetorical principles, and these Quintilian describes as 'artificial' proofs.[2] The earliest Roman rhetorical writers find little to say about non-artificial proofs, and the author of the *Ad Herennium*, evidently writing before the general availability of Aristotle's *Rhetoric*, says nothing about them at all.[3] Quintilian, by contrast, sternly objects that 'those who have failed to include this *genus* in their teachings are very much to be blamed', and proceeds in Book 5 of his *Institutio oratoria* to examine the concept of non-artificial confirmation at considerable length.[4]

Aristotle had argued that the most important methods of non-artificial confirmation are by means of legal documents—especially laws and contracts—and

1. Aristotle 1926, I. 2. 2, p. 14. For a discussion see Serjeantson 2007, pp. 184–5.
2. See Quintilian 2001, 5. 1. 1–2, vol. 2, p. 324 on the distinction between proofs that are *inartificiales* and *artificiales*. Cf. Erasmus 1569, fo. 126ʳ.
3. But Cicero in his *Topica* mentions what he calls 'extrinsic' proofs, and in *De oratore* gives some examples. See Cicero 1949b, II. 8, p. 386 and IV. 24, p. 396. See also Cicero 1942b, II. 6, p. 314 on *testimonia* and Cicero 1942a, II. XXVII. 116, vol. 1, p. 282 on *tabulae* and *testimonia*.
4. Quintilian 2001, 5. 1. 2, vol. 2, p. 324: 'magnopere damnandi qui totum hoc genus a praeceptis removerunt'.

the testimony of trustworthy witnesses.[5] Quintilian takes up each of these topics, but chiefly focuses on the value and usefulness of witnesses, arguing the question on both sides of the case. On the one hand, a skilful advocate can always try to undermine or discredit them:[6] 'A timid witness can be terrorised, a fool deceived, the irascible provoked, the ambitious flattered, the long-winded encouraged in his prolixity.'[7] But on the other hand, 'there is a case for saying that no firmer proof can be given than that which depends on an intimate knowledge of men'.[8] There is therefore a case for saying that the testimony of witnesses—especially if they are numerous and honest[9]—may be capable of providing the strongest confirmation of all. This reflection is only strengthened when we recall that, while forensic arguments may be more or less ingenious, witnesses will usually be giving their evidence under oath.[10]

To this analysis Quintilian adds that some other forms of argument, although not strictly non-artificial, are capable of giving rise to almost the same degree of proof. The most obvious are those that stem from our sense impressions, for 'the primary way in which we take things to be certain is when they are perceived by the senses'.[11] When we cannot doubt that we have seen or heard something, this type of proof is so strong that no scope is left for judicial dispute.[12] Such arguments, at their strongest, are said to be capable of yielding levels of confirmation that Quintilian does not hesitate to describe as indubitable.[13] Richard Rainolde appears to have the same kind of proof in mind when he writes, at the outset of his discussion of 'Confirmacion' in *The Foundacion of Rhetorike*, that one way 'to stablishe and

---

5. Aristotle 1926, I. 15. 1, p. 150 and I. 15. 17, p. 158. For a discussion see Shapiro 2001, pp. 55–9. Joseph 1947, pp. 92–108 examines testimony (and Shakespeare's use of it) but has nothing to say about witnesses.
6. Cicero 1949a has nothing to say about how this can be done, but there are some brief suggestions in *Rhetorica ad Herennium* 1954, II. VI. 9, p. 74.
7. Quintilian 2001, 5. 7. 26, vol. 2, p. 346: 'timidus terreri, stultus decipi, iracundus concitari, ambitiosus inflari, longus protrahi potest'. Here again I avail myself of Donald Russell's fine translation.
8. Quintilian 2001, 5. 7. 4, vol. 2, p. 336: 'nullam firmiorem probationem esse contendit quam quae sit hominum scientia nixa'.
9. Quintilian 2001, 5. 7. 24, vol. 2, p. 346.
10. Quintilian 2001, 5. 7. 33, vol. 2, p. 352.
11. Quintilian 5. 10. 12, vol. 2, p. 372: 'Pro certis autem habemus primum quae sensibus percipiuntur.'
12. Quintilian 2001, 5. 9. 2, vol. 2, p. 358.
13. Quintilian 2001, 5. 9. 2, vol. 2, p. 358 and 5. 10 12, vol. 2, p. 372.

upholde the cause' is to 'Shewe the matter to be manifest', that is, clear to the eye and hence beyond doubt.[14]

From the earliest period at which the study of Roman law was reintroduced in Western Europe, the production of relevant legal documents, together with the sworn testimony of witnesses, came to be regarded as core elements in legal proof.[15] With the revival of classical rhetoric in the Renaissance, the same assumptions began to be more fully developed. Richard Sherry already speaks in detail about such 'unartificiall' forms of proof. He agrees with Quintilian about the importance of documents and witnesses, to which he adds that the testimony of divinations and oracles ought also to be allowed.[16] Abraham Fraunce reformulates Quintilian's basic distinction as a contrast between 'inherent arguments' and those that are 'borrowed elsewhere', and are 'properly called a testimony or witnesse'. Fraunce concedes that, 'in exquisite searching out of the truth' about natural occurrences, the value of witnesses 'is but of small force', but he agrees with Quintilian that, when it comes to civil affairs, this kind of proof 'much prevayleth'. When a witness 'is beleeved, by reason of his vertue, wisedome, &c.' this amounts to an 'inherent' argument and is virtually impossible to overturn or set aside.[17]

The importance of witnesses in the trying of judicial causes began to be similarly emphasized in later sixteenth-century handbooks on common law.[18] When in 1592 William Lambarde reissued his *Eirenarcha*, a guide for justices of the peace originally published in 1581, he included a table of instruction on 'The examination of an offence' in which he not only noted that in 'a conjectural state of a cause' it is sometimes possible to find 'witnesses that prove it', but added that such proofs may sometimes be regarded as 'necessary', and hence as certain as opposed to merely probable.[19] When witnesses pass various tests—appropriate age, known discretion, good reputation, proven trustworthiness—their testimony will undoubtedly be believed, and can thus be treated (as Fraunce had put it) not merely as likely but as an inherent argument.[20]

Although the earliest generation of Roman rhetoricians find little to say about such non-artificial proofs, they give a full account of the contrasting

14. Rainolde 1563, fo. xxx[v].   15. Wickham 2003, pp. 75, 131.
16. Sherry 1550, Sig. E, 7[v]–8[r].   17. Fraunce 1588b, p. 65.
18. On this development see Shapiro 1991, pp. 114–85; Hutson 2007, pp. 72–8, 146–7.
19. Lambarde 1592, pp. 212–13. See Shapiro 2001, pp. 64–6; Hutson 2007, pp. 251–3.
20. On these tests see Shapiro 2000, pp. 14–17.

and 'artificial' forms of confirmation that are held to depend in part on oratorical skill, and may consequently be said to lie, in Quintilian's words, 'wholly within the scope of the art of rhetoric'.[21] They begin by observing that, before deciding on what type of confirmation is best suited to your cause, you need to make sure that you have correctly identified the *constitutio* or 'issue' in which you are involved.[22] Suppose the question at issue is *legalis* or legal in character. As we saw in Chapter 1, this is to say that your cause arises out of a controversy surrounding a legal text.[23] If this is so, then the right way to set about confirming your cause will obviously be to examine and interpret the text itself. As to how this process should be conducted, the rhetoricians offer a number of specific words of advice. You may find it worthwhile, Cicero suggests, to insist that there is something ambiguous about the wording of the text.[24] Or you may find it helpful to claim that there are good reasons for cleaving to the exact wording of the text rather than considering the intentions of the writer, arguing that 'nothing except what is written should be regarded'.[25] Or you may find it possible to challenge the legal standing of the text by invoking a *lex contraria*, a contrary law. If you are in a position to pursue this course, then 'the most important point you must try to make is that the law on which you plan to rest your case is concerned with more important matters' than the contrary law or legal agreement that your adversary has invoked.[26]

Quintilian takes up the same topics in Book 7 of the *Institutio oratoria*, concentrating on questions about the spirit *versus* the letter of the law and on how to handle contrary laws. Discussing the first problem, he is keen to point out that, 'whereas the pleader who focuses on the will of the lawgiver will have to cast doubt on the letter of the law so far as possible, the defender of the letter can attempt to gain help from invoking the will of the lawgiver

21. Quintilian 2001, 5. 8. 1, vol. 2, p. 354: 'quae est tota in arte'.
22. *Rhetorica ad Herennium* 1954, I. XI. 18, p. 32. Cf. Cicero 1949a, I. VIII. 10, p. 20.
23. *Rhetorica ad Herennium* 1954, I. XI. 18, p. 34; Cicero 1949a, I. XI. 14, p. 30; Quintilian 2001, 3. 6. 45, vol. 2, p. 70.
24. Cicero 1949a, II. XL. 116–18, pp. 284–6.
25. Cicero 1949a, II. XLIII. 125, p. 292: 'nihil . . . nisi id quod scriptum spectare oportere'. For his discussion of spirit *versus* letter see Cicero 1949a, II. XLII–XLVIII, 121–43, pp. 290–312.
26. Cicero 1949a, II. XLIX. 145, p. 312: 'Primum igitur . . . considerando . . . magis necessarias res pertinet.' For his discussion of contrary laws see Cicero 1949a, II. XLIX. 144–7, pp. 312–16. For similar lists see *Rhetorica ad Herennium* 1954, I. XI. 19, p. 34; Quintilian 2001, 3. 6. 61, vol. 2, p. 80 and 3. 6. 86–9, vol. 2, p. 92.

as well'.[27] Turning to contrary laws, he argues that, in cases where the legal point is admitted by both parties, the consideration to be borne in mind is whether the enforcement of one law rather than the other 'will lead to a lesser loss'.[28] Closely following Quintilian, Thomas Wilson in his discussion of 'the State legall' in his *Arte of Rhetorique* likewise concentrates on the use that can be made of contrary laws. He observes that 'it often happeneth that lawes seme to have a certaine repugnancie', and he concludes that the first rule to invoke in the process of confirmation must always be to claim that 'the inferioure law must give place to the superiour'.[29]

Suppose, however, that the issue raised by your cause is not *legalis* but *iuridicalis* or juridical in character. Here, as we also saw in Chapter 1, the controversy will revolve around whether something was rightfully or unjustly done.[30] If you are engaged in this type of dispute, the question of how to confirm your side of the argument will in turn depend on whether you are able to present an absolute or merely an assumptive case.[31] If you feel able to maintain that your cause is absolute you will be claiming, in the words of the *Ad Herennium*, that your action was undertaken *recte*, according to what is right, and also *iure*, in accordance with the law and without any *iniuria* or injustice.[32] If that is so, then you can hope to confirm these claims by showing that your conduct was sanctioned by law, or custom, or precedent, or 'the principles of equity and goodness' or 'a bond agreed between parties'.[33] Thomas Wilson agrees that 'when the matter by the awne nature, is defended to bee righte, without any further sekyng', then it is called 'the state absolute'.[34] He further agrees that the most persuasive way of confirming such a claim will be to try to show that the act in question is sanctioned by 'True dealying', or by 'Auncient examples', or by 'Covenauntes and deedes autentique'.[35]

---

27. Quintilian 2001, 7. 6. 3, vol. 3, p. 268: 'Sed ut qui voluntate nitetur scriptum quotiens poterit infirmare debebit, ita qui scriptum tuebitur adiuvare se etiam voluntate temptabit.'
28. Quintilian 2001, 7. 7. 8, vol. 3, p. 274: 'utra minus perdat'.
29. Wilson 1553, Sig. N, 4^{r-v}.
30. *Rhetorica ad Herennium* 1954, I. XIV. 24, p. 42; Cicero 1949a, I. XI. 14–15, p. 30; Quintilian 2001, 3. 6. 45–6, vol. 2, p. 70.
31. *Rhetorica ad Herennium* 1954, I. XIV. 24, p. 42. Cf. Cicero 1949a, II. XXIII. 69, p. 232.
32. On the need for the action to be done *recte* see *Rhetorica ad Herennium* 1954, I. XIV. 24, p. 44. On the need for it to be done *iure* and without *iniuria* see *Rhetorica ad Herennium* 1954, I. XIV. 24, p. 42 and II. XIII. 19, p. 90. Cf. Cicero 1949a, II. XXIII. 69, p. 232.
33. *Rhetorica ad Herennium* 1954, I. XIII. 19. p. 90: 'lege, consuetudine, iudicato, aequo et bono, pacto'. On *ius* arising from *pactum* see also II. XIII. 20, p. 94.
34. Wilson 1553, Sig. O, 1^{v}. 35. Wilson 1553, Sig. O, 1^{v}.

If, however, you are obliged to admit that you have been involved in a crime, and thus that your case is merely assumptive, the only way to establish the justice of your plea will be to argue that you deserve to be excused.[36] As to how this can be done, the author of the *Ad Herennium* is emphatic that you must be sure to mount your case in three connected steps. You must first try to show that you acted under coercion or duress.[37] Next you must try to blame someone else for what happened.[38] Finally, you must affirm that what you did was unavoidable, and that you chose the lesser of two evils.[39] As before, Thomas Wilson closely follows these arguments. He speaks of trying to show, of an action that we hope to excuse, 'that wee did it upon commaundement', that 'evill companie' was to blame, and that either we had to perform the action 'or els have doen worse'.[40]

Suppose, finally, that the issue raised by your cause is neither *legalis* nor *iuridicalis* but *coniecturalis* in character. Here, as we likewise saw in Chapter 1, you will be pleading in a case in which the controversy will be about some matter of fact, and more specifically about some mystery surrounding a matter of fact that needs to be resolved.[41] Here, the right way to confirm your side of the argument will be to form a conjecture about the cause of what happened and go in search of clues until you arrive at the stage at which you are prepared to insist that your initial conjecture has been vindicated. As to what is involved in this process, the clearest answer can be found in Book 2 of the *Ad Herennium*, the argument of which was later developed by Quintilian in Book 5 of the *Institutio oratoria*[42] and subsequently taken up with very little alteration by the legal as well as the rhetorical writers of Shakespeare's England.

From the *Ad Herennium* we learn that there are five stages in the process of rhetorical confirmation in conjectural causes, culminating in a sixth when we simply declare 'that our suspicions have been fully and finally confirmed'.[43] The initial step consists of establishing what is *probabilis* about

36. *Rhetorica ad Herennium* 1954, I. XIV. 24, p. 44. Cf. Cicero 1949a, I. XI. 15, p. 30.
37. *Rhetorica ad Herennium* 1954, I. XV. 25, p. 46. Cf. Cicero 1949a, II. XXVI. 78, p. 242.
38. *Rhetorica ad Herennium* 1954, I. XV. 25, p. 46. Cf. Cicero 1949a, II. XXVIII. 86, p. 252.
39. *Rhetorica ad Herennium* 1954, I. XV. 25, p. 48. Cf. Cicero 1949a, II. XXIV. 72, p. 236.
40. Wilson 1553, Sig. O, 2^r.
41. *Rhetorica ad Herennium* 1954, I. XI. 18, p. 34. Cf. Cicero 1949a, I. VIII. 10, p. 20.
42. *Rhetorica ad Herennium* 1954, II. 2. 4 to II. 5. 8, pp. 62–72. Cf. Quintilian 2001, 5. 10. 33–52, vol. 2, pp. 382–90.
43. *Rhetorica ad Herennium* 1954, II. VI. 9, p. 72: 'Approbatio est qua utimur ad extremum confirmata suspicione.'

our adversary and his case. Here we need to be careful not to misunderstand what the rhetoricians mean by this slippery term. Some critics have been too ready to assume that *probabilis* must always mean 'likely' or 'probable', and thus that the rhetorical culture in which Shakespeare was writing condemned his characters to living in a 'suppositional' world of mere probabilities.[44] It is true that, when Cicero speaks of arguments as *probabilis* he generally means that they are likely as opposed to being necessary or demonstrable.[45] But if we return to the author of the *Ad Herennium* we find him claiming that *probabilis* can also mean provable, that is, susceptible to being tested and confirmed.[46] More specifically, we may be said to attain this level of proof when we manage to establish that our adversary had a motive for committing a crime, when we are able to connect his motive with his previous way of life, and when we manage to point to the benefits that he may have hoped to achieve by his criminal act.[47]

Turning to the next two steps, the author of the *Ad Herennium* expands his earlier account of how to lend verisimilitude to narratives. The second stage is the *conlatio*, when we try to show that our adversary possessed the means and ability to commit his crime, that no one else could have committed it, and that he could not have committed it by any means other than those which he employed.[48] The third stage involves looking for *signa* or signs that our adversary 'sought means favourable to his success'.[49] We must try to demonstrate that he chose a suitable place (*locus*), an appropriate time and space (*tempus*, *spatium*), and had 'hopes of evading detection and hopes of success'.[50]

---

44. See, for example, Altman 2010, pp. 1–3.
45. See, for example, Cicero 1949a, I. XXIX. 44, p. 82.
46. On the link between *probabilis* and *probare* see *Rhetorica ad Herennium* 1954, II. II. 3, p. 62. For the translation of *probabilis* not merely as 'like to the truth' but as 'may be proved to be true' see Veron 1584, Sig. 2K, 4ᵛ; Thomas 1592, Sig. 2P, 7ʳ. The meaning is preserved in the maxim that 'the exception proves the rule'—that is, puts the rule to a probative or confirmatory test.
47. See *Rhetorica ad Herennium* 1954, II. II. 3, p. 62 on *causa* and *commoditas* and II. III. 5, p. 64 on *vita*. Cf. Cicero 1942a, II. V. 17 to II. XI. 37, vol. 1, pp. 180–98. The question of motivation is also discussed under the heading of *narratio* in *Rhetorica ad Herennium* 1954, I. IX. 16, p. 28. See also Cicero 1949a, I. XXI. 29, p. 60; Quintilian 2001, 5. 10. 33–6, vol. 2, pp. 382–4.
48. *Rhetorica ad Herennium* 1954, II. IV. 6, p. 66: 'alium neminem potuisse perficere nisi adversarium, aut eum ipsum aliis rationibus . . . non potuisse'. For similar comments under *narratio* see *Rhetorica ad Herennium* 1954, I. IX. 16, p. 28. See also Cicero 1949a, I. XXI. 29, p. 60.
49. *Rhetorica ad Herennium* 1954, II. IV. 6, p. 66: 'signum est per quod ostenditur idonea perficiendi facultas esse quaesita'.
50. See *Rhetorica ad Herennium* 1954, II. IV. 6, p. 66 on the *locus*, *tempus*, *spatium*, *occasio*, *spes perficiendi*, and *spes celandi*. For similar comments under *narratio* see *Rhetorica ad Herennium* 1954, I. IX. 16, p. 28. See also Cicero 1949a, II. XII. 38–41, pp. 200–2 and Cicero 1949a,

This concern with time, place, space, and so forth is helpfully redescribed by the vernacular rhetoricians as an interest in the 'circumstances' of actions. Richard Sherry offers an extensive list of 'circumstances of the thynges', including 'Cause, place, tyme, chaunce, facultie, instrumente, manour'.[51] Dudley Fenner similarly speaks of 'matter, time, place, persons, and all such circumstances',[52] while George Puttenham refers to 'circumstances of the person, place, time, cause and purpose'.[53] To speak of 'circumstances', in other words, is to recall the Aristotelian and Ciceronian concept of a *topos* or *locus*, a place in which we can hope to find (*invenire*) suitable arguments.[54] The rhetorical concept of the circumstances of actions thus becomes equivalent in effect to the dialectical concept of the topics of arguments. If, for example, you now think of the motive or cause of an action as the name of a 'place', this will have the effect of alerting you to think about possible reasons for some particular action, thereby initiating the process of making it intelligible and solving what may be some mystery about it.[55]

Sometimes the investigation of such circumstances is primarily associated with the stage of the *narratio*. When Thomas Wilson argues that a satisfactory narrative must be sure to respect chronology, he explains that it is always best 'to tell every thyng in order so muche as is nedeful, observyng bothe the tyme, the place, the maner of doyng, and the circumstaunces thereunto belongyng'.[56] But other writers chiefly associate the investigation of circumstances with the *confirmatio*. Leonard Cox advises that, if you are attempting to prove that someone has committed a crime, 'ye must go to the circumstance of the cause/ as that he had leyser ynough thereto/ and place convement and strength withall'.[57] Thomas Wilson subsequently comes round to this way of thinking when he adds (in the course of discussing 'confirmacion in matters of judgement') that we should mark 'the place, the maner of doyng' as well as 'thoportunitie of doyng and the power he had to do this deede'.[58]

Of the two remaining elements in the successful *confirmatio* of a conjectural cause, the first is described in the *Ad Herennium* as the stage at which

I. XXI. 29, p. 60. Quintilian discusses signs in Quintilian 2001, 5. 9. 1–6, vol. 2, pp. 358–64 and questions about about time and place in Quintilian 2001, 5. 10. 37–48, vol. 2, pp. 384–90.
51. Sherry 1550, Sig. F, 2ʳ.
52. [Fenner] 1584, Sig. D, 1ʳ.   53. [Puttenham] 1589, p. 129.
54. For Cicero's adaptation of Aristotle's concept of a *topos*, see Cicero 1949b, II. 7–8, pp. 386–8. Cf. Quintilian 2001, 5. 10. 20–22, vol. 2, pp. 374–6.
55. See Weaver 2008; Hutson 2015.   56. Wilson 1553, Sig. P, 3ʳ.
57. Cox 1532, Sig. E, 5ᵛ.   58. Wilson 1553, Sig. Q, 2ʳ⁻ᵛ.

we look for *argumenta*, the specific kinds of argument that serve 'greatly to increase our suspicion' of the accused.[59] When a crime has been committed, we first need to reflect on the behaviour of the defendant before it occurred. Did he make any preparations, or indicate that he had any accomplices? Next we need to concentrate on the moment when the crime was carried out. Was anything suspicious seen, or were any noises or outcries heard? Lastly, we need to consider the period immediately afterwards. Was anyone seen near the spot, or was anything incriminating left behind, such as an *instrumentum* or implement that could have been put to criminal use?[60]

The final stage is described in the *Ad Herennium* as the *consecutio*.[61] Here we investigate the possible impact of the crime on the person suspected of perpetrating it, trying to establish whether he can be said to exhibit any subsequent signs of guilt.[62] 'The prosecutor must claim if he can', the *Ad Herennium* advises, 'that as soon as people arrived on the scene'[63] the accused behaved in ways 'that are *signa conscientiae*, indications of a guilty conscience'.[64] More specifically, he must try to show that the following terms apply to the demeanour of the suspect: *erubescere, expallescere, titubare*, and *concidere*.[65] Consulting Cooper's *Thesaurus*, we find that in Shakespeare's England *erubescere* was understood to mean 'to blush: to be ashamed';[66] *expallescere* 'to be very pale';[67] *titubare* 'to stagger in speakynge or goinge';[68] and *concidere* 'to fall downe: to die: to fainte'.[69] The aim of the prosecutor is to show that the accused behaved in some or all of these apparently incriminating ways.

The investigation of signs carries us to the heart of the process of confirmation, and the vernacular rhetoricians lay still greater emphasis on

---

59. See *Rhetorica ad Herennium* 1954, II. V. 8, p. 70 on how confirmation can be strengthened 'magis firma suspicione'.
60. *Rhetorica ad Herennium* 1954, II. V. 8, pp. 70–2. Quintilian 2001, 5. 10. 52, vol. 2, p. 390 adds the detail about the *instrumentum*.
61. *Rhetorica ad Herennium* 1954, II. V. 8, p. 72. Cf. Cicero 1949a, II. XII. 42, p. 202.
62. See *Rhetorica ad Herennium* 1954, II. V. 8, p. 72 on 'signa nocentis'.
63. *Rhetorica ad Herennium* 1954, II. V. 8, p. 72: 'Accusator dicet, si poterit, adversarium, cum ad eum ventum sit, . . .'
64. See *Rhetorica ad Herennium* 1954, II. V. 8, p. 72 on 'signa conscientiae'.
65. *Rhetorica ad Herennium* 1954, II. 5. 8, p. 72.
66. Cooper 1565, Sig. 2V, 1ᵛ. On blushing and guilt in Shakespeare see Bevington 1984, pp. 96–8.
67. Cooper 1565, Sig. 2Z, 1ʳ. Cooper mistakenly gives *expallere* (rather than *expallescere*) as the infinitive. For the correct form, and for a similar definition ('to be or waxe very pale') see Thomas 1592, Sig. T, 3ᵛ.
68. Cooper 1565, Sig. 6H, 2ʳ.   69. Cooper 1565, Sig. 2A, 3ᵛ.

it. Leonard Cox maintains that, in seeking to confirm a conjectural issue, our basic aim should be to 'prove it by signes/ whiche are of mervaylouse efficacye in this behalfe'. He goes on to explain that 'here must be noted that sygnes be eyther wordes or dedes that either did go before or els folow the dede'.[70] For example, when investigating the behaviour of a suspect we may find that 'after the dede was done he fled', or that 'whan it was layed to his charge: he blushed or waxed pale or stutted & coulde nat well speke'.[71] Thomas Wilson provides a similar list in his Rule of Reason, later expanding it in his Arte of Rhetorique. It will be suspicious if we find someone 'waxyng pale when he is apprehended, shakynge for feare, or runnyng awaye'.[72] We must also take special note of whether he 'had anye bloude aboute him, or trembled, or stakerde, or was contrarie in tellying of his tale'.[73] More generally, we must consider 'how he kept his countenaunce' and whether 'his coloure chaungeth, his bodye shaketh, and hys tongue foultereth wythin hys mouthe'.[74]

The same preoccupations recur in later sixteenth-century legal texts concerned with the investigation of felonies.[75] Thomas Smith in his chapter on 'Proceedings in Causes Criminal' in De Republica Anglorum notes that judges will generally call as witnesses 'all those who were at the apprehension of the prisoner, or who can give any indices or tokens which we call in our language evidence against the malefactor'.[76] William Lambarde's Eirenarcha and Richard Crompton's handbook for justices of the peace[77] similarly require that, in considering the time subsequent to an alleged offence, the investigating Justice should always look for 'signs' of the accused's probable guilt. Both writers offer particularly elaborate lists, which include 'having blood, or the goods about him: his flying away: his blushing, or change of countenance: his being in company with other offendors: his offer of composition: the measure of his foote: the bleeding of the dead body, etc'.[78]

70. Cox 1532, Sig. E, 5ᵛ.   71. Cox 1532, Sig. E, 6ʳ. See also Sherry 1550, Sig. E, 8ʳ.
72. Wilson 1551, Sig. M, 2ʳ.   73. Wilson 1553, Sig. N, 2ᵛ.   74. Wilson 1553, Sig. N, 3ᵛ.
75. On judicial rhetoric as a basis for legal procedures see Kahn 1989; Goodrich 2001; Mukherji 2006, pp. 4–7.
76. Smith 1982 [1583], pp. 110, 114. See Hutson 2007, pp. 181–2.
77. Crompton's treatise is partly drawn from Anthony Fitzherbert's manual of the 1520s. It was first published in 1583 and reissued in revised form in 1587. My quotations are taken from the 1587 edition (BL copy).
78. Lambarde 1592, pp. 212–13. Crompton 1587, fo. 89ʳ⁻ᵛ reiterates Lambarde's list, while referring us for further details to 'le Lievr del Arte de Rethoricke, compose per Master

This entire process of confirmation in conjectural causes is summarized in the *Ad Herennium* as that of attempting to reach a point of *approbatio* at which we feel able to insist that an initial suspicion has finally been validated.[79] Thomas Wilson picks up the claim about suspicion, arguing that in every conjectural cause there will be some 'matter' being 'examined and tried out by suspicions gathered'.[80] From there it proved a short step to the incorporation into common law texts of this classical understanding of how suspicions can be converted into proofs.[81] Lambarde's table of instructions in his *Eirenarcha* specifies that the correct way to approach any such 'matter' is to focus on the time precedent, the time present, and the time immediately subsequent to any alleged crime. His whole scheme, as he acknowledges, is 'collected out of Cicero, and others',[82] and his pattern of investigation closely follows the *Ad Herennium*. Within a generation, as can be seen from Michael Dalton's *The Countrey Justice*, first published in 1618,[83] the principles originally formulated by the classical rhetoricians had become absorbed, almost without alteration, into the legal instructions offered to magistrates for examining suspects in all types of offence.[84]

The juridical issue

When Shakespeare first became interested in the technicalities of judicial rhetoric, it was the assumptive version of the juridical issue that initially captured his attention. As we saw in Chapter 4, the first such case he considered was that of Lucrece. But before we examine how Lucrece attempts to confirm her assumptive plea, we should first take note of a much earlier work in which Shakespeare had already referred—although only obliquely—to the same rhetorical predicament. The work in question is *The Comedie of Errors*, which may have been written as early as 1590.[85]

Wilson'. On Crompton and Lambarde see Shapiro 2001, p. 65; Hutson 2007, pp. 80, 211–13, 251–3.

79. *Rhetorica ad Herennium* 1954, II. VI. 9, p. 72.   80. Wilson 1553, Sig. N, 1ᵛ.
81. For a full exploration of this theme see Hutson 2007, to which I am much indebted.
82. Lambarde 1592, p. 211.
83. A revision appeared in 1622, and this is the version to which I refer (BL copy).
84. See Dalton 1622, pp. 275–6, a list fuller than Lambarde's but comparable with it.
85. The first recorded performance took place at Gray's Inn on 28th December 1594. Wells and Taylor 1987, pp. 116–17 conjecture that the play must have been written during that year. But King 2005, p. 40 argues for 1590, while Foakes 1962, p. xxiii suggests between 1590 and 1593.

The play begins with a lengthy *narratio* from Egeon, a merchant of Syracuse, who recounts that he has spent five summers roaming through Asia in quest of a long-lost son, and while coasting home has landed at Ephesus.[86] He has arrived, however, in ignorance of a recent law proclaiming that, if anyone from Syracuse be found in Ephesus, he must either pay a fine of a thousand marks or suffer death. The duke of Ephesus opens the scene by informing Egeon of the provisions of the new decree, and concludes by informing him that 'Therefore by Law thou art condemn'd to die.'[87]

Egeon, however, is in a position to offer a *purgatio*, a plea to the effect that he deserves to be excused. As we saw in Chapter 4, to enter such a plea you must show that, even if you have committed an offence, you have not done so *cum consulto*, with intention and foresight. One possibility will be to affirm that your crime arose from an unlucky chance, and this is the excuse that Egeon offers the duke, insisting that his action 'Was wrought by nature, not by vile offence'.[88] This being so, it is open to Egeon to attempt a *confirmatio* of his cause, and the rhetoricians have much to say about how to construct such a defence. But Shakespeare has little use at this stage for such rhetorical minutiae, and we never hear the substance of Egeon's argument. We merely learn from the duke that he has already attempted such a *confirmatio* and been refused: 'Merchant of *Siracusa*, plead no more./ I am not partiall to infringe our Lawes'.[89] Egeon is given a day in which to raise the fine of one thousand marks or face execution.[90]

If we turn, by contrast, to the case of Lucrece, we are confronted with a full-scale attempt to provide a *confirmatio* of an assumptive plea.[91] Lucrece's goal is to show that she was in no way complicit in Tarquin's crime, and she proceeds to confirm her argument with close attention to the rhetorical rules, especially as set out by the author of the *Ad Herennium*. Your first aim, he had declared, should be to attempt a *translatio criminis*, a shifting of guilt. While admitting your involvement in the offence, you must argue 'that you

Bullough 1957–75, vol. 1, p. 3 proposes 1592, which Wiggins and Richardson 2013, p. 206 also regard as the best guess.

86. On Egeon's narrative see Hardy 1997, pp. 33–6.
87. *The Comedie of Errors* TLN 25, p. 293 (1. 1. 25).
88. *The Comedie of Errors* TLN 34, p. 293 (1. 1. 34).
89. *The Comedie of Errors* TLN 3–4, p. 293 (1. 1. 3–4).
90. Hutson 2007, pp. 146–57, 163–72 discusses the impact of Roman new comedy in generating forensic plots in the drama of the 1590s, singling out *The Comedie of Errors* and noting the influence of Plautus.
91. On Lucrece's attempted confirmation see also Weaver 2012, pp. 136–7.

were coerced into doing what you did by the sinful actions of others'.[92] At
the same time, you must develop a narrative in which you explain how the
sinful action took place. As with all narratives, you must seek to be brief and
clear, but above all you must aim for verisimilitude. To this end, 'you must
emphasise the atrocity of the sin of those upon whom the *translatio* of
responsibility for the crime is being made, and must place before the eyes
of your audience the time and place of the crime, together with the *res*'—
the 'matter' at issue between you and your adversary.[93]

Lucrece has already promised to be brief, and she now turns to the crucial
question of verisimilitude. First she speaks about time and place:

> For in the dreadfull dead of darke midnight,
> With shining Fauchion in my chamber came
> A creeping creature with a flaming light,
> And softly cried, awake thou Romaine Dame,
>
> TLN 1625–8, p. 287 (pp. 227–8)

Then she speaks about the *res*, the nature of the demand that Tarquin made
on her, and hence about the 'matter' at issue between them:

> For some hard favour'd Groome of thine, quoth he,
> Unlesse thou yoke thy liking to my will
> Ile murther straight, and then ile slaughter thee,
> And sweare I found you where you did fulfill
> The lothsome act of Lust, and so did kill
>   The lechors in their deed, this Act will be
>   My Fame, and thy perpetuall infamy.
>
> TLN 1632–8, p. 287 (p. 228)

As well as telling us about time and place,[94] Lucrece fixes the scene vividly
ante oculos by means of the figure known to the rhetoricians as *sermocinatio*,
the technique by which, in Henry Peacham's words, 'the Orator faineth a
person and maketh him speake' rather than merely reporting what took
place.[95]

---

92. *Rhetorica ad Herennium* 1954, I. XV. 25, p. 46: 'Aliorum peccatis coactos fecisse'. Cf. Quintilian
    2001, 7. 4. 13, vol. 3, p. 242. See also Wilson 1553, Sig. O, 2^r: our aim should be to show 'that
    wee did it upon commaundement'.
93. *Rhetorica ad Herennium* 1954, II. XV. 22, p. 98: 'peccati atrocitatem proferet in quos crimen
    transferet; rem, locum, tempus ante oculos ponet'.
94. On time and place in Lucrece's narrative see also Weaver 2012, pp. 131–2.
95. Peacham 1593, p. 137.

After supplying these narrative details, Lucrece turns to the *translatio criminis* itself, the claim that she can be absolved of guilt because she acted under coercion and duress:

> With this I did begin to start and cry,
> And then against my heart he set his sword,
> Swearing, unlesse I tooke all patiently,
> I should not live to speake another word.
> So should my shame still rest upon record,
>   And never be forgot in mightie Roome
>   Th'adulterat death of LUCRECE, and her Groome.
>
> TLN 1639–45, p. 287 (p. 228)

Lucrece's shifting of guilt takes the form of the contention that, although she acceded to Tarquin's demands, she only did so because she was left with no alternative but instant death.

The second step in the confirmation of a *purgatio* is the *remotio criminis*. Here, in the words of the *Ad Herennium*, 'we shift culpability away from ourselves' by means of arguing that someone else is to blame for what happened.[96] This is the claim that Lucrece next goes on to make:

> Mine enemy was strong, my poore selfe weake,
> (And farre the weaker with so strong a feare)
> My bloudie Judge forbod my tongue to speake,
> No rightfull plea might plead for Justice there.
> His scarlet Lust came evidence to sweare
>   That my poore beautie had purloin'd his eyes,
>   And when the Judge is rob'd, the prisoner dies.
>
> TLN 1646–52, p. 287 (pp. 228–9)

Lucrece squarely places the blame upon Tarquin, figuring him as a scarlet-robed judge (also scarlet with lust) who refuses to hear a plea, and must therefore take responsibility for the injustice that results.

The third and last stage of confirmation is the *comparatio*. Here we maintain, as the *Ad Herennium* explains, 'that it was necessary to do one of two things, and that the thing we did was the better thing to have done'.[97] This is how Lucrece rests her case:

---

96. *Rhetorica ad Herennium* 1954, I. XV. 25, p. 46: 'a nobis . . . culpam ipsam amovemus'. Cf. Cicero 1949a, II. XXVIII. 86, p. 252. See also Wilson 1553, Sig. O, 2ʳ on 'Blamyng evill companie'.
97. *Rhetorica ad Herennium* 1954, I. XV. 25, p. 48: 'necesse fuisse alterutrum facere, et id quod fecerimus satius fuisse facere'. Cf. Cicero 1949a, II. XXIV. 72, p. 236. See also Wilson 1553, Sig. O, 2ʳ on 'Comparyng the fault, and declaryng that either thei must have doen that, or els have doen worse'.

> O teach me how to make mine owne excuse,
> Or (at the least) this refuge let me finde,
> Though my grosse bloud be staind with this abuse,
> Immaculate, and spotlesse is my mind,
> That was not forc'd, that never was inclind
>   To accessarie yeeldings, but still pure
>   Doth in her poyson'd closet yet endure.
>
> TLN 1653–9, p. 287 (p. 229)

The essence of Lucrece's *comparatio* is that, by choosing to 'take all patiently' and save her life instead of succumbing to Tarquin's sword, she was able to preserve her innocent mind. But, as she shortly reveals, she also had a further reason for wanting to evade immediate death. She wished to make sure of being able to proclaim the name of her violater and call for vengeance. Her final demand to Collatine is 'Be sodainelie revenged on my Foe'.[98]

How successful is Lucrece's confirmation of her plea that she did not act *cum consulto*? Within the world of the poem the answer is twofold, and at this juncture Shakespeare appears to draw specifically on Livy's telling of the tale.[99] Collatine remains speechless with woe,[100] but his attendant lords immediately leap to Lucrece's defence, announcing themselves fully persuaded by her argument:

> With this they all at once began to saie,
> Her bodies staine, her mind untainted cleares,
>
> TLN 1709–10, p. 288 (p. 231)

At the same time they promise Lucrece to exact the revenge for which she has asked:

> At this request, with noble disposition,
> Each present Lord began to promise aide,
> As bound in Knighthood to her imposition,
> Longing to heare the hatefull Foe bewraide.
>
> TLN 1695–8, p. 288 (p. 231)

---

98. *Lucrece*, TLN 1683, p. 288 (p. 230). Weaver 2012, pp. 139–42 additionally stresses that Lucrece ends by moving beyond her engagement with judicial rhetoric, referring instead to her blood as testimony to her innocence. Weaver takes this (p. 139) to be an indication of 'increasing impatience with rhetorical practice'.

99. Livy 1919, I. LVIII. 7–11, vol. 1, p. 202.

100. By contrast with the version in Ovid 1996, II. 829, p. 116, in which Collatinus immediately excuses her on the grounds that she was coerced.

Lucrece's *confirmatio* appears to be a complete rhetorical success. There is one person, however, who is not finally persuaded, and that is Lucrece herself:

> What is the qualitie of my offence
> Being constrayn'd with dreadfull circumstance?
> May my pure mind with the fowle act dispence
> My low declined Honor to advance?
> May anie termes acquit me from this chance?
>   The poyson'd fountaine cleares it selfe againe,
>   And why not I from this compelled staine?
>
> TLN 1702–8, p. 288 (p. 231)

Here Lucrece summarizes the tragic ambiguities that she never fails to detect in her case. On the one hand she insists that she was constrained by circumstances and compelled to receive the stain that she wants to clear. But on the other hand she continues to speak of her offence, and to wonder if any argument can fully acquit her of the foul crime in which she has been involved. Her anxiety is the same as the one later expressed by Claudius in *Hamlet* in the agonized soliloquy in which he confesses to his brother's murder: 'May one be pardoned and retaine th'offence?'[101]

Suddenly, however, these uncertainties disperse, leaving Lucrece with a lucid sense that she must not press her excuse:

> While with a joylesse smile, shee turnes awaie
> The face, that map which deepe impression beares
> Of hard misfortune, carv'd in it with tears.
>   No no, quoth shee, no Dame hereafter living,
>   By my excuse shall claime excuses giving.
>
> TLN 1711–15, p. 288 (p. 231)

As soon as Lucrece feels the justice of this response, she sees that there is no alternative but to kill herself, and her *peroratio* is tragic and brief. Plunging a knife into her breast, she finally recognizes that Tarquin has not merely dishonoured her but caused her death. Although she cannot manage to utter his name, her dying words proclaim 'he he faire Lords, tis he/ That guides this hand to give this wound to me.'[102]

★ ★ ★ ★ ★

---

101. *Hamlet*, TLN 2172, p. 759 (3. 3. 56).   102. *Lucrece*, TLN 1721–2, p. 288 (p. 232).

After taking an early interest in assumptive cases, Shakespeare shifted his attention in his handling of juridical issues almost exclusively to the 'absolute' type in which a plaintiff or defendant insists on the undoubted justice and lawfulness of their cause.[103] The first character to plead in this unequivocal style is Shylocke in the trial scene from Act 4 of *The Merchant of Venice*. Shylocke and Anthonio are in agreement that the issue between them is juridical in character.[104] There is a *quaestio in controversia* to be settled, as Shylocke explicitly acknowledges at the end of the scene when he declares 'Ile stay no longer question'.[105] As with any juridical issue, however, there is no dispute about the salient facts of the case. The two men have entered into a penal bond, the forfeit of which is a pound of flesh, and Anthonio is unable to repay his debt. As a result, Shylocke is now asking, as he says, 'To have the due and forfet of my bond'.[106] The only question is whether Shylocke is acting justly, rightly, and in accordance with the law in pursuing his case.[107]

As soon as Shylocke brings his defiant *prohoemium* to a close, the outraged duke declares that he is ready to dismiss the court unless the learned Bellario is willing to determine the case. He is then handed a letter in which Bellario explains that he is sick and has sent the youthful but learned Dr Balthazer to act in his stead. Bellario's letter informs the court that he has acquainted Balthazer 'with the cause in controversie between the Jew and *Anthonio* the Merchant' and that 'hee is furnished with my opinion' on the legal matter at issue.[108] The young Dr Balthazer (Portia in disguise) then appears:

> DUKE   (*To Portia*) Give me your hand, come you from old *Bellario*?
> PORTIA I did my Lord.
> DUKE   You are welcome, take your place:
> Are you acquainted with the difference
> That holds this present question in the Court.
>
>   TLN 1975–8, p. 501 (4. 1. 165–8)

As the duke indicates, there is a *quaestio iudicii* or question for adjudication arising out of what Bellario has already described as the controversy

---

103. *Rhetorica ad Herennium* 1954, I. XIV. 24, p. 44. Cf. Cicero 1949a, II. XXIII. 69, p. 232.
104. For a strongly contrasting legal appraisal of the scene see Keeton 1967, pp. 132–50.
105. *The Merchant of Venice*, TLN 2152, p. 503 (4. 1. 342).
106. *The Merchant of Venice*, TLN 1845, p. 500 (4. 1. 37).
107. *Rhetorica ad Herennium* 1954, I. XIV. 24, pp. 42, 44.
108. *The Merchant of Venice*, TLN 1962–5, p. 501 (4. 1. 153–5).

between Shylocke and Anthonio. There is consequently a *causa* to be determined, as Portia duly notes when she informs the duke that 'I am enformed throughly of the cause'.[109] She asks for the two parties to be identified: 'Which is the Merchant here? and which the Jew?'[110] When the duke commands Anthonio and Shylocke to stand forth, the stage is set for the matter to be debated *in utramque partem*.

Because the essential facts are not in dispute, Shylocke has no need of a *narratio* designed to appraise the judge of what is at stake. He is in precisely the situation mentioned by Quintilian in proof of his contention that it is a mistake to suppose that narratives are always indispensable in judicial causes. Suppose, Quintilian says, you are in the position of a plaintiff who is simply able to state to the court 'I claim full payment of the loan owed to me in virtue of my contract with the defendant'.[111] If that is so, then it will be sufficient to make this preliminary statement without adding anything more.

Shylocke accordingly proceeds directly to the *confirmatio* of his cause. He regards it as unquestionable that the juridical issue between him and Anthonio is absolute in character. As he dismissively asserts, there can be no doubt that Anthonio has 'A loosing sute'.[112] He sees nothing wrongful about his own plea, nothing that is not *recte* and according to right. As he puts it to the duke, 'What judgment shall I dread doing no wrong?'[113] Nor is there anything about his suit that involves *iniuria* and thereby conflicts with the requirements of justice. When he announces that he has sworn 'To have the due and forfet of my bond',[114] his contention that the penalty is something due to him refers us to the time-honoured legal definition of justice as *ius suum tribuere*, the giving to each their due.

Most important of all, Shylocke continually affirms that his bond is in accordance with *ius*, the dictates of Venetian law. He and Anthonio have entered into a legal agreement, as a result of which he is simply laying claim to what has lawfully become his own property:

> The pound of flesh which I demaund of him
> Is deerely bought, tis mine and I will have it:
>
> TLN 1907–8, p. 500 (4. 1. 99–100)

---

109. *The Merchant of Venice*, TLN 1979, p. 501 (4. 1. 169).
110. *The Merchant of Venice*, TLN 1980, p. 501 (4. 1. 170).
111. Quintilian 2001, 4. 2. 6, vol. 2, p. 220: 'certam creditam pecuniam peto ex stipulatione'.
112. *The Merchant of Venice*, TLN 1870, p. 500 (4. 1. 62).
113. *The Merchant of Venice*, TLN 1897, p. 500 (4. 1. 89).
114. *The Merchant of Venice*, TLN 1845, p. 500 (4. 1. 37).

Shylocke's repeated plea is accordingly to be granted judgement according to the law. To Gratiano's taunts he replies: 'I stand heere for law'.[115] To Portia he responds even more feelingly:

> My deeds upon my head, I crave the law,
> The penalty and forfaite of my bond.
>
> TLN 2012–13, p. 502 (4. 1. 202–3)

After Portia reads the bond and concedes the lawfulness of his demand, he invokes the law yet again:

> I charge you by the law,
> Whereof you are a well deserving piller,
> Proceede to judgement:
>
> TLN 2044–6, p. 502 (4. 1. 234–6)

Nor does Shylocke hesitate to remind the duke of the implications of the fact that his plea is clearly lawful according to the city's decrees. Here Shakespeare follows a hint from one of his sources, Alexander Silvayn's *The Orator*, in which the Jew points out to the judge that he cannot 'breake the credite of trafficke amongst men without great detriment unto the Commonwealth'.[116] Shylocke speaks in strikingly similar terms:

> If you deny it, let the danger light
> Upon your charter and your Citties freedome.
>
> TLN 1846–7, p. 500 (4. 1. 38–9)

Later he repeats the threat when answering the duke's call to show mercy:

> If you deny me, fie upon your Law,
> There is no force in the decrees of Venice:
>
> TLN 1909–10, p. 500 (4. 1. 101–2)

As Shylocke rightly perceives, the duke can hardly fail to take note of the fact that, in a commercial city, it would mark a dangerous precedent if the terms of a contract voluntarily agreed between two men of business were to be set aside.

Faced with this hubristically confident *confirmatio*, Portia eventually breaks the dramatic tension by rebutting Shylocke's contention that the

---

115. *The Merchant of Venice*, TLN 1950, p. 501 (4. 1. 142). On Shylocke's demand for the letter of the law see Tucker 1976.
116. Silvayn 1596, p. 401.

issue between him and Anthonio is in fact *iuridicalis* or juridical in character. Rather, she is able to show, what the court has before it is a *constitutio legalis,* a legal issue, turning as it does on the interpretation of a text. During the legal wrangling preceding this sudden reversal, however, Portia leads Shylocke to believe that she wholly accepts his estimation that the issue is a juridical one, and that his case is absolute. As soon as Shylocke stands forth, she instantly admits that the law cannot fail to uphold his plea:

> PORTIA Is your name *Shylocke*?
> SHYLOCKE   *Shylocke* is my name.
> PORTIA: Of a strange nature is the sute you follow,
> Yet in such rule, that the Venetian law
> Cannot impugne you as you doe proceed.
>
> TLN 1982–5, p. 501 (4. 1. 172–5)

While seeking to persuade Shylocke to withdraw his plea, Portia acknowledges its justice and rounds off her opening statement by reiterating that the court is bound to accept it:

>   I have spoke thus much
> To mittigate the justice of thy plea,
> Which if thou follow, this strict Court of Venice
> Must needes give sentence gainst the Merchant there.
>
> TLN 2008–11, p. 502 (4. 1. 198–201)

Portia concedes that the issue raised by Shylocke is indeed a *constitutio iuridicalis*, and that his case is absolute, so that the court 'must needes' find in favour of him.

This being so, Portia has no hesitation in characterizing Anthonio's predicament. She recognizes that her only recourse will be to enter a *confessio* on Anthonio's behalf, an admission of the charge against him, and a plea for pardon. She cannot even hope to do so in the form of a *purgatio*, a claim to the effect that Anthonio did not make his agreement with Shylocke *cum consulto*, with sufficient forethought. As Anthonio has admitted, he willingly accepted the terms of his bond with Shylocke, as a result of which—as he begins by acknowledging—'no lawfull meanes can carry me/ Out of his envies reach'.[117] Portia has no alternative but to enter a *deprecatio*, an admission that Anthonio has no defence to offer, combined with an appeal for mercy, and she wastes no time in making this move:

---

117. *The Merchant of Venice*, TLN 1817–18, p. 499 (4. 1. 9–10).

> PORTIA You stand within his danger, doe you not.
> ANTHONIO I, so he sayes.
> PORTIA   Doe you confesse the bond?
> ANTHONIO I doe.
> PORTIA   Then must the Jew be mercifull.
>
>   TLN 1986–8, p. 501 (4. 1. 176–8)

Portia is following the advice of the *Ad Herennium* to the letter: she admits that Anthonio knew what he was doing, but she invites Shylocke to recognize, as the *Ad Herennium* puts it, 'that he nevertheless deserves to be treated compassionately', regardless of his desert.[118]

Critics have repeatedly claimed to find in this part of the scene an application of the Aristotelian concept of *epieikeia* or equity,[119] a burgeoning branch of law in sixteenth-century England.[120] The pioneering study of the concept and its place in common law had been furnished by Christopher Saint German in his dialogue *Doctor and Student*, first published in Latin in 1528, translated into English in 1530, and reprinted on at least ten occasions before the end of the century.[121] According to the figure of the Doctor in the first dialogue, to follow the precise words of the law will in some instances be 'both agaynst Justyce & the Common welth: wherfore in some cases it is good and even necessary to leve the wordis of the lawe/ & to folowe that reason and Justyce requyreth/ & to that intent equytie is ordeyned/ that is to say to temper and myttygate the rygoure of the lawe'.[122] The reason for invoking the principle is to ensure that 'all the pertyculer cyrcumstaunces of the dede' are considered, and that the eventual judgement 'is temperyd with the swetnes of mercye'.[123]

There can be no doubt that Shakespeare knew of this doctrine,[124] and he even makes Portia allude to it when she informs Shylocke that she is calling for mercy in order 'To mittigate the justice of thy plea'.[125] But Portia does not call for equity, a concept that makes no appearance in her exchanges

---

118. *Rhetorica ad Herennium* 1954, I. XIV. 24, p. 44: 'et tamen postulat ut sui misereantur'. As Watt 2009, pp. 213–15 notes, this subsequently came to be regarded as Christian mercy.
119. For a list see Bilello 2007, pp. 109–10, to which should be added Mahood 2003, who claims (p. 17) that 'the concept of equity does indeed lie at the heart of the scene', and Platt 2009, pp. 112–15.
120. Hutson 2001, pp. 170–7; Platt 2009, pp. 97–112; Watt 2009.
121. Details from BL catalogue. For Saint German on equity see Guy 1986; Lobban 2007, pp. 20–8.
122. Saint German 1974 [1530], p. 97.   123. Saint German 1974 [1530], p. 95.
124. See Keeton 1967, pp. 144–6; Hutson 2001, pp. 177–91; Zurcher 2010, pp. 208–27.
125. *The Merchant of Venice*, TLN 2009, p. 502 (4. 1. 199).

with Shylocke;[126] rather she mounts a straightforward plea for *misericordia*, pity or compassion for Anthonio's plight. It is true that the exercise of mercy is held to be a consequence of successfully appealing to the ideal of equity as opposed to the letter of the law.[127] But Portia is not advancing a legal plea; the move she makes is strictly a rhetorical one, and she addresses herself not to the judge but to her adversary in the case. Her appeal is not from one jurisdiction to another, but beyond the law; she is asking Shylocke to set aside an undoubted legal right.[128] Given that his plea is *absoluta* or rightfully unqualified, her response on Anthonio's behalf can only be correspondingly *adsumptiva* or concessive, and this can only take the form of a simple call for mercy in place of justice.

Confronted with Portia's demand that he must be merciful, Shylocke instantly retorts 'On what compulsion must I, tell me that.'[129] Portia thereupon responds in the manner recommended by the author of the *Ad Herennium,* who argues that the only possible strategy to adopt in such a tight corner will be to invoke a number of resonantly sententious generalizations on such topics as 'humanity, fortune, mercy and the upheavals and reversals of things'.[130] Portia begins by pronouncing a number of such *sententiae* on the need to temper justice with mercy, mainly taking them from the Bible, the most authoritative source of all:

> The qualitie of mercie is not straind,
> It droppeth as the gentle raine from heaven
> Upon the place beneath: it is twise blest,
> It blesseth him that gives, and him that takes,
> Tis mightiest in the mightiest, it becomes
> The throned Monarch better then his crowne.[131]
>
> TLN 1990–5, p. 501 (4. 1. 180–5)

Next she appeals to an associated Biblical *sententia* about mercy and humanity:

126. As noted in Sokol and Sokol 2000, p. 116. See also Jordan 1982; Bilello 2007, p. 110; Watt 2009, p. 217. For a list of scholars who have expressed scepticism about the role of equity in the scene see Sokol and Sokol 1999, pp. 421–8, to which should be added Bilello 2007, p. 110 and Posner 2013, who stresses that equity is present only as a view about the spirit of the law, not as a legal principle.
127. As noted in Knight 1972, p. 62.   128. As noted in Bilello 2007, p. 114.
129. *The Merchant of Venice*, TLN 1989, p. 501 (4. 1. 179).
130. *Rhetorica ad Herennium* 1954, II. XVII. 26, p. 104: 'Loci communes: de humanitate, fortuna, misericordia, rerum commutatione.'
131. Noble 1935, p. 167 hears an echo of *Ecclesiasticus* 35. 19, where mercy is likened to a cloud of rain.

> But mercie is above this sceptred sway,
> It is enthroned in the harts of Kings,[132]
>
> > TLN 1999–2000, p. 501 (4. 1. 189–90)

Finally she meditates on the requirements of humanity in the face of misfortune:

> > > consider this,
> > That in the course of justice, none of us
> > Should see salvation: we doe pray for mercy,
> > And that same prayer, doth teach us all to render
> > The deedes of mercie.
>
> > TLN 2004–8, p. 502 (4. 1. 194–8)

After this Portia draws to a close with a renewed admission that, if Shylocke is not prepared to show compassion, the court will be bound to give sentence against Anthonio.

There is perhaps something disingenuous about Portia's eloquence, given that she almost immediately encourages Shylocke to stand by the letter of the law.[133] For the moment, however, she is presenting herself as an advocate who has no case to argue, and in consequence has nothing further to offer the court. When Shylocke responds by reiterating his demand for 'The penalty and forfaite of my bond',[134] she announces that she has no alternative but to give up the case. She asks to see the bond, and confirms that it is a lawful document:

> > Why this bond is forfait,
> > And lawfully by this the Jew may claime
> > A pound of flesh,
>
> > TLN 2036–8, p. 502 (4. 1. 226–8)

After Anthonio has made his farewell to his friends, Portia proceeds to judgement:

> > A pound of that same Merchants flesh is thine,
> > The Court awards it, and the law doth give it.
>
> > TLN 2105–6, p. 503 (4. 1. 295–6)

---

132. Noble 1935, p. 167 hears an echo of *Ecclesiasticus* 2. 21, where God's mercy is said to be as great as himself.
133. As noted in Watt 2009, p. 214.
134. *The Merchant of Venice*, TLN 2013, p. 502 (4. 1. 203).

With the passing of this sentence the trial appears to be at an end. To express the outcome in rhetorical terms, Shylocke's contention that his suit is juridical, and that his plea is absolute, appears to have been vindicated.

★ ★ ★ ★ ★

The judicial dispute that Brutus and Antony conduct before the plebeians in Act 3 of *Julius Caesar* likewise hinges on a juridical issue. There is no disagreement as to what Brutus has done: he has engaged in a conspiracy against Caesar and assassinated him. The only question is whether he has acted *recte* and without *iniuria*, rightly and in accordance with the dictates of justice. The controversy between the two men is, in other words, once again absolute in character.[135] Because the facts are not in dispute, Brutus stands in no need of a *narratio*, and like Shylocke he is able to sweep directly from his *prohoemium* to the *confirmatio* of his case. First he insists that the assassination was undoubtedly undertaken *recte* or rightfully. He rose against Caesar because he loved Rome more, and had he not given preference to his country he would have been rude and vile.[136] His action was also performed *iure*, in accordance with law and justice. He sought to ensure that the people of Rome could continue to live as free men instead of dying as slaves, and had he not done so he would have been base.[137] His decision, he assures the plebeians, will therefore be treated as an offence only by those who are themselves rude, vile, or base. When the plebeians assure him that they do not suffer from any of these vices, he feels able to conclude 'Then none have I offended.'[138]

Faced with this *confirmatio*—scarcely less hubristically confident than Shylocke's—Antony affects with lethal irony to admit that Brutus's case is indeed absolute, and thus that his own can be no better than assumptive. He pretends to concede, in other words, that he cannot hope to answer Brutus's argument, and can only offer a *deprecatio*. First he assures his hearers (although his tone belies his words) that he cannot deny the moral excellence of his adversaries:

> They that have done this Deede, are honourable.
> What private greefes they have, alas I know not,

---

135. So pointed is the resulting dispute that it came to be used (for example by Melanchthon) as a text-book example of an *argumentum in utramque partem*. See Jones 1977 p. 16; Hatfield 2005, p. 178.
136. *Julius Caesar*, TLN 1409, 1418, 1420, p. 690 (3. 2. 20, 26, 28).
137. *Julius Caesar*, TLN 1411, 1416, p. 690 (3. 2. 21, 25).
138. *Julius Caesar*, TLN 1423, p. 690 (3. 2. 31).

> That made them do it: They are Wise, and Honourable,
> And will no doubt with Reasons answer you.
>
> TLN 1593–6, p. 692 (3. 2. 202–5)

Next he declares that he cannot hope to provide an effective response, lacking as he does any of the necessary rhetorical skills:

> For I have neyther wit nor words, nor worth,
> Action, nor Utterance, nor the power of Speech,
> To stirre mens Blood.
>
> TLN 1602–4, p. 693 (3. 2. 211–13)

While undercutting his disclaimer with his elegant alliteration, Antony insists that he is without the command of *ornatus* and *pronuntiatio* that will be needed if he is to arouse the emotions of his audience. This being so, his only recourse is to plead for pity to be shown to Caesar and the manner of his death:

> I tell you that, which you your selves do know,
> Shew you sweet *Caesars* wounds, poor poor dum mouths
> And bid them speake for me:
>
> TLN 1605–7, p. 693 (3. 2. 214–16)

With his allusion to the biblical promise that the dumb shall speak, Antony hints at more to come, but for the moment he maintains his pretence of having nothing to say and brings his *deprecatio* to a close.

Suddenly, however, he abandons his pretence and turns to the attack:

> But were I *Brutus*,
> And *Brutus Antony*, there were an *Antony*
> Would ruffle up your Spirits, and put a Tongue
> In every Wound of *Caesar*, that should move
> The stones of Rome, to rise and Mutiny.[139]
>
> TLN 1607–11, p. 693 (3. 2 216–20)

Having appeared to accept Brutus's contention that there was nothing wrongful about the assassination, Antony now assures the plebeians that he is not without a powerfully countervailing argument. What he lacks, he insists, is merely the rhetorical power to ruffle up their spirits in support of his cause. Acknowledging that the issue between him and Brutus is indeed juridical, Antony now suggests that it is not Brutus but he himself who has

---

139. For a discussion of this passage see Alexander 2007, pp. 110–11.

the absolute case. As he has already intimated in his *narratio*, he considers Brutus's conspiracy not merely to be contrary to what is *recte*, since it involved black ingratitude, but also contrary to *ius* or law, since it amounted to an act of treason against Rome, a treason so manifest that any true orator would be able to make the very stones of the city proclaim it.

Antony next presents the *confirmatio* of his claim that Brutus is mistaken in supposing that Caesar sought to tyrannize over Rome. He is able to offer a proof of the type that Aristotle had described as *atechnos*, not dependent on any rhetorical tricks or techniques. To express the point in Quintilian's terms, he calls on a 'non-artificial' proof that is virtually impossible to question, grounded as it is on irrefutable documentary evidence. He produces Caesar's will, which demonstrates that Caesar's plan was not to enslave the people but to make them his lawful heirs:

> To every Roman Citizen he gives,
> To every severall man, seventy five Drachmaes. . . .
> Moreover, he hath left you all his Walkes,
> His private Arbors, and new-planted Orchards,
> On this side Tyber, he hath left them you,
> And to your heyres for ever: common pleasures
> To walke abroad, and recreate your selves.
> Heere was a *Caesar*: when comes such another?
> > TLN 1622–3, 1626–31, p. 693 (3. 2. 231–2, 237–42)

Whereas Brutus had tried to persuade the plebeians that Caesar deserved death, Antony proves that Caesar 'deserv'd your loves', and with this affirmation he draws to a close.[140]

How successful is Antony's *confirmatio*? As soon as he finishes, the first plebeian answers for everyone, showing Antony that he has scored a complete victory. When Antony adds a final rhetorical question, 'when comes such another?' the first plebeian shouts 'Never, never'.[141] Having accepted Antony's argument, they proceed immediately to judgement:

> > come, away, away:
> Wee'l burne his body in the holy place,
> And with the Brands fire the Traitors houses.[142]
> > TLN 1632–4, p. 693 (3. 2. 243–5)

---

140. *Julius Caesar*, TLN 1617, p. 693 (3. 2. 226).
141. *Julius Caesar*, TLN 1632, p. 693 (3. 2. 243).
142. Here Shakespeare closely follows Plutarch 1579, p. 976.

The conspirators are branded as traitors and made an object of immediate revenge. The scene ends with the news that Brutus and Cassius 'Are rid like Madmen through the Gates of Rome.'[143] They will soon be overcome in battle, but they have already lost the war of words.

The legal issue

Shakespeare is less interested in legal than in juridical issues, but the great exception is the trial scene in Act 4 of *The Merchant of Venice*.[144] So far Portia has displayed an apparent willingness to endorse Shylocke's assumption that the issue before the court is wholly juridical, centring on whether his insistence on being granted the forfeit of his bond is legally justifiable. After she delivers her sentence, however, and at the moment when Shylocke steps forward with his knife ('come prepare') she suddenly turns to 'some thing else', namely the precise wording of the bond.[145] As she now reveals, the issue before the court is not juridical after all; rather it is *legalis* or legal, and centres on the interpretation of that particular text.[146] This is the moment at which we may find ourselves reflecting on the significance of Portia's name and its close associations with *porta*, a portal or door. One line of legal argument is suddenly closed off, and a means of entry is given to another and opposing one at the same time.[147]

As we have seen, one question that the rhetoricians always ask when considering the *constitutio legalis* is whether, in the interpretation of a legal document, priority should be given to the spirit or the letter of the law. Throughout the trial Shylocke has shown himself an energetic proponent of the view that what alone matters is the exact wording of his agreement with Anthonio. He first expresses this commitment when Portia asks to see the bond and immediately declares, on the strength of her reading, that 'this bond is forfait'.[148] 'It doth appeare you are a worthy judge', Shylocke comments, 'You know the law, your exposition/ Hath beene most

143. *Julius Caesar*, TLN 1648, p. 693 (3. 2. 259).
144. There is also the long speech in *Henry the Fift* in which the Archbishop of Canterbury interprets for the king a text about the Salic law. See *Henry the Fift*, TLN 166–228, pp. 640–1 (1. 2. 33–95).
145. *The Merchant of Venice*, TLN 2110–11, p. 503 (4. 1. 300–1).
146. Brennan 1986, pp. 45–8 analyses the structure of the scene, but without reference to its rhetorical character.
147. See Tiffany 2002, pp. 360–2.   148. *The Merchant of Venice*, TLN 2036, p. 502 (4. 1. 226).

sound'.[149] The same commitment emerges still more clearly when Anthonio asks the court to pronounce judgement. Portia responds: 'Why than thus it is,/ You must prepare your bosome for his knife'.[150] Shylocke relishes the precision with which she quotes the terms of the agreement:

> I, his breast,
> So sayes the bond, doth it not noble Judge?
> Neerest his hart, those are the very words.
>
> TLN 2058–60, p. 502 (4. 1. 248–50)

Speaking of 'the very words'—*verba ipsa*—Shylocke quotes the phrase that Cicero likes to use when referring to the value of upholding the letter of the law.[151] He reaffirms his commitment yet again when Portia suggests that he summon a surgeon to ensure that Anthonio does not bleed to death.[152] Shylocke is immediately suspicious: 'Is it so nominated in the bond?'[153] Portia reacts impatiently: 'It is not so exprest, but what of that?/ Twere good you doe so much for charitie'.[154] But Shylocke is not happy with any arrangement not specified in the wording of the text: 'I cannot finde it, tis not in the bond'.[155] For Shylocke it is always the letter, never the spirit, that takes precedence.[156]

Faced with Shylocke's insistence on this principle, Portia begins by examining the connection between his bond and the broader framework of Venetian law. As we have seen, Quintilian had observed that, even if you assign priority to the letter of the law, you can gain some help from considering the intentions of the lawgiver, whereas if you focus on recovering the intentions of the lawgiver you will have to cast doubt on the letter of the law so far as possible.[157] Portia avails herself of this helpful asymmetry and starts by considering the intentions underlying the law of contract in Venice. Here she adopts Cicero's suggestion that we should begin by

---

149. *The Merchant of Venice*, TLN 2042–4, p. 502 (4. 1. 232–4).
150. *The Merchant of Venice*, TLN 2050–1, p. 502 (4. 1. 240–1).
151. Cicero 1949a, I. XIII. 17, p. 34 and II. XLII. 121, p. 290.
152. *The Merchant of Venice*, TLN 2063–4, p. 502 (4. 1. 253–4).
153. *The Merchant of Venice*, TLN 2065, p. 502 (4. 1. 255).
154. *The Merchant of Venice*, TLN 2066–7, p. 502 (4. 1. 256–7).
155. *The Merchant of Venice*, TLN 2068, p. 502 (4. 1. 258).
156. Behind this rhetorical commitment some critics have discerned a conflict between the principles of Judaism and Christianity, with Shylocke standing for a Judaic insistence on obedience to law. See, for example, Cooper 1970, pp. 121–4; Tovey 1981, pp. 232–3.
157. Quintilian 2001, 7. 6. 3, vol. 3, p. 268.

arguing that the intent or purpose of a law 'always looks to the same end'.[158]
She closely follows his advice:

> For the intent and purpose of the law
> Hath full relation to the penaltie,
> Which heere appeareth due upon the bond.
>
> TLN 2053–5, p. 502 (4. 1. 243–5)

When, however, Portia turns to the bond itself, she concentrates entirely on
what 'The words expresly are', accepting Shylocke's repeated demand for
the strict letter of the law to be upheld.[159] As soon as she does so, however,
she is able to warn Shylocke to 'Tarry a little'[160] and reflect on what exactly
is and is not said:

> This bond doth give thee heere no jote of blood,
> The words expresly are a pound of flesh:
>
> TLN 2112–13, p. 503 (4. 1. 302–3)

Many critics have seen in these lines the turning point of the case. What
Portia demonstrates, they argue, is that Shylocke 'cannot have the flesh'
after all, and is guilty 'of attempting to enforce a fraudulent contract'.[161] He
has asked for the *verba ipsa* of the bond to be enforced, but 'the very words'
make it impossible to execute.

It is arguable, however, that this reading misunderstands the rhetorical
construction of the scene. As Portia has just made clear, the issue before the
court is not a *constitutio iuridicalis*; rather it is a *constitutio legalis*, in which
the question at issue is the proper interpretation of a legal text. But as we
have seen, one problem that can readily arise in this type of case is that
the wording even of a legally valid text may turn out to be in conflict with
the requirements of a *lex contraria*, a contrary law of superior force. What
Portia next proceeds to demonstrate is that this precise consideration applies
to Shylocke's bond. Shylocke's problem is not that he cannot have the flesh
after all. Portia concedes that his bond remains a valid one: 'The law alowes
it, and the court awards it.'[162] His problem is rather that he has been
unaware of the fact—which Portia now fiercely underlines—that if he

---

158. Cicero 1949a, II. XLII. 122, p. 290: 'sententia . . . semper ad idem spectare'.
159. *The Merchant of Venice*, TLN 2113, p. 503 (4. 1. 303).
160. *The Merchant of Venice*, TLN 2111, p. 503 (4. 1. 301).
161. Brown 1955, p. lii; Benston 1991, p. 179. See also Keeton 1967, p. 140 and further references
     at pp. 147–8; Bilello 2007, pp. 123–4.
162. *The Merchant of Venice*, TLN 2109, p. 503 (4. 1. 299).

takes his pound of flesh, and if in doing so he spills so much as a jot of blood, he will be acting in violation of a *lex contraria* that forbids the shedding of Christian blood, and will thus be exposed to the penalty annexed to the law, which is nothing less than the forfeiture of his lands and goods to the state. Shylocke can still take his pound of flesh in accordance with his bond, and he can even take Antonio's blood as well. But he can only do so if he is willing to incur the penalty for shedding Christian blood, and Portia has evidently calculated that he will judge the stipulated punishment too severe to be contemplated.

The fulcrum of the trial is thus supplied by the passage in which Portia informs Shylocke about the relevant *lex contraria*.[163] Here Shakespeare goes beyond anything in his narrative sources, drawing instead on his own knowledge of judicial rhetoric in order to produce his *coup de théâtre*.[164] First Portia reaffirms Shylocke's legal right: 'Take then thy bond, take thou thy pound of flesh'.[165] But then she draws his attention to the *lex contraria*:

> But in the cutting it, if thou doost shed
> One drop of Christian blood, thy lands and goods
> Are by the lawes of Venice confiscate
> Unto the state of Venice.
>
> TLN 2115–18, p. 503 (4. 1. 305–8)

Shylocke is stunned: 'Is that the law?'[166] Portia responds by further informing him that the relevant *lex contraria* takes the form of an Act of the Venetian state:

> Thy selfe shalt see the Act:
> For as thou urgest justice, be assurd
> Thou shalt have justice more then thou desirst.
>
> TLN 2121–3, p. 503 (4. 1. 310–12)

The significance of the addition is that, as the rhetoricians always emphasize, where there is a conflict of laws, the law that is permitted to prevail must be

---

163. That Portia points to a *lex contraria* has rarely been noted. But see Donawerth 1984, p. 208, and for a discussion of the conflicting laws involved see Holderness 1993, pp. 51–2. Leimberg 2011 also speaks of the *lex contraria*, but argues (p. 193) that 'two laws contradict each other in the written text of the bond', whereas I am arguing that the terms of the bond are contradicted by a different and overriding law.

164. Shakespeare's source here is Fiorentino 1957, but the relevant passage (p. 473) makes no mention of a *lex contraria*.

165. *The Merchant of Venice*, TLN 2114, p. 503 (4. 1. 304).

166. *The Merchant of Venice*, TLN 2120, p. 503 (4. 1. 310).

the one with the greater weight. But it is too obvious to need stating that an
Act of state will always be of greater weight than a private contact, and must
therefore be enforced.

Shylocke is quick to recognize his dilemma. He instantly changes direction and agrees to Bassanio's earlier offer to pay him three times what he is
owed. But Portia intervenes to insist that he has asked for justice according
to his bond, and that this alone is what the court is empowered to award:

> Soft, the Jew shal have all justice, soft no hast,
> He shall have nothing but the penalty . . . .
> Therefore prepare thee to cut of the flesh,
> Shed thou no blood, nor cut thou lesse nor more
> But just a pound of flesh: if thou tak'st more
> Or lesse then a just pound, be it but so much
> As makes it light or heavy in the substance,
> Or the devision of the twentith part
> Of one poore scruple, nay if the scale doe turne
> But in the estimation of a hayre,
> Thou dyest, and all thy goods are confiscate.
>
> TLN 2127–8, 2130–8, p. 503 (4. 1. 317–18, 320–8)

It is true that this elaboration of Portia's initial verdict, although delivered
with triumphant *amplificatio*, might be thought to raise some awkward
questions. What of the fact that, although the *lex contraria* had specified a
confiscation of goods, it had made no mention of a sentence of death? And
what of the common-sensical objection that Shylocke must surely be
permitted the shedding of blood, for otherwise it is impossible to see how
he can be awarded any flesh at all?[167]

To this latter objection, however, Portia has an answer, although it runs
counter to her earlier plea for mercy, for it requires her to be merciless in
reminding Shylocke yet again of the request he has made to the court. He
has insisted on the letter of the law, and he cannot deny that according to
the wording of the bond he is legally permitted flesh and nothing more:

> Thou shalt have nothing but the forfaiture
> To be so taken at thy perill Jew.
>
> TLN 2149–50, p. 503 (4. 1. 339–40)

---

167. Hood Phillips 1972, pp. 92–3 cites several jurists pressing this point.

Shylocke has become the defendant, and like any defendant—in Thomas Wilson's words—he now 'aunswereth at his peril', the peril being the loss of his lands and goods if he insists on the terms of his bond.[168]

Critics have complained that this reversal is too sudden, and that it 'feels unlikely'.[169] No doubt from a legal point of view Portia's handling of the case leaves much to be desired, to say nothing of the fact that she fraudulently presents herself to the court as a legal expert and mendaciously claims to have been sent by Bellario. But rhetorically the scene makes perfect sense. The sudden reversal happens because Portia is able to show that the legal issue around which the trial revolves is not *iuridicalis* but *legalis*. Shylocke is then forced to recognize that, on the strict interpretation of the relevant legal text for which he has asked, he has laid himself open to a pitiless punishment. He immediately announces 'Ile stay no longer question' and prepares to leave the court.[170]

168. Wilson 1553, Sig. M, 3ʳ.   169. See, for example, Margolies 2012, p. 163.
170. *The Merchant of Venice*, TLN 2152, p. 503 (4. 1. 342). On Shylocke's silence at the end of the scene see Rovine 1987, pp. 57–8.

8

Confirmation

The Conjectural Issue

'The conjectural issue', the *Ad Herennium* solemnly informs us, 'is at once the most difficult to handle and the one that most frequently needs to be handled in actual causes'.[1] It must therefore be approached with particular care. As with all types of *constitutiones*, the first task is to pick out the *quaestio iudicii*, the question in controversy that needs to be adjudicated. This can readily be identified in conjectural cases, because the question will always be about some puzzling matter of fact.[2] By way of illustration, the rhetoricians like to appeal to one version of the story of the death of Ajax.[3] Ajax's brother Teucer comes upon Ulysses in the forest standing with a bloody sword in his hand next to the body of Ajax, who has been stabbed to death. Ajax has committed suicide, and Ulysses on finding him has pulled the sword from the corpse. But Teucer is unaware of these facts. As a result, the circumstantial evidence, combined with his knowledge that Ulysses was Ajax's enemy, prompt him to accuse Ulysses of murder.[4] Hereupon, as Cicero says, there arises the issue in controversy and the resulting question for adjudication: 'did he or did he not kill him?'[5]

For the rhetoricians there are two connected morals to be drawn from the tale. One is that, as the *Ad Herennium* says, what distinguishes conjectural

---

1. *Rhetorica ad Herennium* 1954, II. X. 12, p. 80: 'difficillima tractatu est constitutio coniecturalis et in veris causis saepissime tractanda est'.
2. *Rhetorica ad Herennium* 1954, I. XI. 18, p. 34; Cicero 1949a, I. VIII. 11, p. 22; Quintilian 2001, 3. 6. 72–3, vol. 2, p. 84; Wilson 1553, Sig. N, 1ᵛ.
3. As Hutson 2006, pp. 92–3 notes, this version appears to come from a lost tragedy by Pacuvius.
4. *Rhetorica ad Herennium* 1954, I. XI. 18, p. 34 and I. XVII. 26, p. 52; Cicero 1949a, I. VIII. 11, p. 22; Quintilian 2001, 4. 2. 13, vol. 2, p. 224.
5. Cicero 1949a, II. IV. 15, p. 180: 'Occideritne?' Cf. *Rhetorica ad Herennium* 1954, I. XVII. 27, p. 52; Quintilian 2001, 4. 2. 13, vol. 2, p. 224.

issues and serves to label them is that 'the truth has to be sought by way of forming a conjecture' and attempting to confirm it in the light of the available evidence.[6] As Leonard Cox puts it in his *Art or crafte of Rhetoryke*, 'the state of the plee was conjecturall whether Ulisses slew Ajax or nat'.[7] The second moral is that the truth may always be hidden, and may indeed have been hidden on purpose, with the result that the controversy, as the *Ad Herennium* says, 'will be about what in fact took place'.[8] It is important to remember that your initial conjecture may be mistaken, just as Teucer's was in the case of Ajax. As Leonard Cox notes, 'in very dede here was no profe' and 'of truthe Ulisses was nat gylty in the cause', even though the circumstances 'made the mater to be nat a lytle suspect'.[9]

As we saw in Chapter 7, these admonitions are summarized in the form of the claim that confirmation in the case of a conjectural issue must be a matter of searching for clues and trying to uncover what may be a deliberately concealed truth. The verb always used by the classical rhetoricians to describe this process is *quaerere*.[10] According to Thomas Cooper's *Thesaurus*, the word can mean 'to aske: to demaunde', but also 'to search' and 'to seeke for' something.[11] John Veron in his *Dictionarie* agrees that the word can either mean 'to aske, search', or else 'to seeke to have a proofe'.[12] The business of confirmation in conjectural issues may thus be said to take the form of detective work. As Thomas Wilson summarizes, it is a matter of 'searchyng out the substaunce, or nature of the cause'.[13]

Failed confirmation

Shakespeare's most intricate treatment of conjectural issues can be found in *Hamlet*, in which two distinct mysteries are pursued in parallel throughout the first half of the play. Claudius and Polonius are in quest of the truth about the cause of Hamlet's seeming madness, while Hamlet is in quest of the truth about the cause of his father's death. We are introduced to the first

---

6. *Rhetorica ad Herennium* 1954, I. XI. 18, p. 34: 'Hic coniectura verum quaeritur'. Cf. Cicero 1949a, I. VIII. 10, p. 20.
7. Cox 1532, Sig. D, 7ᵛ. Cf also Wilson 1551, Sig. M, 1ᵛ.
8. *Rhetorica ad Herennium* 1954, I. XI. 18, p. 32: 'de facto controversia est'.
9. Cox 1532, Sig. D, 7ᵛ.
10. *Rhetorica ad Herennium* 1954, I. XI. 18, p. 34; Cicero 1949a, I. VIII. 11, p. 22.
11. Cooper 1565, Sig. 5L, 1ᵛ.   12. Veron 1584, Sig. 2L, 6ᵛ.
13. Wilson 1553, Sig. Q, 2ʳ.

of these investigations when Claudius outlines the mystery of Hamlet's behaviour to Rosencrans and Guyldensterne:

> something have you heard
> Of *Hamlets* transformation, so I call it,
> Since not th'exterior, nor the inward man
> Resembles that it was, what it should be,
> More then his fathers death, that thus hath put him
> So much from th'understanding of himselfe
> I cannot deeme of:
>
> TLN 932–8, p. 747 (2. 2. 4–10)

Later he quizzes the pair about their unsatisfactory progress in finding the answer to the puzzle:

> An can you by no drift of circumstance
> Get from him why he puts on this confusion,
> Grating so harshly all his dayes of quiet
> With turbulent and dangerous lunacie?
>
> TLN 1537–40, p. 753 (3. 1. 1–4)

Claudius reminds Rosencrans and Guyldensterne about the conjectural issue, and hence the question for adjudication: what is the cause of Hamlet's dangerous lunacy? He also points out that they need to concentrate on investigating the 'circumstances' of Hamlet's actions if the puzzle is to be solved.

Before Rosencrans and Guyldensterne can set to work, Polonius bustles forward with his own solution. He is excessively confident about his capacity to uncover hidden truths:

> If circumstances leade me, I will finde
> Where truth is hid, though it were hid indeede
> Within the Center.
>
> TLN 1087–9, p. 749 (2. 2. 155–7)

He believes that, if he can uncover the circumstances of Hamlet's actions, he will be able to expose the truth even if it lies buried at the centre of the earth. He then proceeds to develop his theory that Hamlet has become mad as a result of frustrated love for Ophelia.[14] He refers again to the 'circumstances' of Hamlet's behaviour, explaining that Ophelia has told him of his

---

14. Following the advice of the rhetoricians, Polonius already embarks on the confirmation of his conjecture in the course of his narrative.

advances 'by time, by meanes, and place', and he brings forward his purportedly non-artificial proof in the form of Hamlet's letter to Ophelia.[15] But it still remains for him to show that his conjecture can be confirmed by an examination of the *consecutio* or impact on Hamlet in the period—now extending over many weeks—during which Ophelia has been locking herself away from him. He recognizes, as the rhetoricians would say, that he needs to look for further clues to connect Hamlet's distracted state of mind with his conjecture about its cause.

Shakespeare initially likens this process of investigation to that of searching for the head-waters of a river. The prince in *Romeo and Juliet* invokes the image when he commands the tomb to be closed until the mystery of the young lovers' deaths can be traced to its source:

> Seale up the mouth of outrage for a while,
> Till we can cleare these ambiguities,
> And know their spring, their head, their true discent,
>
> TLN 2905–7, p. 411 (5. 3. 216–18)

Claudius recurs to the metaphor when he informs Gertrard about Polonius's alleged discovery:

> He tells me my sweet Queene, that he hath found
> The head and source of all your sonnes distemper.
>
> TLN 982–3, p. 748 (2. 2. 54–5)

Polonius, however, has no use for such pastoral imagery. As soon as he embarks on his quest, he introduces a much more violent metaphor that Hamlet subsequently takes up in his parallel attempt to solve the mystery of his father's death. They both treat the search for clues as a hunt, a process of following a trail to the death.

To illuminate their vocabulary, it may be helpful to turn for a moment to some Elizabethan guides to the hunt. Thomas Cockaine in his *Short Treatise of Hunting* of 1591 provides a survey of 'the order to be observed in hunting the Foxe'. The first step is to 'let loose' the hounds, which should previously have been coupled together.[16] The aim in loosing them all at once is to allow them the best chance of flushing their quarry from its place of

---

15. *Hamlet*, TLN 1056, p. 748 (2. 2. 125).
16. Cockaine 1591, Sig. B, 2ʳ and 4ʳ. On 'loosing' see also Adlington 1566, fo. 78ʳ; Caius 1576, p. 6.

concealment.[17] This further stage is assigned various names, depending on which animal is being chased. George Gascoigne in his *Noble Arte of Venerie* of 1575 runs through the correct technical terms:[18] 'We Herbor and Unherbor a Harte, . . . we lodge & rowse a Bucke, . . . we forme and starte a Hare: . . . we kennell and unkenell a Fox'.[19] Gervase Markham in his *Gentlemans Academie* of 1595 provides a similar list: 'We say, dislodge the Bucke. Start the Hare. Unkennell the Foxe.'[20] Once you have forced your quarry into the open it may be possible to course it, that is, to hunt it in view rather than by scent. 'The surest coursing', Gascoigne explains, 'is when you hunte with houndes, to set your greyhounds underneath the winde very close in some bottom or little playne, & there to course the Fox when he commeth out'.[21] The alternative is to trail your quarry, that is, to follow its scent. Gascoigne admits that this may not always deliver good sport 'bycause the houndes while they trayle, do call on but coldly one after another'.[22] Nevertheless, he says, he wishes to speak 'in prayse of trayling of an Hare from the relief to the Forme' as one of the most satisfying types of chase.[23]

When Polonius informs Claudius of his conjecture about Hamlet's madness he immediately calls up the image of a huntsman following a trail:[24]

> And I doe thinke, or els this braine of mine
> Hunts not the trayle of policie so sure
> As it hath usd to doe, that I have found
> The very cause of *Hamlets* lunacie.
>
> TLN 974–7, p. 748 (2. 2. 46–9)

Claudius is eager to know how Polonius intends to confirm his conjecture: 'How may we try it further?'[25] By way of answer, Polonius next figures himself as a huntsman at the start of a chase:

> POLONIUS You know sometimes he walkes foure houres together Heere in the Lobby.

---

17. On 'quareys' see Gascoigne 1575, p. 170.
18. On Gascoigne see Berry 2001, pp. 4, 10–11, 90–1, 227. See also Bates 2013, pp. 140–4, who stresses Gascoigne's sympathy for the hunted.
19. Gascoigne 1575, p. 239.   20. [Markham] 1595, p. 38.
21. Gascoigne 1575, p. 248.   22. Gascoigne 1575, p. 172.
23. Gascoigne 1575, p. 172.
24. This seems to have been little noticed. Spurgeon 1965, pp. 100–5 discusses Shakespeare's hunting imagery, but without any mention of 'starting' or 'unkennelling'. Berry 2001 concentrates on deer hunting, and has nothing to say about *Hamlet*.
25. *Hamlet*, TLN 1089, p. 749 (2. 2. 157).

> QUEENE   So he dooes indeede.
> POLONIUS   At such a time, Ile loose my daughter to him,
> (*To King*) Be you and I behind an Arras then,
> Marke the encounter,
>
> TLN 1090–4, p. 749 (2. 2. 158–62)

Polonius is planning to set the dogs on Hamlet. He will 'loose' Ophelia upon him, aiming to flush out his feelings from their place of conceal-ment. Meanwhile, he and Claudius will eavesdrop on the encounter, which they will 'mark' for signs or *signa* that Polonius's conjecture about love-madness is correct. Perhaps Hamlet will tremble, perhaps he will turn pale, perhaps he will run away. Whatever happens, they will have supplied themselves with what the rhetoricians regard as the strongest form of non-artificial *confirmatio*, that of their own testimony as witnesses.

Pragmatic as always, Polonius postpones the execution of his plan when Hamlet happens to walk by, and instead takes the opportunity to accost him at once. At first he is not sure that Hamlet recognizes him:

> POLONIUS   Doe you knowe me my Lord?
> HAMLET   Excellent, excellent well, y'are a Fishmonger.
>
> TLN 1103–4, p. 749 (2. 2. 171–2)

Polonius is disconcerted, and even more so when he tries to renew their conversation:

> POLONIUS   Ile speake to him againe. What doe you reade my Lord.
> HAMLET   Words, words, words.
> POLONIUS   What is the matter my Lord.
> HAMLET   Betweene who.
>
> TLN 1121–5, p. 749 (2. 2. 187–91)

Critics sometimes complain about Hamlet's 'contentious quibbling' here,[26] but Hamlet is making an important point. Polonius is enquiring about the subject matter of his reading, but Hamlet pretends to believe that he is asking about a *res in controversia*, a judicial 'matter' in dispute between them. He is figuring Polonius as an adversary who is planning to interrogate him,

---

26. See, for example, Zurcher 2010, p. 247.

which is of course the case. As Polonius is forced to admit, 'Though this be madnesse, yet there is method in't'.[27]

After this unsettling encounter, Polonius and Claudius wait until the following day to pursue their quarry.[28] They now feel fully prepared, as Claudius explains to Gertrard:

> For we have closely sent for *Hamlet* hether,
> That he as t'were by accedent, may heere
> Affront *Ophelia*;
> Her father and my selfe (lawful espials)
> Will so bestow our selves, that seeing unseene,
> We may of their encounter franckly judge,
>
> TLN 1567–72, p. 753 (3. 1. 29–34)

Polonius then 'looses' Ophelia ('walke you heere')[29] and Hamlet makes his entrance, although without giving any indication that he has been closely sent for. Meanwhile, Polonius withdraws with Claudius to see what will happen when Hamlet is 'started'. Hamlet begins ('To be, or not to be,')[30] by meditating on whether it is nobler to suffer or act, bringing his soliloquy to a close with an apparent allusion to his failure to exact revenge. He then catches sight of Ophelia, and a painful encounter ensues in which Hamlet, lapsing into cruelly brisk prose, first assures her that 'I did love you once', only to insist that 'I loved you not'[31] and demand that she get herself to a nunnery and out of his sight.[32] After Hamlet leaves, Ophelia is left to reflect dejectedly on what a noble mind is here o'erthrown.[33]

How far does Polonius's hounding succeed in confirming his conjecture about love-madness? When he first accosts Hamlet he is forced to admit 'how pregnant sometimes his replies are', fleetingly allowing that perhaps Hamlet is not mad after all.[34] But he reassures himself that these are merely instances of 'a happines that often madnesse hits on, which reason and sanity could not so prosperously be delivered of'.[35] He feels further reassured when he reflects that, in the course of their conversation, Hamlet was 'still

---

27. *Hamlet*, TLN 1136–7, p. 749 (2. 2. 200–1).
28. The timing can be established by comparing *Hamlet*, TLN 1471, p. 752 (2. 2. 493) with TLN 1558, p. 753 (3. 1. 21).
29. *Hamlet*, TLN 1581, p. 753 (3. 1. 43).   30. *Hamlet*, TLN 1594, p. 754 (3. 1. 56).
31. *Hamlet*, TLN 1653, 1657, p. 754 (3. 1. 114, 117).
32. *Hamlet*, TLN 1659, 1668, 1675, 1678, 1688, p. 754 (3. 1. 119, 126, 133, 135, 142–3).
33. *Hamlet*, TLN 1689, p. 754 (3. 1. 144).   34. *Hamlet*, TLN 1140–1, p. 749 (2. 2. 203–4).
35. *Hamlet*, TLN 1141–3, p. 749 (2. 2. 204–5).

harping on my daughter', and even more by the fact that 'hee knewe me not at first, a sayd I was a Fishmonger'.[36] As a result, he still feels able to conclude that Hamlet 'is farre gone, farre gone', to which he adds the wistful reflection that 'in my youth, I suffred much extremity for love, very neere this'.[37] Nor is he inclined to abandon his conjecture even after Hamlet declares that he is no longer in love with Ophelia. Modifying his original contention only slightly, he continues to assure Claudius that 'yet doe I believe/ The origin and comencement of this greefe,/ Sprung from neglected love'.[38]

We, the theatre audience, cannot share Polonius's confidence. We may reflect that Hamlet is far from fully in control of his feelings for Ophelia, but we have been alerted to expect apparent signs of insanity ever since he warned Horatio that he might conduct himself strangely.[39] We also know—or we would if we had enjoyed an Elizabethan grammar school education—that Polonius is very far from the mark in supposing Hamlet's declaration 'y'are a Fishmonger'[40] to be an indication of madness. As usual, Polonius lacks any skill at reading signs, and in this instance he comically fails to understand that Hamlet is merely offering him a well-known insult. As any schoolboy in Shakespeare's England would have known, to call a man a fishmonger, as Erasmus had explained in De copia, is to claim that he is the sort of person who blows his nose on his elbow.[41] Hamlet is simply dismissing Polonius, by no means for the only time, as a snivelling old fool.

While Polonius remains obstinate, Claudius sees at once that Polonius's conjecture has been disconfirmed. Having overheard Hamlet and Ophelia together, he is nothing less than contemptuous of the idea that Hamlet is mad for love: 'Love, his affections doe not that way tend'.[42] Nor does he believe that Hamlet is suffering from any form of insanity: 'what he spake, though it lackt forme a little,/ Was not like madnes'.[43] Claudius's scornful

---

36. *Hamlet*, TLN 1117–19, p. 749 (2. 2. 184–6).
37. *Hamlet*, TLN 1119–21, p. 749 (2. 2. 185–7).
38. *Hamlet*, TLN 1715–17, p. 755 (3. 1. 170–2).
39. *Hamlet*, TLN 786–98, p. 746 (1. 5. 168–80). 40. *Hamlet*, TLN 1104, p. 749 (2. 2. 172).
41. Erasmus 1569, fo. 27ᵛ: 'cubito se emungit, salsamentarium indicans'. For 'salsamentarius . . . a fishmonger' see Veron 1584, Sig. 2N, 8ʳ; Thomas 1592, Sig. 2V, 1ʳ. I have not seen any edition in which Hamlet's allusion has been recognized. Hibbard 1987, who finds the remark 'gloriously funny' (p. 212n.), preserves the suggestion (originally owed to Edmond Malone, who offered it as a conjectural emendation) that by 'fishmonger' Hamlet means 'fleshmonger'. The latest Arden editors tell us that Hamlet's 'comic mistake' is simply there to establish that he is feigning madness. See Thompson and Taylor 2006, p. 250n.
42. *Hamlet*, TLN 1701, p. 755 (3. 1. 156). 43. *Hamlet*, TLN 1702–3, p. 755 (3. 1. 157–8).

reaction is partly due to the fact that he has arrived at his own very different and much more disturbing conjecture about the cause of Hamlet's distracted state.[44] He now believes that there is some 'setled matter in his hart' on which his brain is beating, and that this is what 'puts him thus/ From fashion of himselfe.'[45] Hamlet appears to be a man with a cause, and Claudius recognizes that this is likely to be dangerous to himself:

> there's something in his soule
> Ore which his melancholy sits on brood,
> And I doe doubt, the hatch and the disclose
> Will be some danger;
>
> TLN 1703–6, p. 755 (3. 1. 158–61)

The sense in which Hamlet is brooding is not that he is suffering from love-melancholy; rather he is brooding in the manner of a bird hatching an egg. He is hatching a plot, in other words, and Claudius fears the outcome.

The roles have been reversed, and the hunter is feeling hunted. Perhaps we are even to understand that Claudius has come to see that Hamlet knows the truth about the cause of his father's death. Meanwhile, Claudius instantly acts on his own conjecture. He orders that Hamlet be bundled out of the way and sent 'with speede to *England*'.[46] He is planning to dispatch Hamlet to his death, just as he had earlier dispatched his father. Nothing more is heard of Polonius's rival conjecture about love-madness. His attempted *confirmatio* has proved a failure, so that he never gets the chance to deliver a fittingly sententious *peroratio*, in which he would no doubt have had much to say about youth, melancholy, the role of fathers, and the dangerous passion of love.

Ambiguous confirmation

While Polonius is hounding Hamlet, Hamlet is engaged in a parallel act of hunting, trying to uncover what may be the hidden truth about his father's death. The puzzle he needs to solve is whether the ghost is to be believed when he claims that he was murdered. Hamlet's initial conjecture is that the ghost has an honest cause and is telling the truth. As he assures Horatio,

---

44. As noted in Mercer 1987, pp. 206–7.   45. *Hamlet*, TLN 1712–14, p. 755 (3. 1. 167–9).
46. *Hamlet*, TLN 1708, p. 755 (3. 1. 163).

'touching this vision heere,/ It is an honest Ghost that let me tell you'.[47]
Later, however, he begins to experience unsettling doubts:

> The spirit that I have seene
> May be the deale [devil], and the deale hath power
> T'assume a pleasing shape, yea, and perhaps,
> Out of my weakenes, and my melancholy,
> As he is very potent with such spirits,
> Abuses me to damne me;

> TLN 1529–34, p. 753 (2. 2. 551–6)

Facing this deepening anxiety, Hamlet recognizes that he urgently needs to find some independent means of confirming the ghost's narrative, thereby settling the *quaestio iudicii*, the central question that needs to be adjudicated: did his uncle kill his father?

Thomas Wilson had explained that, when we address such questions, we are considering 'the chief grounde of a matter' and 'the chief title & principal ground' of our case.[48] Hamlet echoes his words, acknowledging that he cannot rely on the ghost's mere testimony, and that he needs 'grounds/ More relative then this' if he is to accept the ghost's allegations and act on them.[49] Specifically, he needs to find some means of testing the ghost's veracity by investigating the *consecutio*, the period since Claudius's perpetration of his alleged crime. He needs, in other words, to find some means of forcing Claudius, as the *Ad Herennium* puts it, 'to show some signs of a guilty conscience'.[50]

Like Polonius, Hamlet appeals at this juncture to the image of the hunt. As we have seen, the huntsman's first job is to loose the hounds and, in the case of fox hunting, to 'unkennel' their quarry from its place of conceal-ment, after which it can be coursed. We can even go in pursuit of two-legged foxes. A London preacher had published a tract in 1600 entitled *A toile for two-legged foxes* in which he had called for the persecution of recusant Catholics. One chapter, entitled 'The unkennelling of the Foxe, and the dutie of the terriers', describes how to force guileful papists into the open and ensure that they are coursed and caught.[51] Hamlet invokes the same vocabulary, constructing Claudius as a two-legged fox that he plans, as

---

47. *Hamlet*, TLN 758–9, p. 745 (1. 5. 137–8).   48. Wilson 1553, Sig. M, 3^v–4^r.
49. *Hamlet*, TLN 1534–5, p. 753 (2. 2. 556–7).
50. See *Rhetorica ad Herennium* 1954, II. V. 8, p. 72 on 'signa conscientiae'.
51. Baxter 1600, pp. 121–5.

he says, to 'unkennill' in such a way that his 'occulted guilt' is roused from its hiding place and brought into plain view.[52] Once this act of unkennelling is performed, he has already declared, 'I know my course'.[53] He will course the king and catch him; or rather, he will 'catch the conscience of the King', finally disclosing his guilty conscience to the world.[54]

There remains the question of how this can be done. Here Shakespeare's imagery heavily underscores the parallels he has contrived. Polonius is about to bring Hamlet face to face with Ophelia, hoping to start him into revealing the true state of his feelings. Hamlet stands in need of some analogous means by which he can hope to unkennel the king and prompt him to betray his guilt. Polonius already has a stratagem, and Hamlet needs one. 'About my braine', he says to himself, pondering his next move.[55] A brainwave immediately strikes, evidently as a result of the arrival of the players at Elsinore earlier in the scene.[56] Hamlet warmly welcomes them and immediately puts them through their paces. The first player is persuaded to recite a long piece about Queen Hecuba's flight through the flames of Troy after the death of Priam, but he is overcome by his own recitation, as Polonius observes: 'Looke where he has not turnd his cullour, and has teares in's eyes'.[57] This episode, with its demonstration of the power of theatre, seemingly puts Hamlet in mind of a passage from Thomas North's translation of Plutarch's *Lives* concerning the tyrant Pelopidas:

> being in a Theater, where the tragedy of *Troades* of *Euripides* was played, he went out of the Theater, . . . bicause he was ashamed his people shoulde see him weepe, to see the miseries of *Hecuba* and *Andromacha* played, and that they never saw him pity the death of any one man, of so many of his citizens as he had caused to be slaine. The gilty conscience therefore of this cruell and heathen tyran, did make him tremble.[58]

---

52. *Hamlet*, TLN 1805–6, p. 756 (3. 1. 70–1).   53. *Hamlet*, TLN 1529, p. 753 (2. 2. 551).
54. *Hamlet*, TLN 1536, p. 753 (2. 2. 558).   55. *Hamlet*, TLN 1519, p. 753 (2. 2. 541).
56. But there is a crux here, for Hamlet has already asked the troupe if they can play the murder of Gonzago and promised them an additional speech. See *Hamlet*, TLN 1469, 1472, p. 752 (2. 2. 491, 494). For a proposed solution see Wilson 2000, pp. 31–4.
57. *Hamlet*, TLN 1451–2, p. 752 (2. 2. 477–8). Quintilian 2001, 6. 2. 34–5, vol. 3, p. 62 tells us that he has frequently seen actors in tears after their own performance.
58. Plutarch 1579, pp. 324–5. This source has frequently been noted. See Gaunt 1969, referring to the discovery by Reinhold (1882), subsequently elaborated by Marindin (1896). Gaunt suggests that the reference may not be to Plutarch's *Lives* but rather to the *Moralia*, in which a similar story is told about Alexander of Pherae. See Plutarch 1603, p. 1273. The story is retold (as one about Alexander of Pherae) in Sidney 1595, Sig. F, 1ʳ. Bullough

Plutarch's anecdote is about a murderer whose guilty conscience is stirred by watching a play; specifically, a play about the miseries of Hecuba. Evidently recalling the story, Hamlet suddenly sees a possible means of unkennelling Claudius's guilt:

> I have heard, that guilty creatures sitting at a play,
> Have by the very cunning of the scene,
> Beene strooke so to the soule, that presently
> They have proclaim'd their malefactions:
> For murther, though it have no tongue will speake
> With most miraculous organ: Ile have these Players
> Play something like the murther of my father
> Before mine Uncle,
>
> TLN 1520–7, p. 753 (2. 2. 541–9)

Pursuing his thought about 'giving tongue', Hamlet arranges for the players to re-enact the ghost's account of his own murder, including 'a speech of some dosen or sixteene lines' that he will 'set downe and insert' for them to use.[59]

The classical rhetoricians give strong reasons for believing that such re-enactments can indeed produce the sort of powerful emotional effects that Hamlet hopes to arouse. Cicero speaks of *illustris explanatio*, when an event is so clearly described that 'it is almost as if the deeds are being enacted'.[60] Quintilian refers to this passage,[61] and also introduces from Aristotle's *Rhetoric* the term *enargeia*—clarity or vividness—to describe the same process.[62] He translates *enargeia* as *repraesentatio*, which he defines as the figure we employ when we attempt to picture something instead of merely

1957–75, vol. 7, p. 181 proposes a different source, the anonymous play *A Warning for Faire Women* (1599), in which a woman watching a play about someone who had murdered her husband suddenly confesses to the same crime. Bullough believes (vol. 7, p. 38) that 'this was probably Shakespeare's source', but the Plutarch passage seems to me far more likely.

59. *Hamlet*, TLN 1472–3, p. 752 (2. 2. 493–5).
60. Cicero 1942a, III. LIII. 202, vol. 2, p. 160: 'illustris explanatio rerumque quasi gerantur'. Wilson 1553, Sig. 2A, 3ʳ also speaks of 'illustris explanatio', which he defines as 'an evident declaration of a thyng, as though we sawe it even now done'.
61. Quintilian 2001, 6. 2. 32, vol. 3, p. 60.
62. On Aristotle's account of *enargeia* see Eden 1986, pp. 69–75; on Quintilian's account see Eden 1986, pp. 88–96; Plett 2012, pp. 7–11. Sidney 1595, Sig. D, 1ᵛ–2ʳ likewise draws on Aristotle in commending the 'peerlesse poet' as capable of writing with such vividness as to produce a 'speaking picture'. As Preston 2007, p. 115 notes, *enargeia* was a general term under which several different methods of providing vividness were ranged, including *ekphrasis*.

describing it.[63] As he says when discussing the technique, 'there is great power in being able to give expression to the things we are talking about clearly and in such a way that it seems to our listeners as if they are actually seeing them'.[64] The effect, as he says, will be to penetrate and arouse their emotions with a force that no mere description can ever hope to achieve.[65]

To Elizabethan writers on stage performance, it came to seem that the basic concern of the theatre was with *repraesentatio,* the attempt to re-enact and re-present past events with so much vividness that we feel we are witnessing them. The success of English actors in producing such lifelike representations was even regarded as a matter of national pride. Thomas Nashe in his *Pierce Penilesse* of 1592 boasts that 'our Players are not as the players beyond sea, . . . but our Sceane is more statelye furnish, . . . our representations honourable, and full of gallant resolution'.[66] William Cornwallis in his *Essayes* of 1600 speaks more generally about the moral value of the theatre, and especially about tragedies in which the actors 'give the beholders a more lively representation of vertue, & vice, then the coldnesse of precept'.[67] When Hamlet offers his advice to the players, he adopts the same view of the theatre as an arena in which the world is represented to our gaze. The purpose of playing, he tells them, is 'to holde as twere the Mirrour up to nature, to shew vertue her owne feature; scorne her own Image, and the very age and body of the time his forme and pressure'.[68]

That such acts of representation can arouse particularly intense emotions is no less an article of faith among Elizabethan writers about the stage. Nashe speaks in *Pierce Penilesse* of the theatre as a place in which 'our forefathers valiant acts . . . are revived, and they themselves raised from the Grave of Oblivion, and brought to pleade their aged Honours in open presence'. As he illustrates, the resulting emotional impact can be overwhelming:

> How would it have joyed brave *Talbot* (the terror of the French) to thinke that after he had lyne two hundred yeares in his Tombe, hee should triumphe againe on the Stage, and have his bones newe embalmed with the teares of ten thousand spectators at least, (at

63. Quintilian 2001, 8. 3. 61, vol. 3, p. 374; cf. Aristotle 1926, III. X. 11, p. 404.
64. Quintilian 2001, 8. 3. 62, vol. 3, p. 374. 'Magna virtus res de quibus loquimur clare atque ut cerni videantur enuntiare'.
65. Quintilian 2001, 8. 3. 67, vol. 3, p. 378.   66. Nashe 1592, Sig. F, 4^r.
67. Cornwallis 1600, Sig. 2K, 7^v.   68. *Hamlet*, TLN 1748–51, p. 755 (3. 2. 18–20).

> severall times) who in the Tragedian that represents his person,
> imagine they behold him fresh bleeding.[69]

Nashe even hints that the re-enactment of Talbot's great deeds may be capable of arousing the emotions more powerfully than the deeds themselves.

Shortly before the play in *Hamlet* is performed, Hamlet draws Horatio aside to tell him about the emotions he hopes to excite in Claudius by making him watch just such a *repraesentatio* of his alleged crime:

> There is a play to night before the King,
> One scene of it comes neere the circumstance
> Which I have told thee of my fathers death,
> I prethee when thou seest that act a foote,
> Even with the very comment of thy soule
> Observe mine Uncle, if his occulted guilt
> Doe not it selfe unkennill in one speech,
> It is a damned ghost that we have seene,
>
> TLN 1800–7, p. 755–6 (3. 2. 65–72)

Hamlet is promising that the play will include an account of the 'circumstances' of his father's death—the time, the place, the motive, and the means to bring it about. He is preparing to put his conjecture about the ghost's veracity to what he regards as a decisive test. He hopes that, if Claudius is guilty, a sudden confrontation with the details of his crime will unkennel him. If nothing happens, then the ghost cannot have been telling the truth. But if Horatio watches with sufficient attention, he may see the telltale signs of a guilty conscience finally revealed.

What will count as a satisfactory *confirmatio* of the ghost's narrative? As we have seen, the vernacular rhetoricians, closely followed by a number of legal writers, had proposed a series of tests that any purported confirmation must pass. Shakespeare may have known about these from the legal handbooks, but there is no evidence that he had read them, whereas he was undoubtedly acquainted with the rhetorical texts from which their terminology was largely derived. If we return to the rhetoricians, and in particular to Leonard Cox and Thomas Wilson, we find them singling out three considerations above all. First, we must look to see if the suspected party 'blushed or waxed

---

69. Nashe 1592, Sig. F, 3[r]. For a discussion of this much-quoted passage see Dawson 1996, pp. 32–5.

pale'.[70] Next, we must attend to whether he 'stutted & coulde nat well speke'.[71] Lastly, it will obviously be incriminating if 'after the dede was done he fled'.[72] Thomas Wilson adds that we should also consider more generally 'how he kept his countenaunce'.[73] Hamlet declares, however, that he will consider his conjecture about the ghost's truthfulness fully confirmed if only one of these signs is visible:

> Ile observe his lookes,
> Ile tent him to the quicke, if a but blench
> I know my course.
>
> TLN 1527–9, p. 753 (2. 2. 549–51)

It will be enough for Hamlet if, in Cox's phrase, Claudius merely waxes pale. This will be a sufficient unkennelling of his guilt, and Hamlet will then know what course to follow in order to hunt him to the death.

The time for the performance arrives. The king and queen make their entrance and Claudius steps forward with a seemingly affable greeting. 'How fares our cosin *Hamlet*?'[74] The king is asking Hamlet how he is feeling, but Hamlet affects to believe that Claudius is enquiring about the quality of his fare or food, and responds: 'Excellent yfaith, of the Camelions dish, I eate the ayre, promiscram'd'.[75] The chamelion was believed to live on nothing but the air.[76] Hamlet's remark may at first seem no more than an instance of the kind of riddling to which he is addicted, but something far more aggressive is being conveyed. While it may not be true that Hamlet is living on nothing but the air, he is reminding Claudius that he is living as nothing but the heir, and is therefore feeling undernourished as well as cheated of many promises made to him.[77] His tone may be bantering, but his underlying message is hostile and even threatening. He wants to be something more than the heir, so he wants Claudius out of the way.

The play begins with a dumbshow in which, as Ophelia correctly surmises, we are offered an introduction to the argument:[78]

70. Cox 1532, Sig. E, 6ʳ; cf. Wilson 1553, Sig. M, 2ʳ.
71. Cox 1532, Sig. E, 6ʳ; cf. Wilson 1553, Sig. N, 3ᵛ.
72. Cox 1532, Sig. E, 6ʳ; cf. Wilson 1553, Sig. N, 2ᵛ.   73. Wilson 1553, Sig. N, 2ᵛ.
74. *Hamlet*, TLN 1816, p. 756 (3. 2. 82).   75. *Hamlet*, TLN 1817–18, p. 756 (3. 2. 83–4).
76. See, for example, the entry on the chameleon in Elyot 1538, fo. XVIIIʳ: 'he doth never eate or drynke, but is nourisshed onely by ayre'.
77. For a discussion of punning on air/heir see de Grazia 2007, pp. 89–90. De Grazia treats the play as fundamentally about Hamlet's sense of dispossession. See de Grazia 2007, esp. pp. 1–3. Zurcher 2010, p. 229 goes so far as to suggest that the pun may be present in the opening line of the play, which he writes as 'Who's th'heir'.
78. *Hamlet*, TLN 1861, p. 756 (3. 2. 123).

Enter a King and a Queene, very lovingly; the Queene embracing him, she kneeles, and makes shew of Protestation unto him, he takes her up, and declines his head upon her necke, he layes him downe uppon a bancke of flowers, she seeing him asleepe, leaves him: anon comes in a Fellow, takes off his crowne, kisses it, and pours poyson in the Kings eares, and Exits: the Queene returnes, finds the King dead, and makes passionate action, the poysner with some two or three Mutes comes in againe, seeming to lament with her, the dead body is carried away, the poysner wooes the Queene with gifts, shee seemes loath and unwilling awhile, but in the end accepts his love.[79]

The insertion of this elaborate exercise in *pronuntiatio* raises some puzzles. Speaking earlier to the members of the troupe, Hamlet had expressed contempt for such dumbshows,[80] so why include one at all? The answer seems to be that the players are sadly out of date, and too set in their theatrical ways to be able to give them up. A further and more troubling puzzle is that, while this opening might seem intensely provocative, it does nothing to unkennel the king. He and the queen both remain silent, and after some ribald banter between Hamlet and Ophelia the play itself begins without incident.

Following a prologue, the player king and queen make their entrance. The king is sick, and they speak at length about whether the queen will remarry after his death. The king lies down to sleep, at which point his nephew Lucianus enters. Lucianus evidently begins by following the conventions of revenge drama (making faces, pausing dramatically, miming evil intent, and so on)[81] and does so at such length that Hamlet begins to show considerable impatience: 'Beginne murtherer, pox, leave thy damnable faces and begin'.[82] Propelled into action, Lucianus proceeds to deliver his lines:

> Thoughts black, hands apt, drugges fit, and time agreeing,
> Confiderat season els no creature seeing,
> Thou mixture ranck, of midnight weedes collected,
> With *Hecats* ban thrice blasted, thrice infected,

79. This passage follows the SD at TLN 1858, p. 756 (3. 2. 121).
80. *Hamlet*, TLN 1739, p. 755 (3. 2. 10). Thorne 2000, pp. 112–14 additionally notes that Hamlet is both attracted and repulsed by 'shows'.
81. Felperin 1977, pp. 46–8, 59–60 notes how the play within the play conforms to older models of revenge tragedy. On Lucianus's antics see also de Grazia 2007, pp. 180–2.
82. *Hamlet*, TLN 1969–70, p. 757 (3. 2. 228–9).

> Thy naturall magicke, and dire property,
> On wholsome life usurpe immediatly.

TLN 1972–7, p. 757 (3. 2. 231–6)

Here we have only half a dozen lines, not the dozen or more that Hamlet had promised the players, but it is possible that we are nevertheless intended to think of these as the ones that he had asked leave to insert, if only because they reveal an acquaintance with some of the details that he alone knows from the ghost about how he met his death. Yet more strikingly, they also disclose a precise knowledge of a text to which Hamlet elsewhere refers, the *Rhetorica ad Herennium*, which is here treated in almost parodic terms. As we have seen, in discussing *confirmatio* the *Ad Herennium* had distinguished the *causa*, the *conlatio*, and the *signa*. The *causa* refers to the suspect's motives, the *conlatio* is the stage at which we show that he had the means and ability to commit his crime, and the *signa* are the indications that time, space, and place were all propitious, and that he had hopes of not being detected.[83] Lucianus tells us that he has a motive (thoughts black); that he possesses the means (drugges fit, mixture ranck); that he has the necessary ability (hands apt); that time and place are propitious (confiderat season, time agreeing); and that he has hopes of not being detected (no creature seeing). We wait to see how much of an impact his oration will make, but meanwhile Shakepeare allows himself a touch of satire as he heavy-handedly lays out the formulae for investigating the 'circumstances' of a crime.

With the completion of this *repraesentatio* we come to the *consecutio*, the period when we wait to see if the suspect shows any signs of a guilty conscience. Hamlet has already asked Horatio to pay 'heedfull note' to Claudius, and has promised that 'I mine eyes will rivet to his face'.[84] One thing we need to look for, Thomas Wilson had stressed, is whether the suspect trembles or staggers. There are certainly grounds for suspicion here. As soon as Lucianus pours the poison in the player king's ear, Ophelia calls out: 'The King rises'.[85] Claudius has been 'started', and suddenly rises (perhaps staggers) to his feet. We also need to consider, Wilson had added, how well the suspect keeps his countenance. Claudius does not manage very well. The queen immediately sees that something is wrong:

---

83. On Lucianus and the right or kairotic moment see Beehler 2003, pp. 82–3. Beehler uses the idea of waiting for such a moment to explain Hamlet's delay. On *kairos* in Renaissance thought see also Paul 2014.
84. *Hamlet*, TLN 1809–10, p. 756 (3. 2. 74–5).   85. *Hamlet*, TLN 1982, p. 757 (3. 2. 240).

'How fares my Lord?'[86] The most incriminating thing of all, the rhetoricians agree, will be if the suspect runs away. Claudius next shouts 'away', the courtiers call for lights and he rushes from the scene.[87]

How far is Hamlet's *confirmatio* a success? We, the theatre audience, stand in no need of being persuaded, for we already have good reason to suspect that the ghost has been telling the truth. During the previous scene, when Polonius is setting up his parallel trap for Hamlet, he hands Ophelia a devotional book to read while she is waiting for him:

> *Ophelia* walke you heere, gracious so please you,
> We will bestow our selves; reade on this booke,
> That show of such an exercise may cullour
> Your lonelines; we are oft too blame in this,
> Tis too much proov'd, that with devotions visage
> And pious action, we doe sugar ore
> The devill himselfe.
>
> TLN 1581–7, p. 753 (3. 1. 43–9)

The second half of Polonius's speech is nothing more than another of his maundering references to the art of rhetoric. The rhetoricians have much to say about the sugaring over of our vices to make them appear as virtues. As we have seen, they name the technique *paradiastole* and they sometimes compare it, as does Polonius, to the act of excusing the devil.[88] Polonius's moralizing is, in short, innocent and commonplace. Nevertheless, it has a sensational impact on the king, unintentionally unkennelling him and prompting him to confess in a remorseful aside that he is labouring under a heavy burden of guilt:

> How smart a lash that speech doth give my conscience.
> The harlots cheeke beautied with plastring art,
> Is not more ougly to the thing that helps it,
> Then is my deede to my most painted word:
>
> TLN 1588–91, p. 753 (3. 1. 50–3)

Hamlet and Polonius have been plotting in parallel, but here the lines converge. While Hamlet is hoping to catch the conscience of the king,

---

86. *Hamlet*, TLN 1984, p. 757 (3. 2. 242).   87. *Hamlet*, TLN 1986–7, p. 757 (3. 2. 244–5).
88. See, for example, Susenbrotus 1562, p. 46, where he warns that by this device 'Satan can be transfigured into an Angel of light' ('Satanas transfiguratur in Angelum lucis'). See also *The Triall of true Friendship* (1596), Sig. E, 4ʳ on those 'who are in shapes angels, but in qualities devils'. The prevalence of the trope may have helped to suggest to Shakespeare the name of Angelo in *Measure for Measure*.

Polonius has inadvertently caught it. It is only after Claudius has been publicly unkennelled that he explicitly confesses in soliloquy to 'A brothers murther'.[89] But we have already been alerted to the fact that he has committed some ugly deed, and our suspicions have been strongly aroused as to the probable depth of its ugliness.

There remains the question of how persuasive Hamlet's *confirmatio* appears within the world of the play. Here matters are much more ambiguous and complicated. Hamlet's first effort to unkennel the king is undoubtedly a failure. Claudius does not react to the dumb show in any way, remaining silent until after the player king and queen have delivered their lines, at which point he calmly enquires if the play is about a crime and asks to be told what it is called. Hamlet replies: 'The Mousetrap, mary how? tropically'.[90] The title is a trope (more specifically, a metaphor) but it is also a trap. Hamlet has given up what George Gascoigne calls the noble art of hunting and is now trying to exterminate vermin. But his trap fails to spring, and Hamlet is reduced to taunting Claudius in evident frustration. It is 'a knavish peece of worke', he declares, while sarcastically adding that 'your Majestie, and wee that have free soules, it touches us not, let the gauled Jade winch, our withers are unwrong'.[91]

Much has been made of the failure of the dumbshow to produce any effect.[92] Dover Wilson argued that Claudius cannot have been paying attention, and must have been engaged in a whispered conversation with Polonius and the Queen.[93] Characteristically, he adds that this is the true explanation and the only possible way of playing the scene.[94] But in fact it has no textual warrant at all. Others have argued that the ghost's story must be false,[95] and thus that the dumbshow poses no threat to Claudius. But even if the ghost is nothing but Hamlet's fantasy,[96] we already strongly suspect that it has caused him to believe something true, so that Claudius might still be expected to react on seeing his crime displayed to public gaze. Still others have postulated that Shakespeare simply counts on his audience not to ask why Claudius remains impassive, and is careful not to raise the

89. *Hamlet*, TLN 2154, p. 759 (3. 3. 38).
90. *Hamlet*, TLN 1954, p. 757 (3. 2. 216).   91. *Hamlet*, TLN 1956–9, p. 757 (3. 2. 218–20).
92. For a survey of earlier discussions see Cox 1973, pp. 5–10.
93. Wilson 1934b, pp. 159–60, 183–4.   94. Wilson 1934b, pp. 151, 159, 160.
95. W. W. Greg's suggestion, discussed in Wilson 1934b, pp. 4–7, 150–1 and reformulated in Cavell 2003, pp.179–91. For a discussion see Kerrigan 1996, pp. 77–8.
96. For the dumbshow as the enactment of a primal scene see Cavell 2003, pp. 182–3, 187, 203.

question himself.[97] But the text of the play undoubtedly raises the question, and it cannot simply be left unanswered.

Perhaps we cannot know the solution, but perhaps there is no puzzle to be solved. It is arguable that Claudius's failure to react is just what Hamlet should have expected. He had spoken to Claudius at the start of the scene with sufficient hostility to put anyone on their guard, and even to wonder if some act of aggression might be about to take place. But forewarned is forearmed. 'If a man who is guilty exhibits no signs of guilt',[98] as the *Ad Herennium* observes, the reason may be that 'he was able to think so much beforehand about what might be about to take place that he was able to stop himself from speaking and react with complete confidence'.[99] Perhaps Hamlet's inability to bridle his resentment gave Claudius sufficient warning of the need to steel himself, and this is why his withers remained unwrung.

It might be felt, on the other hand, that Hamlet's second attempt to unkennel the king is no less obviously a success, and that Luciano's rhetoric, by contrast with the failure of the dumbshow, is there to illustrate the incomparably arousing power of speech.[100] But this is not how it seems to Horatio, whom Hamlet regards as someone whose opinion is deeply to be trusted.[101] Before the play scene, Horatio promises Hamlet to watch so closely that nothing will 'scape detecting'.[102] But afterwards he is strikingly unforthcoming about the significance of what he has observed:

> HAMLET Did'st perceive?
> HORATIO Very well my Lord.
> HAMLET Upon the talke of the poysning.
> HORATIO I did very well note him.
>
> TLN 2004–7, p. 758 (3. 2. 261–4)

---

97. Jenkins 1982, p. 504.
98. *Rhetorica ad Herennium* 1954, II. V. 8, p. 72: 'Si reus horum [sc. signs of guilt] nihil fecerit.'
99. *Rhetorica ad Herennium* 1954, II. V. 8, p. 72: 'adeo praemeditatum fuisse quid sibi esset usu venturum ut confidentissime resisteret, responderet'. This, our author adds, is certainly what the person speaking in accusation should try to claim about his adversary.
100. As suggested in Barkan 1995, pp. 345–7. For a different explanation see Zurcher 2010, pp. 264–5.
101. *Hamlet*, TLN 1794, p. 755 (3. 2. 59).
102. *Hamlet*, TLN 1814, p. 756 (3. 2. 79). On the relevance of the conventions of detective stories see Kerrigan 1996.

Despite Hamlet's efforts to prompt him, Horatio refuses to make any declaration to the effect that Claudius's guilt has been confirmed.[103] As usual, Horatio is at his most cautious when Hamlet is at his most intense. He has already warned Hamlet against the ghost, and he will shortly warn him against duelling with Laertes.[104] Here, too, he refuses to be drawn.

Hamlet feels no such doubts, and now claims to be fully convinced. It is true that he ends up by having to rely on additional means to provoke the king, and that Claudius's nerve only cracks when Hamlet interrupts to tell him that 'you shall see anon how the murtherer gets the love of *Gonzagoes* wife.'[105] Without this addition, perhaps Claudius might have weathered Lucianus's speech just as he had earlier weathered the dumbshow. It is also true that, as a student of rhetoric, Hamlet knows that the sort of circumstantial evidence he has marshalled cannot amount to what a Renaissance logician would call a demonstration—which may also be why Horatio refuses to accept that Hamlet's experiment has yielded an unambiguous result.[106] Nevertheless, Hamlet feels able to assure Horatio that the probability that the ghost has been telling the truth now strikes him as so high that he would be prepared to bet a very large sum of money on it: 'O good *Horatio*, Ile take the Ghosts word for a thousand pound'.[107] As Hamlet sees it, the fox has been unkennelled and his own cause has been confirmed. It only remains for him to pronounce a fittingly triumphant *peroratio*.

Successful confirmation

There is a mystery at the beginning of *All's Well That Ends Well* about the countess of Rossillion's young ward Hellen. The countess refers to it as 'The mistrie of your lonelinesse'.[108] Why is Hellen so solitary and sad? The countess believes that she must still be grieving for her father's death, but Rynaldo maintains that the reason for her melancholy is that she has fallen in

---

103. On Horatio's unsureness see Thorne 2000, pp. 110–12.
104. *Hamlet*, TLN 599–604, p. 743 (1. 4. 69–74) and TLN 3431–2, p. 772 (5. 2. 190–1).
105. *Hamlet*, TLN 1980–1, p. 757 (3. 2. 238–9). On this point see Lewis 2012a, pp. 14–15. Kerrigan 1996, p. 186 notes that Hamlet refers to the murderer not as brother but as nephew to the king (i.e. like himself). See also Zurcher 2010, pp. 264–5. Zurcher infers that Claudius reacts to what he perceives as a threat to his own life, not merely a re-enactment of his crime.
106. See Kerrigan 1996, pp. 77–9 on the play as an experiment.
107. *Hamlet*, TLN 2003–4, p. 758 (3. 2. 260–1).
108. *All's Well That Ends Well*, TLN 471, p. 973 (1. 3. 143).

love with Bertram, the countess's unattainable son. The countess resolves to seek a *confirmatio* of this rival conjecture, and Hellen is summoned into her presence.[109]

The countess needs to discover some means of eliciting from the unwilling Hellen the truth about her state of mind. Like Hamlet, she needs some powerful rhetorical technique to 'start' or unkennel her. She puts her faith in the device known to the rhetoricians as *ambiguitas* or *amphibolia*, 'when a word can be taken in two or more senses, but when it is meant to be taken in the sense intended by the person who has spoken'.[110] The countess ingeniously deploys the technique as soon as Hellen makes her appearance, suddenly announcing: 'You know *Hellen/* I am a mother to you'.[111] Critics sometimes speak of this proclamation as a sign of the countess's willingness to welcome Hellen into her family,[112] but this reading fails to recognize that, in speaking ambiguously of herself both as Hellen's mother and as a guardian who has mothered her, the countess is making a rhetorical move. By claiming Hellen as her daughter she is simultaneously affirming that Bertram must be her brother, in which case there can be no future for Hellen's love. The countess is speaking with intentionally disturbing effect, aiming to 'start' Hellen into exhibiting some signs of anxiety at the unspoken implications of what has been said.[113] The stratagem immediately works, as she triumphantly points out:

> Why not a mother? when I sed a mother
> Me thought you saw a serpent, what's in mother,
> That you start at it?

TLN 440–2, p. 973 (1. 3. 112–14)

Like a frightened hare, Hellen has been successfully 'started', and it is now for the countess to discover if she can be made to exhibit any confirmatory signs of guilt at having withheld the truth.

---

109. I have not read any critical work in which it is recognized that the resulting scene is couched in the idiom of the *genus iudiciale*. Desmet 1992 examines the rhetoric of the play, but says nothing about the sources of the countess's eloquence.

110. *Rhetorica ad Herennium* 1954, IV. LIII 67, p. 400: 'Per ambiguum, cum verbum potest in duas pluresve sententias accipi, sed accipitur tamen in eam partem quam vult is qui dixit.' On *ambiguitas/amphibolia* see also Quintilian 2001, 7. 9. 1–15, vol. 3, pp. 280–8; Sherry 1550, Sig. C, 1^r; Peacham 1577, Sig. G, 1^{r-v}.

111. *All's Well That Ends Well*, TLN 437–8, p. 973 (1. 3. 109–10).

112. See, for example, Thomas 1987, p. 145; Desmet 1992, p. 156.

113. As noted in Clark 2007, pp. 64–5. By contrast, Parker 1996, p. 193 sees in the passage a 'scene of incest', a suggestion already found in Wheeler 1981, p. 42 and Hillman 1993, pp. 71–2.

Seeking to catch Hellen's conscience, the countess begins to harass her with the repeated affirmation 'I am your Mother'. Hellen at first manages, as Thomas Wilson would say, to keep her countenance. She daringly responds by picking up the point that this would make Bertram her brother, and explains somewhat duplicitously why this cannot be the case:

> COUNTESSE I say I am your Mother.
> HELLEN   Pardon Madam.
> The Count *Rosillion* cannot be my brother:
> I am from humble, he from honord name:
> No note upon my Parents, his all noble,
> My Master, my deere Lord he is, and I
> His servant live, and will his vassall die:
> He must not be my brother.
>
> TLN 454–60, p. 973 (1. 3. 126–32)

Fully deploying her persuasive arts, Hellen here rounds off with an impassioned rhymed couplet before switching into spondaic metre to give extra weight to her central claim about the social distance between Bertram and herself. But the countess is not to be deflected with such rhetorical tricks. She immediately retorts 'Nor I your mother', and waits to see if this will at last betray Hellen into revealing some signs of guilt.[114]

As we know, Hellen's guilt will be proclaimed if she blushes, or turns pale, or begins to falter in her speech. As soon as the countess says 'Nor I your Mother', she undoubtedly begins to falter:

> You are my mother Madam, would you were
> So that my Lord your sonne were not my brother,
> Indeede my mother, or were you both our mothers,
> I care no more for, then I doe for heaven,
> So I were not his sister, cant no other,
> But I your daughter, he must be my brother.
>
> TLN 461–6, p. 973 (1. 3. 133–8)

As the countess rightly observes, 'daughter and mother/ So strive upon your pulse' that Hellen has ceased to make any sense. When she points this out, Hellen begins to exhibit further signs of guilt: 'what pale agen?/ My feare hath catcht your fondnesse!'[115] Like Hamlet, who had resolved in the case

---

114. *All's Well That Ends Well*, TLN 460, p. 973 (1. 3. 132).
115. *All's Well That Ends Well*, TLN 468–70, p. 973 (1. 3. 140–2).

of Claudius that 'if a but blench' he will judge that he has managed to catch his conscience,[116] the countess takes Hellen's sudden paleness to be suffi-cient evidence that she too has been 'catcht'.

By this stage the countess feels sure that Rynaldo's conjecture has been confirmed, and expresses her confidence in the recurrent image of success-fully tracing a river from the salt sea to its head or source:

> now I see
> The mistrie of your lonelinesse, and finde
> Your salt teares head, now to all sence 'tis grosse:
> You love my sonne,
>
> TLN 470–3, p. 973 (I. 3. 142–5)

Faced with this conclusion, Hellen reacts by blushing, thereby exhibiting a further sign of guilt, as the countess calls on her to admit:

> But tell me then 'tis so, for looke, thy cheekes
> Confesse it 'ton tooth other,
>
> TLN 476–7, p. 973 (I. 3. 148–9)

The countess is now confident that her *confirmatio* has reached the stage of *approbatio* or unquestionable proof:

> You love my sonne, invention is asham'd
> Against the proclamation of thy passion
> To say thou doost not:
>
> TLN 473–5, p. 973 (I. 3. 145–7)

There is nothing that rhetorical *inventio* can hope to achieve, she concludes, in the way of finding any arguments on the other side of the case.

How persuasive is the countess's *confirmatio*? As in the case of Hamlet's unkennelling of Claudius, we stand in no need of being convinced. We have already heard Hellen admit to her hopeless passion for Bertram in soliloquy at the end of the opening scene. When the countess interrogates her, we are simply left to enjoy the spectacle of someone exhibiting a mastery of the rhetorical arts. The scene might indeed be said to be Shakespeare's most purely forensic one. His commitment to illustrating how the precepts of judicial rhetoric can be put to effective use almost threatens to overwhelm his chief dramatic purpose in the scene, that of establishing that the countess is at once a force to be reckoned with and a

116. *Hamlet*, TLN 1528, 1536, p. 753 (2. 2. 550, 558).

character of essential benignity. While we need no convincing, however, we can still ask about the persuasiveness of the countess's speech within the world of the play. Here the answer is that she succeeds so completely that Hellen is left with no option but to confess:

> COUNTESSE   Come, come, disclose
> The state of your affection, for your passions
> Have to the full appeach'd.
> HELLEN   Then I confesse
> Here on my knee, before high heaven and you,
> That before you, and next unto high heaven,
> I love your Sonne:
>
> TLN 489–94, p. 973 (1. 3. 161–6)

With her complex *epanodos* (before/heaven/you; before/you/heaven) Hellen produces a closing rhetorical flourish while admitting defeat.[117] Rynaldo's narrative has finally been confirmed.

Fabricated confirmation

The investigation of conjectural issues normally takes the form of a search for the cause of some puzzling facts. But as we saw in Chapter 1, the classical rhetoricians are not afraid to advise that it may be possible to fabricate such mysteries by making up allegedly puzzling facts and then purporting to explain them. This is what Iago does when he claims to have noticed that Cassio is acting guiltily in Othello's presence. As we know, and as Iago knows, the truth is that Cassio is merely feeling ill at ease. Having fabricated the supposed mystery, however, Iago proceeds to formulate a conjecture—which he knows to be false—by way of explaining it. He insinuates that Cassio must be having an affair with Desdemona, and sets about persuading Othello that this conjecture can be confirmed. He has little doubt that he will succeed:

> trifles light as ayre,
> Are to the jealous, confirmations strong
> As proofes of holy writ,
>
> TLN 1774–6, p. 948 (3. 3. 323–5)

---

117. Horvei 1984, pp. 116–17 classifies the lines as an example of *chiasmus*.

His next task is to conjure out of thin air just such a purportedly strong *confirmatio* of Cassio's guilt. So sure is he of success that he speaks of producing proofs as strong as the 'non-artificial' confirmations that unimpeachable documentary evidence—holy writ itself—can provide.[118]

One reason for Iago's assurance is that Othello's 'unbookish jealousie' makes him credulous;[119] but another is that Othello is too straightforward a character to be skilled at recognizing that appearances can deceive:

> The Moore is of a free and open nature,
> That thinkes men honest, that but seeme to be so:
> And will as tenderly be led bit'h nose—
> As Asses are:
>
> TLN 677–80, p. 936 (1. 3. 381–4)

Like Hercules, of whom Thomas Wilson had said that everyone was so moved by his eloquence that he was able 'to draw them and leade them even as he lusted', Iago is confident of being able to lead Othello in any direction that he may choose.[120]

Some critics have seen an increasing tendency on Shakespeare's part to make use of forensic techniques to show how the rules of evidence can be abused, and have even spoken of the demonization of such techniques in the mature tragedies.[121] If there is indeed such a trajectory to be traced, then Iago stands at the extreme end of it. More than any other character whom Shakespeare endows with rhetorical expertise, Iago illustrates the age-old anxiety voiced by Plato in the *Gorgias* about the morality of the rhetorical arts.[122] Surely what you are saying, Socrates puts it to Gorgias, is that there is no need for the rhetorician to know the truth about things, but merely to have discovered some means of persuading people.[123] As we have seen, Quintilian attempts to head off this criticism by insisting that a good orator cannot fail to be a good man, but even he is obliged to admit that orators sometimes make use of falsehoods to support bad causes, and he does not

---

118. For a full analysis of the resulting 'crisis-scene' (3. 3) see Adamson 1980, pp. 148–74. But Adamson makes no reference to the rhetorical principles around which the scene is structured.

119. *Othello*, TLN 2170, 2227, pp. 952–3 (4. 1. 43, 99).

120. Wilson 1553, Preface, Sig. A, 3ᵛ. On this image of *Hercules Gallicus*, taken from Lucian, see Rebhorn 1995, pp. 66–77; Skinner 1996, pp. 92–3, 389–90.

121. Hutson 2007, pp. 309–10.

122. On Iago as a sophistic rhetor see Crider 2009, pp. 106–21.

123. Plato 2010, 459b, p. 23.

scruple to offer instructions about how to make fabricated cases sound plausible.[124] Within a generation after Shakespeare was writing, these long-standing doubts about the rhetorical arts began to be restated with renewed hostility. Thomas Hobbes was only the most eloquent of many who denounced what he called 'that art of words, by which some men can represent to others, that which is Good, in the likenesse of Evill; and Evill, in the likenesse of Good; and augment, or diminish the apparent greatnesse of Good and Evill; discontenting men, and troubling their Peace at their pleasure'.[125] Shakespeare might even be felt to be anticipating this criticism when he complains in one of his Sonnets about 'What strained touches Rhethorick can lend' by contrast with 'true plaine words'.[126]

Iago deliberately sets out to represent good in the likeness of evil, and from the moment when he first begins to work out his plot he shows himself acutely aware of the rhetorical rules for ensuring that a fabricated *confirmatio* can be made to sound like the truth. As we saw in Chapter 1, Quintilian is particularly interested in how 'false expositions' can be lent an air of verisimilitude.[127] 'To begin with', he writes, 'we must take care that what we are fabricating falls within the bounds of possibility.'[128] This is the prime consideration that Iago has in mind when he begins to formulate his scheme:

> *Cassio*'s a proper man, let me see now,
> To get his place, and to plume up my will,
> In double knavery—how, how, let's see,
> After some time, to abuse *Othelloe*'s eares,
> That he is too familiar with his wife:
> He hath a person and a smooth dispose,
> To be suspected, fram'd to make women false:
>
> TLN 670–6, p. 936 (1. 3. 374–80)

If Cassio is a proper man, young and handsome, and with smooth manners, it is well within the bounds of possibility that Desdemona should find him attractive. As Iago says of her in his next soliloquy, 'That she loves him, tis apt and of great credit'.[129] The allegation is not true, but it is one that will be

---

124. Quintilian 2001, 12. 1. 40, vol. 5, pp. 216–18.
125. Hobbes 2012 [1651], vol. 2, ch. 17, p. 258.
126. Shakespeare 1986, Sonnet 82, lines 10, 12, p. 862 (p. 67).
127. See Quintilian 2001, 4. 2. 88, vol. 2, p. 262 on 'falsae expositiones'.
128. Quintilian 2001, 4. 2. 89, vol. 2, p. 264: 'prima sit curandum ut id quod fingemus fieri possit'.
129. *Othello*, TLN 968, p. 939 (2. 1. 268).

readily believed. The glory of his plot, as Iago gleefully points out, is that it is 'Proball to thinking'; it embodies the crucial quality of likelihood.[130]

We must next make sure, Quintilian goes on, 'that our fabrication fits with the time, the place and the persons involved'.[131] Some suspicious facts about time and place are what Iago points out to Othello when he first insinuates that Cassio is behaving 'guilty-like' in his presence:

> IAGO Did *Michael Cassio* when you wooed my Lady,
> Know of your love?
> OTHELLO He did from first to last:—Why doest thou aske?
>
> TLN 1544–6, p. 945 (3. 3. 93–5)

Iago draws Othello's attention to the fact that Cassio and Desdemona had ample time to get to know each other during Othello's courtship. Othello's response reveals his first flash of suspicion, and Iago pursues his advantage:

> IAGO I did not thinke he had beene acquainted with her.
> OTHELLO O yes, and went betweene us very oft.
> IAGO Indeed?
> OTHELLO Indeed? I indeed, discern'st thou ought in that?
> Is he not honest?
>
> TLN 1549–53, p. 945 (3. 3. 98–102)

Iago is prompting Othello to see that Cassio, in his role as go-between, was also very suitably placed to win Desdemona's confidence. Time, place, and persons all come together, and Othello's questions begin to sound a more suspicious note about Cassio's honesty.

A further thought to bear in mind, Quintilian goes on, is that it will be helpful 'if you can manage to make your falsehoods cohere with something which is true',[132] thereby lending 'colour' to your lies.[133] Iago lays on the necessary colour when, later in the scene, he finally announces his alleged suspicions:

> Receive it from me: I speake not yet of proofe,
> Looke to your wife, observe her well with *Cassio*;
> Weare your eies thus, not jealous, nor secure,
>
> TLN 1648–50, p. 946 (3. 3. 198–200)

---

130. *Othello*, TLN 1338, p. 943 (2. 3. 305).
131. Quintilian 2001, 4. 2. 89, vol. 2, p. 264: 'id quod fingimus . . . personae et loco et tempori congruat'.
132. Quintilian 2001, 4. 2. 89, vol. 2, p. 264: 'si continget, etiam verae alicui rei cohaereat'.
133. See Quintilian 2001, 4. 2. 88, vol. 2, p. 264 on the addition of 'color'.

Having broached his accusation, Iago promptly colours it with two claims about Desdemona. The first concerns the sexual fidelity of Venetian women:

> I know our Countrey disposition well,
> In *Venice* they doe let God see the prankes
> They dare not shew their husbands: their best conscience,
> Is not to leave't undone, but keepe't unknowne.
>
> TLN 1653–6, p. 946 (3. 3. 203–6)

Othello cannot see how this insulting generalization applies to Desdemona, and merely registers bewilderment: 'Doest thou say so.'[134] But Iago is able to link it with some worrying observations that duly give Othello pause:

> IAGO She did deceive her father marrying you;
> And when she seem'd to shake and feare your lookes,
> She lov'd them most.
> OTHELLO And so she did.
> IAGO   Why go too then,
> She that so young, could give out such a seeming,
> To seale her fathers eyes up, close as Oake,
> He thought twas witchcraft:
>
> TLN 1658–63, p. 946 (3. 3. 208–13)

These claims are undoubtedly true, and remind Othello of the disquieting fact that Desdemona is capable of successful deception in matters of the highest importance.[135]

When Othello next enters, he is already fearful that he may have been deceived, and vehemently demands from Iago some proof of Desdemona's faithlessness:

> Villaine, be sure thou prove my Love a whore,
> Be sure of it, give me the oculer proofe, . . .
> Make me to see't, or at the least so prove it,
> That the probation, beare no hinge, nor loope,
> To hang a doubt on: or woe upon thy life.
>
> TLN 1811–12, 1816–18, p. 948 (3. 3. 360–1, 365–7)

With the command that Iago should give him 'the oculer proofe' and 'Make me to see't', Othello is asking to be provided with the most exacting form of

---

134. *Othello*, TLN 1657, p. 946 (3. 3. 207).
135. On Desdemona's lies see Rose 1988, pp. 144–55.

non-artificial 'probation'. He is demanding—on pain of death—to be made a witness of Cassio's guilt and hence of Desdemona's disloyalty.

To Shakespeare's original audience this request would not have seemed strange or excessive. The crime of adultery was handled in the church courts, where higher levels of proof were required than in common law.[136] Richard Cosin in his 1591 *Apologie* for the continued use of ecclesiastical jurisdictions cites from scripture as well as canon law to establish that, in a case of alleged adultery, unless the crime is known to 'the greater part of the whole neighbour-hood or towne', then the establishment of proof as opposed to mere suspicion (which may be aroused simply by 'tokens') requires the sworn testimony of at least *'one good witnesse'*.[137] From Iago's perspective, however, Othello's demand threatens to expose a ruinous weakness in his plot. The problem is not, as some critics have suggested, that the supplying of such a proof would be more than Othello could bear.[138] It is rather that no crime has been committed, so there is no possibility that such a proof could be supplied.

The danger to Iago is serious, but he manages to produce two immediate responses that give him back the initiative. First he retreats into a practical objection to Othello's request. Does he really mean that he wants to watch Cassio and Desdemona making love?

> Would you, the supervisor grossely gape on,
> Behold her topt?...
> What shall I say? where's satisfaction?
> It is impossible you should see this,
>
> TLN 1847–8, 1853–4, pp. 948–9 (3. 3. 396–7, 402–3)

Next he assures Othello that, in spite of this alleged impossibility, he can nevertheless provide a fully persuasive *confirmatio* of Desdemona's guilt:

> But yet I say,
> If imputation and strong circumstances,
> Which leade directly to the doore of truth,
> Will give you satisfaction, you might ha't.
>
> TLN 1857–60, p. 949 (3. 3. 406–9)

136. Ingram 1987, p. 151. See also Ingram 1987, pp. 239, 243, noting that circumstantial evidence was never regarded as sufficient.
137. Cosin 1591, pp. 58, 114. On the need for witnesses see also Maus 1995, pp. 118–19.
138. See, for example, Halio 2002, p. 397.

Here Iago reminds Othello of what the rhetoricians say about adequate levels of proof in judicial causes. As we have seen, they think it may often be sufficient to build up circumstantial evidence about a crime. This requires us to look for signs of a guilty conscience, and also to consider the crime itself and its circumstances—that is, the time, the place, the motive, and the means to commit it. If, in the words of the *Ad Herennium*, we find that 'there are many signs and arguments that come together and cohere with each other',[139] then our conclusion 'ought to be regarded not as a mere expression of suspicion but rather as a clear matter of fact'.[140] Or, as Iago puts it, 'imputation and strong circumstances' can lead 'directly to the doore of truth'. Iago may not be able to conduct Othello into the bedroom, but he can bring him to the door.[141]

For the account of how Iago goes on to fabricate these circumstances, Shakespeare partly relies on his principal source for *Othello*, Giraldi Cinthio's *Hecatommithi*. Cinthio makes the villainous Ensign steal Disdemona's handkerchief with 'great sleight of hand' and leave it in the bedroom of the Corporal with whom, he has assured the Moor, she is conducting an adulterous affair.[142] The Ensign then affirms that the Corporal confessed to him that he received the handkerchief from Disdemona when they were together in bed. When Disdemona cannot explain how she came to lose it, the Moor treats this as sufficient proof of her guilt and resolves on her death.[143]

Shakespeare uses the device of the handkerchief in a not dissimilar but more complicated way. When Desdemona drops it and Iago's wife Emilia picks it up, Iago decides to leave it in Cassio's lodgings in the hope of using it as evidence to excite Othello's jealousy. Critics have frequently seen in the handkerchief the ocular proof of Desdemona's alleged guilt.[144] But this is to misunderstand the rhetorical theory of *confirmatio* on which Shakespeare is drawing in the play. The handkerchief can only count as documentary evidence; it cannot be ocular in the required sense of enabling

---

139. *Rhetorica ad Herennium* 1954, II. VII 11, p. 76: 'multa concurrant argumenta et signa quae inter se consentiant'.
140. *Rhetorica ad Herennium* 1954, II. VII 11, p. 76: 'rem perspicuam, non suspiciosam videri oportere'.
141. As noted in Crider 2009, p. 118.   142. Bullough 1957–75, vol. 7, p. 247.
143. Bullough 1957–75, vol. 7, pp. 248–9.
144. See, for example, Doran 1976, p. 84; Parker 1996, p. 248; Neill 2000, p. 256; McNeely 2004, p. 241.

Othello to witness some event that will give him grounds for believing in Cassio's crime and Desdemona's faithlessness.[145] Iago's plot is more intricate than is often allowed, and the handkerchief plays a subordinate part in it. The confirmation that Iago furnishes comes in two stages, each of which brings forward two purportedly non-artificial proofs. It is only at the end of this process that Iago presents Othello with what he claims to be the kind of ocular proof for which he had initially asked.[146]

Iago embarks on the first step of his *confirmatio* in response to a new and altered demand on Othello's part for some proof of Desdemona's guilt. Pulling back from his insistence that he should be made a witness of Cassio's crime, Othello commands that Iago should 'Give me a living reason, shee's disloyall'.[147] He is asking for what Cicero had described as *illustris explanatio* and Quintilian as *enargeia* or *repraesentatio*—an account of Cassio's crime so vivid and 'living' that it will feel as if he had witnessed it.[148] The vernacular rhetoricians similarly stress the persuasive force of such descriptions, while echoing Othello's idea of 'a living reason' yet more closely. Thomas Wilson speaks of 'the lively settying forthe of any matter',[149] while under the heading of *descriptio* Henry Peacham refers to the means by which we can 'set forth a thing so plainly and lively' that the effect is to 'make a likely shew of life'.[150]

Othello's demand for this kind of non-artificial proof sets Iago a scarcely less exacting test, and at first he feigns reluctance to undertake it. He begins by retreating into his favourite device of *paralepsis*, speaking 'as though he would say nothing in some matter', as Henry Peacham puts it, 'when notwithstanding he speaketh most of all':[151]

> OTHELLO Give me a living reason, shee's disloyall.
> IAGO I doe not like the office,
> But sith I am enter'd in this cause so farre,
> Prickt to't by foolish honesty and love,
> I will goe on:
>
> TLN 1861–5, p. 949 (3. 3. 410–14)

---

145. As noted in Maus 1995, p. 120.
146. For a contrasting analysis see Nicholson 2010, pp. 77–9.
147. *Othello*, TLN 1861, p. 949 (3. 3. 410).
148. Cicero 1942a, III. LIII. 202, vol. 2, p. 160; Quintilian 2001, 8. 3. 61, vol. 3, p. 374.
149. Wilson 1553, Sig. 2A, 3ʳ.   150. Peacham 1593, p. 134.
151. Peacham 1593, p. 130.

While pretending that he does not wish to proceed, Iago cunningly reminds Othello of his standing as 'honest Iago', thereby priming Othello to accept the truth of what he is about to relate.

Shakespeare's ensuing scene transforms Cinthio's narrative, in which the villain simply informs the Moor that Disdemona 'takes her pleasure with him every time he comes to your house' and that the Corporal 'has told me all'.[152] By contrast, Iago provides the kind of 'living reason' for which Othello has asked. As he tells his story, he makes full use of the figures of speech that are said to help narratives sound 'living' and true to life. Henry Peacham had discussed a range of these devices under the heading of *descriptio*,[153] including *sermocinatio*, when 'the Orator faineth a person and maketh him speake',[154] and *prosographia*, when a man's 'doings, affections, and such other circumstances serving to the purpose [are] so described, that it may appeare a plaine and lively picture'.[155] Iago calls on both figures as he boldly embarks on his wholly fictitious tale:

> I lay with *Cassio* lately,
> And being troubled with a raging tooth,
> I could not sleep. There are a kinde of men
> · So loose of soule, that in their sleepes
> Will mutter their affaires, one of this kinde is *Cassio*:
> In sleepe I heard him say. Sweete *Desdemona*,
> Let us be wary, let us hide our loves;
> And then sir, would he gripe and wring my hand,
> Cry oh sweete creature, then kisse me hard,
> As if he pluckt up kisses by the rootes,
> That grew upon my lips, laie his leg ore my thigh,
> And sigh, and kisse, and then cry, cursed fate,
> That gave thee to the Moore.
>
> TLN 1865–77, p. 949 (3. 3. 414–27)

Iago succeeds in painting just such a living picture as the rhetoricians recommend. He not only makes Cassio speak, but imitates his allegedly infatuated tones and makes Othello see how erotically charged is the scene. Feigning reassurance, he immediately adds that 'this was but his dreame'. But Othello is already caught, and insists that 'this denoted a fore-gone conclusion'.[156] Speaking again with pretended reluctance, Iago concedes

---

152. Bullough 1957–75, vol. 7, pp. 245–6.   153. Peacham 1593, pp. 134–43.
154. Peacham 1593, p. 137.   155. Peacham 1593, p. 135.
156. *Othello*, TLN 1879–80, p. 949 (3. 3. 428–9).

that this act of witnessing may indeed 'helpe to thicken other proofes,/ That doe demonstrate thinly'.[157] For the first time, he dares to speak not of circumstantial evidence but of demonstration and proof.

Next Iago stirs in these further proofs. According to the rhetoricians, the other main type of non-artificial *confirmatio* can be furnished by documentary evidence. Iago now supplements his brazen act of false witnessing with a 'document' in the form of Desdemona's handkerchief:

> IAGO   tell me but this,
> Have you not sometimes seene a handkercher,
> Spotted with strawberries in your wives hand.
> OTHELLO I gave her such a one, twas my first gift.
> IAGO I know not that, but such a handkercher,
> I am sure it was your wives, did I to day
> See *Cassio* wipe his beard with.
>
> TLN 1885–91, p. 949 (3. 3. 434–40)

Before introducing this fabrication, Iago has been careful to caution Othello that 'yet we see nothing done', and thus that Desdemona 'may be honest yet'.[158] But he now maintains that something disloyal has been done, for Desdemona has given away Othello's original token of love. As he coolly concludes: 'It speakes against her, with the other proofes'.[159]

Iago now claims to have produced two non-artificial proofs—and hence two separate confirmations—of Cassio's guilt. For Othello this is enough, and he declares himself fully convinced:

> looke here *Iago*,
> All my fond love, thus doe I blow to heaven,—tis gone.
> Arise blacke vengeance, from the hollow hell,
>
> TLN 1896–8, p. 949 (3. 3. 445–8)

The scene ends with Iago agreeing to undertake the murder of Cassio while Othello promises to find some swift means of bringing about Desdemona's death.

Two scenes later, however, when Othello and Iago next enter together, we learn that some considerable time has elapsed, and that Iago's fabricated

---

157. *Othello*, TLN 1882–3, p. 949 (3. 3. 431–2).
158. *Othello*, TLN 1884–5, p. 949 (3. 3. 433–4).
159. *Othello*, TLN 1893, p. 949 (3. 3. 442).

confirmation has not succeeded in stirring Othello to vengeance. This is the moment when the problem of 'double time' in *Othello* becomes of dramatic importance.[160] Admittedly there are critics on hand to assure us that there is no such problem, and that 'from the landing in Cyprus the whole story unfolds in a space of one and a half days'.[161] Certainly Shakespeare conveys the impression that Othello's peace of mind collapses with appalling suddenness. But he also makes it unambiguously clear that many days pass after Othello makes his first resolution to take revenge.[162] Cassio had been present at the beginning of Othello's fatal conversation with Iago, but in the following scene his disappointed mistress Bianca complains that she has not seen him for a week.[163] Still more tellingly, when Iago reminds Othello about the handkerchief he confesses that he had forgotten about it, and that it only now 'comes o're my memory'.[164] Iago begins to press him once more. 'I, what of that?' But Othello merely responds, broodingly but without other sign of emotion, 'That's not so good now'.[165] The days are passing, and Iago's poison has failed to take effect.

As Iago immediately recognizes, he needs to administer a greatly increased dose. He shifts at once from insinuation to outright falsehood, claiming that Cassio has confessed. 'What hath he sayd?' Othello demands,[166] and Iago draws once again on the technique of *aposeopesis* in his stammering response:

> IAGO   Faith that he did—I know not what he did.
> OTHELLO   What? What?
> IAGO   Lye.

---

160. For surveys of this much discussed problem see Sanders 2003, pp. 14–17; Hutson 2013, pp. 77–81.

161. Kermode 1997, p. 1247. See also Margolies 2012, p. 159.

162. Fowler 2003, pp. 39–40 and Margolies 2012, p. 157 warn against anachronism, suggesting that a preoccupation with double time-schemes reflects 'a novel-bound mind-set'. But as Fowler 2003, p. 39 also points out, one of Shakespeare's purposes is clearly to increase dramatic tension. See also Jones 1971, esp. pp. 43, 64–5, on how Shakespeare uses the device to combine longer time spans with a neoclassical sense of scenic continuity. Reflecting on this analysis, Hutson 2006 adds—in a discussion particularly pertinent to *Othello*—that the means by which Shakespeare combines narrative pressure with longer duration is by deploying a rhetorical understanding of narrative.

163. *Othello*, TLN 2099, p. 951 (3. 4. 167).

164. *Othello*, TLN 2147, p. 952 (4. 1. 20). Adamson 1980, pp. 197–8 argues that Othello cannot really have forgotten, but makes no mention of the lapse of time involved.

165. *Othello*, TLN 2150, p. 952 (4. 1. 23).   166. *Othello*, TLN 2158, p. 952 (4. 1. 31).

| OTHELLO | With her? |
| IAGO | With her, on her, what you will. |

TLN 2159–60, p. 952 (4. 1. 32–4)

These lying puns about lying together have a terrifying impact on Othello.[167] They instantly reduce him to a frenzy of questions and exclamations, culminating in the desperate cry 'Confesse? Handkercher? O divell' and the onset of a seizure.[168]

While Iago is waiting for Othello to recover, Cassio enters, and this chance encounter enables Iago, with deadly improvisation, to supply the missing ocular proof.[169] The handkerchief is again used in evidence, but at this stage Shakespeare alters his course. He picks up a further hint from Cinthio's story, in which we are told that one day the Ensign spoke to the Corporal 'while the Moor was standing where he could see them'. When they were 'chatting of quite other matters than the Lady' the Corporal laughed heartily, after which the Ensign assured the Moor that the Corporal had been telling him about his conquest of the Moor's wife.[170] Shakespeare employs the same device of making Othello a secret witness of what Iago claims will be a renewed confession by Cassio of his crime. Iago promises that, while Othello is covertly watching, he will question Cassio about his affair with Desdemona, so that Othello will be able to appraise the marks or signs of Cassio's delinquency, which Iago bids him 'marke'.[171] Othello will thus be provided with the ocular proof for which he originally asked.

As we know, the usual signs of guilt include trembling, turning pale, and being unable to speak. Iago specifically refers to such indications at a later stage in the unfolding of his plot. Deciding that he needs to get rid of Cassio (lest Othello should encounter him) he sets Roderigo on to murder him. Roderigo succeeds in wounding Cassio, and when Bianca appears amid the resulting confusion Iago attempts to inculpate her in the violence. 'Gentlemen all', he announces, 'I doe suspect this trash/ To be a party in this Injurie'.[172] He invites those arriving on the scene to examine her closely:

---

167. On Iago's punning here see Melchiori 1981, pp. 64–5; Menon 2004, p. 110.
168. *Othello*, TLN 2168–9, p. 952 (4. 1. 41).
169. As noted in Calderwood 1989, pp. 63–5. The rhetorical distinction between the two scenes (3. 3 and 4. 1) perhaps needs underlining, if only because some critics (for example, Syme 2012, pp. 246–7) confuse the 'living reason' supplied by Iago's story about Cassio's dream with 'the ocular proof' supplied by Cassio's alleged confession to Iago of his guilt.
170. Bullough 1957–75, vol. 7, pp. 247–9.   171. *Othello*, TLN 2208, p. 953 (4. 1. 80).
172. *Othello*, TLN 2852–3, p. 960 (5. 1. 85–6).

> looke you pale mistrisse?
> Doe you perceive the gastnesse of her eye,
> Nay, an you stare, we shall heare more anon:
> Behold her well I pray you, looke upon her,
> Doe you see Gentlemen? Nay guiltinesse
> Will speake, though tongues were out of use.[173]

TLN 2873–8, p. 961 (5. 1. 105–10)

Bianca is innocent of any crime, but Iago is able to take advantage of the fact that she is pale, aghast, and speechless, all well-known signs of culpability.

During the earlier scene, however, when Iago invites Othello to look for indications of Cassio's guilt, these are not the sort of signs he has in mind. Iago is not interested in showing that Cassio is exhibiting any of the usual marks of a guilty conscience. Like Othello, he thinks of Cassio's alleged conquest of Desdemona as a victory that has left the defeated Othello open to derision and contempt. He knows too that Othello dreads the scorn to which this dishonour will leave him vulnerable. Already Othello has asked him 'Doest thou mocke me?', and expressed the fear that 'A horned man's a monster, and a beast'.[174] The suggestion Iago now puts to Othello is that, if he is looking for marks of Cassio's delinquency, he should be searching for signs of 'notable scornes' directed against him.[175] He should be looking, that is, for indications that Cassio is glorying over him and viewing him with contempt.

The rhetoricians are very interested in these signs as well, and there is general agreement about how to tell whether someone is indeed harbouring feelings of scorn towards us. One of the surest indications, they maintain, will be if they laugh at our plight. 'Laughter', Quintilian explains, 'is never far removed from derision', so that the overriding emotion expressed by it is generally one of disdainful superiority.[176] As he later summarizes, 'the most ambitious way of glorying over others is to deride them'.[177] Thomas Wilson writes in strong agreement, arguing that our aim in provoking laughter is generally to convey 'skorne out right'.[178] By Shakespeare's time, the idea of

---

173. Compare *Hamlet*, TLN 1524, p. 753 (2. 2. 546), where Hamlet says 'murther, though it have no tongue will speake'.
174. *Othello*, TLN 2185, 2187, p. 953 (4. 1. 58, 60).
175. *Othello*, TLN 2208, p. 953 (4. 1. 80).
176. Quintilian 2001, 6. 3. 8, vol. 3, p. 66: 'A derisu non procul abest risus.'
177. Quintilian 2001, 11. 1. 22, vol. 5, p. 20: 'Ambitiosissimum gloriandi genus est etiam deridere.' On the Greek sources of this view of laughter see Halliwell 2008, pp. 264–331.
178. Wilson 1553, Sig. T, 3ʳ.

laughter as a contemptuous expression of triumph and victory had become proverbial. One of the sayings included by John Heywood in his *Two hundred epigrammes* of 1555 declares 'They laugh that wyn, falsly to wyn and keepe'.[179]

Iago knows that, if he can make Othello believe that Cassio is laughing at him, he may finally be able to prove to Othello's satisfaction that Cassio is guilty of having made a conquest of Desdemona. With this in mind, he contrives the required twist to his plot. He resolves to question Cassio about Bianca, whom Cassio views with such amused condescension that, as Iago remarks, 'He, when he heares of her, cannot restraine/ From the excesse of laughter'.[180] But he tells Othello that he is going to ask Cassio about his affair with Desdemona, and invites Othello to hide, mark the encounter, and pass judgement on Cassio's response:

> Do but incave your selfe,
> And marke the Fleeres, the gibes, and notable scornes,
> That dwell in every region of his face;
> For I will make him tell the tale anew,
> Where, how, how oft, how long agoe, and when,
> He hath, and is againe to cope your wife:
>
> TLN 2207–12, p. 953 (4. 1. 79–84)

With his references to where, how, and when, Iago is telling Othello that he is going to ask Cassio for a complete *narratio* of the circumstances attending his crime. Othello will be able to see and mark Cassio's reactions as he tells the tale, and if he displays any fleers or notable scorns Othello will at last be provided with an ocular proof of Cassio's triumph over him and hence of his guilt and iniquity.

With the machinery of his plot in place, Iago enters into conversation with Cassio. He assures him that, according to Bianca, he is going to marry her, to which Cassio responds by laughing out loud. Othello already thinks that Cassio must be glorying over him. 'Doe ye triumph Roman, doe you triumph?'[181] As Cassio reflects on the prospect of marrying someone whom he thinks of as a prostitute he laughs again. Othello in response actually quotes Heywood's proverb about laughter as a reaction to victory. 'So, so, so, so, they laugh that wins'.[182] Iago continues to insist that according to

---

179. Heywood 1555, Sig. D, 4^v, 'Of laughynge'. Cf. Dent 1981, p. 150.
180. *Othello*, TLN 2224–5, p. 953 (4. 1. 96–7).
181. *Othello*, TLN 2244, p. 953 (4. 1. 116).   182. *Othello*, TLN 2248, p. 953 (4. 1. 119).

rumour Cassio will definitely marry Bianca, and again Cassio laughingly expresses his incredulity. Othello takes him to be glorying once more at having scored a victory. 'Ha you scor'd me? Well'.[183] Bianca herself now appears, upset with Cassio for having asked her to copy the embroidery on a handkerchief he had found in his lodgings. Othello recognizes it at once. 'By heaven that should be my handkercher'.[184] Bianca leaves, Iago and Othello are left alone, and it only remains for Iago to offer Othello his interpretation of what has occurred.

Iago now puts together his two non-artificial proofs: the documentary evidence supplied by the handkerchief, and the ocular proof supplied by Othello's secret witnessing of Cassio's triumph over him. Together they enable Iago to present Othello with his clinching *confirmatio* of Cassio's guilt:

> IAGO Did you perceive, how he laughed at his vice?
> OTHELLO O *Iago.*
> IAGO And did you see the handkercher?
> OTHELLO Was that mine?
> IAGO Yours by this hand: and to see how he prizes the foolish
>   woman your wife: she gave it him, and he hath giv'n it his
>   whore.
>
> TLN 2294–2300, p. 954 (4. 1. 163–8)

Here Iago at last feels able to employ the language of witnessing, and hence of ocular proof, asking Othello to reflect on what he has seen and perceived. Othello is only too willing to believe that he has indeed received the proof for which he had asked. His interjections while observing Cassio have already make it clear that he thinks of himself as witnessing an admission of guilt. 'Looke ... his gesture imports it ... oh, I see'.[185] He is not merely convinced but resolved, and determines to kill Desdemona that very night.

How persuasive is Iago's fabricated *confirmatio*? For us the question does not arise. From the outset we have known that we are witnessing the unfolding of a malignant plot, and we may also have reflected that Desdemona's name tells us that she will be unfortunate. We learn in the opening scene that Iago hates Othello, and that his apparent signs of affection all point in the wrong direction:

---

183. *Othello*, TLN 2252, p. 953 (4. 1. 123).   184. *Othello*, TLN 2282, p. 954 (4. 1. 151).
185. *Othello*, TLN 2236, 2261–2, 2266, p. 953 (4. 1. 107, 132–3, 137).

> Tho I doe hate him, as I doe hell paines,
> Yet for necessity of present life,
> I must shew out a flag, and signe of love,
> Which is indeed but signe,
>
> TLN 157–60, p. 930 (1. 1. 153–6)

Repeatedly Iago contrasts his false 'seeming' with how he is in truth:

> In following him, I follow but my selfe.
> Heaven is my judge, not I, for love and duty,
> But seeming so, for my peculiar end.
>
> TLN 58–60, p. 929 (1. 1. 59–61)

Summarizing and glorying in his deceitfulness, he assures us that 'I am not what I am.'[186]

Later Iago even informs us about the mechanics of his plot. After contriving Cassio's dismissal, his plan is to persuade him to petition Desdemona, while at the same time arousing Othello's suspicions about their relationship:

> whiles this honest foole
> Plyes *Desdemona* to repaire his fortune,
> And she for him, pleades strongly to the Moore:
> I'le poure this pestilence into his eare,
> That she repeales him for her bodyes lust;
> And by how much she strives to doe him good,
> She shall undoe her credit with the Moore,
> So will I turne her vertue into pitch,
> And out of her owne goodnesse make the net
> That shall enmesh them all:
>
> TLN 1353–62, p. 943 (2. 3. 320–9)

From this moment we watch the plot unfold exactly as Iago has planned.

There remains the question of the persuasiveness of Iago's fabrication within the world of the play. Othello is not only easily persuaded (much too easily, we may reflect) but is shockingly obdurate. When he interrogates Emilia—Desdemona's companion as well as Iago's wife—she insists that she has never seen anything suspicious, giving her opinion in correct rhetorical form. Hamlet had assured Horatio that he would be prepared to wager a

---

186. *Othello*, TLN 65, p. 929 (1. 1. 66).

thousand pounds on the ghost's veracity. Emilia refers to the same notion of probability, but with much stronger emphasis:

> I durst my Lord, to wager she is honest,
> Lay downe my soule at stake: if you thinke other,
> Remove your thought, it doth abuse your bosome,
>
> TLN 2424–6, p. 955 (4. 2. 11–13)

Emilia is prepared to bet nothing less than her immortal soul that Desdemona has been a faithful wife. But Othello pays no heed, merely remarking that it is strange that she has nothing suspicious to report.[187]

When Othello confronts Desdemona with his accusation she merely expresses bewilderment, but Emilia sees at once that someone must have traduced her, and in Iago's presence she speaks perilously close to the truth:

> I will be hang'd, if some eternall villaine,
> Some busie and insinuating rogue,
> Some cogging, cousening slave, to get some office,
> Have not devisde this slander, I will be hang'd else.
>
> TLN 2545–8, p. 957 (4. 2. 129–32)

Emilia invokes the distinctive vocabulary of judicial rhetoric to drive home the point that, because the charge against Desdemona is false, some slanderous *insinuatio* must have been lodged in Othello's mind. She continues to draw on the same technical vocabulary as she emphasizes the inherent improbability of Othello's charge. If an accusation is to have any likelihood, according to the rhetoricians, we must be able to point to a number of suspicious circumstances surrounding the alleged crime, and in particular to establish the time, the place, and the persons involved. But if we consider Desdemona's case they point to her innocence and not her guilt:

> Why should he call her whore? who keepes her company?
> What place, what time, what forme, what likelihood?
> The Moore's abus'd by some most villanous knave:
>
> TLN 2552–4, p. 957 (4. 2. 136–8)

No one has been visiting Desdemona, and there is no time and place at which the supposed adultery could have taken place. The accusation, in

---

187. *Othello*, TLN 2423, p. 955 (4. 2. 10).

short, carries no likelihood, and the only possible conjecture is that Desdemona is being villainously abused.[188]

The reason why Iago is eventually unmasked is that he fails to heed one final piece of advice that Quintilian had given about how to ensure that our fabrications pass for the truth. 'We must remember', he had warned, 'that the things we fabricate should be confined to claims that cannot be contradicted by a witness'.[189] Iago's wife is the witness who finally contradicts him and lays bare the inner workings of his plot. The unmasking happens as soon as Othello explains why he killed Desdemona:

> *Iago* knowes,
> That she with *Cassio*, hath the act of shame
> A thousand times committed; *Cassio* confest it,
> And she did gratifie his amorous workes,
> With that recognisance and pledge of love,
> Which I first gave her; I saw it in his hand,
> It was a handkercher;
>
> TLN 3114–20, p. 964 (5. 2. 209–15)

Othello appeals to one of Iago's non-artificial proofs, but Emilia has her own and far more telling non-artificial proof to offer in response. Loyal at the last to Desdemona rather than her husband, she presents herself as a witness who knows the truth and has every reason to speak it:

> O thou dull Moore, that handkercher thou speakst of,
> I found by fortune, and did give my husband: ...
> She give it *Cassio*? no alas I found it,
> And I did giv't my husband.
>
> TLN 3129–30, 3134–5, p. 964 (5. 2. 223–4, 228–9)

With this revelation chaos is unleashed. Othello attempts to kill Iago, while Iago stabs and kills Emilia and runs away.

Running away is taken to be a sure sign of guilt, so Iago's purported *confirmatio* is finally disconfirmed. There is consequently no *peroratio* for him to pronounce. He acknowledges as much when he is brought back to face his accusers in the final moments of the play. When Othello demands 'Why

---

188. For a contrasting analysis see Altman 2010, p. 12, who sees in the passage the deployment of a commonplace.
189. Quintilian 2001, 4. 2. 93, vol. 2, p. 266: 'Fingenda vero meminerimus ea quae non cadant in testem.'

he hath thus insnar'd my soule and body?'[190] Iago refuses any further speech:[191]

> Demand me nothing, what you know, you know.
> From this time forth I never will speake word.
>
> TLN 3206–7, p. 965 (5. 2. 300–1)

For once Iago is telling the truth. He listens in silence as his plot is finally revealed, and Othello responds by killing himself.

190. *Othello*, TLN 3205, p. 965 (5. 2. 299).
191. On Iago's 'open' silence see McGuire 1985, pp. xvii–xviii.

9

Refutation and Non-Artificial Proofs

O nce a *confirmatio* has been fully laid out, the case for the prosecution is complete. But what about the case for the defence? According to the *Ad Herennium*, the question of how to respond effectively to an accusation raises no special difficulties. Whatever rhetorical techniques can be used by the prosecution to build up a *confirmatio* can equally well be used by the defence to produce a *refutatio* or rebuttal of what has been alleged. The *Ad Herennium* accordingly concludes that the topics of confirmation and refutation should be treated 'conjointly with one another'.[1] Thomas Wilson agrees, concluding that 'in confutyng of causes, the like maie be had, as we used to prove'. The obvious reason is that 'as thynges are alleged, so thei maie be wrested, and as houses are buylded, so thei maie bee overthrowen'.[2]

Cicero does not wholly endorse this simple view, and devotes much space in Book 1 of *De inventione* to outlining some distinctive ways in which arguments can be refuted.[3] Quintilian likewise has a lot to say about the special task of speaking in defence, and offers some detailed advice about the most effective means of rebutting an adversary's case.[4] Nevertheless, they agree that *confirmatio* and *refutatio* should basically be considered together.[5] As a result, neither has any quarrel with the view that the construction of a *refutatio*, no less than a *confirmatio*, requires the marshalling of appropriate non-artificial as well as artificial proofs. They accept that the relevant non-artificial proofs will need to take the form of documents or trustworthy

---

1. See *Rhetorica ad Herennium* 1954, II. I. 2, p. 58 on speaking 'coniuncte de confirmatione et confutatione'.
2. Wilson 1553, Sig. Q, 2ᵛ.   3. Cicero 1949a, I. XLII. 79 to I. LI. 96, pp. 124–44.
4. Quintilian 2001, 5. 13. 4–55, vol. 2, pp. 468–96.
5. Cicero 1949a, I. XLII. 78, p. 122; Quintilian 2001, 5. 13. 56, vol. 2, p. 496.

witnesses, and that whatever artificial proofs are brought to bear will need to follow the same pattern as in a *confirmatio*, centring on the *signa*, the *argumentum*, and the *consecutio*. The only difference is that, when speaking in defence, we shall be looking for disconfirming clues from the time when the crime took place, and trying to establish the absence and not the presence of suspicious signs from the period afterwards.

Shakespeare's dramaturgical practice shows that he fully endorses this view of how to develop a *refutatio* in a judicial cause. As he does not fail to notice, however, this commitment leaves him with an intractable challenge. Among his forensic plays there are three major scenes in which a *confirmatio* is constructed out of supposed signs of guilt, after which the case for the prosecution is successfully challenged and overturned. But if we now imagine a scene in which the prosecution first examines the *signa*, the *argumentum*, and the *consecutio*, after which the defence attempts to demolish each of these lines of argument in turn, it becomes all too easy to see that a great deal of overlap and undramatic exposition will result. Shakespeare was of course alive to the difficulty, and when he first confronted it he hit on a solution that seems to have satisfied him completely, for he subsequently repeats it in each of the other scenes in which he dramatizes a successful *refutatio*. He begins by constructing a *confirmatio* out of alleged signs of guilt, but he then produces a *refutatio* at a single stroke by means of a non-artificial proof, either in the form of irrefutable documentary evidence or the testimony of an unimpeachable witness. As we shall see, this not only enables him to avoid repetition and to vary the dramatic pace, but to bring each scene to a sudden and rhetorically satisfying close.

Refutation by documentary evidence

Shakespeare first dramatizes a judicial *refutatio* in the closing scene of *Romeo and Juliet*, in which the *dénouement* begins with the arraignment of Friar Lawrence and Balthazer before the prince. There is a mystery to be explained, as the Chief Watchman indicates as soon as the prince appears on the scene:

> Soveraine, here lies the County *Paris* slain,
> And *Romeo* dead, and *Juliet* dead before,
> Warme and new kild.

> TLN 2884–6, p. 411 (5. 3. 195–7)

How have the young lovers and Paris met their deaths? This is what the rhetoricians would call the central question to be adjudicated. As the prince immediately recognizes, he is dealing with a conjectural issue in a judicial cause, and his aim must now be to 'seeke & know how this foule murder comes'.[6]

The correct procedure is to put forward a conjecture and look for evidence to confirm it. When the Chief Watchman arrives at the scene of the crime he immediately calls for such a hunt:

> The ground is bloudie, search about the Churchyard.
> Go some of you, who ere you find attach.
>
> TLN 2861–2, p. 411 (5. 3. 172–3)

As some of the watchmen leave he repeats his order to the others:

> Go tell the Prince, runne to the *Capulets*,
> Raise up the *Mountagues*, some others search,
>
> TLN 2866–7, p. 411 (5. 3. 177–8)

While the hunt gets under way, the Chief Watchman ruminates on the task confronting him, sententiously rising from blank to rhymed verse:

> We see the ground whereon these woes do lye,
> But the true ground of all these piteous woes
> We cannot without circumstance descry.
>
> TLN 2868–70, p. 411 (5. 3. 179–81)

With his pun on 'ground', the Chief Watchman reveals his understanding of the skills required to produce a confirmation in a conjectural issue. He knows that he must focus not merely on the bloody ground but on what Thomas Wilson had called 'the chief title & principal ground' of the case.[7] He also sees that this will require him, as he says, to descry the circumstances of the crime. He will need, that is, to enquire into time, place, and persons, and thereafter consider the *argumentum* and *consecutio* in relation to what may have occurred.

The enquiry that Shakespeare goes on to dramatize has no parallel in Arther Brooke's *Romeus and Juliet*,[8] but it closely follows the analysis in the *Ad Herennium*.[9] We first need to ask 'whether anyone had any helpers or

---

6. *Romeo and Juliet*, TLN 2887, p. 411 (5. 3. 198).   7. Wilson 1553, Sig. M, 4ʳ.
8. For the parallel passage see Brooke 1562, fos. 78ᵛ–79ʳ.
9. As noted in Baldwin 1944, vol. 2, p. 78.

accomplices',[10] and 'whether it was unusual for such a person to be in such a place at such a time'.[11] When the members of the Watch return from their search, they report finding Romeo's servant in the churchyard together with a Friar. They appear, that is, to have come upon a suspect and an accomplice, both of whom might be thought to be there at an unusual time. Next, what about the instant of the crime itself? Is it possible to say if anything suspicious 'was perceived by any of the senses'?[12] The Chief Watchman undoubtedly saw something suspicious, for when Paris's page guided him to the tomb he found a torch burning there.[13] We also need to ask 'if anything was left behind after the event', including any *instrumentum* that could have been put to criminal use.[14] Here too the members of the Watch have something incriminating to report. While arresting the Friar, they 'tooke this Mattocke and this Spade from him,/ As he was comming from this Church-yards side'.[15] 'A great suspition', comments the Chief Watchman, adding the order 'stay the Frier too'.[16] He evidently feels that he is beginning to assemble the kind of 'firmer suspicions' to which the rhetoricians refer, and when the prince arrives he informs him that the Friar and Romeo's servant have been discovered 'With Instruments upon them, fit to open/ These dead mens Tombes'.[17] Finally, we need to ask 'whether the suspect betrayed any signs of a guilty conscience when people arrived on the scene'.[18] Did he, for example, blush, turn pale, falter or faint?[19] Pointing to the figure of Friar Lawrence, the third watchman has a further suspicious circumstance to reveal: 'Here is a Frier that trembles, sighes, and weepes'.[20]

The prince now enters, eager to establish that he is appearing in his public *persona* as chief magistrate:

---

10. *Rhetorica ad Herennium* 1954, II. V. 8, p. 70: 'num quid habuerit de consciis, de adiutoribus'.
11. *Rhetorica ad Herennium* 1954, II. V. 8, p. 70: 'num quo in loco praeter consuetudinem fuerit aut alieno tempore'.
12. *Rhetorica ad Herennium* 1954, II. V. 8, p. 70: 'num quid aliquo sensu perceptum sit'.
13. *Romeo and Juliet*, TLN 2860, p. 411 (5. 3. 171).
14. *Rhetorica ad Herennium* 1954, II. V. 8, p. 70: 'num quid re transacta relictum sit'. Quintilian 2001, 5. 10. 52, vol. 2, p. 390 adds the detail about the *instrumentum*.
15. *Romeo and Juliet*, TLN 2874–5, p. 411 (5. 3. 185–6).
16. *Romeo and Juliet*, TLN 2876, p. 411 (5. 3. 187).
17. *Romeo and Juliet*, TLN 2889–90, p. 411 (5. 3. 200–1).
18. See *Rhetorica ad Herennium* 1954, II. V. 8, p. 72 on the need to look for 'signa conscientiae' at the moment 'cum ad eum ventum sit'.
19. *Rhetorica ad Herennium* 1954, II. 5. 8, p. 72.
20. *Romeo and Juliet*, TLN 2873, p. 411 (5. 3. 184).

> What misadventure is so early up,
> That calls our person from our morning rest?
>
> TLN 2877–8, p. 411 (5. 3. 188–9)

The Chief Watchman tells him what has happened, and by bringing forward Friar Lawrence and Balthazer he indicates that he has arrived at a conjecture about who may be to blame. The prince agrees that they must undoubtedly be regarded as 'the parties of suspition',[21] and they are left with the task of attempting a *refutatio* of the plausible *confirmatio* that the Chief Watchman and his men have succeeded in building up.

The Friar first takes the stage, beginning by admitting that circumstances point to his guilt. As he has already acknowledged in his *prohoemium*, he is 'most suspected as the time and place/ Doth make against me'.[22] But as he embarks on his lengthy *narratio* he takes pains to follow the advice of the rhetoricians on how best to exonerate himself. He recounts how he planned to reunite Romeo and Juliet; how he gave Juliet a potion that produced the form of death; and how she awoke to find Romeo dead and thereupon killed herself. The prince then calls on Balthazer to present a supplementary narrative. 'Wheres *Romeos* man? what can he say to this?'[23] Balthazer, who has been silent ever since the arrival of the Watch, responds with a prompt and precise account of his role:

> I brought my maister newes of *Juliets* death,
> And then in poste he came from *Mantua*,
> To this same place, to this same monument.
> This Letter he early bid me give his Father,
> And threatned me with death, going in the Vault,
> If I departed not, and left him there.
>
> TLN 2961–6, p. 412 (5. 3. 272–7)

With these narratives the Friar and Balthazer are able to go some way towards defending themselves, as they are able to provide an explanation of Juliet's death that leaves them both exonerated. It is true that, although Friar Lawrence is innocent, his efforts to manage the young lovers' lives might be thought somewhat lacking in prudence and foresight, but this is not a question that the play ever addresses, except possibly in the prince's

---

21. *Romeo and Juliet*, TLN 2911, p. 411 (5. 3. 222).
22. *Romeo and Juliet*, TLN 2913–14, p. 411 (5. 3. 224–5).
23. *Romeo and Juliet*, TLN 2960, p. 412 (5. 3. 271).

closing warning that 'Some shall be pardond, and some punished'.[24] Meanwhile, neither he nor Balthazer are able to shed any light on the deaths of
Paris and Romeo, and it might additionally be thought that they stand in
need of a much fuller *refutatio* if they are to succeed in vindicating even their
basic innocence.

At this juncture, however, the remaining puzzles are suddenly solved.
First the prince calls a witness:

> Where is the Counties Page that raisd the Watch?
> Sirrah, what made your maister in this place?
>
> TLN 2968–9, p. 412 (5. 3. 279–80)

The page in his deposition is able to clarify one of the mysteries by giving an
explanation of Paris's death:

> He came with flowers to strew his Ladies grave,
> And bid me stand aloofe, and so I did,
> Anon comes one with light to ope the Tombe,
> And by and by my maister drew on him,
> And then I ran away to call the Watch.
>
> TLN 2970–4, p. 412 (5. 3. 281–5)

As we already know, and as the prince is now able to infer, Paris must have
been killed by Romeo after he drew his sword on him. The prince now
turns to the other form of non-artificial proof he has been offered in the
form of the letter handed to him by Balthazer:

> This Letter doth make good the Friers words,
> Their course of Love, the tidings of her death,
> And here he writes, that he did buy a poyson
> Of a poore Pothecarie, and therewithall,
> Came to this Vault, to die and lye with *Juliet*.
>
> TLN 2975–9, p. 412 (5. 3. 286–90)

As the prince notes, this vital piece of documentary evidence serves to
'make good' the claims in Friar Lawrence's narrative, and the mystery of
Romeo's death is finally resolved. As we already know, and as the letter
makes clear to the prince, Romeo killed himself after finding Juliet seemingly dead.

24. *Romeo and Juliet*, TLN 2997, p. 412 (5. 3. 308).

How conclusive is this *refutatio* of the Chief Watchman's conjecture? For us the question does not arise. We have already witnessed the circumstances of the lovers' deaths, and we may even feel that Friar Lawrence's *narratio*, from which we learn nothing that we did not already know, is somewhat overextended. If we ask, however, about the role of the *refutatio* within the world of the play, the answer is that it is wholly conclusive. The firmest kind of non-artificial proof, everyone agrees, takes the form of a combination of witnessing and the reading of relevant depositions and documents.[25] This is the combination that the prince eventually succeeds in assembling, and it enables him to draw the judicial investigation to a close. It only remains for him to pronounce a fittingly sombre *peroratio* to bring the tragedy to an end.

Refutation by an unimpeachable witness

Senator Brabantio confronts the duke and senators of Venice in Act 1 of *Othello* with what he takes to be a conjectural issue in a judicial cause. He declares that he is facing a mystery, a shocking and extraordinary mystery, concerning a matter of fact. The undoubted fact is that Desdemona has eloped with Othello and married him without his permission or even his knowledge. The mystery is to understand what could possibly have caused her to do such a monstrous and self-destructive thing. Brabantio raises this *quaestio iudicii* while addressing his adversary in openly racist terms:[26]

> Whether a maide so tender, faire, and happy, . . .
> Would ever have (t'incurre a general mocke)
> Runne from her gardage to the sooty bosome
> Of such a thing as thou?
>
> TLN 253, 256–8, p. 931 (1. 2. 66, 69–71)

Subsequently Brabantio reiterates the question for adjudication when presenting his accusation to the duke. How could Desdemona have fallen in love 'with what she fear'd to looke on?'[27]

As a state councillor evidently well-versed in judicial rhetoric, Brabantio knows that he must put forward a conjecture to explain the mystery and

---

25. See Syme 2012, pp. 22, 33–9, 46–52, where he goes so far as to privilege representation over presence.
26. Sokol 2008, pp. 128–32 emphasizes Brabantio's combination of racist and social objections.
27. *Othello*, TLN 384, p. 933 (1. 3. 98).

then attempt to confirm it. As we know, his conjecture is that Desdemona must have been abused in one of two criminal ways. First he suggests that Othello must have subjected her to magical powers: 'Dambd as thou art, thou hast inchanted her'.[28] Next he argues that he must also have 'Abus'd her delicate Youth, with Drugs or Minerals,/ That weakens Motion.'[29] Finally, when laying his accusation before the duke and senators he combines the two charges:

> She is abus'd, stolne from me and corrupted,
> By spels and medicines, bought of mountebancks,
> For nature so preposterously to erre,
> (Being not deficient, blind, or lame of sense,)
> Saunce witchcraft could not.
>
> TLN 346–50, p. 933 (1. 3. 60–4)

He ends by mentioning, for the first time, the particularly grave accusation that he believes Othello to be guilty of practising witchcraft.

While mounting his attack, Brabantio begins at the same time to develop a *confirmatio* of his conjecture. Critics sometimes dismiss his denunciation of Othello as mere hysteria,[30] but Brabantio is careful to craft his argument according to the rhetorical rules, presenting it in two distinct instalments. When he first encounters Othello he immediately speaks of the kind of sensory confirmation that—as Quintilian had argued—we can regard as virtually certain even though it may not amount to a non-artificial proof.[31] He warns Othello that 'ile referre me to all things of sense' and insists that such tests already show Othello's guilt to be probable.[32] He thinks it obvious to the sight that Desdemona must have been enchanted, for she would never voluntarily have 'Runne from her gardage to the sooty bosome/ Of such a thing as thou'.[33] He also thinks, although without explaining himself, that his conjecture is 'palpable', obvious to the touch.[34] Visibly as well as palpably an object of fear rather than delight, Othello is so evidently guilty according to Brabantio that the whole world will be bound to endorse his appeal to

---

28. *Othello*, TLN 250, p. 931 (1. 2. 63).   29. *Othello*, TLN 261–2, pp. 931–2 (1. 2. 74–5).
30. See, for example, McNeely 2004, p. 228.
31. See Quintilian 2001, 5. 10. 12, vol. 2, p. 372, and cf. *Rhetorica ad Herennium* 1954, II. V. 8, p. 70. This view about the veridical character of sensory impressions was beginning to come under pressure. For the view to which Brabantio still adheres see Clark 2007, pp. 9–20.
32. *Othello*, TLN 251, 263, pp. 931–2 (1. 2. 64, 76).
33. *Othello*, TLN 257–8, p. 931 (1. 2. 70–1).   34. *Othello*, TLN 263, p. 932 (1. 2. 76).

the sensory evidence: 'Judge me the world, if 'tis not grosse in sense,/ That thou hast practis'd on her with foule Charmes'.[35]

Later, when Brabantio mounts his accusation before the duke, he concentrates on what the *Ad Herennium* describes as the first stage in the production of a *confirmatio*, the stage at which we seek to establish what is *probabilis* about our adversary and his case.[36] If, Brabantio maintains, Othello is to show that Desdemona voluntarily married him, he will need to demonstrate that she had a *causa*, a reason or motive for marrying him. But according to Brabantio she had no such motive:

> a maide so tender, faire, and happy,
> So opposite to marriage, that she shund
> The wealthy curled darlings of our Nation,
>
> TLN 253–5, p. 931 (I. 2. 66–8)

Next, her elopment will have to be shown to be coherent with her *vita*—her nature and her general mode of life. But Brabantio sees no such coherence:

> A maiden never bold:
> Of spirit so still and quiet, that her motion
> Blusht at her selfe:
>
> TLN 380–2, p. 933 (I. 3. 94–6)

Lastly, it will have to be shown that Desdemona expected some *commoditas* or benefit from her marriage. But according to Brabantio it is obvious that she can expect no such benefit. He warns Othello that she will 'incurre a general mocke';[37] he objects that Othello will fill her with fear rather than delight;[38] and he later tells the duke that he expects the marriage to lose her not merely her credit but everything.[39]

One of the senators now formally restates the *quaestio iudicii* and calls on Othello to defend himself:

> But *Othello* speake,
> Did you by indirect and forced courses,
> Subdue and poison this young maides affections?
> Or came it by request, and such faire question,
> As soule to soule affoordeth?
>
> TLN 396–400, p. 933 (I. 3. 110–14)

---

35. *Othello*, TLN 259–60, p. 931 (I. 2. 72–3).
36. *Rhetorica ad Herennium* 1954, II. II. 3, p. 62 on *causa* and *commoditas* and II. III. 5, p. 64 on *vita*. See also Cicero 1942a, II. V. 17 to II. XI. 37, vol. I, pp. 180–98.
37. *Othello*, TLN 256, p. 931 (I. 2. 69).   38. *Othello*, TLN 258, p. 931 (I. 2. 71).
39. *Othello*, TLN 383, p. 933 (I. 3. 97).

By way of response Othello launches into his *narratio*, entering at the same time into the process of trying to refute his adversary's *confirmatio* of his charge. As we saw in Chapter 6, he seeks to establish that Desdemona was indeed bewitched, but only by the entrancing story of his adventurous life, and he succeeds to such an extent that the duke feels able to call on Brabantio to abandon his case.

As Brabantio correctly points out, however, Othello has not yet supplied a *refutatio* of the accusation against him. He accordingly continues to demand some proof that Desdemona 'was halfe the wooer' and that she willingly consented to marry Othello without being compelled.[40] This brings their court battle to a climax, but Othello is able to claim the victory by refuting Brabantio's charge of coercion at a stroke. He has already asked for Desdemona to be summoned, and as he concludes his *narratio* she makes her entrance. 'Here comes the Lady', he announces, 'let her witnesse it'.[41] He feels so confident that his cause is not foul but honest, and that Desdemona's testimony will exonerate him, that he declares his willingness to suffer death 'If you doe finde me foule in her report'.[42]

It is now for Brabantio as prosecutor to interrogate the witness, and he proceeds to set about the task:

> Come hither gentle mistresse:
> Doe you perceive in all this noble company,
> Where most you owe obedience?
>
> TLN 463–5, p. 934 (1. 3. 176–8)

Desdemona's reply has sometimes been treated as an attempt at mediation,[43] but this misses the forensic context of Brabantio's request. When Desdemona responds with an unequivocal proclamation of her loyalty to Othello, she is at the same time repudiating Brabantio's contention that she must have been coerced:

> I am hitherto your daughter, But heere's my husband:
> And so much duty as my mother shewed
> To you, preferring you before her father,
> So much I challenge, that I may professe,
> Due to the Moore my Lord.
>
> TLN 470–4, p. 934 (1. 3. 183–7)

---

40. *Othello*, TLN 461, p. 934 (1. 3. 174).
41. *Othello*, TLN 455, p. 934 (1. 3. 169). On Desdemona as witness see Doran 1976, pp. 74–6.
42. *Othello*, TLN 403, p. 933 (1. 3. 117).   43. See, for example, Snow 1988, p. 232.

Brabantio has already made it clear that he will consider Desdemona to be an unimpeachable witness:

> If she confesse that she was halfe the wooer,
> Destruction on my head, if my bad blame
> Light on the man.
>
> TLN 461–3, p. 934 (I. 3. 174–6)

Having heard her testimony, he now concedes that there is no alternative but to give up his case:

> God bu'y, I ha done:
> Please it your Grace, on to the State affaires;
>
> TLN 474–5, p. 934 (I. 3. 187–8)

Desdemona and Othello remain silent as Brabantio formally acknowledges their marriage. Were it not for the lurking figure of Iago, who has already declared his hatred for Othello,[44] we might feel that we have reached the end of a Shakespearean comedy. The lovers have engaged in a courtship, successfully overcome their differences, frustrated the attempts of an obstructive father to forbid their marriage, and are ready to depart in pursuit of their happiness.[45]

How conclusive is Othello's *refutatio* of Brabantio's charge that Desdemona must have been 'wrought upon' and coerced?[46] Within the play no one expresses any doubt that Desdemona's act of witnessing confirms Othello's case, so that it only remains for the duke to round off the argument with a suitably healing *peroratio*. Among Shakespeare's original audience, however, some might have felt the matter to be more ambiguous and complicated. Othello lays before the Senate a version of his love-story in which his conquest of Desdemona is treated as a victory for the power of eloquence. But as the rhetoricians always liked to boast, the force of rhetoric is always partly coercive.[47] When Cicero speaks at the start of *De inventione* about the impact of *oratio* when combined with *ratio*, he describes the original founders of cities as 'inducing men to follow a useful and honest

---

44. *Othello*, TLN 6–8, p. 929 (I. 1. 7–8).
45. Snyder 1979, pp. 70, 73–4; cf. Watson 1990, pp. 337–8.
46. *Othello*, TLN 392, p. 933 (I. 3. 106).
47. On the importance for the rhetoricians of knowing how to inflame hearts and minds see Vickers 1988, pp. 73–80; on early modern discussions about the power of the passions to overcome reason see James 1997, pp. 225–52.

way of life, even though at first they cried out against the change because they were not used to it'.[48] The combination of reason with eloquence forced them to do things they would never otherwise have done. Yet more suggestive is Thomas Wilson's assessment at the beginning of his *Arte of Rhetorique* of how king Pyrrhus waged war against Rome. As we saw in Chapter 1, Wilson explains how Pyrrhus liked to send the orator Cineas to persuade the towns he was besieging to give up without a fight. From this story he goes on to draw a lofty moral about the power of rhetoric:

> What worthier thing can there be, then with a word to winne cities & whole countries? If profite may perswade, what greater gayne can we have, then withoute bloudshed to achive a conquest? If pleasure may provoke us, what greater delite do we know, then to see a whole multitude with the onely talke of a man ravished & drawen whiche waye him liketh best to have them?[49]

Here rhetoric is explicitly figured as a compelling force. While those who succumb to it are not physically overpowered, they are nevertheless made to submit. Moreover, as the reference to ravishment implies, they are overpowered in the manner of a woman yielding to a seducer who sweeps aside her resistance and makes a conquest of her. She may not be the victim of a violent assault, but nor is her acquiescence entirely voluntary.[50]

As a footnote it is worth recalling that, at the time when Shakespeare was writing *Othello*, he was lodging with a family called Mountjoy in their house on Silver Street in the Cripplegate district of London.[51] The family wanted their former apprentice Stephen Belott to marry their daughter Mary, and Shakespeare became involved in their plans, as is clear from a deposition he made on oath in the Court of Requests in May 1612. The plaintiff in the case in which Shakespeare was called as a witness was Belott, who testified that he had been promised a dowry on marrying Mary in 1604, but that the money had never been paid. Shakespeare affirms in a brief deposition—the only source in which we can read his spoken words—that he was asked by Mary's mother to help bring about the match:

---

48. Cicero 1949a, I. II. 2, p. 6: 'rem inducens utilem atque honestam primo propter insolentiam reclamantes'.
49. Wilson 1553, Epistle, Sig. A, 1ᵛ.
50. On rhetoric and rape see Rebhorn 1995, pp. 158–70; on the violence of rhetoric see Crider 2009, pp. 79–82.
51. My information here is taken from Nicholl 2007, pp. 3–5.

> And further this deponent sayethe that the said defftes wyeffe did sollicitt and entreat this deponent to move and perswade the said Complainant to effect the said Marriadge and accordingly this deponent did move and perswade the complainant therunto:[52]

The couple duly got married, and the person who successfully moved and persuaded the initially reluctant Belott was Shakespeare, who was writing at much the same time about how Othello moved and persuaded Desdemona to marry him. To have been moved and persuaded by Shakespeare at the height of his powers must have been quite an experience for a young apprentice. When Shakespeare's words of persuasion produced their desired effect, it would be interesting to know if he felt any sense that he might have forcibly drawn and pulled Belott, as Thomas Wilson would put it, in the direction that he himself best liked.[53]

Double refutation: documents and witnesses

With the opening of the final scene in *All's Well That Ends Well* a calm descends after the frenetic events of the previous Act, in which we have witnessed the working out of Hellen's plot. Count Bertram believes that he has successfully seduced Diana, although he has in fact been duped by the bed trick, and has unknowingly made love to Hellen, with whom he has exchanged rings in bed.[54] Hellen has meanwhile given it out that she has succumbed to her grief at the loss of Bertram and died. We learn this news from a conversation between two of Bertram's companions in Florence, the lords Dumaine. The second Lord wants to know on what authority Hellen is believed to be dead, and the first Lord explains:

> The stronger part of it by her owne Letters, which makes her storie true, even to the poynt of her death: her death it selfe, which could not be her office to say, is come: was faithfully confirm'd by the Rector of the place.

> TLN 1995–9, p. 989 (4. 3. 47–50)

---

52. Nicholl 2007, p. 290.   53. Wilson 1553, Epistle, Sig. A, 1^v.

54. See *All's Well That Ends Well*, TLN 1921–3, p. 988 (4. 2. 60–2), where we are told that this exchange of rings formed part of the bed trick. On rings in Shakespeare see Bevington 1984, pp. 57–60; Kinney 2006, pp. 51–76. On the sexual significance of a woman's yielding her 'ring' see Mukherji 2006, pp. 32–51. On the bed trick see Desens 1994; Mukherji 2006, pp. 48–50, 207–8, 225–7.

Hellen's death has been attested by the two most conclusive forms of non-artificial proof: by documentary evidence, and by the testimony of a witness whose standing proclaims his trustworthiness. When the second Lord asks whether Bertram has been informed, the first Lord assures him that he knows 'the particular confirmations, point from point, to the full arming of the veritie'.[55]

As the rhetoricians would say, this only goes to show that confirmation is not the same as certainty. Hellen is far from being dead; she is on her way back to Rossillion to bring about the *dénouement* of the plot. The ensuing scene is one of extreme forensic complexity, and in writing it Shakespeare departs very far from his principal source, William Painter's *The Palace of Pleasure*. Painter's tale ends with a feast held by Count Beltramo at Montpellier, at which Giletta arrives in her pilgrim's garb, prostrates herself before the count and returns his family ring, upon which he accepts her as his lawful wife.[56] Shakespeare makes two major additions to the story: one is the appearance of Diana and her mother to mount their accusation against Count Bertram; the other is the introduction of a second ring, a ring given to Hellen by the king that has mysteriously come into Bertram's possession. While Diana and her mother pursue their *constitutio iuridicalis* against Bertram, with the king acting as judge, the king is pursuing a *constitutio coniecturalis* on his own account, attempting to uncover the truth about how Bertram acquired his ring. The resulting tumultuous scene owes nothing to Painter or Boccaccio and everything to Shakespeare's by now well-honed skills at drawing on the principles of judicial rhetoric for dramatic effect.

While Hellen is journeying to Rossillion, Count Bertram and the court have already arrived there, and the king has forgiven Bertram his abandonment of Hellen. Her death is mourned by everyone, and particularly by the older generation, who have been her natural allies throughout. But the main and more cheerful business of the day is to solemnize the marriage between Bertram and Maudlin, the daughter of Lord Lafew. Bertram informs the king that Maudlin was his original choice, and the king indicates that the marriage can now go ahead, making his declaration in a rhymed couplet with an appropriate tone of finality:

---

55. *All's Well That Ends Well*, TLN 2001–2, p. 989 (4. 3. 52–3). For a discussion see Baldwin 1944, vol. 2, pp. 86–7.
56. Painter 1566, fo. 100[r-v]; cf. Bullough 1957–75, vol. 2, p. 396.

The maine consents are had, and heere wee'l stay
To see our widdowers second marriage day:

> TLN 2588–9, p. 995 (5. 3. 69–70)

Lord Lafew next asks Bertram to seal the bargain by handing over a suitable token of his commitment:

Come on my sonne, in whom my houses name
Must be digested: give a favour from you
To sparkle in the spirits of my daughter,
That she may quickly come.

> TLN 2592–5, p. 995 (5. 3. 73–6)

Complying with his request, and seemingly rounding off this phase of the action, Bertram hands Lord Lafew a favour in the form of a ring.

With this gesture the calm of the scene is suddenly shattered.[57] Lord Lafew at once recognizes the ring as one that Hellen used to wear:

Helen that's dead
Was a sweet creature: such a ring as this,
The last that ere I tooke her leave at Court,
I saw upon her finger.

> TLN 2596–9, p. 995 (5. 3. 77–80)

Bertram attempts to deny it ('Hers it was not') but the king intervenes on Lord Lafew's side:

Now pray you let me see it. For mine eye,
While I was speaking, oft was fasten'd too't:
This Ring was mine, and when I gave it *Hellen*,
I bad her if her fortunes ever stoode
Necessitied to helpe, that by this token
I would releeve her.

> TLN 2600–5, p. 995 (5. 3. 81–6)

Again Bertram denies it ('The ring was never hers') but the countess now adds her voice to that of the king:

Sonne, on my life
I have seene her weare it, and she reckon'd it
At her lives rate.

> TLN 2608–10, p. 995 (5. 3. 89–91)

---

57. Haley 1993, pp. 237–53 provides a full analysis of the rest of the scene, although without reference to its rhetorical structure.

Bertram realizes that his bluster has failed and that he will have to make up a
story to satisfy them:

> You are deceiv'd my Lord, she never saw it:
> In Florence was it from a casement throwne mee,
> Wrap'd in a paper, which contain'd the name
> Of her that threw it:
>
> TLN 2611–14, p. 995 (5. 3. 92–5)

With this outright and perfidious lie Bertram evidently hopes to draw the
increasingly awkward discussion to a close.

The king, however, refuses to be fobbed off. He not only reaffirms that he
himself gave Hellen the ring, but makes it clear that he regards it as sinister that
Bertram should somehow have acquired it. The reason is not merely because
he presented it to Hellen as a pledge of his willingness to help her; it is also
because of a solemn vow that, he now reveals, she made at the time:

> She call'd the Saints to suretie,
> That she would never put it from her finger,
> Unlesse she gave it to your selfe in bed,
> Where you have never come: or sent it us
> Upon her great disaster.
>
> TLN 2627–31, p. 995 (5. 3. 108–12)

When Bertram repeats his denial ('She never saw it') the king loses patience:
'Thou speak'st it falsely, as I love mine Honor'.[58] He is fully convinced—
correctly, as we know—that the ring in Bertram's possession is undoubtedly
the one that Hellen received from him.

As the king now perceives, he is confronting a conjectural issue in a
judicial cause. The indisputable fact, as he sees it, is that Bertram has
somehow come into possession of Hellen's ring. The mystery is to explain
how he could have acquired it when Hellen would never have given it to
him unless they were together in bed, an event that (so far as the king is
aware) has never taken place. As the rhetoricians would say, this raises the
central question for adjudication, and the king puts it directly to Bertram:

> Had you that craft to reave her
> Of what should stead her most?
>
> TLN 2605–6, p. 995 (5. 3. 86–7)

---

58. *All's Well That Ends Well*, TLN 2632, p. 995 (5. 3. 113).

The king is asking Bertram to confirm or deny that he must have found means to deprive Hellen of her ring, and thus of her ultimate means of security.

The king knows that he needs to form a conjecture about what may have happened and search for evidence to confirm it.[59] He discloses that he has already arrived at some conclusions that are giving him serious cause for alarm, and he actually describes them as his 'conjecturall feares'. He believes, although he falters and can hardly bring himself to state his suspicion clearly, that Bertram may have murdered Hellen, and that this is how he may have acquired her ring:

> Thou speak'st it falsely, as I love mine Honor,
> And mak'st conjecturall feares to come into me,
> Which I would faine shut out; if it should prove
> That thou art so inhumane, 'twill not prove so:
> And yet I know not, thou didst hate her deadly,
> And she is dead, which nothing but to close
> Her eyes my selfe, could win me to beleeve,
> More then to see this Ring.
>
> TLN 2632–9, p. 995 (5. 3. 113–20)

A few moments later he reiterates his anxiety to the countess: 'I am a-feard the life of *Hellen* (Ladie)/ Was fowly snatcht.'[60]

Announcing his conjecture, the king begins at the same time to build up a *confirmatio* of his belief that he is adjudicating in a foul cause. Bertram undoubtedly had a motive for killing Hellen ('thou didst hate her deadly'), and the fact that he now has her ring is a further indication of guilt. The next step, the king recognizes, must be to search for additional signs and clues. As he declares, 'Wee'l sift this matter further'.[61] But meanwhile he feels that, whatever the outcome of his enquiry into the 'matter', he will have no reason to treat his original fears as groundless:

> My fore-past proofes, how ere the matter fall
> Shall taxe my feares of little vanitie,
>
> TLN 2640–1, p. 995 (5. 3. 121–2)

59. As noted in Altman 2010, pp. 352–3.
60. *All's Well That Ends Well*, TLN 2673–4, p. 996 (5. 3. 151–2).
61. *All's Well That Ends Well*, TLN 2643, p. 995 (5. 3. 124).

The king regards the existing proofs as strong enough to justify his fears, and Bertram is accordingly placed under arrest and led away under guard.

The king's conjecture, however, is almost immediately overturned. The *refutatio* is provided by Diana in the course of attesting that Bertram seduced and abandoned her after promising marriage. She proclaims that the ring was hers, that she gave it to Bertram 'being a bed' with him, and proceeds to offer two non-artificial proofs.[62] The first takes the form of what the rhetoricians would call a piece of documentary evidence, a ring that Bertram gave her as a reciprocal pledge. She now holds out this second ring to be inspected by the court:

> O behold this Ring,
> Whose high respect and rich validitie
> Did lacke a Paralell:
>
> TLN 2712–14, p. 996 (5. 3. 189–91)

The countess immediately recognizes the Rossillion family ring, and treats the fact that Bertram gave it to Diana as conclusive proof that he must indeed have promised marriage:

> He blushes, and 'tis hit:
> Of sixe preceding Ancestors, that Jemme;
> Confer'd by testament to'th sequent issue
> Hath it beene owed and worne. This is his wife,
> That Ring's a thousand proofes.
>
> TLN 2716–20, p. 996 (5. 3. 193–7)

The countess has two reasons for believing that Diana's accusation has been proved a thousandfold. One is that Bertram would never have given away such an important family heirloom except as a correspondingly important pledge. The other is that to blush as Bertram does on seeing the ring is one of the best-known signs of guilt: 'He blushes, and 'tis hit'. The countess aptly figures Diana as a huntress and Bertram as her quarry wounded in flight.

Diana's second non-artificial proof is yet more conclusive. She promises to hand back Bertram's family ring if he will return the ring she gave him 'being a bed'. The king tells her that, according to Bertram, he acquired it when 'you threw it him/ Out of a Casement'.[63] But Diana solemnly

---

responds 'I have spoke the truth': she gave it to him in bed.[64] This is a lie, of course, but the luckless Bertram (hoodwinked by the bed trick) believes it to be true, and is forced into a confession, thereby making good Diana's claim without any need of further proof: 'My Lord, I do confesse the ring was hers'.[65] The king replies contemptuously: 'You boggle shrewdly, every feather starts you'.[66] Bertram is figured as a frightened horse shying at the slightest thing. Diana's contention has 'started' him, arousing his guilty conscience and finally constraining him to abandon his ignoble evasions and tell the truth.

The fact that Bertram has confessed might appear sufficient, but the king next encourages Diana to bring forward a further non-artificial proof of her claim that Bertram promised to marry her: 'Me thought you saide/ You saw one heere in Court could witnesse it'.[67] Diana has not in fact told the king, or at least not in our hearing, of any plans to summon a witness. But at this point she tentatively suggests that she wishes to do so, and that his name is Parrolles. She is about to subject Count Bertram to the indignity of hearing testimony brought against him by one of his own most dubious followers, someone whose name already informs us that he lacks any substance and amounts to nothing but words.

Bertram, however, knows how to head off this further threat. As the *Ad Herennium* advises, the best thing to do in this kind of situation is to try to discredit the witness before he can bring forward any evidence. You must object 'to his disgraceful way of life and the unreliability of what he will say'.[68] Bertram duly follows this advice:

> He's quoted for a most perfidious slave
> With all the spots a'th world, taxt and debosh'd,
> Whose nature sickens, but to speake a truth:
> Am I, or that or this for what he'l utter,
> That will speake any thing.

TLN 2726–30, p. 996 (5. 3. 203–7)

64. *All's Well That Ends Well*, TLN 2752, p. 996 (5. 3. 228).
65. *All's Well That Ends Well*, TLN 2753, p. 997 (5. 3. 229).
66. *All's Well That Ends Well*, TLN 2754, p. 997 (5. 3. 230).
67. *All's Well That Ends Well*, TLN 2720–1, p. 996 (5. 3. 197–8).
68. *Rhetorica ad Herennium* 1954, II. VI. 9, p. 74: 'Contra testes: secundum vitae turpitudinem, testimoniorum inconstantiam.'

Diana is obliged to admit that she is loath 'to produce/ So bad an instrument', and it looks as if this element in her *confirmatio* will have to be given up.[69]

The king, however, strictly enjoins Parrolles to tell the truth, promising him immunity if he will do so, and Parrolles thereupon confirms everything that Diana has said: 'I was in that credit with them at that time, that I knewe of their going to bed, and of other motions, as promising her marriage, and things which would derive mee ill will to speake of, therefore I will not speake what I know.'[70] This is quite sufficient for the king: 'Thou hast spoken all alreadie'.[71] Like the countess, he now believes Diana's accusations to be fully justified.

The king acknowledges that his initial conjecture about how Bertram acquired Hellen's ring has been refuted, but he also sees that he is now confronting a new and different conjectural issue. If Diana presented Bertram with the ring that he originally gave to Hellen, how did Diana come by it? There is a new mystery and a new question for adjudication, and the king puts it to Diana directly:

> KING This Ring you say was yours.
> DIANA   I my good Lord.
> KING Where did you buy it? Or who gave it you?
>   TLN 2790–1, p. 997 (5. 3. 260–1)

As Diana gives him increasingly riddling answers, the conjecture at which the king arrives is that, as Bertram had originally alleged, she may after all be nothing more than a prostitute associated with the military camp. 'I do not like her now', he tells the court, and to Diana he says 'I thinke thee now some common Customer', a disreputable person whose testimony cannot be trusted.[72] Like Bertram, Diana is placed under arrest, and with the additional threat that, if she refuses to explain how she came into possession of the ring, she will be executed within the hour.

Diana is able, however, to respond with an immediate *refutatio* of the king's new conjecture. She produces a non-artificial proof of her innocence in the form of an unimpeachable witness who is in a position to explain

69. *All's Well That Ends Well*, TLN 2722–3, p. 996 (5. 3. 199–200).
70. *All's Well That Ends Well*, TLN 2782–6, p. 997 (5. 3. 254–7).
71. *All's Well That Ends Well*, TLN 2787, p. 997 (5. 3. 258).
72. *All's Well That Ends Well*, TLN 2801, 2806, p. 997 (5. 3. 271, 276).

everything. 'Great King I am no strumpet', she declares,[73] and by way of confirmation she explains how Bertram was deceived by the bed trick, speaking in rhymed verse in what Quintilian calls the *genus grande* or grand style[74]:

> He knowes himselfe my bed he hath defil'd,
> And at that time he got his wife with childe:
> Dead though she be, she feeles her yong one kicke:
> So there's my riddle, one that's dead is quicke,
> And now behold the meaning.

TLN 2820–4, p. 997 (5. 3. 290–4)

The meaning is that Hellen substituted for her in the bed trick, and Hellen now makes her appearance to confirm this crucial fact. Before the astonished king, who asks 'Is't reall that I see?', Hellen explains that it was she and not Diana who was in bed with Bertram.[75] 'Oh my good Lord', she tells Bertram, 'when I was like this Maid,/ I found you wondrous kinde'.[76] It was therefore she, and not Diana, who received from Bertram the Rossillion family ring in return for the ring given to her by the king. 'There is your Ring', she now says to Bertram, handing it back.[77]

How conclusive is this *refutatio* of the king's conjecture? For us the question does not arise. We have been party to Hellen's plot from the outset, and by this stage we may even find ourselves reflecting that its implications could perhaps have been worked out rather more economically. But within the world of the play the *dénouement* not only brings a moment of high drama but a generally satisfying air of finality. Hellen is able to announce in triumph that she has finally met the conditions laid out in the dreadful letter that Bertram left for her when he escaped to Italy:

> And looke you, heeres your letter: this it sayes,
> When from my finger you can get this Ring,
> And are by me with childe, &c. This is done,
> Will you be mine now you are doubly wonne?

TLN 2831–4, p. 997 (5. 3. 301–4)

---

73. *All's Well That Ends Well*, TLN 2812, p. 997 (5. 3. 282).
74. Quintilian 2001, 12. 10, 58–62, vol. 5, pp. 312–14.
75. *All's Well That Ends Well*, TLN 2826, p. 997 (5. 3. 296).
76. *All's Well That Ends Well*, TLN 2829–30, p. 997 (5. 3. 299–300).
77. *All's Well That Ends Well*, TLN 2830, p. 997 (5. 3. 300). But Hellen may be pointing to the ring we last saw in the hands of Diana when she held it out to be inspected by everyone. See TLN 2712, p. 996 (5. 3. 189).

Next the king indicates his willingness to accept the story of the bed trick, and hence the honesty of Diana's cause: 'For I can guesse, that by thy honest ayde,/ Thou keptst a wife her selfe, thy selfe a Maide'.[78] Bertram remains to be satisfied, but he suddenly informs the king that he is now willing to be persuaded, rising from blank to rhymed verse to underline the strength of his commitment:

> If she my Liege can make me know this clearly,
> Ile love her dearely, ever, ever dearly.
>
> TLN 2835–6, p. 997 (5. 3. 305–6)

Nothing has prepared us for this sudden change of heart, but Bertram's couplet signals an ending, and Hellen seems confident of being able to convince him that she has told the truth:

> If it appeare not plaine, and prove untrue,
> Deadly divorce step between me and you.
>
> TLN 2837–8, p. 998 (5. 3. 307–8)

These mutual assurances are Bertram's and Hellen's final words.

It is true that this ending can hardly be said to meet the usual expectations of comedy, several of which appear to be deliberately flouted and undermined.[79] It is not clear that Hellen and Bertram make a good match, and their final declarations of love are far from being unconditional and passionate in the way that the conventions require.[80] Bertram promises to love Hellen if she can make good her case, and Hellen speaks of divorce if he remains unsatisfied. Nevertheless, Hellen has at last got what she wants, and the king acknowledges that the case is closed. It only remains for him to pronounce a suitably celebratory *peroratio*.

---

78. *All's Well That Ends Well*, TLN 2849–50, p. 998 (5. 3. 319–20).
79. For a discussion see Margolies 2012.   80. Frye 1965, p. 72.

10

The Peroration and Appeal to Commonplaces

The theory of *loci communes*

When we come to the *peroratio*, Quintilian writes, 'we are allowed to open up the full flood of our eloquence'.[1] We must be sure to provide a summary of our case, but our principal aim should be to engage in a process of *amplificatio* designed to arouse the emotions of our audience to their highest pitch. 'The amplification of what we have argued', as Quintilian puts it, 'constitutes the main part of any conclusion, and at this moment it is appropriate not merely to give voice to ornate and magnificent *sententiae* but to clothe these thoughts in ornate and magnificent words.'[2] Cicero had already spoken in similar terms in *De inventione*, in which he proposes that, after enumerating the points we have argued, we should divide our peroration into two further sections, in each of which we should aim to amplify our cause. In the first, the *indignatio*, we should employ every device of *amplificatio* to excite hatred for our adversaries.[3] In the second, the *conquestio*, we should attempt to induce feelings of sympathy on the part of the judge for our own side of the case.[4] Both writers add that, as Quintilian puts it, we must never speak in low or colloquial tones; we must always ensure that our *peroratio* is constructed in a grand and rhythmical style.[5]

---

1. Quintilian 2001, 6. 1. 51, vol. 3, p. 42: 'totos eloquentiae aperire fontes licet'. See also Quintilian 2001, 4. 1. 28, vol. 2, p. 192.
2. Quintilian 2001, 6. 1. 52, vol. 3, p. 42: 'maxima pars epilogi amplificatio, verbis atque sententiis uti licet magnificis et ornatis'.
3. Cicero 1949a, I. LIII. 100–1, pp. 150–2.
4. Cicero 1949a, I. LIII. 100 and I. LV. 106, pp. 150, 156.
5. Quintilian 2001, 11. 1. 6, vol. 5, p. 10.

The most effective method of amplifying a judicial cause is said to be by appealing to *loci communes*, common 'places' of argument.[6] Cicero lays it down that the best means of exciting sympathy in our closing *conquestio* will be to deploy such *loci* 'with gravity and sententiousness'.[7] The *Ad Herennium* goes so far as to conclude that the basic purpose of the peroration should be 'to insert amplifications by means of *loci communes*'.[8] It might well be felt, however, that both these terms—*locus* as well as *communis*—stand in need of some further explication. First, what does it mean to speak of *loci* or 'places' of argument? Cicero has little to say about this question in *De inventione*, but in his *Topica* he provides what eventually became the standard answer. Drawing on Aristotle's treatment of *topoi*, he explains that 'when there is some argument that we want to track down, we need to know its *loci*, this being the name assigned by Aristotle to the seats or dwelling-places, as one might say, from which arguments can be drawn forth'.[9] Quintilian virtually quotes this passage, likewise telling us that the *loci* are 'the dwelling-places of arguments, in which they lie concealed, and from which they need to be sought out'.[10] The underlying image of hunting and gathering is enthusiastically picked up by the rhetorical theorists of the Renaissance.[11] Erasmus in his *De copia* describes the young student 'as resembling a diligent bee, for he will fly through the gardens of every different author, alighting upon every flower, and gathering no little nectar from each'.[12] Thomas Wilson in his *Rule of Reason* prefers a more predatory simile. When skilled hare-finders

---

6. On the Renaissance theory of commonplaces see Lechner 1962; Moss 1996; Moss 2001; Plett 2004, pp. 131–46; Peltonen 2013, pp. 80–3. Kennedy 1942, pp. 134–5 treats conclusions exclusively as summaries and has nothing to say about commonplaces.

7. See Cicero 1949a, I. LV. 106, p. 156 on 'loci communes' and the need to deliver them 'graviter et sententiose'.

8. *Rhetorica ad Herennium* 1954, III. VIII. 15, p. 182: 'amplificationes interponemus per locos communes'.

9. Cicero 1949b, II. 7–8, p. 386: 'cum pervestigare argumentum aliquod volumus, locos nosse debemus; sic enim appellatae ab Aristotele sunt eae quasi sedes, e quibus argumentum promuntur'. See also Cicero 1942a, II. XXXIX. 166, vol. 1, pp. 316–18.

10. Quintilian 2001, 5. 10. 20, vol. 2, p. 374: 'sedes argumentorum, in quibus latent, ex quibus sunt petenda'. See also Quintilian 2001, 5. 10. 119, vol. 2, p. 426 and cf. Lechner 1962, pp. 130–2.

11. See Plett 2004, pp. 118–20; Altman 2010, pp. 141–3.

12. Erasmus 1569, fo. 149[r]: 'itaque studiosus ille, velut apicula diligens, per omnes autorum hortos volitabit, flosculis omnibus adsultabit undique succi nonnihil colligens'. He appears to be drawing on the account of the life of bees in Pliny 1940, XI. IV. 11 to XI. XXIII. 70, vol. 3, pp. 438–74. But Crane 1993, p. 59 notes that Plutarch may be another source, and there are similar passages in Horace 2004, 4. 2. 25–32, p. 222 and (even closer) in Seneca 1920, LXXXIV. 3–5, pp. 276–8.

'see the grounde beaten flatte round about' they will 'gesse by al likelihod that the hare was there a litle before'. The process is much the same as trying to find the 'places' in which good arguments lie concealed, 'for these places be nothyng els but covertes or boroughes'.[13]

Next, what do the rhetoricians mean when they speak of these *loci* as 'common'? Here they tend to shift from talking about the places in which arguments can be found to talking about the arguments themselves.[14] One reason why we speak in these terms, according to the *Ad Herennium*, is because the arguments we uncover will frequently be common to both sides of a case.[15] This aspect of the theory was likewise picked up by the rhetoricians of Shakespeare's time. Richard Sherry explains that the notion of a 'place' primarily refers to 'seates of argumentes', which are said to be 'common' because they can 'be entreated of, of both partes'.[16] For example, 'he that is fore spoken agaynste by witnesses' will attempt to persuade us that they cannot be trusted, whereas 'he that is helpen' will argue in favour of them.[17] Richard Rainolde agrees that 'a common place, serveth bothe for the accuser and the defender'. When speaking in prosecution we must attempt to deploy inflammatory *loci communes* 'to exasperate and move the Judges', whereas in defence we must try 'to pulle doune and deface the contrarie alledged'.[18]

Of greater significance is the associated idea that *loci communes* are common in the sense of being commonly believed. Aristotle adumbrates this aspect of the theory when he observes in his *Art of Rhetoric* that rhetoricians typically reason on the basis of generally accepted principles.[19] Cicero discusses the idea in Book 2 of *De inventione*, where he explains that a *locus communis* 'takes the form of an amplified statement of something undisputed'.[20] Subsequently he comments that any generalizations about matters

13. Wilson 1551, Sig. J, 5ᵛ–6ʳ.
14. Wels 2008, p. 153 notes this slide. For a clear instance see *Rhetorica ad Herennium* 1954, II. VI. 9, pp. 72–4, where *loci* are described as 'places' of argument, and compare *Rhetorica ad Herennium* 1954, II. XVII. 26, p. 104, where generalizations about such matters as fortune and humanity are likewise described as *loci communes*. The alternatives are well distinguished in Quintilian 2001, 5. 10. 20, vol. 3, p. 374. Among Renaissance rhetoricians, Agricola is particularly emphatic in speaking of *loci* less as places of argument than as arguments in themselves. See Moss 1996, pp. 73–82; Rhodes 2004, pp. 152–3.
15. *Rhetorica ad Herennium* 1954, II. VI. 9, p. 72. See also Cicero 1949a, II. XV. 48, pp. 208–10; Quintilian 2001, 4. 1. 71, vol. 2, p. 214.
16. Sherry 1550, Sig. F, 4ʳ⁻ᵛ.   17. Sherry 1550, Sig. F, 4ʳ.
18. Rainolde 1563, fo. xxxiiiᵛ.   19. Aristotle 1926, I. I. 12, p. 10.
20. Cicero 1949a, II. XV. 48–50, pp. 208–10: 'certae rei quandam continet amplificationem'.

of acknowledged importance 'are what we nowadays call commonplaces'.[21] Quintilian prefers to cleave to the original use of the term to refer to 'places' of arguments, but he agrees that 'nowadays the word is usually understood to mean an oration on adultery or luxury or some such general theme'.[22] Here again the Renaissance writers underline the point. Vives thinks of commonplaces as 'traditionally accepted maxims' on such topics as cruelty, fortune, the passage of time, and so on,[23] while Rainolde claims that commonplaces can actually be defined as orations in which 'the matter... doeth agree universally to all menne'.[24]

According to some Renaissance rhetoricians, the reason why the maxims embodied in *loci communes* tend to be widely accepted is that, as Melanchthon argues, such *loci* should not be regarded merely as elegant formulations of conventional wisdom but rather as receptacles of truths about the world. Melanchthon's first handbook on rhetoric, the *De rhetorica libri tres* of 1519, already argues that *loci communes* are as much dialectical as rhetorical in character. They are not simply useful for purposes of amplification but amount to proofs in their own right, adumbrating as they do some basic structures of the moral and natural world.[25] He goes so far as to conclude that the right way of thinking about commonplaces is to recognize 'that they constitute the forms and rules of all things'.[26]

If we are looking for such deep and widely applicable principles, what are the 'places' in which we have best chance of finding them? Cicero and Quintilian provide an answer that had a profound impact on Renaissance discussions of *loci communes*, especially in the writings of Erasmus, Melanchthon, Vives, and their many disciples.[27] Analysing rhetorical proofs in his *De inventione*, Cicero contends that 'every matter is confirmed in argument by referring to the attributes either of persons or actions'.[28] Quintilian

21. Cicero 1962a, XII. 47, p. 48: 'qui nunc communes appellantur loci'.
22. Quintilian 2001, 5. 10. 20, vol. 2, p. 374: 'Locos ... vulgo nunc intelleguntur in luxuriam et adulteriam et similia'.
23. Vives 1913 [1531], p. 184.   24. Rainolde 1563, fo. xxxiii^r.
25. Moss 1996, pp. 121–4. Melanchthon developed the implications in his *Rhetorices Elementa*. See Melanchthon 1539, p. 54, where he speaks of how *loci communes* can be applied 'ad probandum' as well as 'ad amplificandum'.
26. Melanchthon 1519, p. 72: 'formae sunt seu regulae omnium rerum'. On this view of commonplaces see Altman 2010, pp. 143–5. For a survey of Melanchthon's rhetorics see Mack 2011, pp. 106–22.
27. For Erasmus on *loci* see Trousdale 1982, pp. 31–8; on the Erasmian programme see Nauert 2006, pp. 154–71.
28. Cicero 1949a, I. XXIV. 34, p. 70: 'Omnes res argumentando confirmantur aut ex eo quod personis aut ex eo quod negotiis est attributum.'

greatly enlarges on the claim, declaring that 'there can never be a *quaestio* that does not arise either from a thing or a person, nor can there be any *loci* of arguments that do not arise from persons or things'.[29] The relevant attributes of persons, he goes on, are such matters as birth, nationality, education, physique, fortune, and so on.[30] The relevant properties of things are extremely numerous, but the most important relate to the motivations for human action, and hence to such passions as anger, hatred, envy, avarice, hope, ambition, audacity, and fear.[31]

According to Erasmus, one of Quintilian's most valuable contributions was to put together these comprehensive lists of 'places' in which arguments can be found.[32] If, for example, you are trying to think of memorable *sententiae* with which to denounce an adversary in court, you will now be conscious of a number of helpful places in which to look. Recalling Quintilian's catalogue, you will know to search under such headings as ambition, anger, audacity, avarice, and so on, tracking your quarry through the entire alphabet of human weaknesses. As Thomas Wilson puts it, we have been provided with 'a marke whiche giveth warnyng to our memory', and we can now hope to delve into it with a better chance of finding appropriate *sententiae* with which to embellish our case.[33]

To this analysis the Renaissance writers make one important addition, and here their chief inspiration appears to have been Erasmus's *De copia*.[34] If you wish to master the application of *loci*, Erasmus lays down, you not only need to hunt and gather them; you also need to record them in a convenient and systematic way.[35] The most effective means of doing so, he suggests, will be to construct a commonplace book with headings (*tituli*) relating to each *locus* of argument.[36] Following Quintilian, he adds that these headings should be derived 'partly from the types and elements of the virtues and vices, and partly from those things which are of the greatest importance in

29. Quintilian 2001, 5. 8. 4, vol. 2, p. 356: 'neque ulla quaestio quae non sit aut in re aut in persona, neque esse argumentorum loci possunt nisi in iis quae rebus aut personis accidunt'.
30. Quintilian 2001, 5. 10. 23–7, vol. 2, pp. 376–8.
31. Quintilian 2001, 5. 10. 34, vol. 2, p. 382: 'ira odium invidia cupiditas spes ambitus audacia metus'. On early modern discussions of the character of the passions see James 1997, pp. 71–81.
32. As noted in Hutson 2007, pp. 78–80.
33. Wilson 1551, Sig. J, 5ᵛ. On *sententiae* see Donker 1992, pp. 1–21.
34. Moss 1996, pp. 101–15. For an outline of *De copia* see Mack 2011, pp. 80–8.
35. On 'gathering' and 'framing' see Crane 1993, pp. 3–4, 72–4.
36. See Erasmus 1569, fo. 148ᵛ on the need for *tituli*, the need for these to be placed *in ordinem*, and the need for everything to be *annotata*. On notebooks as memory aids see Yeo 2008.

mortal affairs'.[37] They must then be appropriately subdivided, so that under the *titulus* of liberality, for example, you must be sure to distinguish between suitable and unsuitable benefits, single and mutual benefits, worthy and unworthy recipients, and so on.[38] Erasmus thinks it will be helpful to pair off each major virtue with an opposing vice,[39] although he allows that you can simply follow alphabetical order if you prefer.[40] With this framework in place, you will then be ready to look for commonplaces in the best authors, and will be able to expand your collection by embellishing it with your own observations on life.[41] As he summarizes, 'once you have supplied yourself with as many headings as necessary, and laid them out in whatever order you want, you will be able to keep adding further *loci communes* or *sententiae*, copying each of them down in its appropriate place'.[42] You will then be able to fetch them out as necessary from the places in which you have stored them, 'just as if you are turning them into ready cash'.[43]

This proposal about the construction of commonplace books was enthusiastically taken up by the booksellers, who began to reissue a number of traditional *florilegia* or collections of literary 'flowers' in Erasmus's preferred style.[44] Nanus Mirabellius's *Polyanthea*, originally published as a *florilegium* in 1503, was subsequently reorganized along strictly Erasmian lines.[45] The virtues were grouped together and broken down into their constituent parts, while the *sententiae* themselves (as later title pages boast) were presented 'under appropriate *tituli* and *loci* in every case'.[46] Among these restructured *florilegia*, one of the most widely used was Octavianus Mirandula's *Illustrium Poetarum Flores,* first printed in Venice in 1507 and reworked

---

37. Erasmus 1569, fo. 147^{r-v}: 'partim a generibus, ac partibus vitiorum, virtutumque; partim ab his, quae sunt in rebus mortalium praecipua'.
38. Erasmus 1569, fo. 148^v.
39. See Erasmus 1569, fo. 147^v on the need to follow the 'ratio affinitatis & pugnantiae'.
40. Erasmus 1569, fo. 147^v: 'si malit elementorum ordinem sequatur'.
41. On the allegedly transformative effect of this exercise see Crane 1993, pp. 61–4. Schleiner 1970, pp. 170–85 outlines an earlier but comparable method—used in medieval biblical *claves*—in which key terms are set apart, broken down into positive and negative senses, and then amplified.
42. Erasmus 1569, fo. 148^v: 'posteaquam tibi titulos compararis, quot erunt satis, eosque in ordinem quem voles digesseris, deinde ... addideris locos communes sive sententias ... suo loco annotabis'.
43. Erasmus 1569, fo. 147^r: 'velut in numerato possimus habere'.
44. On the use of such commonplace books in schools see Green 2009, pp. 241–9.
45. On Mirabellius see Moss 1996, pp. 93–7.
46. Mirabellius 1600, title page: 'suis quibusque locis & titulis collocatae'. Cf. Moss 1996, pp. 206–7.

as a collection of *loci communes* in 1538.[47] When it eventually appeared in London in 1598 the title page duly noted that the *flores* had been 'arranged into common places'.[48] Still more popular in Elizabethan England was Hermann Germbergius's *Carminum Proverbialium*, first published in London in 1577 and frequently reprinted, in which we are assured that the *loci communes* have been specially selected for the instruction of the young.[49]

By this time a number of vernacular collections had also begun to appear. Some of these continued to uphold the tradition, popularized by Melanchthon, of treating the Bible as the most obvious source of authoritative *loci communes*. Thomas Cogan's *Well of Wisedome*, in which 'chosen sayings' from the Old and New Testaments were 'bestowed in usuall common places', was one such work,[50] while John Marbeck produced a comparable but much larger collection entitled *A Booke Of Notes and Common places* in 1581.[51] No less popular were the collections drawn from predominantly secular and especially classical sources. Here the pioneer was Thomas Heywood, whose best-selling compilation of proverbial wisdom was initially published in 1546 and went through at least six editions before the final version was included in his *Woorkes* in 1566.[52] Less popular, but more strictly Erasmian in conception, was Thomas Blague's *A schole of wise Conceytes*, first issued in 1569 and reprinted in 1572. As the title page promises, the book is 'set forth in commonplaces' with the *loci* in alphabetical order, beginning with abstinence, ambition, and arrogance and ending with vainglory and wisdom.[53] The most successful of these collections was William Baldwin's *Treatice of morall philosophy*, first published in 1547 and reissued on an enlarged scale at least a dozen times before the end of the century.[54] Baldwin's title suggests a systematic treatise, but his work is yet another compilation of 'woorthy sentences, notable preceptes, counsailes, parables

---

47. Moss 1996, pp. 95, 189. Baldwin 1944, vol. 2, pp. 409–13 suggests that Shakespeare may have known this text.
48. Mirandula 1598, title page: 'in locos communes digesti'.
49. Germbergius 1577, title page: 'loci communes, in gratiam iuventutis selecti'.
50. Cogan 1577, title page.
51. Marbeck 1581. See also Cawdray 1600, another compilation of biblical quotations and paraphrases described on the title page as 'collected into Heads and Common places'.
52. Heywood 1566.
53. Blague 1572, pp. 6, 8, 11, 165, 174.
54. Baldwin's original text was revised and extended by Thomas Paulfreyman in the 1560s. This version was enlarged and reissued four times and, in its final form, first published in 1579, went through at least five further printings before the end of the century.

and semblables'.[55] They are arranged in twelve books under appropriate *tituli*, beginning with God and the soul of man, continuing with a series of *sententiae* on law and order, and thereafter centring on the cardinal virtues and the seven deadly sins.

A further trio of commonplace books appeared in the closing years of Elizabeth's reign. The moving spirit behind this venture was Nicholas Ling, who later became known as the publisher of the two Quarto versions of *Hamlet*.[56] Ling began by assembling some materials collected by John Bodenham,[57] which he issued in 1597 as *Politeuphuia. Wits Common wealth,* producing an augmented version in 1598.[58] The anthology is constructed along strictly Erasmian lines, with an alphabetical index to guide the reader to the various *loci*, and with the commonplaces largely organized according to the contrasts between the leading virtues and vices. Ling announced in 1598 that he was planning further instalments,[59] and later in the same year there appeared Francis Meres's *Palladis Tamia*, advertised as a sequel to *Politeuphuia*.[60] Meres's work is heavily indebted to Erasmus's *Parabola sive Similiae*, but it nevertheless won him posthumous fame because of its concluding section in which he compares the poets of antiquity with those of his own day, singling out William Shakespeare as 'the most excellent' writer of tragedies and comedies currently at work.[61] The final volume in Ling's series was published as *Bel vedere or the Garden of the Muses* in 1600. The book is dedicated to John Bodenham, who is praised in the opening epistle as the 'first causer and collectour' of the work.[62] As in *Politeuphuia*, an alphabetical index guides the reader to the various *loci*, which largely centre as before on the connections and contrasts between the leading virtues and vices. Love and hate are considered in turn, as are concord and war, fame and infamy, good and evil deeds, and finally youth, age, life, and death.[63]

55. Baldwin 1579, title page.   56. On Ling as publisher see Johnson 1985.
57. This is noted by Ling himself in [Ling] 1598, Sig. A, 2^r. On Ling's and Bodenham's compilations see Stallybrass and Chartier 2007, pp. 43–53.
58. [Ling] 1598, title page.   59. [Ling] 1598, Sig. A, 3^r.
60. Meres 1598, title page. But while the work is described as 'the Second part of Wits Common wealth' it was not published by Ling.
61. Meres 1598, p. 282.
62. [Bodenham] 1600, Epistle Dedicatory, n. p. We are told that Bodenham laboured for many years on the task, which is why I treat him as the author.
63. [Bodenham] 1600, p. 234.

Erasmus can hardly have been averse to the publishing phenomenon that his *De copia* did so much to promote, but he seems to have been more interested in persuading diligent students to compile commonplace books for themselves. He offers a number of hints about how to set about this task, and these were influentially developed by Melanchthon in *De rhetorica libri tres*[64] and by Vives in *De tradendis disciplinis*.[65] They all agree that a two-step process is involved.[66] First of all, Erasmus writes, the student 'must collect from as many authors as possible' a wide range of *sententiae*,[67] to which 'he can add new ones of his own as may be required'.[68] Every item of interest that he comes across, whether in reading or observation, must be jotted down at once.[69] Melanchthon agrees that at this stage the student is merely taking notes 'about anything he may happen to encounter by chance,'[70] following the injunction that '*sententiae* should be diligently piled up'.[71] He adds that what he specifically has in mind is the collecting of '*loci communes* on the vices, the virtues, fortune, death, literary riches and similar themes'.[72] Whenever the student comes across a *sententia* on any of these topics, he must be sure to jot it down *in tabulas*, that is, on the writing tables that he needs to carry around with him for this purpose.[73]

As Erasmus concedes, however, the fruits of this process can hardly fail to be anything more than 'a confused collection of items without any arrangement', and it still remains to digest and organize them.[74] To attain this further goal, the student must already have completed his other major task, that of laying out the headings of a commonplace book in which he can write down (*adscribere*) whatever notes he may have managed to scribble

---

64. The chapter on *loci communes* in Melanchthon's *De rhetorica* partly takes the form of a long quotation from Erasmus' *De copia*. See Melanchthon 1519, pp. 69–72 and cf. Erasmus 1569, fos. 147ʳ–148ʳ. On Melanchthon's rhetorics see Vickers 1988, pp. 192–6.
65. See Vives 1913 [1531], pp. 107–9, another discussion indebted to Erasmus' account. For further instructions see the discussion in Goyet 1993, pp. 412–14.
66. See Stallybrass et al. 2004; Lewis 2012b, pp. 615–16.
67. Erasmus 1569, fo. 152ᵛ: 'tot scriptoribus colligi'.
68. Erasmus 1569, fo. 152ᵛ: 'verum etiam pro re novas [sententias] parere licet'.
69. Erasmus 1569, fo. 151ʳ.
70. Melanchthon 1519, p. 69: 'quicquid inciderit forte fortuna'.
71. Melanchthon 1519, p. 71: 'sententiae diligenter coacervandae sunt'.
72. Melanchthon 1519, p. 6: 'locos communes, vitiorum, virtutum, fortunae, mortis, divitiarum literarum & similes'.
73. Melanchthon 1519, p. 7. See Cooper 1565, Sig. 6E, 5ʳ for *tabula* as 'A booke or regester for memorie of thinges'. For additional details see Stallybrass et al. 2004, pp. 411–12.
74. Erasmus 1569, fo. 148ᵛ: 'indigesta rerum turba'.

(*annotare*) on his writing tables.[75] Melanchthon agrees that we need to distinguish between taking notes (*notare*) and properly recording them (*recordare*). The student should begin by jotting down whatever strikes him as interesting, but at a later stage 'each *sententia*, each adage, each useful apophthegm which you excerpt, and which is scribbled on your *tabulae* or writing-tables, you must now record in its proper *locus* or place'.[76]

Hamlet was at some stage a student at the University of Wittenberg, where we are to imagine him studying the basic syllabus of grammar, rhetoric, and logic (the so-called Trivium), even if he proceeded no further. Melanchthon was teaching rhetoric at Wittenberg from the early 1520s, and his lectures on the subject began to be published around that time, including his views about commonplaces.[77] Hamlet seems to have been a student some time before the action of the play takes place, but a number of habits from his university days remain with him.[78] The most obvious is that he carries around with him a pair of *tabulae* or writing tables, and at the end of the scene in which he first encounters the ghost they are very much on his mind. He speaks of his 'tables', and alludes to the familiar metaphor of the human heart as a writing table on which good or evil actions can equally well be inscribed. Among many invocations of this theme, Edward Knight in *The triall of truth* of 1580 had offered a particularly elaborate comparison between 'the heartes of men' and 'a payre of writing tables, which serve for to noate in all remembrances' and must be 'cleane wiped out before wee may wryte good things therein'.[79] Hamlet adjusts the metaphor, figuring his memory rather than his heart as a writing table, but he follows a similar train of thought when he promises the ghost that he will produce a *tabula rasa*, wiping everything from it in order to be sure of remembering what has been demanded of him:

> Yea, from the table of my memory
> Ile wipe away all triviall fond records,
> All sawes of bookes, all formes, all pressures past

---

75. Erasmus 1569, fo. 151ʳ.
76. Melanchthon 1519, p. 7: 'si quam sententiam, si quod adagium, si quod apophthegm dignum, quod in tabulas referatur exceperis, suo recordas loco'.
77. See Melanchthon 1519, and cf. Moss 1996, p. 126 on the publication of Melanchthon's lectures on rhetoric as *Institutiones rhetoricae* in 1521.
78. Hamlet appears to be thirty years old at the time of the action of the play. See *Hamlet*, TLN 3115 and 3129, p. 769 (5. 1. 123–4 and 137–8). For a discussion of his age see de Grazia 2007, pp. 82–4.
79. Knight 1580, p. 53.

> That youth and observation coppied there,
> And thy commandement all alone shall live,
> Within the booke and volume of my braine
> Unmixt with baser matter,
>
> TLN 715–21, p. 745 (1. 5. 98–104)

As Hamlet here acknowledges, the ghost has just entrusted him with a judicial 'matter' of such importance that it must take precedence over everything else.[80] He accordingly needs to expunge any 'triviall' notes of the kind that youthful students of the Trivium would have been encouraged to copy down in their first year at Wittenberg. He needs to make sure that any records of the 'sawes' he has encountered are wiped away in order to guarantee that sufficient space is left in the tables of his memory for the matter he needs above all to recall.

Despite his promise not to clutter up his tables, Hamlet remains very much the humanist student, and as soon as he thinks about Claudius he decides that there is something he must not fail to jot down. Earlier in the day he had watched the king greet the members of his court with confidence and affability, but he has now been told that Claudius is an adulterer, a murderer, and the usurper of the Danish throne. The disparity between the hidden truth and how Claudius presents himself to the world suddenly strikes Hamlet with the force of an epiphany:

> O villaine, villaine, smiling damned villaine,
> My tables,
> My tables, meet it is I set it downe
> That one may smile, and smile, and be a villaine,
> At least I'm sure it may be so in Denmarke.
>> *He writes*
> So Uncle, there you are,
>
> TLN 723–8, p. 745 (1. 5. 106–10)

Hamlet has fetched out his writing tables and scribbled a note about smiling villainy. 'So Uncle, there you are', he concludes, as if Claudius's character has now been fixed. If, however, he remembers the full instructions provided by Melanchthon in his lectures at Wittenberg, he will know that he still has a further task to perform. He must enter a fair copy of his note into his book of *loci communes* in the appropriate 'place'. One of the headings in

---

80. Wilder 2010, pp. 102–4, 110–13 detects an association 'between table-books and sexually compromised female bodies'.

Ling's *Politeuphuia* is 'Presumption', under which he includes an observation about those who are capable of 'a shamelesse smile'.[81] Perhaps we are to imagine Hamlet inscribing his own observation in a similar 'place'.

Shakespearean commonplaces

We must do our best, Desdemona jokingly tells Iago, to avoid producing a 'lame and impotent conclusion'.[82] The rhetoricians strongly agree that we must be sure to end on a high and rousing note. As we have seen, the most effective means of doing so, they argue, is to call on a series of resonant *loci communes*, deploying them in the grand style with the aim of exciting the emotions of our hearers to their highest pitch. If we turn to Shakespeare's practice, however, we find him evidently uneasy about such emphatic and definitive forms of closure.[83] Some of his most intensely forensic scenes come to an end without any such *peroratio*, and it also seems significant that, when he chooses to write formal conclusions, he usually puts them in the mouths of characters who are not only old but old-fashioned, and who generally have an interest in trying to impose some specious order on some awkward and complex events. Although these figures may speak magnificently, they are severely limited by their acceptance of the rhetorical assumption that the surest means to arouse the emotions of our hearers will be to echo their most deeply entrenched beliefs. As a result, their sentiments tend to be commonplace not merely in the rhetorical but in the pejorative sense of the term.

Besides revealing these doubts, Shakespeare likes to loosen and unsettle the classical conventions about formal endings in two related ways. The rhetoricians take it for granted that judicial *perorationes* will always be delivered in open court. Shakespeare usually endorses this assumption, but by no means in every case. Sometimes he stages judicial causes in which the setting is conversational or even domestic, and in these instances he uses the conclusion as a moment for private meditation on what has taken place. The other unquestioned assumption had been that any plaintiff or defendant will always present a complete judicial oration, including a suitable *prohoemium*, a *narratio*

---

81. [Ling] 1598, fo. 267ᵛ.   82. *Othello*, TLN 846, p. 938 (2. 1. 158).
83. I owe a particular debt to Colin Burrow for helping me to reconsider the direction of my argument in the sections that follow.

of the facts, a *confirmatio* or *refutatio*, and a *peroratio* in the grand style. But to allow a character in a play to speak uninterruptedly at such length would obviously be unwieldy and undramatic, and Shakespeare never writes any such full-scale speeches in the *genus iudiciale*. He invariably distributes the individual sections between two different speakers, and the *peroratio* is never delivered by the character who initially introduces the cause.

When the setting is domestic, Shakespeare employs the same principle of distribution in each case. He assigns the *prohoemium* and *narratio* to the character who brings forward the accusation, after which a different speaker takes up the cause, supplying the *confirmatio* as well as the *peroratio* of the speech. The first play in which this pattern is followed is *Hamlet*. After watching the performance of *The Mousetrap* in Act 3, Hamlet feels that he has succeeded in provoking a final *confirmatio* of the ghost's charge, and as soon as Claudius and the courtiers depart he pronounces his *peroratio* at once:

> Why let the strooken Deere goe weepe,
>> The Hart ungauled play,
> For some must watch while some must sleepe,
>> So runnes the world away.
>
> TLN 1988–91, p. 758 (3. 2. 246–9)

This, somewhat bewilderingly, is Hamlet's complete *peroratio*. The effect seems deliberately anti-climactic, and the rhetorical conventions are followed only in a minimal way. Although he speaks in rhymed verse, and thus in the heightened style appropriate to the culmination of a judicial speech, his diction is far from sonorous or grand, and while the two concluding lines might at a pinch be described as a *locus communis*, the 'sentence' he pronounces is so lacking in sententiousness that it finds no place in any Elizabethan book of commonplaces.

Hamlet instead uses his peroration as a means of reflecting on the different persons involved in his cause. The stricken deer is perhaps the queen, whom Hamlet is about to strike down, as he tells us, by speaking daggers to her.[84] But the deer may instead be the king, who confesses in soliloquy in the next scene to being stricken with guilt.[85] Hamlet himself appears to be the hart who remains ungalled. Although he knows that he is being hunted, he has

---

84. *Hamlet*, TLN 2113, p. 759 (3. 2. 357).   85. *Hamlet*, TLN 2156, p. 759 (3. 3. 40).

just assured Claudius that neither of them can be described as a galled jade.[86] Meanwhile, the characters most deeply involved in his cause have been watching rather than sleeping: the king and queen have been watching the play, while he and Horatio have been watching the king and queen. At the end it is Claudius who, like the world, runs away—shouting to his courtiers 'away'.[87]

Hamlet's peroration is far from resounding; rather it initiates a scene in which, as Guyldensterne complains, he appears unable to put his discourse into any kind of frame.[88] He continues in the same hectic vein as he talks to Horatio about what they have just observed, producing a further quatrain of verse before switching into prose to assure Horatio that he would now wager a thousand pounds that the ghost has been telling the truth. While his manner may be distracted, however, Hamlet makes it plain that he considers the long judicial investigation on which he has been engaged to be at an end. His peroration may be strange and inadequate from a rhetorical point of view, but he definitely offers it as a final rounding-off.

The other play in which Shakespeare stages a judicial investigation in a domestic setting is *All's Well That Ends Well*. Rynaldo begins by putting forward the *prohoemium* and *narratio* of his charge that Hellen is concealing a secret passion for Bertram. As soon as the countess reflects on what Rynaldo has told her, she recognizes that her own suspicions have been confirmed and accepts that Rynaldo has uncovered the truth. She thereupon takes up the investigation of the cause herself, producing a *confirmatio* by wresting a confession from Hellen and adding a *peroratio* in which she meditates in soliloquy on her young ward's unrequited love.

The commonplace books have a great deal to say about the pangs of young love.[89] Under the heading 'Youth', we learn from Meres that 'young yeares are incident to the heat of love'[90] and from Bodenham that 'Love is youths plague'.[91] If we turn to the heading 'Love', we find much more to the same effect. Germbergius tells us that 'there are as many griefs in love as

---

86. *Hamlet*, TLN 1959, p. 757 (3. 2. 220).   87. *Hamlet*, TLN 1986, p. 757 (3. 2. 244).
88. *Hamlet*, TLN 2024–5, p. 758 (3. 2. 279–80).
89. Here and in subsequent quotations I shall generally be citing commonplaces, not proverbs. There is much proverbial wisdom in Shakespeare, and this topic has been extensively covered. See, for example, Hulme 1962, pp. 39–88; Dent 1981. Less has been said about commonplaces. As we shall see, some were also proverbial, but few invoked by Shakespeare can be found in the books of proverbs of his time.
90. Meres 1598, fo. 66ʳ.   91. [Bodenham] 1600, p. 220.

there are flowers in a meadow.'[92] Meres warns that 'love doth pierce deadly',[93] and Bodenham adds that 'Love is in prime of youth, a Rose'.[94] Ling similarly declares that love involves 'treading upon thornes', that it is 'a heate full of coldnes, a sweete full of bitternes', and that it 'byteth first the flourishing blossomes of youth'.[95] These are the somewhat hackneyed sentiments that likewise pass through the countess's mind as she waits to talk to Hellen:[96]

> Even so it was with me when I was yong:
>   If ever we are natures, these are ours, this thorne
> Doth to our Rose of youth rightlie belong:
>   Our bloud to us, this to our blood is borne,
> It is the show, and seale of natures truth,
> Where loves strong passion is imprest in youth,
> By our remembrances of daies forgon,
> Such were our faults, or then we thought them none,
>
> TLN 428–35, p. 973 (I. 3. 100–7)

As the countess's rhyming pentameters settle into couplets, she presents her reflections in a particularly elevated form of the grand style, transforming the familiar metaphors into a more complex image of youth itself as a rose with wounding thorns. For the content of her thought, however, she remains entirely dependent on the tritest *sententiae* about youthful passion to be found in some of the more wearying sections of the commonplace books. As a result, in spite of the grandeur of her verse, she is made to sound somewhat trite and weary herself.[97]

Except for these two instances, Shakespeare endorses the classical assumption that the proper arena for delivering an oration in the *genus iudiciale* will normally be a court of law. When he stages judicial speeches in this setting he again divides the individual sections among different speakers, but the pattern of distribution differs from the one I have so far explored. The character who appears as plaintiff or defendant invariably expounds the entire case, beginning with a formal *prohoemium*, proceeding to a *narratio* of the facts

92. Germbergius 1577, p. 9: 'quot campo flores, tot sunt in amore dolores'.
93. Meres 1598, fo. 134ᵛ.   94. [Bodenham] 1600, p. 32.
95. [Ling] 1598, fos. 15ᵛ, 16ʳ.
96. Note that, because she has already been convinced by Rynaldo's *narratio*, she delivers her *peroratio* at once. Such a positioning is recommended in the *Rhetorica ad Herennium* 1954, II. XXX. 47, p. 144.
97. On the platitudes voiced by the king as well as the countess, see Price 1979, esp. p. 95. On the significance of the countess's age see Cloud 1991.

and turning to a *confirmatio* if he or she is speaking in prosecution or a *refutatio* in defence.[98] It is only at this juncture that the flow is interrupted. Whenever Shakespeare includes a formal *peroratio*, this is never spoken by the plaintiff or the defendant, but always by the judge of the case. The effect is to enable him to pronounce sentence in two separable meanings of the term. He announces his verdict, but he also takes the opportunity to insert a number of *sententiae* to round off the case and in some instances to bring the play to a close.

Sometimes, however, Shakespeare does not wish his judicial scenes to end on such a conventionally resonant note, and in these cases he omits a formal *peroratio* altogether. This is what happens after Antony puts forward the *prohoemium*, the *narratio*, and the *confirmatio* of his charge that Brutus has conspired against Rome. Antony concludes by reading Caesar's will, demonstrating that Caesar had no wish to enslave the people, as Brutus had alleged, but rather to benefit them. 'Heere was a *Caesar*', he ends, 'when comes such another?'[99] The judges of his cause are the plebeians, and according to the rhetoricians this would be the moment for one of them to pronounce a grand *peroratio* in which the virtues of stable government and the values of princely liberality could equally well have been extolled. But this would obviously have slackened the dramatic pace, and Shakespeare prefers to press on with the violent action to which Antony's speech immediately gives rise:

> 2. PLEBEIAN Go fetch fire.
> 3. PLEBEIAN Plucke downe Benches.
> 4. PLEBEIAN Plucke downe Formes, Windowes, any thing.[100]
>
> TLN 1636–8, p. 693 (3. 2. 247–9)

Nor does Antony feel that anything further needs to be said. Action is what he wants himself, as he ends by pointing out: 'Now let it worke: Mischeefe thou art a-foot,/ Take thou what course thou wilt'.[101]

There is one other court scene in which Shakespeare altogether dispenses with a formal *peroratio*. Portia manages in Act 4 of *The Merchant of Venice* to produce a *refutatio* of Shylocke's contention that his plea is an instance of a

---

98. Strictly speaking the *confirmatio* in the closing scene of *All's Well That Ends Well* is jointly produced by Diana and Hellen when the former provides the cue for the latter's entrance at the end.

99. *Julius Caesar*, TLN 1631, p. 693 (3. 2. 242).

100. As before, I follow the numbering of the plebeians given in the First Folio. See Shakespeare 1996, *Julius Caesar*, TLN 1795–7, p. 731.

101. *Julius Caesar*, TLN 1639–40, p. 693 (3. 2. 250–1).

constitutio iuridicalis, after which the case moves quickly to a close. The duke grants Shylocke his life, upon which Anthonio petitions him to remit the state's share of Shylocke's goods and gains permission to make use of the other half himself. Anthonio further demands that Shylocke become a Christian, and that he bequeath his possessions at his death to Lorenzo and Jessica. Agreeing to these conditions, the defeated Shylocke finally leaves the court. It only remains for the duke, as judge, to conclude with a fittingly sententious *peroratio.* But when Shylocke asks for the deed of gift to be sent for him to sign, the duke's sole response is 'Get thee gone, but doe it'.[102] He then turns to the learned young Dr Balthazer. 'Sir I entreate you home with me to dinner'.[103] Portia excuses herself, explaining that she must return to Padua and needs to leave at once. The duke expresses polite disappointment:

> I am sorry that your leysure serves you not.
> *Anthonio,* gratifie this gentleman,
> For in my mind you are much bound to him.
>
> TLN 2211–13, p. 504 (4. 1. 401–3)

This would be the moment for the duke to add a ringing *peroratio* on such obviously relevant themes as justice, mercy, magnanimity, and gratitude. But Portia has already regaled us with a considerable number of such *loci communes,* and Shakespeare has no use for another conventionally eloquent speech. Having reminded Anthonio of how much he owes to Dr Balthazer, the duke and his attendants simply sweep out.

If we now turn by contrast to the remaining court scenes I have discussed, we find in each instance that, after the plaintiff or defendant has developed a *confirmatio* or *refutatio,* the judge duly proceeds to pronounce a *peroratio* in the grand style. The earliest play in which this pattern is followed is *Romeo and Juliet.* After Friar Lawrence's narrative has been confirmed, the prince steps forward with a fittingly sombre *peroratio,* beginning with some reflections on the mutual hatred between the Mountagues and Capulets. The commonplace books have much to say about the power of such hostilities to destroy civic peace. Blague notes that 'by concorde small things increase' and by discord 'great things waste and consume.'[104] Ling agrees that 'cittizens in a Common-weale, by their concord maintain the state, but by their hatreds

---

102. *The Merchant of Venice,* TLN 2203, p. 504 (4. 1. 393).
103. *The Merchant of Venice,* TLN 2207, p. 504 (4. 1. 397).   104. Blague 1572, p. 34.

destroy it',[105] adding that 'concord maketh small thinges mightily to increase, but discord maketh great things sodainly to decay'.[106] These are likewise the thoughts that echo in the prince's mind as he turns to the parties involved:

> Where be these enemies? *Capulet, Mountague?*
> See what a scourge is laide upon your hate?
> That heaven finds means to kil your joyes with love,
> And I for winking at your discords too,
> Have lost a brace of kinsmen, all are punisht.
>
> TLN 2980–4, p. 412 (5. 3. 291–5)

Like the countess in *All's Well*, the prince converts the clichés of the commonplace books into a new and compacted image. The joys are the young lovers who have died, and heaven has additionally punished their families by causing their children to die for love. For the substance of the speech, however, the prince remains content to follow the rhetorical principle that the best way to arouse the feelings of an audience is simply to repeat familiar beliefs in lofty tones. As a result, he has nothing to add to the well-worn *topos*, originally owed to Sallust, that civic discord inevitably brings destruction upon all.[107]

After this preliminary judgement, the second part of the prince's *peroratio* brings the play to an end. He acknowledges that the tragedy has at last prompted the Mountagues and Capulets to make a declaration of peace. But, as the commonplace books regularly point out, such an outcome can hardly be regarded as a happy or even a stable one. Cogan warns that 'the longer the strife endureth, the more it burneth',[108] while Ling adds that 'Deere and unprofitable is the peace, that is bought with guiltlesse blood'.[109] These anxieties are likewise at the forefront of the prince's mind as he launches into his highly charged conclusion, the closing sestet of a Sonnet:

> A glooming peace this morning with it brings,
>   The Sun for sorrow will not shew his head:
> Go hence to have more talke of these sad things,
>   Some shall be pardond, and some punished.

---

105. [Ling] 1598, fo. 7ᵛ.   106. [Ling] 1598, fo. 8ʳ.
107. The source of the *topos* to which Blague and Ling both refer is Sallust's *Bellum Iugurthinum*. See Sallust 1931, X. 6, p. 148: 'concordia parvae res crescunt, discordia maxumae dilabuntur'.
108. Cogan 1577, p. 106.   109. [Ling] 1598, fo. 7ʳ.

> For never was a Storie of more wo,
> Then this of *Juliet* and her *Romeo*.
>
> TLN 2994–9, p. 412 (5. 3. 305–10)

Although the warring families have promised to live in harmony, the final couplet recalls not their hopes but the tragic events of the immediate past, and the play ends on a rhetorically conventional as well as a profoundly cheerless note.

A classical *peroratio* likewise brings to a close the court scene in Act I of *Othello*. After Desdemona's *confirmatio* of her love for Othello, Brabantio's accusation is dismissed. He is prostrated with grief, but there is no legal remedy and the only remaining question is how to cope with his defeat. The commonplace books have an endless number of determinedly optimistic suggestions to make. Sometimes they point out that, once misfortune has struck, you can at least be said to know where you stand.[110] But their chief admonition is that if you resign yourself to sorrow you will only make things worse. Cogan offers the warning 'take no heaviness to heart',[111] and Ling adds that 'the comforting of griefe, is phisick to maintaine griefe'.[112] Meanwhile we are exhorted to muster as much patience as possible. Blague notes the saying that 'a wise man will stoutly beare out that which by no meanes can be avoided',[113] and Baldwin adds that 'one of the vertues that a wise man ought to have' is 'that he can suffer well'.[114] We are also said to have good reason for displaying fortitude. 'Patience', Germbergius explains, 'is a noble form of conquering, for he who suffers also scores a triumph'.[115] Ling is particularly emphatic about the importance of appearing not to care. Under the heading 'Patience' we read that 'the sweetest salve to mishap is patience, & no greater revenge can be offered to fortune, then to rest content in the midst of misery',[116] while under the heading 'Fortune' we are told that 'there can be no greater check to the pride of Fortune, then with a resolute courage to passe over her crosses without care'.[117]

---

110. See, for example, [Ling] 1598, fo. 121^r. Dent 1981, p. 261 notes that 'To know the worst is good' was a proverb.

111. Cogan 1577, p. 22, quoting *Ecclesiasticus* 38. 20.

112. [Ling] 1598, fo. 159^v. A French proverb. See Delamothe 1595, p. 43: 'He that comfortes a greefe, makes it renew againe.'

113. Blague 1572, p. 129.   114. Baldwin 1579, fo. 149^r.

115. Germbergius 1577, p. 159: 'Nobile vincendi genus est patientia: vincit, qui patitur.' Cf. Baldwin 1579, fo. 148^v.

116. [Ling] 1598, fo. 60^r.

117. [Ling] 1598, fo. 113^r. For similar reflections see also [Bodenham] 1600, pp. 100, 151.

These are precisely the reflections that occur to the duke of Venice as he
turns to comfort Brabantio. He begins by announcing that he will 'lay a
sentence' upon him, and he does so in both senses of the term.[118] He has
already given his verdict on the case, which is that Brabantio must 'Take up
this mangled matter at the best'.[119] He now draws the trial to a close by
delivering a *peroratio* replete with encouraging 'sentences':

> When remedies are past, the griefes are ended,
> By seeing the worst, which late on hopes depended,
> To mourne a mischeife that is past and gone,
> Is the next way to draw new mischiefe on;
> What cannot be preserv'd when fortune takes,
> Patience her injury a mockery makes.
> The rob'd that smiles, steales something from the thiefe,
> He robs himselfe, that spends a bootelesse griefe.
>
> TLN 487–94, p. 934 (1. 3. 200–7)

Like the countess in *All's Well*, and like the prince in *Romeo and Juliet*, the
duke follows the rhetorical principle that the surest way to make a successful
emotional appeal will be to call on images and assumptions already familiar
to one's audience. As a result, and despite the grandeur of his verse, the
content of his speech again veers towards the commonplace in the pejorative no less than the technical sense of the term.

I turn lastly to the court battle that occupies the closing scene of *All's Well
That Ends Well*. After Hellen's *confirmatio* of her claim that Bertram has
unknowingly slept with her, Bertram finally seems to welcome her love and
it only remains for the king of France to offer a celebratory *peroratio*. The idea
that a happy ending may be all the happier if, as in Hellen's case, some
intervening bitterness has been overcome, is one that frequently recurs in the
commonplace books. Under the heading 'Content', Ling includes the maxim
'the ende of calamitie is the beginning of content, & after misery, always ensues
most happy felicitie'.[120] Meres is especially interested in such joyful reversals
of ill-fortune and offers numerous *sententiae* on the theme. One promises that
'of harde beginninges proceedeth great pleasure',[121] while another maintains
that 'of the greatest and sorest labours comes the sweetest fruits'.[122]

---

118. *Othello*, TLN 484, p. 934 (1. 3. 197).   119. *Othello*, TLN 458, p. 934 (1. 3. 171).
120. [Ling]1598, fo. 210ʳ.   121. Meres 1598, fo. 208ᵛ.
122. Meres 1598, fo. 208ᵛ. The underlying proverb is of course (in Heywood's formulation) 'all is
     well that endeth well'. See Heywood 1546, Sig. C, 3ᵛ. Dent 1981, p. 48 mentions earlier
     instances.

These are likewise the sentiments with which the king of France, addressing himself to Diana, brings the play to an end:

> Let us from point to point this storie know,
> To make the even truth in pleasure flow:
> If thou beest yet a fresh uncropped flower,
> Choose thou thy husband, and Ile pay thy dower.
> For I can guesse, that by thy honest ayde,
> Thou keptst a wife her selfe, thy selfe a Maide.
> Of that and all the progresse more and lesse,
> Resolvedly more leasure shall expresse:
> All yet seemes well, and if it end so meete,
> The bitter past, more welcome is the sweet.

TLN 2845–54, p. 998 (5. 3. 314–23)

The king speaks in rhymed couplets in the grand style, and offers a handsome tribute to the honesty of Diana's cause. Like the duke in *Othello*, however, he never rises above the commonplace wisdom on which his speech is based. More troublingly, he does not even seem sure that the bitter past is indeed over, and thus that the happy present can be welcomed by everyone. The most he feels able to say is that all seems to be well, and the play ends on this doubtful and irresolute note.[123]

From commonplaces to the commonplace

It often seems that Shakespeare has a constitutional antipathy towards the conclusive and the disambiguated, and this may help to explain his tendency to avoid definitive perorations and conventionally resonant commonplaces. He was also writing at a time when the practice of searching for such *sententiae* and reasoning on the basis of their authority was beginning to be called into question, and there are several signs that he may to some degree have shared these doubts. Although Hamlet keeps a commonplace book, he sounds less than enthusiastic about the sort of wisdom that such compilations generally contain. He voices his scepticism early in the play when Claudius and Gertrard are attempting to persuade him that he is mourning excessively for his father's death. The question of how much grief it is

---

123. On these closing moments and their ambiguities see Donaldson 1977, pp. 48–9, 53–4; Lewis 1990, pp. 165–7.

proper to display was one that greatly preoccupied the compilers of commonplace books, and they tended to take the view—with which Claudius
firmly agrees—that it is unmanly and perhaps even impious to mourn too
long. The main reason they give is that death is so omnipresent that we
ought not to pay it any special heed. Under the heading 'Death' we find this
sentiment monotonously repeated: 'it is evident that all must die'; 'neces-
sarilie die all we must'; 'it is common to die'; 'what thing soever lives, is sure
to die'.[124] Gertrard duly urges Hamlet to 'cast thy nightly colour off',[125] and
seeks to hearten him with the relevant *topos*: 'Thou know'st tis common all
that lives must die'.[126] But Hamlet responds with what sounds like exas-
peration as well as weariness: 'I Maddam, it is common'.[127] Death is indeed
common, but the observation is so commonplace as to have lost any force.

I have been much concerned throughout this book with the idea that
forensic arguments depend in part for their persuasiveness on their specific
place in a speech. If this is so, then it is perhaps not surprising that Gertrard's
sententia, bereft as it is of any judicial context, appears somewhat flat and
stale. Sometimes, however, what Shakespeare seems to doubt is whether *loci
communes*, wherever they are placed in a speech, have any value at all. He
raises the question most explicitly at the moment in Act 1 of *Othello* when
the duke pronounces his *peroratio*, calling on Brabantio to show fortitude in
the face of his grief. His intention is to round off Othello's trial, but
Brabantio refuses to accept that the process is at an end. No sooner has
the duke delivered his purportedly encouraging words than Brabantio reacts
with a determined repudiation of the very idea that it is possible to comfort
anyone with such banal *sententiae*.[128] As we have seen, Shakespeare normally avoids set pieces that have the effect of holding up the dramatic action,
but in this case he deliberately brings the scene to a halt by inserting a further
peroratio in which Brabantio echoes the duke's sonorous couplets while
rebuking their complacency at the same time:

> He beares the sentence well that nothing beares,
> But the free comfort, which from thence he heares:
> But he beares both the sentence and the sorrow,

---

124. Blague, 1572, p. 113; Marbeck, 1581, p. 294; Mirandula 1598, p. 502; [Bodenham] 1600,
     p. 232. Cf. Donker 1992, pp. 133–4, noting that Erasmus' *Declamatio de morte* treats the same
     theme.
125. *Hamlet*, TLN 224, p. 739 (1. 2. 68).   126. *Hamlet*, TLN 228, p. 739 (1. 2. 72).
127. *Hamlet*, TLN 230, p. 739 (1. 2. 74).
128. For a discussion see Nicholson 2010, pp. 75–6.

That to pay griefe, must of poore patience borrow.
These sentences to sugar, or to gall,
Being strong on both sides, are equivocall:
But words are words, I never yet did heare,
That the bruis'd heart was pierced through the eare:

TLN 497–504, p. 934 (I. 3. 210–17)

The duke's 'sentences', Brabantio defiantly retorts, have no power to bear him up. Referring to the two main elements in the theory of *loci communes*, he first observes that, as the rhetoricians had conceded, such *sententiae* are common in the sense of being available to both parties in a dispute. But if they are 'strong on both sides', as Brabantio puts it, they can scarcely be said to offer any unequivocal help or support. No less deluded is the belief that mere words can ever hope to lance and thereby cure the ills of the heart. With his dismissal of words as mere words, Brabantio comes close to treating the entire theory of commonplaces with contempt.

Brabantio's doubts were beginning to be voiced much more generally at around the same time. Montaigne speaks with memorable scorn when he comments in his *Essayes* (in John Florio's translation of 1603) that 'these rapsodies of common places, wherewith so many stuffe their study' amount to nothing more than 'a ridiculous-fond fruite of learning', giving rise to 'bookes made of things neither studied nor ever understood'. He does not hesitate to dismiss the entire practice as 'weake, childish and absurde'.[129] Etienne Molinier in his *Mirrour for Christian States* similarly rails against the 'ornaments' of rhetoric 'wherewith we seeke to conceale manifest defects', including the use of 'borrowed common places ill applied out of the povertie of a barren and constrained discourse'.[130] Churchmen were particularly advised to avoid the highflown and evasive language in which *loci communes* were habitually expressed. John Dove in his 1601 tract on divorce warns that 'true preaching doth not consist in heaping up of common places, in prolixity and length of speech', while the elder Antoine Arnauld in his attack on the Jesuits, translated in 1602, denounces them for 'seeking out large fields of plausible common places' and thereby refusing to argue and 'come to the poynt'.[131] A generation later, we find John Donne speaking in his Sermons in yet more contemptuous terms of 'Common

---

129. Montaigne 1603, Bk. 3, ch. 12, p. 629.
130. Molinier 1635, p. 345. On Molinier and pulpit oratory see Bayley 1980, esp. pp. 91–8.
131. Dove 1601, Sig. A, 8ʳ; Arnauld 1602, p. 79.

placers' who merely collect 'ragges and fragments' and patch them together 'for their purpose, and to serve their turne'.[132]

These doubts soon broadened out into a critique of rhetorical invention as a whole. The theory of *loci communes* had been based on the premise that in legal and political debate the aim should be to 'invent' and apply whatever arguments are already believed to carry persuasive force. But this cardinal assumption about the importance of arguing from accepted principles now began to come under powerful attack. The most destructive assault was launched by Thomas Hobbes in *The Elements of Law*, which he circulated in 1640.[133] Hobbes introduces a fundamental distinction between teaching the truth and merely persuading people to entertain beliefs. It is mere persuasion when writers accept as principles 'those opinions which are already vulgarly received', so that they simply 'take up maxims from their education, and from the authority of men' instead of using scientific methods of reasoning to arrive at new truths.[134] To 'invent' arguments in this rhetorical style, and thereby 'take the habitual discourse of the tongue for ratiocination', is no longer regarded by Hobbes as a valid species of argument.[135] If there is a process of 'invention' to be followed, it cannot consist of uncovering something already there; it must take the form of discovering or devising new ways of doing things for the first time. Hobbes is one of the earliest writers to make consistent use of the term 'invention' in this novel and to us more familiar sense, as when he speaks about the invention of the alphabet or the later invention of printing.[136] Once this contrasting understanding of what it means to speak of inventing something began to take hold, the central role played by rhetorical *inventio* in English education could no longer be sustained. The phase in the cultural history of the Renaissance with which I have been concerned finally came to an end.

132. Donne 1953–62, vol. VI, p. 56. On this passage see Ettenhuber 2011, p. 50. Ben Jonson similarly equates commonplaces with the commonplace when he makes Jack Daw in *Epicoene* dismiss Aristotle as 'a mere common place fellow'. See Jonson 1620, Sig. D, 3ᵛ.

133. For Hobbes's attack on the theory of rhetorical invention see Skinner 1996, pp. 257–67 and Bassakos 2010. For further reflections on the turn against rhetoric see Vickers 1988, pp. 196–213; Skinner 2002b; Mann 2012, pp. 201–18.

134. Hobbes 1969 [1640], 13. 3–4, pp. 66–7.   135. Hobbes 1969 [1640], 13. 4, p. 67.

136. Hobbes 2012 [1651], vol. 2, ch. 4, p. 48.

Appendix: The Date of *All's Well That Ends Well*

It used to be generally agreed that the terminal date for the completion of *All's Well That Ends Well* was 1603 or 1604.[1] Then a number of commentators began to voice a preference for 1605.[2] Both suggestions have now been thrown into doubt. The challenge originated with an article published by Macdonald Jackson in *Notes and Queries* in 2001 in which he declared that '*All's Well That Ends Well* cannot have been composed earlier than mid-1606.'[3] As Laurie Maguire and Emma Smith rightly observe in their 2012 essay about the authorship of *All's Well*, 'Jackson's post-1606 dating is winning widespread acceptance.'[4] Wells and Taylor in their revised version of *The Complete Works* propose a new terminal date of 1607.[5] Jonathan Bate and Eric Rasmussen in their 2007 edition countenance a terminal date of 1606.[6] Catherine Alexander in her collection of 2009 on Shakespeare's last plays unequivocally assigns *All's Well* to 1607.[7] Lois Potter in her biography of 2012 notes that the play has been redated, refers her readers to Jackson's article and discusses *All's Well* in her chapter on the years 1606–09.[8] Maguire and Smith are enthusiastic about this recent tendency to shift the date of the play, as they put it, 'from 1602–03 to 1606–07 (or later)'.[9] Perhaps too enthusiastic, for hardly anyone has defended a terminal date of earlier than 1603 or later than 1607. Nevertheless, when challenged by Brian Vickers and Marcus Dahl, Maguire and Smith felt sufficiently confident to respond by dismissing them as 'flat-earthers' who 'cling to an old date for *AWEW* (1604 rather than 1607 or later)'.[10]

Maguire and Smith's proposed re-dating is bound up with their claim that Shakespeare wrote *All's Well* jointly with Thomas Middleton, a collaboration that in turn suggests a date considerably later than the traditional one. This alleged collaboration, however, has been persuasively questioned by Vickers and Dahl,

---

1. For 1603 as the terminal date see Chambers 1930, vol. 1, p. 451; Bullough 1957–75, vol. 2, p. 375. This judgement is still endorsed in Blakemore Evans 1997, pp. 85, 536, and Leggatt 2003, p. 11. For 1604 see Hunter 1959, p. xxv. The exceptions are Haley, 1993, pp. 9, 256, who argues for 1600, and Melchiori 1994, p. 443, who argues for 1602.
2. For 1605 as the terminal date see Fraser 1985, p. 5; Wells and Taylor 1987, pp. 126–7; Snyder 1993, pp. 23–4. This is the judgement accepted in Greenblatt 1997, p. 3386.
3. Jackson 2001, p. 299.   4. Maguire and Smith 2012a, p. 13.
5. Shakespeare 2005, p. x.   6. Bate and Rasmussen 2007, p. 587.
7. Alexander 2009, p. xiii.   8. Potter 2012, pp. 335, 358.
9. Maguire and Smith 2012a, p. 13.   10. Maguire and Smith, 2012b, p. 6.

who have concluded that *All's Well* is wholly Shakespeare's work.[11] The effect is to return us to Jackson's original reason for proposing a date for the play of no earlier than mid 1606. Jackson's argument centres on the moment in Act 2 when Parrolles boasts that he was responsible for inflicting a scar on the left cheek of 'one Captaine *Spurio*'.[12] According to Jackson, the only other play from Shakespeare's time in which the name Spurio occurs is Thomas Middleton's *The Revenger's Tragedy*, and Jackson conjectures that 'if one dramatist was influenced by another's introduction of the name Spurio to the English stage, Shakespeare must surely have been the debtor'.[13] Middleton's play, Jackson notes, was written and first performed in the spring of 1606. Hence his conclusion that *All's Well* cannot have been composed earlier than the middle of that year.

It is not clear, however, why we should assume that Shakespeare must have taken the name Spurio from some other writer as opposed to thinking of it for himself. This possibility is strengthened by the fact that the name is obviously a joke. The Latin *spurius*, in Italian *spurio*, basically means 'bastard'. Thomas Cooper in his Latin–English *Thesaurus* of 1565 offers as his first definition of *spurius* 'Borne of a common woman: base borne: that knoweth not who is his father'.[14] John Florio in *A Worlde of Wordes*, his Italian–English dictionary of 1598, similarly offers as his first definition of *spúrio* 'a whores sonne whose father is not know, a bastard, one base borne'.[15]

There is a further layer to the joke, and one that suggests even more strongly that the name must be Shakespeare's own conceit. This is the fact that it offers him such a good means of commenting on the character of Parrolles. A secondary way in which the word 'spurious' was used in Shakespeare's time was to refer to anything false or counterfeit, anything sham or made up. Cooper offers 'counterfayte' as his second definition,[16] and Florio agrees that the word is 'used for a counterfeit'.[17] But as Hellen warns us in the opening scene of *All's Well*, Parrolles is 'a notorious Liar' and 'solie a coward'.[18] With the name Spurio, Shakespeare appears to be alerting us to the strong probability that the wounded Captain may be no more than a figment of Parrolles's imagination.[19] Parrolles himself is certainly a spurious character, whose pretentious dress and mendacious speech might well be said—as Ben Jonson says of Crispinus in *Poetaster*—to be marked by 'spurious Snotteries'.[20]

Suppose, however, we accept Jackson's unargued assumption that Shakespeare cannot have made up the name, but must have taken it from some other source.

11. They responded in the *Times Literary Supplement* 5693 (11 May 2012), but for the full presentation of their evidence see the *Institute of English Studies* website at http://www.ies.sas.ac.uk/about-us/news/middleton-and-shakespeare
12. *All's Well That Ends Well*, TLN 600–1, p. 975 (2. 1. 41).   13. Jackson 2001, p. 299.
14. Cooper 1565, Sig. 6A, 3ʳ.   15. Florio 1598, p. 393. See also Perceval 1599, p. 224.
16. Cooper 1565, Sig. 6A, 3ʳ.   17. Florio 1598, p. 393.
18. *All's Well That Ends Well*, TLN 100–1, p. 970 (1. 1. 88–9).
19. For a similar suggestion see Potter 2012, p. 337.   20. Jonson 1602, Sig. M, 3ᵛ.

This still gives us no reason to conclude that he must have taken it from Middleton. Shakespeare adapted much of the plot of *All's Well* from William Painter's *Palace of Pleasure* of 1566. The tale appears as novell thirty-eight in the collection,[21] but Shakespeare would only have needed to glance through the earlier part of the book to come upon novell five, taken from Livy, which tells the tragic story of Virginia's sufferings at the hands of Appius Claudius. There he would have found the name Spurius as the opening word of the story, with the initial 'S' rendered in a fine and eye-catching woodcut.[22] It could easily have caught his eye.

A yet more probable source is Alexander Silvayn's collection of declamations, which had been translated and published by Lazarus Piot under the title *The Orator* in 1596.[23] Silvayn's ninety-fifth declamation is entitled: '*Of a Jew, who would for his debt have a pound of the flesh of a Christian*'.[24] Shakespeare drew on this passage in writing *The Merchant of Venice*, in which he echoes several of Piot's turns of phrase.[25] If he had paused at the fifth declamation while looking through the collection, he would have seen that it was entitled: '*Of Spurius Servilius, who defended himself against the people, being by them accused for his cowardly fighting*'.[26] Parrolles likewise faces a charge of cowardly fighting, and when his courage is tested it turns out to be as spurious as everything else about him.

An obvious objection is that the name in both the cases I have cited is Spurius rather than Spurio. But there are several other instances in which Shakespeare comes upon a Latin name in one of his sources and converts it into its Italian form. This happens in *Romeo and Juliet*, in which he draws most of his plot from Arther Brooke's poem of 1562. There the hero appears as Romeus, which Shakespeare translates into Romeo.[27] Something similar happens in *Othello*, in which several details are taken from Richard Knolles's *The Generall Historie of the Turke* of 1603. Knolles speaks of Angelus Sorianus,[28] the commander of a Venetian galley at the time of the invasion of Cyprus.[29] Shakespeare turns him into Signior Angelo, from whom a report is received about a possible Turkish attack on Rhodes.[30] The same thing happens again in *All's Well*. Shakespeare's sources speak of Spurius, but Parrolles makes it clear that his alleged encounter with the Captain took place in Italy,[31] so Shakespeare translates Spurius into Spurio.

Jackson's speculations about the name Spurio give us no reason, in short, to accept a date for *All's Well* as late as 1606, to say nothing of later. To what date, then, should the play be assigned? It seems to me that the balance of evidence still tells heavily in favour of the conclusion widely accepted before Jackson made his intervention: that *All's Well* was almost certainly written in the latter half of 1604 or the early months of 1605.

---

21. Painter 1566, fos. 95ʳ–100ᵛ.   22. Painter 1566, fo. 13ʳ.   23. Silvayn 1596.
24. Silvayn 1596, p. 400.   25. Silvayn 1596, pp. 401, 402.   26. Silvayn 1596, p. 34.
27. Brooke 1562.   28. Knolles 1603, p. 839.
29. Bullough 1957–75, vol. 7, p. 262 and note.
30. *Othello*, TLN 300–2, p. 932 (1. 3. 14–16).
31. *All's Well That Ends Well*, TLN 585, 599–601, pp. 974–5 (2. 1. 26, 40–1).

Before offering my evidence, I need to note the implications of endorsing this earlier date. The effect is to disjoin *All's Well* from its alleged connections—recently much emphasized[32]—with Shakespeare's so-called late romances, and to realign it with *Othello* and *Measure for Measure*, both of which are generally agreed to have been written between 1603 and 1604.[33] As for the evidence that *All's Well* was written at around the same time, it is strong and varied in character. First, it is worth recalling three stylistic tests that have been applied to the canon as a whole. Eliot Slater published an analysis in 1977 of word links between *All's Well* and Shakespeare's other plays. Of the two tests he used, one showed a statistically significant excess of links with only two plays, *Troilus and Cressida* and *Measure for Measure*, while his other revealed that the closest links were with *Measure for Measure* and *Othello*.[34] Next, John Fitch produced a statistical survey in 1981 of sense-pauses within complete blank verse lines,[35] refining and correcting Chambers's pioneering analysis of 1930.[36] The resulting percentages turned out to be almost identical for *Othello* and *All's Well*, the next closest plays being *Timon of Athens* and *Measure for Measure*.[37] Finally, the colloquialism-in-verse test reported by Wells and Taylor in 1987 suggests, once again, that the play closest in time to *All's Well* is *Measure for Measure*.[38]

The conclusion to which these linguistic tests point is that *All's Well* must have been written later than—but not much later than—*Measure for Measure*.[39] If we now recall the plotting and organization of the two plays, we come upon further evidence to the same effect. Both plots hinge around a bed trick, with the exposure of the victim occupying much of the closing scene. A further parallel is that a character named Mariana appears in both plays to comment on the infidelity of men,[40] while other names—Escalus, Lodowick—of importance in *Measure for Measure* recur more incidentally in *All's Well*, as if Shakespeare were drawing on a stock already in his mind.[41] Most significant is the fact that in both plays, as well as in *Othello*, the dramaturgy is extensively indebted to the classical theory of rhetorical invention in 'conjectural' and 'juridical' causes. A further word needs to be said about this final point.

As I try to show in the body of this book, two distinct 'conjectural' causes are pursued in *Othello*. Brabantio attempts in Act 1 to confirm his conjecture that

---

32. See, for example, McMullan 2009, p. 10; Altman 2010, pp. 39–41; Maguire and Smith, 2012a, p. 13.
33. For references see above, ch. 2, notes 52–7.   34. Slater 1977, pp. 109–12.
35. Fitch 1981, pp. 289–307.   36. Chambers 1930, vol. 2, pp. 401–2.
37. Fitch 1981, p. 300.   38. Wells and Taylor 1987, pp. 101–6, 127.
39. This in itself seems sufficient to dismiss the dating of 1600 proposed in Haley 1993.
40. As noted in Walker 1982.
41. Escalus is Angelo's second-in-command in *Measure for Measure*. For the recurrence of the name see *All's Well That Ends Well*, TLN 1570, p. 985 (3. 5. 70). Lodowick is the name assumed by the Duke in *Measure for Measure*. For its recurrence see *All's Well That Ends Well*, TLN 2105, p. 990. (4. 3. 138). For Mariana see *Measure for Measure*, TLN 1318, p. 909 (3. 1. 200) and *All's Well That Ends Well*, TLN 1502, p. 984 (3. 5. 8).

Othello must have practised witchcraft on Desdemona, while Iago succeeds in Act 3 in persuading Othello of his fabricated conjecture that Desdemona is conducting a love affair with Cassio. In *Measure for Measure* Shakespeare turns to 'juridical' causes, invoking the classical rules to provide the structure of two crucial scenes. In Act 2 Isabella comes before Angelo to plead an assumptive case, while in Act 5 she presents the duke with what she claims to be an absolute form of a *constitutio iuridicalis,* accusing Angelo of misusing his office and attempting to establish the rightfulness of her charge.

With one exception, no other play from Shakespeare's Jacobean years reflects any similar concern with the classical principles of forensic eloquence. The exception is *All's Well,* in which the rules are deployed in the same way as in *Othello* and *Measure for Measure,* although at a new level of complexity. In Act I Rynaldo presents a *constitutio coniecturalis,* offering a conjecture about the cause of Hellen's melancholy that the countess is able to confirm. In Act 5 Diana and her mother introduce another *constitutio iuridicalis* when they appear before the king of France to present an absolute case against Count Bertram. Meanwhile, the king engages in a yet further *constitutio coniecturalis,* addressing himself in the closing scene to the mystery of how Count Bertram came into possession of Hellen's ring.

To insist that Shakespeare wrote *All's Well* in 1606 (or even later) is to ask us to believe that, after exhibiting such a fascination with judicial rhetoric in *Othello* and *Measure for Measure* between 1603 and 1604, he lost any interest in its dramaturgical possibilities for several years, only to return to the same rhetorical techniques in *All's Well,* after which he lost interest in them once again. This seems inherently less probable than that all three plays were composed during the same period of Shakespeare's intense absorption in the theory of forensic eloquence.

If we combine these considerations with the other pieces of evidence I have assembled, we are brought back to something like the conclusion voiced in the Arden edition of *All's Well* as long ago as 1959: that *Measure for Measure* and *All's Well* are 'obvious twins'.[42] The metaphor admittedly embodies an exaggeration, since no one believes that they were conceived on the same date. But they undoubtedly stand in a close relationship with one another, so close as to suggest that they must have taken shape in Shakespeare's mind at around the same time. I conclude that, just as *Measure for Measure* was probably written soon after *Othello,* so *All's Well* was probably written soon after *Measure for Measure,* and I date its completion to the early months of 1605.[43]

42. Hunter 1959, p. xxiii.
43. This Appendix is based on Skinner 2013 and appears here by kind permission of the editors of *Notes and Queries* and Oxford University Press.

Bibliography

PRIMARY SOURCES

Adlington, William (1566). *The xi. bookes of the Golden asse . . . enterlaced with sondrie pleasaunt and delectable tales*, London.

Arber, Edward (1875–94). *A Transcript of the Registers of the Company of Stationers of London; 1554–1640AD*, London.

Aristotle (1926). *The 'Art' of Rhetoric*, trans. John Henry Freese, London.

Arnauld, Antoine (1602). *A Discourse*, trans. William Watson, London.

Aubrey, John (1898). *Brief Lives, chiefly of Contemporaries*, ed. Andrew Clark, 2 vols, Oxford.

Augustine, Saint (1610). *St. Augustine, Of the Citie of God*, trans. John Healey, London.

Baldwin, William (1579). *A treatice of morall philosophy contaynynge the sayinges of the wyse, . . . whose woorthy sentences, notable preceptes, counsailes, parables and semblables, doe hereafter followe*, London.

[Baxter, J.] (1600). *A toile for two-legged foxes Wherein their noisome properties; their hunting and unkenelling, with the duties of the principall hunters and guardians of the spirituall vineyard is livelie discovered*, London.

Blague, Thomas (1572). *A schole of wise Conceytes . . . set forth in common places by order of the Alphabet*, London.

[Bodenham, John] (1600). *Bel vedere or the Garden of the Muses*, London.

Brinsley, John (1622). *A Consolation for our Grammar Schooles*, London.

Brooke, Arther (1562). *The Tragicall Historye of Romeus and Juliet*, London.

Butler, Charles (1598). *Rhetoricae Libri Duo Quorum Prior de Tropis & Figuris, Posterior de Voce & Gestu Praecipit*, Oxford.

Caius, John (1576). *Of Englishe Dogges*, trans. Abraham Fleming, London.

Campion, Thomas (1602). *Observations in the Art of English Poesie*, London.

Castiglione, Baldassare (1612). *De Curiali Sive Aulico, Libri quatuor*, London.

——(1994). *The Book of the Courtier*, ed. Virginia Cox, London.

Cawdray, Robert (1600). *A Treasurie or store-house of Similes . . . Newly collected into Heads and Common places*, London.

Chapman, George (1594). *The Shaddow of Night: Containing Two Poeticall Hymnes*, London.

——(1611). *The Iliads of Homer Prince of Poets*, London.

Chapman, George (1614). *Homer's Odysses*, London.

Churchyard, Thomas (1579). *A generall rehearsall of warres*, London.

Cicero, Marcus Tullius (1481). *M. T. Ciceronis . . . Rhetoricae veteris liber I . . . rhetoricorum veterum liber ultimus . . . M. Tullii Ciceronis Rhetoricae novae ad Herenium*, Venice.

——(1539). *Rhetoricorum M. Tullii Ciceronis ad C. Herennium Libri IIII . . . Eiusdem M. Tullii Ciceronis de inventione rhetorica libri II*, Cologne.

——(1546). *Rhetoricorum ad C. herennium libri IIII. incerto auctore. Ciceronis De Inventione libri II*, Venice.

——(1550). *Rhetoricum ad C. Herennium libri Quattuor. Eiusdem M. Tullii Ciceronis de inventione rhetorica libri duo*, Cologne.

——(1570). *Rhetoricorum ad C. Herennium libri quatuor. M. T. Ciceronis de Inventione libri duo, Johannis Michaelis Bruti animadversionibus illustrati*, Lyon.

——(1574). *Rhetoricorum M. T. Ciceronis ad C. Herennium, Libri IIII . . . Eiusdem M. T. Ciceronis de Inventione Rhetorica, Libri II*, London.

——(1579a). *Rhetoricorum ad C. Herennium Libri Quattuor. M. T. Ciceronis De Inventione Libri Duo*, London.

——(1579b). *Orationum Marci Tul. Ciceronis*, London.

——(1579c). *De Officiis Libri Tres. Cato maior, vel de Senectute. Laelius, vel de Amicitia. Paradoxa stoicorum sex. Somnium Scipionis, ex libro de Rep.*, London.

—— et alii (1584). *Sententiae Ciceronis, Demosthenis, Ac Terentii*, London.

——(1942a). *De oratore*, trans. E. W. Sutton and H. Rackham, 2 vols, London.

——(1942b). *De partitione oratoria*, trans. H. Rackham, London.

——(1949a). *De inventione*, trans. H. M. Hubbell, London.

——(1949b). *Topica*, trans. H. M. Hubbell, London.

——(1962a). *Brutus*, trans. H. M. Hubbell, rev. edn, London.

——(1962b). *Orator*, trans. H. M. Hubbell, rev. edn, London.

Cockaine, Thomas (1591). *A Short Treatise of Hunting*, London.

Cogan, Thomas (1577). *The Well of Wisedome, conteining chiefe and chosen sayings . . . bestowed in usuall common places in order of A. B. C.*, London.

Cooper, Thomas (1565). *Thesaurus Linguae Romanae & Britannicae*, London.

Copie of a Letter, The (1588). London.

Cornwallis, William (1600). *Essayes*, London.

[Cosin, Richard] (1591). *An Apologie for Sundrie Proceedings by Jurisdiction Ecclesiasticall*, London.

Cox, Leonard (1532). *The Art or crafte of Rhetoryke*, London.

Crompton, Richard (1587). *Loffice & aucthoritie de Justices de Peace*, London.

Dalton, Michael (1622). *The Countrey Justice . . . Newly corrected and inlarged*, London.

Day, Angel (1592). *A Declaration of all such Tropes, Figures or Schemes, as for excellencie and ornament in writing, are specially used in this Methode*, London.

Delamothe, G. (1595). *The Treasure of the French toung. Containing the rarest Sentences . . . set in order, after the Alphabeticall maner*, London.

Donne, John (1953–62). *The Sermons of John Donne*, ed. George R. Potter and Evelyn M. Simpson, 10 vols, Berkeley, CA.

Dove, John (1601). *Of divorcement*, London.

Elyot, Thomas (1531). *The boke named the Governour*, London.

——(1538). *The dictionary of syr Thomas Eliot knight*, London.

Erasmus, Desiderius (1569). *De duplici copia verborum, et rerum, Commentarii duo*, London.

[Fenner, Dudley] (1584). *The Artes of Logike and Rethorike*, Middelburg.

Fiorentino, Giovanni (1957). *Il pecorone*, trans. Geoffrey Bullough in *Narrative and Dramatic Sources of Shakespeare*, vol. 1, London, pp. 463–76.

Florio, John (1598). *A Worlde of Wordes, Or Most copious, and exact Dictionarie in Italian and English*, London.

Fraunce, Abraham (1588a). *The Arcadian rhetorike: or The praecepts of rhetorike made plaine by examples*, London.

——(1588b). *The Lawiers Logike, exemplifying the praecepts of Logike by the practise of the common Lawe*, London.

Gascoigne, George (1575). *The Noble Arte of Venerie*, London.

Germbergius, Hermann (1577). *Carminum Proverbialium . . . Loci Communes, in gratiam iuventutis selecti*, London.

Greene, Robert (1584). *The myrrour of modestie*, London.

——(1592). *Greenes, groats-worth of witte, bought with a million of repentance*, London.

Guazzo, Stefano (1581). *The civile conversation of M. Steeven Guazzo . . . translated out of French by George Pettie, devided into foure books*, London.

Guicciardini, Francesco (1599). *The Historie of Guicciardin . . . Reduced into English by Geffray Fenton*, London.

Harington, John (1591). *Orlando Furioso in English Heroical Verse*, London.

Heywood, John (1546). *A Dialogue conteinyng the number in effect of all the proverbs in the englishe tongue*, London.

——(1555). *Two hundred epigrammes, upon two hundred proverbes, with a thyrde hundred newely added*, London.

——(1566). *John Heywoodes woorkes*, London.

Hobbes, Thomas (1969). *The Elements of Law Natural and Politic*, ed. Ferdinand Tönnies, Introd. M. M. Goldsmith, London.

——(2012). *Leviathan*, ed. Noel Malcolm, 3 vols, Oxford.

Horace (2004). *Odes and Epodes*, trans. Niall Rudd, London.

Jonson, Ben (1602). *Poetaster or The Arraignment*, London.

——(1605). *Sejanus His Fall*, London.

——(1620). *Epicoene, or The Silent Woman*, London.

Kempe, William (1588). *The Education of children in learning: Declared by the Dignitie, Utilitie, and Method thereof*, London.

Knight, Edward (1580). *The triall of truth, wherein are discovered three greate enemies unto mankinde, as pride, private grudge, and private gaine*, London.

Knolles, Richard (1603). *The Generall Historie of the Turke*, London.

Lambarde, William (1592). *Eirenarcha: or of The office of the Justices of Peace . . . revised, corrected, and enlarged*, London.

[Ling, Nicholas] (1598). *Politeuphuia. Wits Common wealth*, London.

Lipsius, Justus (1594). *Sixe Bookes of Politickes or Civil Doctrine, . . . Done into English by William Jones*, London.

Livy (1919). *History of Rome Books I–II*, trans. B. O. Foster, London.

Longinus (1995). *On the Sublime*, trans. W. H. Fyfe, rev. Donald Russell, London, pp. 159–307.

Marbeck, John (1581). *A Booke Of Notes and Common places*, London.

[Markham, Gervase] (1595). *The Gentelmans Academie*, London.

Melanchthon, Philipp (1519). *De rhetorica libri tres*, Basel.

——(1539). *Rhetorices Elementa*, Lyon.

Meres, Francis (1598). *Palladis Tamia. Wits Treasury Being the Second part of Wits Common wealth*, London.

Mirabellius, Nanus (1600). *Polyanthea*, Lyon.

Mirandula, Octavianus (1598). *Illustrium Poetarum Flores . . . in locos communes digesti*, London.

Molinier, Etienne (1635). *A Mirrour for Christian States*, trans. William Tyrwhit, London.

Montaigne, Michel de (1603). *The Essayes Or Morall, Politike and Millitarie Discourses*, trans. John Florio, London.

Nashe, Thomas (1592). *Pierce Penilesse his Supplication to the Divell*, London.

Ovid (1582). *Metamorphoseon libri XV*, London.

——(1583a). *Fastorum Lib. VI. Tristium Lib. V. De Ponto Lib. IIII. In Ibim. Ad Liviam*, London.

——(1583b). *Heroidum Epistolae. Amorum Libri III. De arte amandi Libri III. De Remedio Amoris, Libri II*, London.

——(1996). *Fasti*, trans. James George Frazier, rev. G. P. Goold, London.

Painter, William (1566). *The Palace of Pleasure*, London.

Peacham, Henry (1577). *The Garden of Eloquence*, London.

——(1593). *The Garden of Eloquence . . . Corrected and augmented*, London.

Perceval, Richard (1599). *A dictionarie in Spanish and English, . . . Now enlarged and amplified*, London.

Philibert de Vienne (1575). *The Philosopher of the Court*, trans. George North, London.

Plato (2010). *Gorgias, Menexenus, Protagoras*, ed. Malcolm Schofield, trans. Tom Griffith, Cambridge.

Pliny (1940). *Natural History*, vol. 3, trans. H. Rackham, London.

Plutarch (1579). *The Lives of the Noble Grecians and Romanes . . . translated . . . into Englishe, by Thomas North*, London.

——(1603). *The Philosophie, commonlie called, The Morals*, trans. Philemon Holland, London.

[Puttenham, George] (1589). *The Arte of English Poesie*, London.

Quintilian (2001). *The Orator's Education (Institutio oratoria)*, trans. and ed. Donald
    A. Russell, 5 vols, London.
Rainolde, Richard (1563). *A booke called the Foundacion of Rhetorike*, London.
Ramus, Petrus (1964). *Dialectique*, ed. Michel Dassonville, Geneva.
Regius, Raphael (1492). *Ducenta problemata*, Venice.
Rhetorica ad Herennium (1954). Trans. and ed. Harry Caplan, London.
Rich, Barnabe (1959). *Rich's Farewell to Military Profession 1581*, ed. Thomas
    M. Cranfill, Austin, TX.
Saint German, Christopher (1974). *Doctor and Student*, ed. T. F. T Plucknett and
    J. L. Barton, London.
Sallust (1931). 'Bellum Jugurthinum', in *Sallust*, trans. J. C. Rolfe, revised edn,
    London, pp. 132–380.
Seneca (1920). *Epistles 66–92*, trans. Richard M. Gummere, London.
Shakespeare, William (1593). *Venus and Adonis*, London.
——(1594). *Lucrece*, London.
——(1597). *An Excellent conceited Tragedie of Romeo and Juliet. As it hath been often
    (with great applause) plaid publiquely, by the right Honourable the L. of Hunsdon his
    Servants*, London.
——(1600). *The most excellent historie of the merchant of Venice . . . As it hath beene
    divers times acted by the Lord Chamberlaine his Servants*, London.
——(1603). *The tragicall historie of Hamlet Prince of Denmarke by William Shake-speare.
    As it hath beene diverse times acted by his Highnesse servants in the cittie of London: as
    also in the two universities of Cambridge and Oxford, and else-where*, London.
——(1604). *The Tragicall Historie of Hamlet Prince of Denmarke. By William Shake-
    speare. Newly imprinted and enlarged to almost as much againe as it was, according to the
    true and perfect Coppie*, London.
——(1985). *All's Well That Ends Well*, ed. Russell Fraser (The New Cambridge
    Shakespeare), Cambridge.
——(1986). *The Complete Works: Original-Spelling Edition*, gen. eds Stanley Wells
    and Gary Taylor, Oxford.
——(1990). *King Henry VIII*, ed. John Margeson (The New Cambridge Shake-
    speare), Cambridge.
——(1991). *Measure for Measure*, ed. Brian Gibbons (The New Cambridge Shake-
    speare), Cambridge.
——(1996). *The First Folio of Shakespeare*, ed. Charlton Hinman, 2nd edn, Introd.
    Peter W. M. Blayney, New York, NY.
——(1998). *The First Quarto of Hamlet*, ed. Kathleen O. Irace (The New Cam-
    bridge Shakespeare), Cambridge.
——(2001). *Timon of Athens*, ed. Karl Klein (The New Cambridge Shakespeare),
    Cambridge.
——(2003). *Hamlet, Prince of Denmark*, ed. Philip Edwards (The New Cambridge
    Shakespeare), Cambridge.
——(2003). *King Richard II*, ed. Andrew Gurr (The New Cambridge Shakespeare),
    Cambridge.

Shakespeare, William (2003). *Othello*, ed. Norman Sanders (The New Cambridge Shakespeare), Cambridge.

——(2003). *Romeo and Juliet*, ed. G. Blakemore Evans (The New Cambridge Shakespeare), Cambridge.

——(2003). *The Merchant of Venice*, ed. M. M. Mahood (The New Cambridge Shakespeare), Cambridge.

——(2003). *Troilus and Cressida*, ed. Anthony B. Dawson (The New Cambridge Shakespeare), Cambridge.

——(2003) *Twelfth Night or What You Will*, ed. Elizabeth S. Donno (The New Cambridge Shakespeare), Cambridge.

——(2004). *Julius Caesar*, ed. Marvin Spevack (The New Cambridge Shakespeare), Cambridge.

——(2005). *King Henry V*, ed. Andrew Gurr (The New Cambridge Shakespeare), Cambridge.

——(2005). *The Comedy of Errors*, ed. T. S. Dorsch (The New Cambridge Shakespeare), Cambridge.

——(2005). *The Complete Works*, ed. Stanley Wells and Gary Taylor, 2nd edn, Oxford.

——(2006). *The Poems*, ed. John Roe (The New Cambridge Shakespeare), Cambridge.

——(2006). *The Sonnets*, ed. G. Blakemore Evans (The New Cambridge Shakespeare), Cambridge.

——(2007). *The Winter's Tale*, ed. Susan Snyder and Deborah T. Curren-Aquino (The New Cambridge Shakespeare), Cambridge.

——(2009). *Love's Labour's Lost*, ed. William C. Carroll (The New Cambridge Shakespeare), Cambridge.

——(2012). *The Second Part of King Henry VI*, ed. Michael Hattaway (The New Cambridge Shakespeare), Cambridge.

Sherry, Richard (1550). *A Treatise of Schemes & Tropes*, London.

Sidney, Philip (1595). *The Defence of Poesie*, London.

——(1598). *The Countesse of Pembrokes Arcadia*, London.

Silvayn, Alexander (1596). *The Orator: Handling a hundred severall Discourses, in forme of Declamations*, trans. L[azarus] P[iot], London.

Smith, Thomas (1982). *De Republica Anglorum*, ed. Mary Dewar, Cambridge.

Spenser, Edmund (1596). *The Faerie Queene. Disposed into twelve bookes, Fashioning XII. Morall vertues*, London.

Sturm, Johannes (1538). *De Literarum Ludis Recte Aperiendis Liber*, Strasbourg.

Susenbrotus, Johann (1562). *Epitome troporum ac schematum*, London.

Talon, Omer (1631). *Rhetorica*, Cambridge.

Thomas, Thomas (1592). *Dictionarium Linguae Latinae et Anglicanae*, London.

Triall of true Friendship, The (1596). London.

Turberville, George (1575). *The booke of faulconrie or hauking*, London.

Veron, John (1584). *A Dictionarie in Latine and English*, London.

Vives, Juan Luis (1913). *Vives: On Education: A Translation of the De Tradendis Disciplinis*, trans. Foster Watson, Cambridge.

Whetstone, George (1578). *The right excellent and famous historye, of Promos and Cassandra devided into two commicall discourses*, London.

Wilson, Thomas (1551). *The rule of Reason, conteinyng the Arte of Logique*, London.

——(1553). *The Arte of Rhetorique, for the use of all suche as are studious of Eloquence*, London.

SECONDARY SOURCES

Ackroyd, Peter (2005). *Shakespeare: The Biography*, London.

Adamson, Jane (1980). *Othello as Tragedy: Some Problems of Judgment and Feeling*, Cambridge.

Adamson, Sylvia, Gavin Alexander, and Katrin Ettenhuber (eds) (2007). *Renaissance Figures of Speech*, Cambridge.

Adelman, Janet (1989). 'Bed Tricks: On Marriage as the End of Comedy in *All's Well That Ends Well* and *Measure for Measure*', in *Shakespeare's Personality*, ed. Norman N. Holland, Sidney Homan, and Bernard J. Paris, Berkeley, CA, pp. 151–74.

Alexander, Catherine (ed.) (2009). *The Cambridge Companion to Shakespeare's Last Plays*, Cambridge.

Alexander, Gavin (2007). 'Prosopopoeia: The Speaking Figure', in *Renaissance Figures of Speech*, ed. Sylvia Adamson, Gavin Alexander, and Katrin Ettenhuber, Cambridge, pp. 95–112.

Altman, Joel B. (1978). *The Tudor Play of Mind: Rhetorical Inquiry and the Development of Elizabethan Drama*, Berkeley, CA.

——(2010). *The Improbability of Othello: Rhetorical Anthropology and Shakespearean Selfhood*, Chicago, IL.

Armitage, David, Conal Condren, and Andrew Fitzmaurice (eds) (2009). *Shakespeare and Early Modern Political Thought*, Cambridge.

Attar, Karina Feliciano (2011). 'Genealogy of a Character: A Reading of Giraldi's Moor', in *Visions of Venice in Shakespeare*, ed. Laura Tosi and Shaul Bassi, Farnham, pp. 47–64.

Baldwin, T. W. (1944). *William Shakspere's 'Small Latine & Lesse Greeke'*, 2 vols, Urbana, IL.

Barkan, Leonard (1995). 'Making Pictures Speak: Renaissance Art, Elizabethan Literature, Modern Scholarship', *Renaissance Quarterly* 48, pp. 326–51.

Barker, William (2001). 'Abraham Fraunce', in *British Rhetoricians and Logicians 1500–1650, First Series*, ed. Edward A. Malone, Detroit, MI, pp. 140–56.

Bassakos, Pantelis (2010). '*Ambiguitas* instead of *Ambigere*; Or, What Has Become of *Inventio* in Hobbes', *Redescriptions* 14, pp. 15–30.

Bate, Jonathan (2008). *Soul of the Age: The Life, Mind and World of William Shakespeare*, London.

—— and Eric Rasmussen (eds) (2007). *Complete Works* (The RSC Shakespeare), Basingstoke.

Bates, Catherine (2013). *Masculinity and the Hunt: Wyatt to Spenser*, Oxford.

Baumlin, Tita French (2001). 'Thomas Wilson', in *British Rhetoricians and Logicians 1500–1650, First Series*, ed. Edward A. Malone, Detroit, MI, pp. 282–306.

Bawcutt, N. W. (1991). General Introduction to *Measure for Measure* (The Oxford Shakespeare), Oxford, pp. 1–63.

Bayley, Peter (1980). *French Pulpit Oratory, 1598–1650*, Cambridge.

Bednarz, James P. (2001). *Shakespeare and the Poets' War*, New York, NY.

Beehler, Sharon A. (2003). '"Confederate Season": Shakespeare and the Elizabethan Understanding of *Kairos*', in *Shakespeare Matters: History, Teaching, Performance*, ed. Lloyd Davis, Newark, NJ, pp. 74–88.

Belton, Ellen (2007). '"To make the 'not' eternal": Female Eloquence and Patriarchal Authority in *All's Well, That Ends Well*', in *All's Well, That Ends Well: New Critical Essays*, ed. Gary Waller, London, pp. 125–39.

Benabu, Joel (2013). 'Shakespeare and the Rhetorical Tradition: Toward Defining the Concept of an "Opening"', *Rhetoric Review* 13, pp. 27–43.

Bennett, Robert B. (2000). *Romance and Reformation: The Erasmian Spirit of Shakespeare's Measure for Measure*, Newark, NJ.

Benston, Alice N. (1991). 'Portia, the Law, and the Tripartite Structure of *The Merchant of Venice*', in *The Merchant of Venice: Critical Essays*, ed. Thomas Wheeler, New York, NY, pp. 163–94.

Berry, Edward (2001). *Shakespeare and the Hunt: A Cultural and Social Study*, Cambridge.

Berry, Philippa (1992). 'Woman, Language, and History in *The Rape of Lucrece*', *Shakespeare Survey* 44, pp. 33–9.

Bevington, David (1984). *Action Is Eloquence: Shakespeare's Language of Gesture*, Cambridge, MA.

Bilello, Thomas C. (2007). 'Accomplished with What She Lacks: Law, Equity, and Portia's Con', in *The Law in Shakespeare*, ed. Constance Jordan and Karen Cunningham, Basingstoke, pp. 109–26.

Binns, J. W. (1990). *Intellectual Culture in Elizabethan and Jacobean England: The Latin Writings of the Age*, Leeds.

Blakemore Evans, G. (ed.) (1997). *The Riverside Shakespeare*, 2nd edn, Boston, MA.

——(2003). Introduction to *Romeo and Juliet* (The New Cambridge Shakespeare), Cambridge, pp. 1–62.

——(ed.) (2006). *The Sonnets* (The New Cambridge Shakespeare), Cambridge.

Boas, Frederick S. (1896). *Shakspere and his Predecessors*, London.

Bradley, A. C. (2007). *Shakespearean Tragedy*, 4th edn, Basingstoke.

Bradshaw, Graham (1993). *Misrepresentations: Shakespeare and the Materialists*, Ithaca, NY.

Brennan, Anthony (1986). *Shakespeare's Dramatic Structures*, London.

Briggs, Julia (1994). 'Shakespeare's Bed-tricks', *Essays in Criticism* 44, pp. 293–314.

Brook, G. L. (1976). *The Language of Shakespeare*, London.

Brown, John Russell (1955). Critical Introduction to *The Merchant of Venice* (The Arden Shakespeare), London, pp. xxxvii–lviii.

Brown, Keith (1979). '"Form and Cause Conjoin'd": "Hamlet" and Shakespeare's Workshop', in *Aspects of Hamlet*, ed. Kenneth Muir and Stanley Wells, Cambridge, pp. 39–48.

Bullough, Geoffrey (1957–75). *Narrative and Dramatic Sources of Shakespeare*, 8 vols, London.

Bulman, James C. (1996). 'Introduction: Shakespeare and Performance Theory', in *Shakespeare, Theory, and Performance*, ed. James C. Bulman, London, pp. 1–11.

Burrow, Colin (1998). 'Life and Work in Shakespeare's Poems', in *Proceedings of the British Academy* 97, pp. 15–50.

——(2002). Introduction to *William Shakespeare: The Complete Sonnets and Poems* (The Oxford Shakespeare), Oxford, pp. 1–158.

——(2004). 'Shakespeare and Humanistic Culture', in *Shakespeare and the Classics*, ed. Charles Martindale and A. B. Taylor, Cambridge, pp. 9–27.

——(2013). *Shakespeare and Classical Antiquity*, Oxford.

Bushnell, Rebecca W. (1996). *A Culture of Teaching: Early Modern Humanism in Theory and Practice*, Ithaca, NY.

Calderwood, James L. (1989). *The Properties of Othello*, Amherst, MA.

Caplan, Harry (1954). Introduction to Cicero, *De inventione*, London, pp. vii–lviii.

Carroll, William C. (2009). Introduction to *Love's Labour's Lost* (The New Cambridge Shakespeare), Cambridge pp. 1–54.

Cavell, Stanley (2003). *Disowning Knowledge In Seven Plays of Shakespeare*, Updated edn, Cambridge.

Chambers, E. K. (1930). *William Shakespeare: A Study of Facts and Problems*, 2 vols, Oxford.

Charlton, Kenneth (1965). *Education in Renaissance England*, London.

Cheney, Patrick (2004). *Shakespeare, National Poet-Playwright*, Cambridge.

——(2008). *Shakespeare's Literary Authorship*, Cambridge.

Clark, Ira (2007). *Rhetorical Readings, Dark Comedies, and Shakespeare's Problem Plays*, Gainesville, FL.

Clark, Stuart (2007). *Vanities of the Eye: Vision in Early Modern European Culture*, Oxford.

Cloud, Random (1991). '"The Very Names of the Persons": Editing and the Invention of Dramatick Character', in *Staging the Renaissance: Reinterpretations of Elizabethan and Jacobean Drama*, ed. David S. Kastan and Peter Stallybrass, London, pp. 88–96.

Colclough, David (2009). 'Talking to the Animals: Persuasion, Counsel and their Discontents in *Julius Caesar*', in *Shakespeare and Early Modern Political Thought*, ed.

David Armitage, Conal Condren, and Andrew Fitzmaurice, Cambridge, pp. 217–33.

Cole, Howard C. (1981). *The All's Well Story from Boccaccio to Shakespeare*, Chicago, IL.

Collins, Stephen (2001). 'Dudley Fenner', in *British Rhetoricians and Logicians 1500–1650, First Series*, ed. Edward A. Malone, Detroit, MI, pp. 117–25.

Connolly, Joy (2007). *The State of Speech: Rhetoric and Political Thought in Ancient Rome*, Princeton, NJ.

Cook, Victor William (2001). 'Charles Butler', in *British Rhetoricians and Logicians 1500–1650, First Series*, ed. Edward A. Malone, Detroit, MI, pp. 81–90.

Cooper, John R. (1970). 'Shylock's Humanity', *Shakespeare Quarterly* 21, pp. 117–24.

Corbeill, Anthony (2002). 'Rhetorical Education in Cicero's Youth', in *Brill's Companion to Cicero: Oratory and Rhetoric*, ed. James M. May, Leiden, pp. 23–48.

Cormack, Bradin (2007). *A Power to Do Justice: Jurisdiction, English Literature, and the Rise of Common Law, 1509–1625*, Chicago, IL.

—— Martha C. Nussbaum, and Richard Strier (eds) (2013). *Shakespeare and the Law: A Conversation among Disciplines and Professions*, Chicago, IL.

Cox, Lee S. (1973). *Figurative Design in Hamlet: The Significance of the Dumb Show*, n.p.

Crane, Mary Thomas (1993). *Framing Authority: Sayings, Self and Society in Sixteenth-Century England*, Princeton, NJ.

Crider, Scott F. (2009). *With What Persuasion: An Essay on Shakespeare and the Ethics of Rhetoric*, New York, NY.

Cross, M. Claire (1953). 'The Free Grammar School of Leicester', *Department of English Local History Occasional Papers No. 4*, [University College of Leicester], Leicester.

Curtis, Cathy (2002). 'Richard Pace's *De fructu* and Early Tudor Pedagogy', in *Reassessing Tudor Humanism*, ed. Jonathan Woolfson, Basingstoke, pp. 43–77.

Daniell, David (1998). Introduction to *Julius Caesar* (The Arden Shakespeare), London, pp. 1–147.

Dawson, Anthony B. (1996). 'Performance and Participation: Desdemona, Foucault, and the Actor's Body', in *Shakespeare, Theory, and Performance*, ed. James C. Bulman, London, pp. 29–45.

—— and Gretchen E. Minton (2008). Introduction and Appendix 2 in *Timon of Athens* (The Arden Shakespeare), London, pp. 1–145 and 401–7.

De Grazia, Margreta (2007). *Hamlet Without Hamlet*, Cambridge.

Dent, R. W. (1981). *Shakespeare's Proverbial Language: An Index*, London.

Desens, Marliss C. (1994). *The Bed-Trick in English Renaissance Drama: Explorations in Gender, Sexuality, and Power*, London.

Desmet, Christy (1992). *Reading Shakespeare's Characters: Rhetoric, Ethics, and Identity*, Amherst, MA.

Dewar, Mary (1982). Introduction to Thomas Smith, *De Republica Anglorum*, Cambridge, pp. 1–9.

Donaldson, Ian (1977). '*All's Well That Ends Well*: Shakespeare's Play of Endings', *Essays in Criticism* 27, pp. 34–55.

—— (1982). *The Rapes of Lucretia: A Myth and its Transformations*, Oxford.

——(2011). *Ben Jonson: A Life*, Oxford.

Donawerth, Jane (1984). *Shakespeare and the Sixteenth-Century Study of Language*, Chicago, IL.

Donker, Marjorie (1992). *Shakespeare's Proverbial Themes: A Rhetorical Context for the Sententia as Res*, Westport, CT.

Doran, Madeleine (1976). *Shakespeare's Dramatic Language*, Madison, WI.

Dowling, Maria (1986). *Humanism in the Age of Henry VIII*, Beckenham.

Drakakis, John (2010). Introduction to *The Merchant of Venice* (The Arden Shakespeare), London, pp. 1–159.

Dubrow, Heather (1987). *Captive Victors: Shakespeare's Narrative Poems and Sonnets*, Ithaca, NY.

Duncan-Jones, Katherine (2001). *Ungentle Shakespeare: Scenes from his Life,* London.

Eden, Kathy (1986). *Poetic and Legal Fiction in the Aristotelian Tradition*, Princeton NJ.

——(1997). *Hermeneutics and the Rhetorical Tradition: Chapters in the Ancient Legacy & Its Humanist Reception*, New Haven, CT.

Edwards, Philip (2003). Introduction to *Hamlet, Prince of Denmark* (The New Cambridge Shakespeare), Cambridge, pp. 1–82.

Elam, Keir (1984). *Shakespeare's Universe of Discourse: Language-Games in the Comedies*, Cambridge.

Empson, William (1979). *The Structure of Complex Words*, London.

Enders, Jody (1992). *Rhetoric and the Origins of Medieval Drama*, Ithaca, NY.

Enterline, Lynn (2012). *Shakespeare's Schoolroom: Rhetoric, Discipline, Emotion*, Philadelphia, PA.

Erne, Lukas (2003). *Shakespeare as Literary Dramatist*, Cambridge.

——(2013). *Shakespeare and the Book Trade*, Cambridge.

Ettenhuber, Katrin (2011). *Donne's Augustine: Renaissance Cultures of Interpretation*, Oxford.

Evans, Robert O. (1966). *The Osier Cage: Rhetorical Devices in Romeo & Juliet*, Lexington, KY.

Felperin, Howard (1977). *Shakespearean Representation: Mimesis and Modernity in Elizabethan Tragedy*, Princeton, NJ.

Fitch, John G. (1981). 'Sense-Pauses and Relative Dating in Seneca, Sophocles and Shakespeare', *The American Journal of Philology* 102, pp. 289–307.

Fitzmaurice, Andrew (2009). 'The Corruption of *Hamlet*', in *Shakespeare and Early Modern Political Thought*, ed. David Armitage, Conal Condren, and Andrew Fitzmaurice, Cambridge, pp. 139–56.

Foakes, R. A. (1962). Introduction to *The Comedy of Errors* (The Arden Shakespeare), London, pp. xi–lv.

Forker, Charles R. (2002). Introduction to *King Richard II* (The Arden Shakespeare), London, pp. 1–169.

——(2004). 'How did Shakespeare come by His Books', *Shakespeare Yearbook* 14, pp. 109–20.

Fowler, Alastair (2003). *Renaissance Realism: Narrative Images in Literature and Art*, Oxford.

Fraser, Russell (1985). Introduction to *All's Well That Ends Well* (The New Cambridge Shakespeare), Cambridge, pp. 1–37.

Frye, Northrop (1965). *A Natural Perspective: The Development of Shakespeare's Comedy and Romance*, New York, NY.

Gaunt, D. M. (1969). 'Hamlet and Hecuba', *Notes and Queries*, New Series 16, pp. 136–7.

Gibbons, Brian (1980). Introduction to *Romeo and Juliet* (The Arden Shakespeare), London, pp. 1–77.

——(1991). Introduction to *Measure for Measure* (The New Cambridge Shakespeare), Cambridge, pp. 1–72.

Gillespie, Stuart (2001). *Shakespeare's Books: A Dictionary of Shakespeare's Sources*, London.

Gless, Darryl J. (1979). *Measure for Measure, the Law, and the Convent*, Princeton, NJ.

Goldberg, Jonathan (1983). *James I and the Politics of Literature: Jonson, Shakespeare, Donne and Their Contemporaries*, Baltimore, MD.

Goodrich, Peter (2001). 'Law', in *Encyclopedia of Rhetoric*, ed. Thomas O. Sloane, Oxford, pp. 417–26.

Gowland, Angus (2006). *The Worlds of Renaissance Melancholy: Robert Burton in Context*, Cambridge.

Goyet, Francis (1993). 'Les diverses acceptions de *lieu* et *lieu commun* à la Renaissance', in *Lieux Communs: topoi, stéréotypes, clichés*, ed. Christian Plantin, Paris, pp. 410–22.

Graham, Kenneth (1994). *The Performance of Conviction: Plainness and Rhetoric in the Early English Renaissance*, Ithaca, NY.

Green, Ian (2009). *Humanism and Protestantism in Early Modern English Education*, Farnham.

Green, Lawrence D. and James J. Murphy (2006). *Renaissance Rhetoric Short-Title Catalogue 1460–1700*, 2nd edn, Aldershot.

Greenblatt, Stephen (1988). *Shakespearean Negotiations: The Circulation of Social Energy in Renaissance England*, Oxford.

——(ed.) (1997). *The Norton Shakespeare*, New York, NY.

——(2001). *Hamlet in Purgatory*, Princeton, NJ.

Greg, W. W. and Boswell, E. (1930). *Records of the Court of the Stationers' Company 1576 to 1602*, London.

Grendler, Paul F. (1989). *Schooling in Renaissance Italy: Literacy and Learning, 1300–1600*, Baltimore, MD.

Gurr, Andrew (1992). *The Shakespearean Stage 1574–1642*, 3rd edn, Cambridge.

Gurr, Andrew (2003). Introduction to *King Richard II* (The New Cambridge Shakespeare), Cambridge, pp. 1–60.

——(2005). Introduction to *King Henry V* (The New Cambridge Shakespeare), Cambridge, pp. 1–55.

Guy, John (1986). 'Law, Equity and Conscience in Henrician Juristic Thought', in *Reassessing the Henrician Age: Humanism, Politics and Reform 1500–1550*, ed. Alistair Fox and John Guy, Oxford, pp. 179–98.

Haley, David (1993). *Shakespeare's Courtly Mirror: Reflexivity and Prudence in All's Well That Ends Well*, Newark, NJ.

Halio, Jay L. (2002). 'Reading *Othello* Backwards', in *Othello: New Critical Essays*, ed. Philip C. Kolin, London, pp. 391–400.

Halliwell, Stephen (2008). *Greek Laughter: A Study of Cultural Psychology from Homer to Early Christianity*, Cambridge.

Hamilton, Charles (1986). *In Search of Shakespeare: A Study of the Poet's Life and Handwriting*, London.

Hampton, Timothy (2009). *Fictions of Embassy: Literature and Diplomacy in Early Modern Europe*, Ithaca, NY.

Hanson, Elizabeth (1998). *Discovering the Subject in Renaissance England*, Cambridge.

Hardy, Barbara (1997). *Shakespeare's Storytellers: Dramatic Narration*, London.

Harmon, A. G. (2004). *Eternal Bonds, True Contracts: Law and Nature in Shakespeare's Problem Plays*, Albany, NY.

Hatfield, Andrew (2005). *Shakespeare and Republicanism*, Cambridge.

Hattaway, Michael (2012). Introduction to *The Second Part of King Henry VI* (The New Cambridge Shakespeare), Cambridge, pp. 1–69.

Hawkins, Harriett (1987). *Measure for Measure*, Brighton.

Heath, Malcolm (2009). 'Codifications of Rhetoric', in *The Cambridge Companion to Ancient Rhetoric*, ed. Erik Gunderson, Cambridge, pp. 59–73.

Helmholz, R. H. (1987). *Canon law and the law of England*, London.

Henderson, Judith Rice (2001). 'Angel Day', in *British Rhetoricians and Logicians 1500–1650, First Series*, ed. Edward A. Malone, Detroit, MI, pp. 99–107.

Hesk, Jon (2009). 'Types of Oratory', in *The Cambridge Companion to Ancient Rhetoric*, ed. Erik Gunderson, Cambridge, pp. 145–61.

Hibbard, G. R. (1987). General Introduction to *Hamlet* (The Oxford Shakespeare), Oxford, pp. 1–28.

Hillman, Richard (1993). *William Shakespeare: The Problem Plays*, New York, NY.

Holderness, Graham (1993). *The Merchant of Venice*, Harmondsworth.

——(2010). *Shakespeare and Venice*, Farnham.

Holmer, Joan O. (1995). *The Merchant of Venice: Choice, Hazard and Consequence*, Basingstoke.

Honigmann, E. A. J. (1980). 'Shakespeare's "Bombast"', in *Shakespeare's Styles: Essays in Honour of Kenneth Muir*, ed. Philip Edwards, Inga-Stina Ewbank, and G. K. Hunter, Cambridge, pp. 151–62.

Honigmann, E. A. J. (1993). 'The First Quarto of *Hamlet* and the Date of *Othello*', *The Review of English Studies*, New Series, 44, pp. 211–19.

——(1997). Introduction and Appendix I in *Othello* (The Arden Shakespeare), London, pp. 1–111 and 344–50.

Hood Phillips, Owen (1972). *Shakespeare and the Lawyers*, London.

Horvei, Harald (1984). *The Chev'ril Glove: A Study in Shakespearean Rhetoric*, Bergen.

Howell, Wilbur S. (1956). *Logic and Rhetoric in England, 1500–1700*, Princeton, NJ.

Hulme, Hilda M. (1962). *Explorations in Shakespeare's Language: Some Problems of Word Meaning in the Dramatic Text*, London.

Hunter, G. K. (1959). Introduction to *All's Well That Ends Well* (The Arden Shakespeare), London, pp. xi–lix.

——(1994). 'Rhetoric and Renaissance Drama', in *Renaissance Rhetoric*, ed. Peter Mack, Basingstoke, pp. 103–18.

Hutson, Lorna (2001). 'Not the King's Two Bodies: Reading the "Body Politic" in Shakespeare's *Henry IV*, Parts 1 and 2', in *Rhetoric and Law in Early Modern Europe*, ed. Victoria Kahn and Lorna Hutson, London, pp. 166–98.

——(2006). 'Forensic Aspects of Renaissance Mimesis', *Representations* 94, pp. 80–109.

——(2007). *The Invention of Suspicion: Law and Mimesis in Shakespeare and Renaissance Drama*, Oxford.

——(2013). '"Lively Evidence": Legal Inquiry and the *Evidentia* of Shakespearean Drama', in *Shakespeare and the Law: A Conversation among Disciplines and Professions*, ed. Bradin Cormack, Martha C. Nussbaum, and Richard Strier, Chicago, IL, pp. 72–97.

——(2015). 'Rhetoric and Law', in *Oxford Handbook of Rhetorical Studies*, ed. Michael MacDonald, Oxford (forthcoming).

Ingram, Michael (1987). *Church Courts, Sex and Marriage in England, 1570–1640*, Cambridge.

Irace, Kathleen O. (1998). Introduction to *The First Quarto of Hamlet* (The New Cambridge Shakespeare), Cambridge, pp. 1–27.

Jackson, MacDonald P. (2001). 'Spurio and the Date of *All's Well That Ends Well*', *Notes and Queries*, New Series, 48, pp. 298–9.

James, Susan (1997). *Passion and Action: The Emotions in Seventeenth-Century Philosophy*, Oxford.

Jardine, Lisa (1977). 'Lorenzo Valla and the Intellectual Origins of Humanist Dialectic', *Journal of the History of Philosophy* 15, pp. 143–63.

Javitch, Daniel (1972). 'Poetry and Court Conduct: Puttenham's *Arte of English Poesie* in the Light of Castiglione's *Cortegiano*', *Modern Language Notes* 87, pp. 865–82.

Jenkins, Harold (1982). Introduction to *Hamlet* (The Arden Shakespeare), London, pp. 1–159.

Johnson, D. (1985). 'Nicholas Ling, publisher 1580–1607', *Studies in Bibliography* 38, pp. 203–14.

Jones, Emrys (1971). *Scenic Form in Shakespeare*, Oxford.
——(1977). *The Origins of Shakespeare*, Oxford.
Jordan, Constance and Karen Cunningham (eds) (2007). *The Law in Shakespeare*, Basingstoke.
Jordan, William C. (1982). 'Approaches to the Court Scene in the Bond Story: Equity and Mercy or Reason and Nature', *Shakespeare Quarterly* 33, pp. 49–59.
Joseph, Miriam (1947). *Shakespeare's Use of the Arts of Language*, New York, NY.
Jowett, John (2004). Introduction to *The Life of Timon of Athens* (The Oxford Shakespeare), Oxford, pp. 1–153.
Kahn, Victoria (1989). 'Rhetoric and the Law', *Diacritics* 19, pp. 21–34.
Kahneman, Daniel (2011). *Thinking, Fast and Slow*, London.
Kamaralli, Anna (2005). 'Writing about Motive: Isabella, the Duke and Moral Authority', *Shakespeare Survey* 58, pp. 48–59.
Kapust, Daniel (2011). 'Cicero on Decorum and the Morality of Rhetoric', *European Journal of Political Theory* 10, pp. 92–112.
Kay, Margaret M. (1966). *The History of Rivington and Blackrod Grammar School*, 2nd edn, Manchester.
Keeton, George W. (1967). *Shakespeare's Legal and Political Background*, London.
Keller, Stefan (2009). *The Development of Shakespeare's Rhetoric: A Study of Nine Plays*, Tübingen.
Kennedy, George (1972). *The Art of Rhetoric in the Ancient World 300 BC–AD 300*, Princeton, NJ.
Kennedy, Milton B. (1942). *The Oration in Shakespeare*, Chapel Hill, NC.
Kennedy, William J. (1978). *Rhetorical Norms in Renaissance Literature*, New Haven, CT.
Kermode, Frank (1997). 'Othello, The Moor of Venice', in *The Riverside Shakespeare*, ed. G. Blakemore Evans, 2nd edn, Boston, MA, pp. 1246–50.
Kerrigan, John (1996). *Revenge Tragedy: Aeschylus to Armageddon*, Oxford.
——(2001). *On Shakespeare and Early Modern Literature: Essays*, Oxford.
——(2012). 'Coriolanus Fidiussed', *Essays in Criticism* 62, pp. 319–53.
Kiernan, Pauline (1996). *Shakespeare's Theory of Drama*, Cambridge.
King, Ros (2005). Introduction to *The Comedy of Errors*, ed. T. S. Dorsch (The New Cambridge Shakespeare), Cambridge, pp. 1–53.
Kinney, Arthur F. (2006). *Shakespeare and Cognition: Aristotle's Legacy and Shakespearean Drama*, London.
Kirwood, A. E. M. (1931). 'Richard Field, Printer, 1589–1624', *The Library*, Fourth series, 12, pp. 1–39.
Klein, Karl (2001). Introduction to *Timon of Athens* (The New Cambridge Shakespeare), Cambridge, pp. 1–66.
Kliman, Bernice (1982). 'Isabella in "Measure for Measure"', *Shakespeare Studies* 15, pp. 137–48.
Knight, W. Nicholas (1972). 'Equity and Mercy in English Law and Drama (1405–1641)', *Comparative Drama* 6, pp. 51–66.

Knowles, Ronald (1999). Introduction to *King Henry VI Part 2* (The Arden Shakespeare), pp. 1–141.

Langer, Ullrich (1999). 'Invention', in *The Cambridge History of Literary Criticism*, vol. 3, *The Renaissance*, ed. Glyn P. Norton, Cambridge, pp. 136–44.

Lechner, Joan M. (1962). *Renaissance Concepts of the Commonplaces*, New York, NY.

Lees-Jeffries, Hester (2013). *Shakespeare and Memory*, London.

LeFanu, W. R. (1959–64). 'Thomas Vautrollier, Printer and Bookseller', *Proceedings of the Huguenot Society of London*, 20, pp. 12–25.

Leggatt, Alexander (1988). 'Substitution in *Measure for Measure*', *Shakespeare Quarterly* 39, pp. 342–59.

—— (2003). Introduction to *All's Well That Ends Well*, ed. Russell Fraser (The New Cambridge Shakespeare), Cambridge, pp. 1–43.

Leimberg, Inge (2011). *'What May Words Say . . . ?' A Reading of The Merchant of Venice*, Lanham, MD.

Levenson, Jill L. (2004). 'Shakespeare's *Romeo and Juliet*: The Places of Invention', in *Shakespeare and Language*, ed. Catherine Alexander, Cambridge, pp. 122–38.

Lever, J. W. (1965). Introduction to *Measure for Measure* (The Arden Shakespeare), London, pp. xi–xcviii.

Lewis, Cynthia (1990). '"Derived Honesty and Achieved Goodness": Doctrines of Grace in *All's Well That Ends Well*', *Renaissance and Reformation* 26, pp. 147–70.

Lewis, Rhodri (2012a). 'Shakespeare's Clouds and the Image Made by Chance', *Essays in Criticism* 62, pp. 1–24.

——(2012b). 'Hamlet, Metaphor, and Memory', *Studies in Philology* 109, pp. 609–41.

Lobban, Michael (2007). *A History of the Philosophy of Law in the Common Law World, 1600–1900,* Dordrecht.

Lucking, David (1997). *Plays Upon the Word: Shakespeare's Drama of Language*, Lecce.

Lyne, Raphael (2011). *Shakespeare, Rhetoric and Cognition*, Cambridge.

Mack, Peter (1993). *Renaissance Argument: Valla and Agricola in the Traditions of Rhetoric and Dialectic,* Leiden.

——(2002). *Elizabethan Rhetoric: Theory and Practice*, Cambridge.

——(2010). *Reading and Rhetoric in Montaigne and Shakespeare*, London.

——(2011). *A History of Renaissance Rhetoric 1380–1620*, Oxford.

Maguire, Laurie (2007). *Shakespeare's Names*, Oxford.

——and Emma Smith (2012a). 'Many Hands: A New Shakespeare Collaboration?' *Times Literary Supplement* 5690, 20 April, pp. 13–15.

——and Emma Smith (2012b). 'All's Well That Ends Well', *Times Literary Supplement* 5697, 8 June, p. 6.

Mahood, M. M. (2003). Introduction to *The Merchant of Venice* (The New Cambridge Shakespeare), Cambridge, pp. 1–65.

Mann, Jenny C. (2012). *Outlaw Rhetoric: Figuring Vernacular Eloquence in Shakespeare's England*, Ithaca, NY.

Maquerlot, Jean-Pierre (1995). *Shakespeare and the Mannerist Tradition: A Reading of Five Problem Plays*, Cambridge.

Margeson, John (1990). Introduction to *King Henry VIII* (The New Cambridge Shakespeare), Cambridge, pp. 1–59.

Margolies, David (2012). *Shakespeare's Irrational Endings: The Problem Plays*, Basingstoke.

Marino, James J. (2011). *Owning William Shakespeare: The King's Men and Their Intellectual Property*, Philadelphia, PA.

Marsh, Nicholas (2003). *Shakespeare: Three Problem Plays*, Basingstoke.

Martindale, Charles and Michelle (1990). *Shakespeare and the Uses of Antiquity: An Introductory Essay*, London.

Maus, Katharine E. (1995). *Inwardness and Theater in the English Renaissance*, Chicago, IL.

McCandless, David (1997). *Gender and Performance in Shakespeare's Problem Comedies*, Bloomington, IN.

McDonald, Russ (2001). *Shakespeare and the Arts of Language*, Oxford.

——(2006). *Shakespeare's Late Style*, Cambridge.

McGuire, Philip C. (1985). *Speechless Dialect: Shakespeare's Open Silences*, Berkeley, CA.

McKerrow, R. B. (ed.) (1968). *A Dictionary of Printers and Booksellers in England, Scotland and Ireland, and of Foreign Printers of English Books, 1557–1640*, London.

McMullan, Gordon (2000). Introduction and Appendix 3: Attribution and Composition in *King Henry VIII (All Is True)* (The Arden Shakespeare), London, pp. 1–199, 448–9.

—— (2009). 'What is a "Late Play"?', in *The Cambridge Companion to Shakespeare's Last Plays*, ed. Catherine Alexander, Cambridge, pp. 5–27.

McNeely, Trevor (2004). *Proteus Unmasked: Sixteenth-Century Rhetoric and the Art of Shakespeare*, London.

Medine, Peter E. (1986). *Thomas Wilson*, Boston, MA.

Meek, Richard (2009a). 'Shakespeare and Narrative', *Literature Compass* 6, pp. 482–98.

——(2009b). *Narrating the Visual in Shakespeare*, Farnham.

Meerhoff, Kees (1994). 'The Significance of Philip Melanchthon's Rhetoric in the Renaissance', in *Renaissance Rhetoric*, ed. Peter Mack, Basingstoke, pp. 46–62.

Melchiori, Giorgio (1981). 'The Rhetoric of Character Construction in "Othello"', *Shakespeare Survey* 34, pp. 61–72.

—— (1992). 'Hamlet: The Acting Version and the Wiser Sort', in *The 'Hamlet' First Published (Q1, 1603): Origins, Form, Intertextualities*, ed. Thomas Clayton, Newark, NJ, pp. 195–210.

——(1994). *Shakespeare: Genesi e struttura delle opere*, Bari.

Menon, Madhavi (2004). *Wanton Words: Rhetoric and Sexuality in English Renaissance Drama*, Toronto.

Menzer, Paul (2008). *The Hamlets: Cues, Qs, and Remembered Texts*, Newark NJ.

Mercer, Peter (1987). *Hamlet and the Acting of Revenge*, Basingstoke.

Miola, Robert S. (2000). *Shakespeare's Reading*, Oxford.

Moschovakis, Nicholas (2002). 'Representing Othello: Early Modern Jury Trials and the Equitable Judgments of Tragedy', in *Othello: New Critical Essays*, ed. Philip C. Kolin, London, pp. 293–323.

Moss, Ann (1996). *Printed Commonplace-Books and the Structuring of Renaissance Thought*, Oxford.

——(2001). 'Commonplaces and Commonplace books', in *Encyclopedia of Rhetoric*, ed. Thomas O. Sloane, Oxford, pp. 119–24.

Moss, Jean Dietz and William A. Wallace (2003). *Rhetoric & Dialectic in the Time of Galileo*, Washington, DC.

Mukherji, Subha (2006). *Law and Representation in Early Modern Drama*, Cambridge.

Munro, Lucy (2005). *Children of the Queen's Revels: A Jacobean Theatre Repertory*, Cambridge.

Nauert, Charles G. (2006). *Humanism and the Culture of Renaissance Europe*, 2nd edn, Cambridge.

Neill, Michael (2000). *Putting History to the Question: Power, Politics, and Society in English Renaissance Drama*, New York, NY.

—— (2006). Introduction and Appendix A: The Date of the Play in *Othello, the Moor of Venice* (The Oxford Shakespeare), Oxford, pp. 1–179 and 399–404.

Newman, Karen (1985). *Shakespeare's Rhetoric of Comic Character: Dramatic convention in Classical and Renaissance Comedy*, London.

Nicholl, Charles (2007). *The Lodger: Shakespeare on Silver Street*, London.

Nicholson, Catherine (2010). '*Othello* and the Geography of Persuasion', *English Literary Renaissance* 40, pp. 56–87.

Noble, Richard (1935). *Shakespeare's Biblical Knowledge and Use of the Book of Common Prayer*, London.

Nuttall, A. D. (1983). *A New Mimesis: Shakespeare and the Representation of Reality*, London.

Ong, Walter J. (1965). 'Ramist Rhetoric', in *The Province of Rhetoric*, ed. Joseph Schwartz and John A. Rycenga, New York, NY, pp. 226–55.

Orgel, Stephen (1996). Introduction to *The Winter's Tale* (The Oxford Shakespeare), Oxford, pp. 1–83.

—— (2006). Introduction to *The Sonnets*, ed. G. Blakemore Evans (The New Cambridge Shakespeare), pp. 1–22.

Pafford, J. H. P. (1963). Introduction to *The Winter's Tale* (The Arden Shakespeare), London, pp. xv–lxxxix.

Palonen, Kari (2008). 'Speaking Pro et Contra: The Rhetorical Intelligibility of Parliamentary Politics and the Political Intelligibility of Parliamentary Rhetoric', in *The Parliamentary Style of Politics*, ed. Suvi Soininen and Tapani Turkka, Helsinki, pp. 82–105.

Parker, Patricia (1987). *Literary Fat Ladies: Rhetoric, Gender, Property*, London.

——(1996). *Shakespeare from the Margins: Language, Culture, Context*, Chicago, IL.

Paul, Joanne (2014). 'The Use of *Kairos* in Renaissance Political Philosophy', *Renaissance Quarterly* 67, pp. 43–78.

Pearlman, E. (2002). 'Shakespeare at Work: The Invention of the Ghost', in *Hamlet: New Critical Essays*, ed. Arthur F. Kinney, London, pp. 71–84.

Peltonen, Markku (2003). *The Duel in Early Modern England: Civility, Politeness and Honour*, Cambridge.

——(2013). *Rhetoric, Politics and Popularity in Pre-Revolutionary England*, Cambridge.

Percival, W. Keith (1983). 'Grammar and Rhetoric in the Renaissance', in *Renaissance Eloquence: Studies in the Theory and Practice of Renaissance Rhetoric*, ed. James J. Murphy, Berkeley, CA, pp. 303–30.

Peters, Julie Stone (2000). *Theatre of the Book 1480–1880: Print, Text, and Performance in Europe*, Oxford.

Pincombe, Mike (2001). *Elizabethan Humanism: Literature and Learning in the Later Sixteenth Century*, London.

Platt, Peter G. (1999). 'Shakespeare and Rhetorical Culture', in *A Companion to Shakespeare*, ed. David S. Kastan, Oxford, pp. 277–96.

—— (2009). *Shakespeare and the Culture of Paradox*, Farnham.

Plett, Heinrich F. (2004). *Rhetoric and Renaissance Culture*, New York, NY.

——(2012). *Enargeia in Classical Antiquity and the Early Modern Age*, Leiden.

Posner, Richard A. (2013). 'Law and Commerce in *The Merchant of Venice*', in *Shakespeare and the Law: A Conversation among Disciplines and Professions*, ed. Bradin Cormack, Martha C. Nussbaum, and Richard Strier, Chicago, IL, pp. 147–55.

Potter, Lois (2012). *The Life of William Shakespeare: A Critical Biography*, Oxford.

Preston, Claire (2007). 'Ekphrasis: Painting in Words', in *Renaissance Figures of Speech*, ed. Sylvia Adamson, Gavin Alexander, and Katrin Ettenhuber, Cambridge, pp. 115–29.

Price, John Edward (1979). 'Anti-Moralistic Moralism in *All's Well That Ends Well*', *Shakespeare Studies* 12, pp. 95–111.

Prosser, Eleanor (1971). *Hamlet and Revenge*, 2nd edn, Stanford, CA.

Rackley, Erika (2008). 'Judging Isabella: Justice, Care and Relationships in *Measure for Measure*', in *Shakespeare and the Law*, ed. Paul Raffield and Gary Watt, Oxford, pp. 65–79.

Raffield, Paul and Gary Watt (eds) (2008). *Shakespeare and the Law*, Oxford.

Ratcliffe, Stephen (2010). *Reading the Unseen: (Offstage) Hamlet*, Denver, CO.

Rebhorn, Wayne A. (1995). *The Emperor of Men's Minds: Literature and the Renaissance Discourse of Rhetoric*, Ithaca, NY.

Rhodes, Neil (2004). *Shakespeare and the Origins of English*, Oxford.

Roberts, Caroline (2002). 'The Politics of Persuasion: *Measure for Measure* and Cinthio's *Hecatommithi*', *Early Modern Literary Studies* 7, pp. 1–17.

Roe, John (2006). Introduction to *The Poems* (The New Cambridge Shakespeare), Cambridge, pp. 1–80.

Rose, Mary Beth (1988). *The Expense of Spirit: Love and Sexuality in English Renaissance Drama*, Ithaca, NY.

Ross, Lawrence J. (1997). *On Measure for Measure: An Essay in Criticism of Shakespeare's Drama*, Newark, NJ.

Rovine, Harvey (1987). *Silence in Shakespeare: Drama, Power, and Gender*, Ann Arbor, MI.

Ryle, S. F. (2003). 'Leonard Cox', in *British Rhetoricians and Logicians 1500–1650, Second Series*, ed. Edward A. Malone, Detroit, MI, pp. 58–67.

Salingar, Leo (1974). *Shakespeare and the Traditions of Comedy*, Cambridge.

Sanders, Norman (2003). Introduction to *Othello* (The New Cambridge Shakespeare), Cambridge, pp. 1–61.

Saunders, W. H. (1932). *A History of the Norwich Grammar School*, Norwich.

Schleiner, Winfried (1970). *The Imagery of John Donne's Sermons*, Providence, RI.

Serjeantson, Richard (2007). 'Testimony: The Artless Proof', in *Renaissance Figures of Speech*, ed. Sylvia Adamson, Gavin Alexander, and Katrin Ettenhuber, Cambridge, pp. 179–94.

Serpieri, Alessandro (2002). 'Reading the Signs: Towards a Semiotics of Shakespearean Drama', in *Alternative Shakespeares*, ed. John Drakakis, 2nd edn, London, pp. 121–46.

Shapiro, Barbara J. (1991). *'Beyond Reasonable Doubt' and 'Probable Cause': Historical Perspectives on the Anglo-American Law of Evidence*, Berkeley, CA.

——(2000). *A Culture of Fact: England, 1550–1720*, Ithaca, NY.

——(2001). 'Classical Rhetoric and the English Law of Evidence', in *Rhetoric and Law in Early Modern Europe*, ed. Victoria Kahn and Lorna Hutson, London, pp. 54–72.

Shapiro, James (2005). *1599: A Year in the Life of William Shakespeare*, London.

Sharon-Zisser, Shirley (2001). 'Richard Sherry', in *British Rhetoricians and Logicians 1500–1650, First Series*, ed. Edward A. Malone, Detroit, MI, pp. 235–47.

Shrank, Cathy (2004). *Writing the Nation in Reformation England 1530–1580*, Oxford.

Shuger, Debora K. (1988). *Sacred Rhetoric: The Christian Grand Style in the English Renaissance*, Princeton, NJ.

——(2001). *Political Theologies in Shakespeare's England: The Sacred and the State in Measure for Measure*, Basingstoke.

Simon, Joan (1966). *Education and Society in Tudor England*, Cambridge.

Skinner, Quentin (1978). *The Foundations of Modern Political Thought*, 2 vols, Cambridge.

——(1995). 'The Vocabulary of Renaissance Republicanism: A Cultural *longue-durée?*', in *Language and Images of Renaissance Italy*, ed. Alison Brown, Oxford, pp. 87–110.

——(1996). *Reason and Rhetoric in the Philosophy of Hobbes*, Cambridge.

——(2002a). *Visions of Politics*, vol. 1, *Regarding Method*, Cambridge.

——(2002b). 'Moral Ambiguity and the Renaissance Art of Eloquence', in *Visions of Politics*, vol. 2, *Renaissance Virtues*, Cambridge, pp. 264–85.

——(2002c). 'Hobbes on Rhetoric and the Construction of Morality', in *Visions of Politics*, vol. 3, *Hobbes and Civil Science*, Cambridge, pp. 87–141.

——(2007). 'Paradiastole: Redescribing the Vices as Virtues', in *Renaissance Figures of Speech*, ed. Sylvia Adamson, Gavin Alexander, and Katrin Ettenhuber, Cambridge, pp. 147–63.

Skinner, Quentin (2009). 'Shakespeare and Humanist Culture', in *Shakespeare and Early Modern Political Thought*, ed. David Armitage, Conal Condren, and Andrew Fitzmaurice, Cambridge, pp. 271–81.

——(2013). 'A Spurious Dating for *All's Well That Ends Well*', *Notes and Queries*, New Series, 60, pp. 429–34.

Slater, Eliot (1977). 'Word Links with *All's Well That Ends Well*', *Notes and Queries*, New Series, 24, pp. 109–12.

Smith, Shawn (2001). 'Henry Peacham', in *British Rhetoricians and Logicians 1500–1650, First Series*, ed. Edward A. Malone, Detroit, MI, pp. 188–201.

Snow, Edward A. (1988). 'Sexual Anxiety and the Male Order of Things in *Othello*', in *Othello: Critical Essays*, ed. Susan Snyder, New York, NY, pp. 213–49.

Snyder, Susan (1979). *The Comic Matrix of Shakespeare's Tragedies: Romeo and Juliet, Hamlet, Othello and King Lear*, Princeton, NJ.

——(1992). 'Naming Names in *All's Well That Ends Well*', *Shakespeare Quarterly* 43, pp. 265–79.

——(1993). Introduction to *All's Well That Ends Well* (The Oxford Shakespeare), Oxford, pp. 1–65.

——and Deborah T. Curren-Aquino (2007). Introduction to *The Winter's Tale* (The New Cambridge Shakespeare), Cambridge, pp. 1–72.

Sokol, B. J. (2008). *Shakespeare and Tolerance*, Cambridge.

——and Mary Sokol (1999). 'Shakespeare and English Equity Jurisdiction: The Merchant of Venice and the Two Texts of King Lear', *Review of English Studies* 50, pp. 417–39.

—— (2000). *Shakespeare's Legal Language: A Dictionary*, London.

Spevack, Marvin (2004). Introduction to *Julius Caesar* (The New Cambridge Shakespeare), Cambridge, pp. 1–45.

Spurgeon, Caroline F. E. (1965). *Shakespeare's Imagery and What it Tells Us*, Cambridge.

Stallybrass, Peter, J. Franklin Mowery, and Heather Wolfe (2004). 'Hamlet's Tables and the Technologies of Writing in Renaissance England', *Shakespeare Quarterly* 55, pp. 379–419.

——and Roger Chartier (2007). 'Reading and Authorship: The Circulation of Shakespeare 1590–1619', in *A Concise Companion to Shakespeare and the Text*, ed. Andrew Murphy, Oxford, pp. 35–56.

Stamp, A. E. (1930). *The Disputed Revels Accounts (1604–5 and 1611–12)*, London.

Starnes, DeWitt T. (1954). *Renaissance Dictionaries: English–Latin and Latin–English*, Austin, TX.

Stevenson, David L. (1959). 'The Role of James I in Shakespeare's *Measure for Measure*', *ELH: A Journal of English Literary History* 26, pp. 188–208.

Struever, Nancy S. (1988). 'Shakespeare and Rhetoric', *Rhetorica* 6, pp. 137–44.

Syme, Holger S. (2012). *Theatre and Testimony in Shakespeare's England: A Culture of Mediation*, Cambridge.

Thomas, Vivian (1987). *The Moral Universe of Shakespeare's Problem Plays*, London.

Thomas, Vivian (2005). 'Shakespeare's Sources: Translations, Transformations, and Intertextuality in *Julius Caesar*', in *Julius Caesar: New Critical Essays*, ed. Horst Zander, Oxford, pp. 91–110.

Thompson, Ann and Neil Taylor (2006). Introduction to *Hamlet* (The Arden Shakespeare), London, pp. 1–137.

Thorne, Alison (2000). *Vision and Rhetoric in Shakespeare: Looking through Language*, Basingstoke.

Tiffany, Grace (2002). 'Names in *The Merchant of Venice*', in *The Merchant of Venice: New Critical Essays*, ed. John W. Mahon and Ellen Macleod Mahon, London, pp. 353–67.

Tovey, Barbara (1981). 'The Golden Casket: An Interpretation of *The Merchant of Venice*', in *Shakespeare as Political Thinker*, ed. John Alvis and Thomas G. West, Durham, NC, pp. 215–37.

Traversi, Derek (1969). *An Approach to Shakespeare*, 3rd edn, 2 vols., London.

Tribble, Evelyn B. (2005). 'Distributing Cognition in the Globe', *Shakespeare Quarterly* 56, pp. 135–55.

Trousdale, Marion (1982). *Shakespeare and the Rhetoricians*, Chapel Hill, NC.

Tucker, E. F. J. (1976). 'The Letter of the Law in "The Merchant of Venice"', *Shakespeare Survey* 29, pp. 93–101.

van Es, Bart (2013). *Shakespeare in Company*, Oxford.

Vasoli, Cesare (1968). *La dialettica e la retorica dell'Umanesimo: Invenzione e metodo nella cultura del XV e XVI secolo*, Milan.

Vaughan, Virginia Masson (2011). 'Supersubtle Venetians: Richard Knolles and the Geopolitics of Shakespeare's *Othello*', in *Visions of Venice in Shakespeare*, ed. Laura Tosi and Shaul Bassi, Farnham, pp. 19–32.

Vickers, Brian (1968). *The Artistry of Shakespeare's Prose*, London.

——(1988). *In Defence of Rhetoric*, Oxford.

——(2002). *Shakespeare, Co-Author: A Historical Study of Five Collaborative Plays*, Oxford.

Walker, Alice (1982). 'Six Notes on *All's Well That Ends Well*', *Shakespeare Quarterly* 33, pp. 339–42.

Ward, Ian (1999). *Shakespeare and the Legal Imagination*, London.

Ward, John O. (1983). 'Renaissance Commentators on Ciceronian Rhetoric', in *Renaissance Eloquence: Studies in the Theory and Practice of Renaissance Rhetoric*, ed. James J. Murphy, Berkeley, CA, pp. 126–73.

——(1999). 'Cicero and Quintilian', in *The Cambridge History of Literary Criticism*, vol. 3, *The Renaissance*, ed. Glyn P. Norton, Cambridge, pp. 77–87.

Watson, Curtis B. (1960). *Shakespeare and the Renaissance Concept of Honor*, Princeton, NJ.

Watson, Robert N. (1990). 'Tragedy', in *The Cambridge Companion to English Renaissance Drama*, ed. A. R. Braunmuller and Michael Hattaway, Cambridge, pp. 301–51.

Watson, Walter (2001). 'Invention', in *Encyclopedia of Rhetoric*, ed. Thomas O. Sloane, Oxford, pp. 389–404.

Watt, Gary (2009). *Equity Stirring: The Story of Justice Beyond Law*, Portland, OR.

Weaver, William P. (2008). '"O teach me how to make mine own excuse": Forensic Performance in *Lucrece*', *Shakespeare Quarterly* 59, pp. 421–49.

——(2012). *Untutored Lines: The Making of the English Epyllion*, Edinburgh.

Weimann, Robert and Douglas Bruster (2008). *Shakespeare and the Power of Performance: Stage and Page in the Elizabethan Theatre*, Cambridge.

Wells, Stanley and Gary Taylor, with John Jowett and William Montgomery (1987). *William Shakespeare: A Textual Companion*, Oxford.

Wels, Volkhard (2008). 'Melanchthon's Textbooks on Dialectic and Rhetoric as Complementary Parts of a Theory of Argumentation', in *Scholarly Knowledge: Textbooks in Early Modern Europe*, ed. Emidio Campi, Simone de Angelis, Anja-Silvana Goeing, and Anthony T. Grafton, Geneva, pp. 138–56.

Wheeler, Richard P. (1981). *Shakespeare's Development and the Problem Comedies: Turn and Counter-Turn*, Berkeley, CA.

Whigham, Frank (1984). *Ambition and Privilege: The Social Tropes of Elizabethan Courtesy Theory*, Berkeley, CA.

Whitaker, J. (1837). *The Statutes and Charter of Rivington School*, London.

Whitaker, Virgil (1953). *Shakespeare's Use of Learning: An Inquiry into the Growth of his Mind & Art*, San Marino, CA.

Wickham, Chris (2003). *Courts and Conflict in Twelfth-Century Tuscany*, Oxford.

Wiggins, Martin with Catherine Richardson (2013). *British Drama 1533–1642. A Catalogue*, Vol. 3: *1590–1597*, Oxford.

Wilder, Linn P. (2010). *Shakespeare's Memory Theatre: Recollection, Properties, and Character*, Cambridge.

Willcock, Gladys and Alice Walker (1970). Introduction to George Puttenham, *The Arte of English Poesie*, Cambridge, pp. ix–cii.

Williams, Grant (2001). 'Richard Rainolde', in *British Rhetoricians and Logicians 1500–1650, First Series*, ed. Edward A. Malone, Detroit, MI, pp. 223–34.

Wills, Garry (2011). *Rome and Rhetoric: Shakespeare's Julius Caesar*, New Haven, CT.

Wilson, John Dover (1934a). *The Manuscript of Shakespeare's Hamlet and the Problems of its Transmission: An Essay in Critical Bibliography*, 2 vols, Cambridge.

—— (1934b). *What Happens in Hamlet*, Cambridge.

Wilson, Luke (2000). *Theaters of Intention: Drama and the Law in Early Modern England*, Stanford, CA.

Wilson, Rawdon (1995). *Shakespearean Narrative*, Newark, NJ.

Wisse, Jacob (2002). '*De oratore*: Rhetoric, Philosophy, and the Making of the Ideal Orator', in *Brill's Companion to Cicero: Oratory and Rhetoric*, ed. James M. May, Leiden, pp. 375–400.

Yates, Frances (1966). *The Art of Memory*, London.

Yeo, Richard (2008). 'Notebooks as Memory Aids: Precepts and Practices in Early Modern England', *Memory Studies* 1, pp. 115–36.

Zurcher, Andrew (2010). *Shakespeare and Law*, London.

Index